Miracles and the Venerable Bede

WILLIAM D. McCREADY

With a degree of unanimity rare in scholarly circles, it is generally agreed today that the career of the Venerable Bede (672/673-735) represents the most noteworthy expression of the culture that flourished in Northumbria in the seventh and eighth centuries. Exegete, historian, hagiographer, scientist: for the following medieval centuries Bede was a scholar whose importance and influence knew few rivals. This study seeks to elucidate one aspect of his legacy by examining his treatment of the miracles of modern saints. The principal sources are his *Ecclesiastical History* and his *Lives of St Cuthbert*, but both are read in the light of his exegetical and other works, and Bede's thought in turn is examined against the backdrop provided by the fund of patristic and early medieval sources on which he drew.

The volume follows upon an earlier study of Gregory the Great, and focuses largely on the same issues, including Bede's understanding of the natural realm and the order it possesses, his view of the purpose of miracles both in the New Testament and in his own times, the degree of scepticism or credulity with which he viewed modern wonders, and the truth value that he attached to the miracle stories he judged worthy of narrating. Deeply respectful of all the fathers of the church, Bede reserved a special veneration for Gregory, whom he regarded as the apostle to the English. With the possible exception of the commentary on 1 Kings (1 Samuel), he knew all of Gregory's major works, including both the *Homilies on the Gospels* and the *Dialogues*. A detailed comparison reveals that Bede was profoundly influenced by both the *Dialogues* and Gregory's other works. However, his dependence was far from servile. In addition to recording his indebtedness to Gregory, *Miracles and the Venerable Bede* identifies a number of points where Bede's treatment takes on a character of its own, and needs to be understood in its own terms.

STUDIES AND TEXTS 118

Miracles and the Venerable Bede

WILLIAM D. McCREADY

PONTIFICAL INSTITUTE OF MEDIAEVAL STUDIES

ACKNOWLEDGMENT

This book has been published with the help of a
grant from the Canadian Federation for the Humanities
using funds provided by the Social Sciences and
Humanities Research Council of Canada.

BT
97.2
.M32
1994

CANADIAN CATALOGUING IN PUBLICATION DATA

McCready, William D. (William David), 1943–
Miracles and the Venerable Bede

(Studies and texts, ISSN 0082-5328 ; 118)
Includes bibliographical references and index.
ISBN 0-88844-118-5

1. Bede, the Venerable, Saint, 673–735 – Views on miracles.
2. Miracles.   3. Gregory I, Pope, ca. 540–604 – Influence.
I. Pontifical Institute of Mediaeval Studies.   II. Title.
III. Series: Studies and texts
(Pontifical Institute of Mediaeval Studies) ; 118

BT97.2.M33 1994   231.7'3   C94-932424-8

Printed by
Edwards Brothers Incorporated, Michigan, USA

To my parents

Contents

Preface   ix

Abbreviations   xv

Introduction   1

1. Science and Literary Culture   9

2. Scepticism, Credulity and Belief   44

3. The Age of Miracles   75

4. The Purpose of Miracle   105

5. The Virtue of the Saints   124

6. Bede and the Hagiographical Tradition   154

7. The Legacy of the *Dialogues*   176

8. Vera Lex Historiae   195

9. Truth and Its Limits   214

Conclusion   230

Bibliography   235

Index of Citations   263

General Index   275

Preface

The subject of this book is the concept of miracle in the thought of the Venerable Bede. Its specific focus is Bede's understanding of the miracles of modern saints, miracles of the sort that he himself describes for us in his *Ecclesiastical History*. The book has been designed as a self-contained treatment of the issue, and it can be appraised simply on its own merits. It has also, however, been conceived as a sequel to an earlier volume: *Signs of Sanctity: Miracles in the Thought of Gregory the Great*, published by the Pontifical Institute of Mediaeval Studies in 1989. *Signs of Sanctity* focuses primarily on the miracle stories recorded in Gregory's *Dialogues*, although it is not a book about the *Dialogues per se*. It is really Gregory's larger concept of miracle that *Signs of Sanctity* seeks to clarify. Hence it attempts to read the *Dialogues* in the light of Gregory's letters, homilies and other theological works, and to assess as carefully as possible the late antique/early medieval context in which his view of miracles developed.

The immediate stimulus for *Signs of Sanctity* was the sense of puzzlement that many have experienced with the *Dialogues*, and that has given rise to a considerable literature. Whereas an older generation of scholars —best represented by Dudden, perhaps—was content to read the *Dialogues* literally, and to castigate their author for his blind and childish credulity, more recent critics have tended to adopt the opposite premise. They have argued that a man of Gregory's culture and sophistication could not have intended such apparently naive wonder-tales to be received as a factual account, and therefore that, as Bolton puts it, it is to the supra-historical sense that Gregory would have us direct our attention. *Signs of Sanctity* arose out of a sense of dissatisfaction with both alternatives. The question that needed to be addressed squarely was whether Gregory seriously believed the stories he related. Among recent commentators, Pierre Boglioni was alone in having given the issue significant attention.[1]

---

1   Frederick Homes Dudden, *Gregory the Great: His Place in History and Thought*, 2 vols. (1905; repr. New York, 1967); W.F. Bolton, "The Supra-Historical Sense in the Dialogues of Gregory 1," *Aevum* 33 (1959): 206-213; Pierre Boglioni, "Miracle et nature chez Grégoire le Grand," in *Cahiers d'études médiévales* 1: *Epopées, légendes et miracles* (Montreal, 1974), pp. 11-102.

In tackling this central question, *Signs of Sanctity* touches on a number of related issues as well. The main thrust of the argument, however, can be summarized as follows. On balance, modern critics are correct when they point to the larger, spiritual significance with which Gregory would invest his miracle stories. The didactic import of these episodes is clear. They are vehicles by which Gregory intends to convey lessons of a doctrinal or moral nature. These same critics are mistaken, however, if they think that the empirical status of these tales can safely be ignored, or that Gregory was engaging in a kind of moralizing, historical fiction, putting into the mouths of his alleged informants stories borrowed from St Augustine, Sulpicius Severus or some other source. Not only can such borrowing not be established, it would be impossible to reconcile with Gregory's deepest convictions on matters of truth and falsity. The conclusion, therefore, is clear. Whatever we may think of the historicity of Gregory's miracle stories (an issue on which *Signs of Sanctity* ventures no opinion), Gregory himself believed them, and intended his readers to believe them as well.

It was shortly before the completion of *Signs of Sanctity* that Francis Clark published his major, two-volume study, *The Pseudo-Gregorian Dialogues*, a book that has invigorated Gregorian scholarship with an uncustomary degree of controversy.[2] Because of the recent appearance of Clark's work, *Signs of Sanctity* does not take it into account. It simply announces that the book arrived too late, and that in any case its argument is not persuasive. According to Clark, the *Dialogues* are not to be credited to Gregory the Great at all: they are the product of a forger working in the latter part of the seventh century, approximately a hundred years after the *Dialogues* are usually thought to have been written, although this imposter (the "Dialogist") had access to, and incorporated into his forgery, genuine and otherwise unpublished Gregorian material. Clark's argument is based on external evidence of a textual or manuscript nature that would point to a relatively late date for the appearance of the *Dialogues*, and internal evidence suggesting that, given their character, the *Dialogues* could not possibly have been written by Gregory. It is the latter, the second part of his argument, that Clark considers the "essential core" of his case. The arguments there advanced, he claims, "demonstrate a clear and irreconcilable contrast between the author of the *Dialogues* and the St Gregory the

---

2   Francis Clark, *The Pseudo-Gregorian Dialogues* (Leiden, 1987).

Great who is intimately known to us through his profound theological commentaries and pastoral writings."[3]

Hitherto Clark has had a hostile reception. In addition to the usual reluctance to jettison well-established views, among Benedictines one suspects a natural disinclination to have the only biographical source for the founder of their order consigned to the historical ash-heap.[4] For the most part, however, criticism has focused on Clark's study of the external evidence. In this category, for example, is the insistence that the testimony of Paterius and Tajo is to be taken at face value, as is Gregory's famous letter to Maximian of Syracuse; or that the evidence of Jonas of Bobbio and Isidore of Seville confirms that the *Dialogues*

---

3   Clark, "The Renewed Debate on the Authenticity of the Gregorian Dialogues," *Augustinianum* 30 (1990): 75-105 at 80 & 78.

4   Major critiques have been offered by Adalbert de Vogüé, "Grégoire le Grand et ses 'Dialogues' d'après deux ouvrages récents," *Revue d'histoire ecclésiastique* 83 (1988): 281-348; Paul Meyvaert, "The Enigma of Gregory the Great's *Dialogues*: A Response to Francis Clark," *Journal of Ecclesiastical History* 39 (1988): 335-381; and Robert Godding, "Les *Dialogues* ... de Grégoire le Grand. A propos d'un livre récent," *Analecta Bollandiana* 106 (1988): 201-229. See also two additional essays by de Vogüé: "La mort dans les monastères: Jonas de Bobbio et les Dialogues de Grégoire le Grand," in *Mémorial Dom Jean Gribomont (1920-1986)* (Rome, 1988), pp. 593-619; and "'Martyrium in occulto'. Le martyre du temps de paix chez Grégoire le Grand, Isidore de Séville et Valerius du Bierzo," in *Fructus Centesimus. Mélanges offerts à Gerard J.M. Bartelink à l'occasion de son soixante-cinquième anniversaire*, ed. A.A.R. Bastiaensen, A. Hilhorst & C.H. Kneepkens, (Dordrecht, 1989), pp. 125-140. Additional review articles include Pierre Minard, "Les Dialogues de Saint Grégoire et les origines du monachisme bénédictin. A propos d'un livre récent," *Revue Mabillon* 61 (1986-1988): 471-481; Pierre-Patrick Verbraken, "Les Dialogues de saint Grégoire le Grand sont-ils apocryphes? A propos d'un ouvrage récent," *Revue Bénédictine* 98 (1988): 272-277; Pius Engelbert, "Hat Papst Gregor der Große die «Dialoge» geschrieben? Bemerkungen zu einem neuen Buch," *Erbe und Auftrag* 64 (1988): 255-265; idem, "Neue Forschungen zu den «Dialogen» Gregors des Großen. Antworten auf Clarks These," *Erbe und Auftrag* 65 (1989): 376-393; Giuseppe Cremascoli, "Se i *Dialogi* siano opera di Gregorio Magno: due volumi per una *vexata quaestio*," *Benedictina* 36 (1989): 179-192; and Robert Gillet, "Les *Dialogues* sont-ils de Grégoire?" *Revue des études augustiniennes* 36 (1990): 309-314.

For Clark's detailed response, in addition to the work cited above in n. 3, see "The Authorship of the Gregorian Dialogues: An Old Controversy Renewed," *Heythrop Journal* 30 (1989): 257-272; "St. Gregory and the Enigma of the *Dialogues*: A Response to Paul Meyvaert," *Journal of Ecclesiastical History* 40 (1989): 323-343 (followed by Meyvaert's comment on pp. 344-346); and "The Renewed Controversy about the Authorship of the Dialogues," in *Gregorio Magno e il suo tempo* (Rome, 1991), 2:5-25.

were clearly known, and known to be Gregory's, in the first half of the seventh century. Despite their alleged centrality, Clark's arguments on internal grounds have received relatively less attention. In fact, one or two critics, while vigorously defending Gregory's authorship of the *Dialogues*, have acknowledged the same tension between the *Dialogues* and Gregory's other works that Clark develops at length.

In his comprehensive and detailed review of Clark, Meyvaert notes that the *Dialogues* are not cited in any of Gregory's theological works. Contrary to Gregory's usual practice, he does not seem to have provided them with a dedicatory letter either. Possibly, Meyvaert conjectures, the *Dialogues* were never released for general distribution, either because Gregory wished to avoid attracting praise that could have imperiled his soul, or because he had had second thoughts about the value of their stories. Following Meyvaert's lead, Engelbert too thinks that Gregory may have had reservations, including reservations about his miracle stories possibly pandering to debased tastes. Neither critic, it would seem, sees any spiritual significance in the stories that would clearly have rendered them worthy of publication: apparently their sole value consists in establishing that holiness might on occasion be rewarded with miraculous gifts. The result of such a perspective is additional reinforcement for Clark's central contention, that the *Dialogues* are somehow or other unworthy of Gregory.[5]

---

5   Meyvaert, "Enigma," pp. 372-373, 378; Engelbert, "Neue Forschungen," pp. 392-393. Cf. "Papst Gregor der Große," p. 265, where Engelbert seems to regard much of the *Dialogues*, book two excepted, as beneath the dignity of Gregory. He suggests the influence of a secretary.

   For an opposed view, see Pearse Aidan Cusack, "Authenticity of the Dialogues of Gregory the Great," *Cistercian Studies* 24 (1989): 339-342 at 342. Cusack points out that Clark's critique adopts the following structure: "Gregory would not do such things. ... The Dialogist was guilty of them; therefore the work cannot be the work of Gregory." He argues that such specious logic can be disarmed by recognizing the *Dialogues* for what (he claims) they are: "The Dialogues are not history but legend. ... [They] need not be taken literally; they can have a spiritual sense which it is rewarding to discover; indeed, the book is replete with symbolism and typology, as is the Bible."

   On the specific matters of the missing dedicatory letter and Gregory's silence concerning the *Dialogues*, Meyvaert has been answered by Adalbert de Vogüé, "Les dialogues, oeuvre authentique et publiée par Grégoire lui-même," in *Gregorio Magno e il suo tempo* 2:27-40.

In this context one virtue of *Signs of Sanctity* is that it provides an alternate reading of the internal evidence, and in so doing challenges directly the heart of Clark's case. It was not part of the original purpose of *Signs of Sanctity* to reinforce the Gregorian authorship of the *Dialogues*. The book was written on the almost universally shared assumption that Gregory was indeed the author, and focuses instead on the conception of miracle entailed by the stories there related. In the context of the debate engendered by the Clark thesis, however, *Signs of Sanctity* has the effect of confirming Gregorian authorship by showing that the leading ideas of the *Dialogues* are in harmony with those recorded elsewhere in Gregory's works. The *Dialogues* are the product of a coherent world view not unworthy of one of the best educated and most cultured minds of the sixth century.

From a study of miracles in the thought of Gregory the Great there is a natural progression to a consideration of Bede's handling of the same issue. Miracles figure as prominently in Bede's works as they do in Gregory's, and over the years they have attracted a comparable amount of scholarly interest.[6] In Gregory's case the principal sources are the *Dialogues* and the *Homilies on the Gospels*; in Bede's they are the *Ecclesiastical History* and the *Lives of St Cuthbert*. In each case as well there is the same prospect of extended study bearing dividends. The principal sources do not have to be read in isolation, as is frequently the case with hagiographical literature. Both Gregory and Bede have left a rich legacy of other writings that collectively are invaluable in establishing an intellectual context. Particularly significant are their works of exegesis, for their comments on biblical miracles provide important guidance on how the modern miracles they record elsewhere are to be

---

6   See, for example, Bertram Colgrave, "Bede's Miracle Stories," in *Bede: His Life, Times, and Writings. Essays in Commemoration of the Twelfth Centenary of His Death*, ed. A. Hamilton Thompson (1935; repr. Oxford, 1969), pp. 201-229; C. Grant Loomis, "The Miracle Traditions of the Venerable Bede," *Speculum* 21 (1946): 404-418; Joel T. Rosenthal, "Bede's Use of Miracles in 'The Ecclesiastical History,'" *Traditio* 31 (1975): 328-335; Benedicta Ward, "Miracles and History: A Reconsideration of the Miracle Stories Used by Bede," in *Famulus Christi: Essays in Commemoration of the Thirteenth Centenary of the Birth of the Venerable Bede*, ed. Gerald Bonner (London, 1976), pp. 70-76; Laurence Stearns Creider, "Bede's Understanding of the Miraculous" (Ph.D. dissertation, Yale University, 1979); Gail Ivy Berlin, "Bede's Miracle Stories: Notions of Evidence and Authority in Old English History," *Neophilologus* 74 (1990): 434-443.

regarded. Perhaps the strongest reason, however, for following a study of Gregory with one of Bede is Bede's veneration of Gregory, and his known dependence on him in his theological works. Given the nature of their relationship, it is a reasonable working hypothesis that on the issue of miracles specifically Gregory's views could have had significant and perhaps determining influence on the Anglo-Saxon scholar. An important objective of the present volume is to test this hypothesis as systematically as possible.

Abbreviations

CCL	Corpus Christianorum. Series Latina. Turnhout: Brepols, 1953— .
CSEL	Corpus scriptorum ecclesiasticorum latinorum. Vienna, 1866— .
EHD 1	*English Historical Documents* 1: *c. 500-1042*. Ed. Dorothy Whitelock. 2nd edition. New York: Oxford University Press, 1979.
HE	Bede, *Historia ecclesiastica gentis Anglorum*. Ed. and trans. Bertram Colgrave and R.A.B. Mynors. Oxford: Clarendon, 1969.
MGH, SRM	Monumenta Germaniae Historica. Scriptores rerum Merovingicarum. Hannover: Hahn, 1885— .
PG	Patrologiae cursus completus. Series Graeca. Ed. J.P. Migne. Paris, 1857-1866.
PL	Patrologiae cursus completus. Series Latina. Ed. J.P. Migne. Paris, 1844-1864.
Plummer, *Opera Historica*	*Venerabilis Baedae Opera Historica*. Ed. Carolus Plummer. 2 vols. Oxford: Oxford University Press, 1896.
SC	Sources chrétiennes. Paris: Cerf, 1942— .
Signs of Sanctity	Wm.D. McCready, *Signs of Sanctity: Miracles in the Thought of Gregory the Great*. Studies and Texts 91. Toronto: Pontifical Institute of Mediaeval Studies, 1989.
VCA	*Vita S. Cuthberti auctore anonymo*. Ed. and trans. Bertram Colgrave. *Two Lives of Saint Cuthbert*, pp. 59-139. Cambridge: Cambridge University Press, 1940.
VCM	Bede, *Vita S. Cuthberti (metrica)*. Ed. Werner Jaager. *Bedas metrische Vita s. Cuthberti*. Palaestra 198. Leipzig: Mayer & Müller, 1935.
VCP	Bede, *Vita S. Cuthberti (prosaica)*. Ed. and trans. Bertram Colgrave. *Two Lives of Saint Cuthbert*, pp. 141-307. Cambridge: Cambridge University Press, 1940.
Zimmermann	Gregory the Great, *Dialogues*. Trans. Odo John Zimmerman. Fathers of the Church 39. New York, 1959.

Introduction

Little is known of the life of Bede save what Bede himself records in the brief biographical statement at the end of his *Ecclesiastical History*. There he tells us that he was a mere seven years of age when he was entrusted by his kinsmen to the care of Abbot Benedict and the brethren of the monastery of St Peter at Wearmouth so that he might be educated. When the sister institution of St Paul's was established at Jarrow, the young Bede accompanied the small group of monks transferred there under the leadership of Ceolfrith. Shortly thereafter occurred the famous incident recorded in the anonymous *Life of Ceolfrith*, an outbreak of pestilence that so reduced the population of Jarrow that there was no one left to sing the offices save Ceolfrith himself and one small boy. According to Colgrave, "there can be no doubt that the little boy was Bede himself. It is typical of Bede's modesty that, in his *History of the Abbots*, he omits the incident altogether."[1] Apart from a few short trips, Bede spent his entire life at Jarrow. He was ordained deacon at the tender age of nineteen and priest at the age of thirty, each time by Bishop John of Hexham, later known as John of Beverley; but he never attained a position of leadership in the community. He seems never to have aspired to one. Instead he applied himself entirely to a life of quiet study and contemplation. "Amid the observance of the discipline of the Rule and the daily task of singing in the church," he tells us, "it has always been my delight to learn or to teach or to write."[2] Since he was in his fifty-ninth year in 731 when he completed the *Ecclesiastical History*, he must have been born in 672 or 673. His death on 25 May 735, the eve of Ascension Day, has been lovingly recorded by his disciple, Cuthbert, a later abbot of the combined monastery of Wearmouth-Jarrow. "All who heard or saw the death of our saintly father Bede," says Cuthbert, "declared that they had never seen a man end his days in such great holiness and peace."[3]

---

1 *Vita Ceolfridi*, chap. 14, Plummer, *Opera Historica* 1:393. Bertram Colgrave, *HE*, p. xx; cf. Plummer, *Opera Historica* 1:xii.
2 *HE* 5.24, p. 567.
3 *Epistola de obitu Bedae*, ed. & trans. Colgrave & Mynors, *HE*, pp. 579-587 at 585-587.

Although located at the very edge of the inhabited world as it was then known, Northumbria was far from being a cultural backwater in the late seventh and early eighth centuries.[4] Bede's monastery in particular benefited from the enterprise and scholarly interests of its founder and patron, Benedict Biscop, whose trips to Rome and the continent resulted in an excellent working library particularly rich in theological sources. The collection developed even further under Benedict's successor, the abbot Ceolfrith, whose departure in 717 to spend his last days in Rome occasioned much distress on Bede's part. In addition to Ambrose, Jerome, Augustine and Gregory the Great, the four great Fathers of the western church, Bede had access to other Latin sources like Cyprian of Carthage or Hilary of Poitiers, and to some Greek patristic authors—Gregory Nazianzen and John Chrysostom, for example—as well. It is almost sixty years now since Laistner endeavoured to reconstruct the holdings of this library (or at least of the books to which Bede somehow or other had access) from the references or citations in Bede's works, and the inevitable result is that his list is badly out of date.[5] The subsequent appearance of modern critical editions of several items in the Bede corpus would now require both the addition of some titles and the deletion of others. One suspects, however, that the changes introduced in any revised edition of the list would not alter the validity of Laistner's general assessment. The catalogue of the books that Bede was able to consult was both "impressive in length and for his age unique."[6]

4   See, for example, David M. Wilson, "The Art and Archaeology of Bedan North-umbria," in *Bede and Anglo-Saxon England. Papers in Honour of the 1300th Anniversary of the Birth of Bede, Given at Cornell University in 1973 and 1974*, ed. Robert T. Farrell (Oxford, 1978), pp. 1-22.
5   M.L.W. Laistner, "The Library of the Venerable Bede," in *Bede: His Life, Times, and Writings*, pp. 237-266. Roger Ray, "What Do We Know about Bede's Commentaries?" *Recherches de théologie ancienne et médiévale* 49 (1982): 5-20, has announced that he and Paul Meyvaert "intend to produce the needed revision" (n. 18).
6   Laistner, "Library of the Venerable Bede," p. 260. See Bede's own remarks in the epistle to Acca that prefaces his commentary on Genesis. Here Bede mentions the Fathers (Basil, Ambrose and Augustine) who commented on Genesis before him, and then notes how rich a collection their works represent: "Verum quia haec tam copiosa tam sunt alta ut vix nisi a locupletioribus tot volumina adquiri, vix tam profunda nisi ab eruditioribus valeant perscrutari, placuit vestrae sanctitati id nobis officii iniungere ut de omnibus his, velut de amoenissimis late florentis paradisi campis, quae infirmorum viderentur necessitati sufficere decerperemus" (*In Gen.*, Praef., CCL 118A:1).

Bede took full advantage of the opportunity, and in the process became by common agreement the most important and influential scriptural scholar between Gregory the Great and Thomas Aquinas.[7] Unsurprisingly, Bede's own claims are considerably more modest. "From the time I became a priest until the fifty-ninth year of my life," he tells us, "I have made it my business, for my own benefit and that of my brothers, to make brief extracts from the works of the venerable fathers on the holy Scriptures, or to add notes of my own to clarify their sense and interpretation."[8] In Bede's own judgment, his work is largely derivative, very much overshadowed by the Fathers. At one time this assessment was frequently endorsed in the secondary literature as well. Bede himself, however, is not the best judge in such matters, and especially over the last twenty years or so scholars have been coming around to a rather different view.[9] Bede's devotion to the Fathers was real, but it is not, as Ray points out, to be confused with "scholarly deference, personal reticence, or even monastic humility. It was programmatic."[10] Bede's calling was primarily that of a teacher, providing materials for an Anglo-Saxon church still in its infancy. To meet the need at hand Bede quite reasonably followed the works of his great predecessors, adapting and explaining where necessary to make the message intelligible for his less cultured countrymen.

In so doing, it was never Bede's practice slavishly to endorse whatever view happened to be at hand. Initially, he tells us, he was somewhat dazzled by the splendour of his authorities. But as confidence and experience grew he found himself prepared to correct their errors and misjudgments. His reputed distrust of Isidore of Seville, overstated though it may be, is only the most striking illustration of his independent spirit that comes to mind.[11] Rather than merely stringing citations

7 On the diffusion of Bede's influence, beginning in his own lifetime, see, for example, Dorothy Whitelock, *After Bede* (Jarrow, 1960); Ansgar Willmes, "Bedas Bibelauslegung," *Archiv für Kulturgeschichte* 44 (1963): 281-314, esp. 306-314; and M.B. Parkes, *The Scriptorium of Wearmouth-Jarrow* (Jarrow, 1982).
8 *HE* 5.24, p. 567.
9 See, for example, Paul Meyvaert, "Bede the Scholar," in *Famulus Christi*, pp. 40-69, an important essay that summarizes some earlier views.
10 Ray, "Bede's Commentaries," p. 12.
11 *Retr. Act. Apost.* 1.13, CCL 121:107: "auctoritatem magnorum sequens doctorum, quae in illorum opusculis inveni, absque scrupulo suscipienda credidi." See Meyvaert, "Bede the Scholar," p. 58. With regard to Bede's use of Isidore specifically,

together in a *catena Patrum*, choices had to be made, a task that Bede
faced with both discernment and sensitivity, placing a strong personal
stamp on his material while shaping it as his needs dictated. Meyvaert
points out that "it has somehow become more coherent in his hands; the
sum is greater than its parts. It takes a kind of genius to do this sort of
thing well, a kind of genius which Bede undoubtedly possessed."[12]
When necessary he was also willing to venture his own personal
contribution to the elucidation of the sacred text. As Holder explains:

> We should not let Bede's humility prevent us from recognizing the full
> extent of his creative genius. ... When he could find an ancient text that
> expressed his own convictions well, he would quote it gladly; otherwise, he
> did not hesitate to exercise his own sanctified imagination in the service of
> true doctrine. [13]

Holder lays to rest as well Bede's alleged reluctance to consider original
approaches to complex issues. The existence of texts like *De templo* and
De tabernaculo establish the point. These thematically conceived
treatises were innovations on Bede's part; they constitute strong evidence
that he was considerably more creative than he gives himself credit for.

In referring to the venerable Fathers in whose footsteps he was
content to follow, Bede was thinking primarily of Ambrose, Jerome,
Augustine and Gregory the Great. These were his principal guides. Of
the four, Ambrose seems clearly to have had the least influence on
Bede's exegesis. Of the others, depending on the standard of measurement used, one could argue with some plausibility for either Jerome or
Augustine being his major authority. According to Laistner, Bede knew
eighteen of Augustine's works.[14] Of no other patristic author had he
read as much. These eighteen, however, represent only a small percentage of Augustine's total output, and even of these there is some

---

Meyvaert points out that he "only mentions the name of Isidore three times, and
each time it is to correct him. ... Dante placed Bede and Isidore together in Paradise. He might have hesitated, had he been more fully aware of Bede's true senti-
ments ..." (pp. 58-60). Cf. Laistner, "Library of the Venerable Bede," p. 256; and
Roger Ray, "Bede's *vera lex historiae*," *Speculum* 55 (1980): 1-21 at 15-17.

12   Meyvaert, "Bede the Scholar," p. 62. Cf. Ray, "Bede's Commentaries," p. 11.

13   Arthur G. Holder, "New Treasures and Old in Bede's 'De Tabernaculo' and 'De
Templo,'" *Revue Bénédictine* 99 (1989): 237-249 at 249.

14   Laistner, "Library of the Venerable Bede," p. 263.

question about how many he knew directly.[15] Although additional research may require some modification of the picture in Jerome's case as well, as things now stand Bede seems to have had direct knowledge of most of Jerome's writings, and he also seems to have cited him more frequently.[16]

If pride of place is to be conceded to one of the four, however, then by general acknowledgment it should be granted to Gregory the Great.[17] The special respect that Bede accorded to Gregory is evident at every turn in his work, nowhere more clearly than in the introduction to the final book of his commentary on the Canticle of Canticles:

> In our exposition of the Canticle of Canticles, which we have set forth in five books—for the first part of the work is directed specifically against Julian [of Eclanum], and [is written] in defence of the grace of God, which he attacked, and from the lack of which he perished—we have so followed in the footsteps of the Fathers that for the moment we have left unexamined the works of our father, beloved of God and men, Pope Gregory. We thought it would be more pleasing to readers if we were to bring together equally and place in one book everything, scattered here and there throughout all his works, that Pope Gregory had to say in explanation of

15 See Paul-Irénée Fransen, "D'Eugippius à Bède le Vénérable: à propos de leurs florilèges augustiniens," *Revue Bénédictine* 97 (1987): 187-194. Fransen provides a comparison of the extracts from Augustine found in the florilegium of Eugippius with those found in Bede's commentary on the Apostle (the forthcoming *Collectio ex opusculis sancti Augustini in epistulas Pauli Apostoli*, CCL 121B). On this basis he argues that some of the titles mentioned by Laistner may have been known to Bede only from Eugippius's extracts. The strongest doubts probably surround *Contra Faustum* and *De doctrina christiana*. He also argues, however, that Bede's dependence on Eugippius was far from servile: "Tout en s'inspirant d'Eugippius, Bède fraie son propre chemin. Il puise largement dans des œuvres augustiniennes que ne cite pas Eugippius. Bien plus: même s'il emprunte à Eugippius certains extraits d'une œuvre augustinienne, il n'en cite pas moins d'autres extraits de la même œuvre non sélectionnés par Eugippius" (p. 192).

16 See Thomas R. Eckenrode, "The Venerable Bede and the Pastoral Affirmation of the Christian Message in Anglo-Saxon England," *Downside Review* 99 (1981): 258-278 at 270. Eckenrode has surveyed the sources identified in the Corpus Christianorum editions of *In Lucam, In Marcam, In Ezram et Neemiam, In 1 Samuhelis* and *De tabernaculo*, and has concluded that Jerome is cited four times as frequently as Augustine.

17 See, for example, Paul Meyvaert, *Bede and Gregory the Great* (Jarrow, 1964), esp. pp. 13-19; and Alan Thacker, "Bede's Ideal of Reform," in *Ideal and Reality in Frankish and Anglo-Saxon Society: Studies Presented to J.M. Wallace-Hadrill*, ed. Patrick Wormald, Donald Bullough & Roger Collins (Oxford, 1983), pp. 130-153.

this book, for his works are many and his comments abundant. With God's help, this is what we are now about to do. A seventh book on the Canticle of Canticles has, therefore, been prepared, a book brought together by our labour, but composed of the words and teaching of the blessed Gregory, so that if perchance there is anyone of the view that our work ought properly to be rejected, he may have at hand for his reading the comments of one who is by no means ever to be spurned. If, however, there is some reader especially enamoured of our efforts, let it be as though our humble building were to receive a golden roof at the hand of a great master-builder.[18]

In view of the special interest that Gregory took in the conversion of the Anglo-Saxons, it is unsurprising that Bede should have honoured him especially and devoted a chapter of the *Ecclesiastical History* to his biography. "We can and should by rights call him our apostle," says Bede, "for though he held the most important see in the whole world and was head of Churches which had long been converted to the true faith, yet he made our nation, till then enslaved to idols, into a Church of Christ, so that we may use the apostle's words about him, 'If he is not an apostle to others yet at least he is to us, for we are the seal of his apostleship in the Lord.'"[19] Bede's veneration was not a matter of mere sentiment, however. Meyvaert speaks of a "spiritual affinity" linking Gregory and Bede in a subtle fashion,[20] the product presumably of the common perspective they shared on the exegete's task. Neither is known for the insight he brought to abstract questions of speculative theology. It was the moral sense of Scripture to which they both were drawn. The issues that particularly commanded their

18 *In Cant.* 6, CCL 119B:359: "In expositione cantici canticorum quam libris quinque explicavimus, nam primum huius operis volumen contra Iulianum pro defensione gratiae Dei quam ille impugnavit unde et hac destituente periit specialiter confecimus, ita patrum vestigia secuti sumus ut interim opuscula dilecti Deo et hominibus papae ac patris nostri Gregorii relinqueremus intacta iocundius fore legentibus rati si ea quae ille in explanationem huius voluminis per cuncta opuscula sua sparsim disseruit quia plurima sunt et copiose dicta quasi in unum collecta volumen pariter omnia poneremus quod modo adiuvante domino sumus facturi. Cudatur ergo septimus in cantica canticorum liber nostro quidem labore collectus sed beati Gregorii sermonibus et sensu compositus ut si quis forte sit qui nostra opuscula iure spernenda aestimet habeat in promptu legenda eius dicta qui constat nullatenus esse spernendus. Si quis vero haec quoque nostra si quis captus amore legat sit ut marmoreis nostrae parvitatis aedificiis aureum tantus architectus culmen imponat."
19 *HE* 2.1, p. 123.
20 Meyvaert, *Bede and Gregory the Great*, p. 19.

attention were those relating to the immediately practical concerns of the Christian life.[21]

With the possible exception of his commentary on 1 Kings (1 Samuel),[22] Bede knew all of Gregory's major works and drew from them liberally. His knowledge clearly extended to Gregory's *Dialogues* as well. At the beginning of the *Historia abbatum* he appropriates the *Dialogues'* description of Benedict of Nursia for his own portrait of Benedict Biscop; throughout the *Ecclesiastical History* the verbal echoes of the *Dialogues* are frequent enough for Wallace-Hadrill to suggest that they were "constantly in Bede's mind."[23] Indeed, Loomis has suggested that Bede employed them as a touchstone of authenticity to help him distinguish the credible from the fantastic:

> For years he amassed materials for his *Historia*. Both written and oral facts and fictions came to his hand. The items of native wonder-lore must have been very numerous. Faced with the task of selection, and fully aware of the miracle traditions of the Celts, he turned for guidance to the *Dialogues* of Gregory, whose authority and fame, both as the progenitor of English Christianity and as an unimpeachable historian of Church lore, were incontestably established. When Bede found English miracles too much tinged with the colors of a primitive and unbridled imagination, he chose to lay them quietly aside.[24]

Bede's knowledge of the *Dialogues* clearly familiarized him with the miracle stories that had been told by Gregory. When combined with his command of Gregory's more strictly theological works, it also left him well prepared fully to appreciate the nuances of Gregory's concept of the miraculous and its role in the early medieval church. Given his esteem of "the apostle to the English," it is reasonable to assume that Bede's

---

21 Cf. Willmes, "Bedas Bibelauslegung," p. 292.

22 See below, p. 18, n. 26.

23 *Historia abbatum* 1.1, Plummer, *Opera Historica* 1:364: "Qui ut beati papae Gregorii verbis, quibus cognominis eius abbatis vitam glorificat, utar: 'Fuit vir vitae venerabilis, gratia Benedictus et nomine, ab ipso pueritiae suae tempore cor gerens senile, aetatem quippe moribus transiens, nulli animum voluptati dedit." Cf. *Dial.* 2 Prol. 1, SC 260:126. J.M. Wallace-Hadrill, *Bede's Ecclesiastical History of the English People* (Oxford, 1988), p. 173.

24 Loomis, "Miracle Traditions," p. 418. On the formative influence of the *Dialogues* on early medieval English hagiography, see Theodor Wolpers, *Die englische Heiligenlegende des Mittelalters* (Tübingen, 1964), p. 44; and David W. Rollason, *Saints and Relics in Anglo-Saxon England* (Oxford, 1989), pp. 63-64.

own perspective was materially shaped by Gregory's. The present volume has been designed to determine to what extent that was the case. Hence it deals with largely the same set of issues as *Signs of Sanctity*, and in basically the same terms, although the emphasis tends to fall at different points, and the order of the discussion is somewhat altered.

Chapter One begins by considering briefly the intellectual background and perspective that Bede brought to his work, before examining more closely the place of miracles in his view of the natural realm and the kind of order it contains. Subsequent chapters consider the degree of scepticism or credulity that Bede brought to the issue, as well as his thoughts on the history of miracles, the purpose they serve in the eighth-century church, and their relationship to saintly virtue. The last four chapters all address the question of the truth value of Bede's miracle stories. Can we assume that Bede himself accepted as factually true whatever he chose to include in his narrative, or is there reason to believe that factual veracity may sometimes have been sacrificed to other, higher considerations? Since Gregory the Great is questioned on the same set of issues in *Signs of Sanctity*, throughout this book comparisons between Bede and Gregory are frequent. The book is not, however, intended simply as an essay on Gregorian influence in the early medieval centuries. Indeed, it is primarily an essay on Bede himself, who deserves more than merely being read and judged by Gregorian standards. His status as the fifth great father of the Latin church demands that every effort be made to understand him on his own terms.

1

Science and Literary Culture

The twin monastery of Wearmouth-Jarrow that constituted Bede's home for over fifty years was located in the remote stretches of an island province that itself lay at the extreme north-western limit of the inhabited world as it was then known. However, the monastery's physical isolation was not accompanied by the cultural deprivation that one otherwise might have expected. Through the patronage of its remarkable founder, Benedict Biscop, it was quickly brought into the cultural mainstream of the seventh century, with the result that Bede, its most celebrated product, was able to acquire a level of education that was the envy of his contemporaries. In the late seventh century, of course, the foundation of such an education was grammar, which Bede mastered to a degree rivalled by few others. Although it was a second language for Bede, one based initially at least on the study of the Psalter, he came to acquire a Latinity perfectly modelled to the purpose it had to serve and a worthy rival to that of Gregory the Great. "In addition to [its] extraordinary efficiency ... in transmitting and exemplifying the essentials of literacy," says Wetherbee, "its simplicity and purity and its freedom from stylistic self-consciousness constitute in themselves a positive contribution to the development of a medieval Christian humanism."[1]

In one respect at least, his knowledge of Greek, Bede came to surpass Gregory. Gregory describes himself as being virtually ignorant of the language, something of an overstatement perhaps given his period of service as papal *apocrisiarius* in Constantinople. But even when allowances are made for the traditional *confessiones humilitatis*, it remains clear that his command of the language was limited.[2] Bede, on the other hand, possessed a working knowledge of it, and one that improved measurably over the years. In view of the Greek/Latin and Latin/Greek dictionaries that were then available and that Bede himself used in his *De orthographia*, Gribomont maintains that there is no reason to think that

---

1   Winthrop Wetherbee, "Some Implications of Bede's Latin Style," in *Bede and Anglo-Saxon England*, pp. 23-31 at 23.
2   *Signs of Sanctity*, p. 178.

his expertise was exceptional for the time. More recently, Dionisotti has argued that it was a remarkable and extraordinary achievement. In all probability, she suggests, Bede was self-taught, his knowledge being based upon word-for-word study of the Greek and Latin Scriptures, in addition to what could have been culled from Latin patristic sources.[3] Whether exceptional or not, however, his accomplishment remains noteworthy. Early in his career, as a reading of his commentary on the Acts of the Apostles demonstrates, Bede's knowledge of Greek was largely passive, dependent on early patristic sources and on Greek/Latin interlinear texts. In his mature work, as his book of *Retractions* exemplifies, he was capable of working to a much higher standard, even if he still lacked the easy facility of the accomplished scholar. As Lynch puts it, no longer was he "bound to accept passively the version of a single interlinear. He clearly had an extensive biblical Greek vocabulary and could read the Greek text well enough to know when it was correctly expressed in Latin."[4]

---

3   Cf. Jean Gribomont, "Saint Bède et ses dictionnaires grecs," *Revue Bénédictine* 89 (1979): 271-280; and Anna Carlotta Dionisotti, "On Bede, Grammars, and Greek," *Revue Bénédictine* 92 (1982): 111-141, esp. 128. Bede himself describes the blossoming of Greek studies at Canterbury after the arrival of Theodore and Hadrian, adding: "usque hodie supersunt de eorum discipulis, qui Latinam Graecamque linguam aeque ut propriam in qua nati sunt norunt" (*HE* 4.2, p. 334). On the accuracy of his assessment, however, see Michael Lapidge, "The Study of Greek at the School of Canterbury in the Seventh Century," in *The Sacred Nectar of the Greeks: The Study of Greek in the West in the Early Middle Ages*, ed. Michael W. Herren & Shirley Ann Brown (London, 1988), pp. 169-194.

4   Kevin M. Lynch, "The Venerable Bede's Knowledge of Greek," *Traditio* 39 (1983): 432-439, esp. 437. For a contrasting view, see W.F. Bolton, "An Aspect of Bede's Later Knowledge of Greek," *Classical Review* n.s. 13 (1963): 17-18. In the catalogue of his writings appended to the *Ecclesiastical History* Bede lists a life of St Anastasius that seems to have been lost: "librum vitae et passionis sancti Anastasii male de Greco translatum et peius a quodam inperito emendatum, prout potui, ad sensum correxi" (*HE* 5.24, pp. 568-570). Although this might be taken to support the conclusion suggested by his exegetical works, the most recent scholarship on this issue would suggest caution. See Carmela Vircillo Franklin & Paul Meyvaert, "Has Bede's Version of the «Passio S. Anastasii» Come Down to Us in «BHL» 408?" *Analecta Bollandiana* 100 (1982): 373-400. Franklin and Meyvaert have identified the faulty Latin translation as *BHL* (*Bibliotheca Hagiographica Latina*) 410b, which survives in the single exemplar, MS F.III.16 (ff. 14-23) of the Biblioteca Nazionale of Turin. With regard to Bede's version they suggest only that "the possibility of attributing *BHL* 408 to Bede deserves very serious consideration" (p. 395). Interestingly, however, *BHL* 408 was made by someone

If Bede surpassed Gregory in his grasp of language, however, Gregory had a greater familiarity with the world of literature. According to Bonner, who reflects the established scholarly consensus, the essential difference between Bede's cultural world and that of the Fathers was that "Bede had no foundation of classical literature such as they enjoyed." Bede learned his Latin for essentially spiritual purposes, to enable him to fulfil his vocation as a monk and a priest. His textbooks, therefore, had been the standard grammars used by many before him, supplemented, of course, by Sacred Scripture itself. There is no indication that, like the classically trained Fathers, Bede went on to the second stage of grammatical study by examining directly the major literary works of antiquity. He would not have had the means even if he had had the inclination. The library of Wearmouth-Jarrow was overwhelmingly theological in nature. Its collection was that of an institution whose rule made much less provision for liberal studies than would have been the case at Cassiodorus's Vivarium in the mid-sixth century.[5] Hence, apart from Vergil, Pliny and, of course, the grammarians, Bede's knowledge of classical texts was basically second hand. Indeed, in recent years even his direct knowledge of Vergil has been seriously challenged.[6]

Although it would be perilous to suggest that the matter is settled, the result of Wright's most recent investigation of the issue has been to reinstate Bede in his knowledge of Vergil. His quotations of Vergilian material are indeed often taken from the late Latin grammarians. But there is also compelling evidence of direct use of the poet, sufficient to warrant the conclusion that his knowledge extended to *Eclogues*, *Georgics* and *Aeneid*. More recently Irvine has gone on to argue *inter alia* for his firsthand knowledge of Ovid's *Metamorphoses* and Seneca's *Epistulae* as well, pointing to the centrality of grammar in the intellectual life of the time. "Bede's use of classical texts," he maintains, "must be understood in the context of a culture that depended on grammatical methodology at every level of learning from elementary literacy to advanced studies in exegesis." In this context the literature of antiquity retained its value and utility, and Bede clearly demonstrated his firsthand exposure

---

who did not have access to the Greek original, and thus "could only judge the Latin of *BHL* 410b on its own face value" (p. 392).

5   Gerald Bonner, "Bede and Medieval Civilization," *Anglo-Saxon England* 2 (1973): 71-90 at 76 & 80.

6   See Peter Hunter Blair, "From Bede to Alcuin," in *Famulus Christi*, pp. 239-260 at 243-250.

to it.[7] The most recent statements on the issue, therefore, provide what may be a necessary corrective, and restore to Bede some direct knowledge of the literature of the ancient world. The fundamental picture, however, remains much as it was. Bede may not have been totally ignorant of Vergil or even Ovid and Seneca. But his firsthand knowledge of classical literature was still limited in comparison with Augustine's or Gregory's. Grammar may have retained its central, determining role in the intellectual life of the seventh and eighth centuries, as Bede, the author of grammatical texts, would well have known. But its character had changed — "Purely vocational in purpose, the sole end of grammar was now an understanding of Scripture so profound that its truth would become the means of sustaining the monk's spiritual life"[8]—and as a result less room was left for the antique literary tradition.

A closer look at particular works bears out the general conclusion. In *De arte metrica* Bede does quote from a number of classical authors, principally Vergil. Since his subject matter was practical instruction in pronunciation, non-Christian sources would not have appeared particularly threatening. Even so, however, he frequently substitutes selections from Christian poets for the Vergilian extracts contained in his sources. Christian poets have displaced classical authors as the main sources of Bede's literary culture; it is they who are identified as *nostrates poetae*.[9] In *De schematibus et tropis* the same broad trend is clear. Indeed, apart from one extract from Sedulius and an unidentified but probably

---

7   Neil Wright, "Bede and Vergil," *Romanobarbarica* 6 (1981): 361-379; Martin Irvine, "Bede the Grammarian and the Scope of Grammatical Studies in Eighth-Century Northumbria," *Anglo-Saxon England* 15 (1986): 15-44, esp. 40. Roger Ray, "Bede and Cicero," *Anglo-Saxon England* 16 (1987): 1-15, argues that Bede's rhetorical sophistication was such as to suggest a firsthand knowledge of Cicero's *De inventione*. However, Helmut Gneuss, "The Study of Language in Anglo-Saxon England," *Bulletin of the John Rylands University Library* 72 (1990): 3-32, esp. 29, regards the evidence as inconclusive. Cf. Luigi Piacente, "Un nuovo frammento ciceroniano in Beda," *Romanobarbarica* 9 (1986-1987): 229-245.

8   Margo H. King, "*Grammatica mystica*: A Study of Bede's Grammatical Curriculum," in *Saints, Scholars and Heroes: Studies in Medieval Culture in Honour of Charles W. Jones*, ed. Margot H. King & Wesley M. Stevens (Collegeville MN, 1979), 1:145-159 at 153.

9   *De arte metrica* 14, CCL 123A:123; cf. ibid. 3, p. 91: "in nostratibus poematibus." See Bruno Luiselli, "Il *De arte metrica* di Beda di fronte alla tradizione metricologica tardo-latina," in *Grammatici latini d'età imperiale: Miscellanea filologica* (Genova, 1976), pp. 169-180.

Christian hexameter, even the Christian poets disappear. There is one additional selection from the *Moralia* of Gregory the Great, but all other illustrative examples are taken from the Bible. Although the Greeks may pride themselves on having invented figures or tropes, says Bede, his intent is to illustrate that they were anticipated by Sacred Scripture:

> In order that you and all who wish to read this work may know that Holy Writ surpasses all other writings not merely in authority because it is divine, or in usefulness because it leads to eternal life, but also for its age and artistic composition (*sed et antiquitate et ipsa ... positione dicendi*), I have chosen to demonstrate by means of examples collected from Holy Writ that teachers of secular eloquence have not been able to furnish us with any figures and tropes of this kind that did not first appear in Scripture.[10]

King takes some of the force out of the latter example by suggesting that *De schematibus et tropis* was really a theological work rather than the rhetorical treatise it has generally been considered. It was intended, says King, to provide "an introduction to exegesis by means of a study of the literary devices used in Scripture."[11] Even so, however, the general drift of Bede's thought is clear. Although he worked comfortably in the languages of the ancient world, and developed his competence in Latin to a very high degree, he was not able fully to appropriate its culture. He followed in the footsteps of Gregory the Great, and took the tendencies there noticeable one stage further. For the most part the classical allusions or quotations detectable in his work betray no attachment to the literature of antiquity but are simple echoes of the training he received in Latin grammar. They occur in writings dating primarily from the early part of his career, and are largely absent from

---

10 *De schematibus et tropis* 1, CCL 123A:142-143; trans. Gussie Hecht Tannenhaus, in *Readings in Medieval Rhetoric*, ed. Joseph M. Miller, Michael H. Prosser & Thomas W. Benson (Bloomington, 1973), p. 97 (revised). The inspiration was Augustinian. See *De doctrina christiana* 3.29.40, CCL 32:100-101; cf. Antonio Isola, "Il *De schematibus et tropis* di Beda in rapporto al *De doctrina Christiana* di Agostino," *Romanobarbarica* 1 (1976): 71-82. In addition to acknowledging the marked Christian and biblical character of Bede's treatise, Ulrich Schindel, "Die Quellen von Bedas Figurenlehre," *Classica et Mediaevalia* 29 (1968): 169-186, points to the traditional nature of the teaching it contains: "Abgesehen von den Beispielen benutzt Beda ... durchaus das traditionelle Lehrgut der saecularis eloquentia, deren Anspruch auf Originalität er so entschieden zurückweist" (pp. 169-170). His principal source, in Schindel's judgment, was none other than Donatus.

11 King, "*Grammatica mystica*," p. 150.

his mature theological works.[12] The cultural and intellectual world inhabited by the mature Bede was one in which the images of ancient literature had largely lost their power. It was overwhelmingly Christian, and primarily biblical.

Was Bede also an opponent of secular culture? Like Gregory the Great, he has certainly been read that way; and although nuance has now refined the harsh judgments of a half-century ago,[13] they have by no means been reversed. Even among the most sympathetic of modern observers one can find references to Bede's at least occasional hostility to pagan authors.[14] Indeed, Bede himself provides those so inclined with the opportunity. At one point in *De arte metrica* he refuses to include extracts from the works of the poet Porphyrius because of their pagan status.[15] In his commentary on Genesis he finds an appropriate figure for worldly wisdom and eloquence in the bricks prepared for the

12 Bede's grammatical works (*De orthographia, De arte metrica, De schematibus et tropis*) are generally assigned an early date. Kendall, their editor, suggests 701 or 702 for *De arte metrica* and *De schematibus et tropis*. However, recent scholarship has advanced a dissenting view. Irvine, "Bede the Grammarian," pp. 41-43, argues that in the absence of hard evidence there is no reason to consider the grammatical treatises either immature or dating from early in Bede's career. Dionisotti, "On Bede, Grammars, and Greek," maintains of *De orthographia* specifically that it was neither an early work nor a mere text-book, but rather "a reference work for the library, or scriptorium, or the desk of the studious monk" (p. 122).

13 See, for example, D. Bernard Capelle, "Le rôle théologique de Bède le Vénérable," *Studia Anselmiana* 6 (1936): 1-40, esp. 8-9 & 13, who sees in Bede's work evidence of a radical and inflexible anti-classicism. For a more balanced assessment reflecting the most recent scholarship, see George Hardin Brown, *Bede the Venerable* (Boston, 1987), pp. 30-31.

14 See, for example, Wright, "Bede and Vergil," p. 377: "his occasional hostility to pagan authors suggest[s] that Bede shared with many Christian writers a basic mistrust of the Classics." Cf. p. 362. According to Bonner, "Bede and Medieval Civilization," p. 82, Bede was "notoriously" hostile to the classics, "more hostile than his master, Gregory the Great."

15 *De arte metrica* 24, CCL 123A:138: "Reperiuntur quaedam et in insigni illo volumine Porphyrii poetae, quo ad Constantinum Augustum misso meruit de exilio liberari. Quae, quia pagana erant, nos tangere non libuit." Elsewhere in *De arte metrica* Bede does not hesitate to provide short quotations from pagan authors to illustrate what he has to say about metre. What is at issue, therefore, is the inappropriateness of including extensive extracts, comparable to those he provides from Christian sources. Note also that he refers to the "distinguished" volume of Porphyrius.

building of the tower of Babel.[16] But if his language sometimes appears harsh and his judgment uncompromising, a full examination of the context usually reveals a more specific point to be at issue than the global condemnation of secular culture as a whole.

Bede's commentary on Luke 15:16-17 can be offered as a typical example. Here he refers dismissively to worldly wisdom, describing it as *inanis philosophia* and likening it to pods suitable for the feeding of swine. But, viewed in context, these comments turn out to be something less than a summary judgment. The chapter in question contains the story of the Prodigal Son, who, in his straightened circumstances, "would gladly have fed on the pods that the swine ate," and who asks himself: "How many of my father's hired servants have bread enough and to spare, but I perish here with hunger." Says Bede:

> The servants of the father have bread in abundance, because those who strive to perform good works with a view to future reward are refreshed by the daily sustenance of heavenly grace. But those who, excluded from the father's dwelling, eagerly fill their bellies with pods, perish from hunger, for living without faith they seek after the blessed life by the vain study of philosophy. Just as the bread that strengthens the heart of man is likened to the word of God by which his soul is restored, so the pod, which is tender on the outside but empty within, and which does not nourish the body but fills it, so that it is more burden than use, is not inappropriately compared to secular wisdom, whose discourse resounds to the applause of eloquence, but is void of the virtue of utility.[17]

If Bede speaks contemptuously of worldly philosophy, what is at issue is philosophy that would offer itself as a substitute for faith, the kind of

---

16 *In Gen.* 3, CCL 118A:159. Babylon, where the tower was located, represents the city of the reprobate, to which Jerusalem, the city of the faithful, is contrasted. Hence Bede refers to the "compositionem et ornatum eloquentiae secularis, ... per quam civitas superba diaboli, sive in philosophia fallaci seu in haeretica versutia, multum ad tempus videtur erigi, sed in examine districti iudicis quam sit damnabilis et confusione digna patebit."

17 *In Luc.* 4, CCL 120:289: "Mercennarii ergo patris abundant panibus quia qui futurae mercedis intuitu digna operari satagunt cotidianis supernae gratiae reficiuntur alimoniis. At vero fame pereunt qui extra patris aedes positi ventrem cupiunt implere de siliquis, id est qui sine fide viventes vitam beatam inanis philosophiae studiis inquirunt. Sicut enim *panis* qui *cor hominis confirmat* [cf. Ps. 103(104):15] verbo Dei quo mentem reficiat assimilatur, ita siliqua quae et ipsa intus inanis foris mollis est et corpus non reficit sed implet ut sit magis oneri quam usui saeculari sapientiae non inmerito comparatur cuius sermo facundiae plausu sonorus sed virtute utilitatis est vacuus."

enquiry undertaken by those who, without committing themselves to the Christian life, would presume to pronounce on the meaning of human existence or the source of ultimate blessedness. In his commentary on Gen. 7:20 his point is much the same. In speaking of the pride or arrogance of secular philosophy, what he has in mind is a spirit of enquiry that, trespassing into areas where it has no licence, needs to be reminded of the limited range of its competence.[18]

Bede speaks disparagingly of pagan philosophy on a few other occasions as well, but only in the context of its being used to deride simple faith or to contradict Christian teaching. Hence the pagan philosophers brought to mind by the words of Prov. 15:2: "The mouths of fools pour out folly," are thinkers like Porphyry and Julian: "contra ecclesiae doctores stultitiae suae fluenta fundebant."[19] Philosophy itself is not the object of Bede's contumely; the word itself is not a term of opprobrium for him. Indeed, in one noteworthy passage he acknowledges that the pagan philosophers were motivated by the pursuit of truth and wisdom, and were inspired by the search for the true God.[20] He does succumb, and not infrequently, to the temptation to associate philosophy with heterodoxy. This seems especially true in his commentary on Ezra and Nehemiah, where philosophy, rhetoric and dialectic are all presented as instruments of heretical depravity.[21] But if philosophy has been used by misbelievers to attack the faith, it can also be employed to

---

18   *In Gen.* 2, CCL 118A:119. In Gen. 7:20 we read that the waters of the flood covered the tops of the mountains to a depth of fifteen cubits. The number fifteen, Bede tells us, results from the addition of seven and eight, whose significance is revealed by the fact that the Lord rested in his tomb on the seventh day of the week, and on the eighth day, the first day of the new week, was raised from the dead. The number seven, therefore, represents the rest of the souls of the blessed after the death of their bodies, while eight is a figure for the time of the resurrection. He then continues: "Quindecim ergo cubitis, id est septem et octo, aqua montes excelsos transcendit, quia fides ecclesiae, quae fonte lavacri salutaris sanctificatur, spe futurae requiei et inmortalitatis antecellit omni fastui philosophiae carnalis, quae de mundi quidem creatura novit subtiliter disputare, sed de creatore mundi et ea quae supra mundum in illa est vita sanctorum nihil dicere novit."

19   *In Prov.* 2, CCL 119B:86-87; cf. *In 1 Sam.* 1, CCL 119:23.

20   *In Cant.* 2, CCL 119B:231: "Haec autem gentilitatis fuisse vota Deum scire cupientis sed necdum scientis testantur studia philosophorum qui pro indagine veritatis ac sapientiae tot lustravere terras tanta condidere volumina."

21   See his comments on Ezra 4:14-15 (*In Ezram et Neemiam* 1, CCL 119A:285-286) and Nehemiah 13:23-24 (ibid. 3, CCL 119A:391). Cf. ibid. 2, CCL 119A:327, where he refers to "hereses et superstitiosas philosophorum sectas."

support Christian orthodoxy and overcome its adversaries. Bede acknowledges a positive role in the church for those of philosophical temperament or training, one that consists primarily of refuting the apologists for perverse teaching;[22] and in the *Chronica Maiora* he provides specific examples of individuals whose philosophical acumen or rhetorical skill have served the church well.[23]

In the second book of his commentary on 1 Samuel Bede stakes out a similarly positive appraisal of the value of pagan literature. In 1 Sam. 14:24ff Saul orders his troops to abstain from nourishment until the Philistine army has been run to ground. Despite the temptations of discovered honey, everyone but Jonathan obeys the royal injunction. "Jonathan had not heard his father charge the people with the oath; so he put forth the tip of the staff that was in his hand, and dipped it in the honeycomb, and put his hand to his mouth; and his eyes became bright." Jonathan can be taken as a figure for the Christian teacher, says Bede, who partakes of the honeycomb when he finds his mouth sweetened by the taste of secular literature. Indeed, his eyes thereby become brighter as well, not for the perception of new truths so much as for the more effective articulation of what he already knows. Although the content of secular literature is often offensive, Bede seems to be saying, there is much that the Christian teacher can learn from its style and form to enable him to express Christian ideas more forcefully and persuasively.[24]

---

22 Cf. ibid. 2, CCL 119A:317; and *In Cant.* 5, CCL 119B:351. In the latter text he comments as follows on Cant 8:9: "*Si ergo murus est*, inquit, soror nostra *aedificemus super eam propugnacula argentea*, ac si aperte dicat, Si idonea est ecclesia gentium in aliquibus suis membris perversorum contraire doctrinis habens acutos ad dicendum viros vel naturae videlicet ingenio callentes vel institutione philosophica instructos nequaquam his velim dicendi ministerium tollamus quin potius iuvemus eos datis scripturarum sanctarum paginis quo fortius possint ac facilius infirmos quosque atque indoctos ab insidiis custodire vel doctrinae fallentis vel exempli corrumpentis."

23 See, for example, *Chronica Maiora* = *De temp. ratione* 66.383, CCL 123B:506: "Marcion dissertissimus Antiochenae presbiter ecclesiae, quippe *qui in eadem urbe rethoricam docuerat*, adversus Paulum de Samosathae, qui Antiochiae episcopus dogmatizabat Christum communis naturae hominem tantum fuisse, accipientibus notariis disputavit, qui dialogus usque hodie extat." Bede's source is Jerome, *De viris illustribus* 71, PL 23:719, who refers, however, to 'Malchion'. Cf. *De temp. ratione* 66.389, CCL 123B:507.

24 *In 1 Sam.* 2, CCL 119:120: "Intinxit autem Ionathan favo silvestri virgam qua vel ad equum vel ad viandi praesidium utebatur et sic eam manu ad os convertit suum. Et magister quilibet non numquam auctoritatem potentiae qua vel subditos regere vel se ipsum sine offensione gerere curabat argumentis sive sententiis gentilium credit adiuvandam mellitoque ut ita dixerim ex his ore illuminantur quidem quasi

On occasion, Bede tells us, some Christian teachers have cultivated a greater attachment than is appropriate to such literature; and without mentioning Jerome by name he goes on to say that once such a teacher was summoned in a vision before the divine tribunal and chastised for being more of a Ciceronian than a Christian. Although modern scholars may doubt that Jerome's vision is to be taken seriously, Bede does not.[25] What is at issue, however, is only the excessive love of secular eloquence, not secular literature itself. He flatly rejects the notion of any prohibition, pointing to the examples of Moses and Daniel profiting from the thought and letters of the Egyptians and Chaldaeans, and acknowledging that even St Paul did not disdain to quote pagan poets when he thought it appropriate. Bede was indeed aware of the dangers lurking in the non-Christian heritage, and he counsels us accordingly: "multo cautius necesse est acutis rosa in spinis quam mollibus lilium colligatur in foliis multo securius in apostolicis quam in Platonicis quaeritur consilium salubre pagellis." His final position on the matter, however, is broadly Augustinian in nature, and similar to that of Gregory the Great, who also was prompted to discuss the issue in his commentary on 1 Kings (1 Samuel).[26] Although he is far from recognizing any indepen-

---

favosa compositione verborum oculi mentis ad enuntiandum quae recte noverint acutius sed retardantur plerumque mentis eiusdem incessus recordata sensuum vanitate a persequendis pravorum sive actuum sive dogmatum cultoribus. Quod cavens psalmista [Ps. 118(119):85-86], *Narraverunt mihi*, inquit, *iniqui fabulationes sed non ita ut lex tua domine omnia mandata tua veritas.*" Pierre Riché, *Education and Culture in the Barbarian West: Sixth Through Eighth Centuries*, trans. John J. Contreni (Columbia SC, 1976), p. 389, interprets this as a condemnation of secular letters. According to Riché, "Bede placed himself outside the tradition of the Fathers, who had hoped that the liberal arts would be used in the service of Christian thought" (p. 388). For a fundamentally different reading, however, see Ray, "Bede and Cicero," pp. 2-5.

25 *In 1 Sam.* 2, CCL 119:119-121, esp. 120; cf. Jerome, *Ep.* 22.30, CSEL 54:189-191. On the modern scholarly reaction to Jerome's dream, see, for example, Jacqueline Amat, *Songes et visions: l'au-delà dans la littérature latine tardive* (Paris, 1985), pp. 217-222.

26 Cf. Gregory the Great, *In 1 Reg.* 5.84-85, CCL 144:471-473. Whether Bede was familiar with this Gregorian text is at best unclear. The judgment of the editor of his *In 1 Sam.* (CCL 119, Praef., p. v) is that indeed he was, a conclusion shared by Judith McClure, "Bede's Old Testament Kings," in *Ideal and Reality in Frankish and Anglo-Saxon Society*, pp. 76-98; and Manlio Simonetti, "La tecnica esegetica di Beda nel *Commento a 1 Samuele*," *Romanobarbarica* 8 (1984/85): 75-110, esp. 105-108. For a contrasting view, however, see Pierre-Patrick Verbraken, "Le com-

dent value in classical thought and learning, as though these things could be studied for their own sake, he clearly recognizes their worth when properly subordinated to Christian purposes. In addition to being open to the culture of the ancient world and prepared to learn from it, Bede was even more responsive to the natural world around him and sensitive to its rhythms. Bede's scientific interests have long been recognized,[27] interests that he developed to a point achieved by few of his contemporaries. Not unexpectedly, his science does display many of the weaknesses of what passed for scientific thinking in his time. Frequently, especially in his early writings, he is content to copy from the works of venerable authorities like Isidore and Pliny. Even there, however, evidence of his intellectual independence and analytical ability, qualities that developed significantly over the length of his career, is not entirely lacking. Unlike either Augustine or Gregory, Bede actually investigated nature himself, and consequently was able to make original contributions to both cosmology and chronology. His work on the ocean tides is particularly noteworthy, even though he advanced no new theories to account for them. Careful empirical observation enabled him to show how tidal variation could be predicted with a corrected nineteen-year lunar cycle.[28]

Such studies left Bede with a strong sense of the regularity in nature and our ability to grasp it. He believed that the universe was an orderly place, one "whose phenomena, whether observed in the skies or experienced on the earth, were all capable of rational explanation and not

---

mentaire de Saint Grégoire sur le Premier Livre des Rois," *Revue Bénédictine* 66 (1956): 159-217 at 161; Paul Meyvaert, "A New Edition of Gregory the Great's Commentaries on the Canticle and 1 Kings," *Journal of Theological Studies* n.s. 19 (1968): 215-225 at 225; and Adalbert de Vogüé, "Les plus anciens exégètes du Premier Livre des Rois: Origène, Augustin et leurs épigones," *Sacris Erudiri* 29 (1986): 5-12.

27 See, for example, Franz Strunz, "Beda in der Geschichte der Naturbetrachtung und Naturforschung," *Zeitschrift für deutsche Geistesgeschichte* 1 (1935): 311-321. For a recent assessment, see Wesley M. Stevens, *Bede's Scientific Achievement* (Jarrow, 1985).

28 See the studies of Thomas R. Eckenrode: "Venerable Bede as a Scientist," *American Benedictine Review* 22 (1971): 486-507; "Venerable Bede's Theory of Ocean Tides," *American Benedictine Review* 25 (1974): 56-74; and "The Growth of a Scientific Mind: Bede's Early and Late Scientific Writings," *Downside Review* 94 (1976): 197-212.

merely the outcome of caprice."[29] Of course, his sense of the kind of coherence that could be found in nature was quite different from what has prevailed since the Scientific Revolution. Modern science invests order in a series of mathematically conceived natural laws governing the behaviour of objects of the most diverse kinds. For Bede, as for Augustine and Gregory the Great before him and for Aquinas after, order in the universe was a function of God's having endowed each specific kind of creature with its own distinctive nature. Common to both views, however, is the fact that natural phenomena are the product of natural causes, and are to be explained in terms of the principles of order embedded in the cosmos at creation.

In Augustine's thought, especially in *De Genesi ad litteram*, the idea is captured in the notion of the *rationes seminales*. It is they that assure that each creature will develop according to its own kind—that an acorn will become an oak tree, for example, and not a maple—and that it will be capable of fulfilling the role assigned it in the design of Providence. Bede did not possess Augustine's metaphysical temperament, and so it is unsurprising that he has left us no sustained discussion of the issue. Although he knew and used extensively *De Genesi ad litteram*, in his own commentary on Genesis there is only one reference to the seminal reasons, and that to explain how God could be said to have created all things at once. The answer he gives is Augustine's: they were created in potency in the seminal reasons, and then brought forth at the appropriate time.[30] Elsewhere, however, it is clear that Bede has grasped Augustine's governing idea. The seminal reasons are basic structural principles infused in nature and responsible for its order.[31]

As one could only expect, Bede is also prompt to acknowledge God's presence in the universe, for he is the author of nature and of whatever

29 Peter Hunter Blair, *The World of Bede* (London, 1970), p. 262; cf. idem, *Northumbria in the Days of Bede* (London, 1976), pp. 66-67.
30 *In Gen.* 1, CCL 118A:40-41.
31 See the chapter "De quadrifario Dei opere" in *De natura rerum* 1, CCL 123A:192. Here as well Bede addresses the issue of simultaneous creation: "Tertio, quod eadem materies, secundum causas simul creatas non iam simul, sed distinctione sex primorum dierum in caelestem terrestremque creaturam, formatur." However, immediately thereafter we read: "Quarto, quod eiusdem creaturae seminibus et primordialibus causis totius seculi tempus naturali cursu peragitur, ubi Pater usque nunc operatur et Filius, ubi etiam *corvos pascit* et *lilia vestit* Deus." Cf. Augustine, *De Genesi ad litteram* 9.17, CSEL 28.1:291-292.

coherence it possesses. The Saviour himself proclaimed: "My father is working still, and I am working," not, as Bede explains, by calling new kinds of creatures into being, but by upholding the structure he has already established.[32] Without God's sustaining presence, the entire universe would face immediate and complete collapse: "etsi unaquaeque pars potest esse in toto cuius pars est, ipsum tamen totum non est nisi in illo a quo conditum est."[33] It is against this background that Bede can speak of God as being responsible for the daily rising and setting of the sun. He knew perfectly well that there were natural forces according to which this took place, forces that were accessible to human reason, and that it did not require each day a separate act of divine governance. His point, therefore, is that these forces possess no inherent necessity but are contingent upon the divine will.[34] At the same time, however, he would also acknowledge that sometimes the divine presence manifests itself more immediately and directly. His interest in matters scientific notwithstanding, Bede was profoundly cognizant of the pitfalls that await when we lose sight of our inherent human limits and overreach ourselves.[35] Nature was orderly because created by God, and it was worthy of study because of the way scientific knowledge could enhance Christian understanding of the universe and our place in it. But Bede was never threatened by the modern temptation to think that in principle everything can be reduced to our ordered categories. He was too much aware of the realm of mystery that lay beyond our ken, depths of being that were ultimately unfathomable; and it was this, of course, that left him open to the reality of the miraculous.

Given the absence of philosophical or metaphysical titles in his library, it is unsurprising that, like Gregory the Great, Bede had no strong inclination to treat miracles on the ontological level. In his surviving works one looks in vain for any extensive, theoretical discussion. This does not mean that he lacked ideas, but only that they must be pieced together from scattered observations, primarily on the miracles of Scripture. Like most Christian thinkers, Bede adopted as his basic premise the idea that miracles are a manifestation of divine power.

32 John 5:17; *Hom. Evan.* 1.23, CCL 122:167-168.
33 *Exp. Act. Apost.* 17.28, CCL 121:73; cf. *In Gen.* 1, CCL 118A:35.
34 Cf. *In Gen.* 1, CCL 118A:5 and *In Reg. Quaest.* 25, CCL 119:316-317.
35 See, for example, *In Prov.* 3, CCL 119B:130: "Evenit enim saepe ut qui maiore scientia praediti fulgebant ad ultimum plus volentes sapere quam fragilitati humanae concessum est in insipientiae foveam deciderent."

Whereas Christ performed them on his own authority, the apostles could do so only in virtue of the power he entrusted to them.[36] Indeed, strictly speaking the apostles worked no miracles at all. It was God who did so, operating through them. In the *Ecclesiastical History* and the *Life of St Cuthbert* Bede does not show any of the ambivalence of some early medieval hagiographers, as if the saints could be credited with an intrinsic, autonomous miraculous power of their own.[37] The miracles witnessed at St Fursa's tomb were performed, not by Fursa, but by God himself; and what St Cuthbert offered to suppliants at his shrine was not miracles performed in his own right but simply the benefit of his influence in heaven. Hence, when Baduthegn, a monk from Lindisfarne, visited the holy site, he "prostrated himself before the body of the man of God, praying with devout fervour that the Lord, through Cuthbert's intercession, would be propitious to him."[38]

In his comments on the individual miracles of Christ Bede frequently draws attention to the suddenness with which they achieved their effect.[39] When Christ rebuked the fever afflicting Peter's mother-in-law (Mark 1:30-31; Luke 4:38-39), it left her immediately. Usually, says Bede, people recovering from illness of this sort are oppressed with weariness, and continue to suffer discomfort. In this case, however, recovery was instantaneous, and the woman was able to rise from her sick bed and minister to Christ and those who had accompanied him. The subsequent healing of the leper was achieved in a similarly sudden

---

36	*In Marc.* 2, CCL 120:504. Cf. ibid. 1, CCL 120:448; *In Luc.* 2, CCL 120:111.

37	On Gregory of Tours, for example, see Giselle de Nie, *Views from a Many-Windowed Tower: Studies of Imagination in the Works of Gregory of Tours* (Amsterdam, 1987), pp. 95-96, 100, 199-200.

38	On Fursa, see *HE* 3.19, p. 276: "merita illius multis saepe constat Deo operante claruisse virtutibus." On Cuthbert, see *HE* 4.31, pp. 446-447: "prosternens se ad corpus viri Dei, pia intentione per eius auxilium Dominum sibi propitium fieri precabatur."

39	See *De templo* 1, CCL 119A:184, where Bede offers a general observation while commenting on Cant. 5:14: "*Manus eius tornatiles aureae plenae hyacinthis.* Tornatiles quippe sunt manus eius quia apparens in carne sanitates et miracula quaecumque voluit absque omni morarum tarditate absque ullis errorum ambagibus Dei virtus et sapientia perfecit." Cf. *In Cant.* 4, CCL 119B:290-291, where his treatment of the same verse entails a more specific comment on John 5:8-9: "Manus ergo domini tornatiles sunt quia in promptu habet facere quae vult quia dicit et fiunt; denique dixit: *Surge tolle grabbatum tuum et ambula,* nec mora surgens *sustulit grabbatum et ambulabat* qui duos de quadraginta annos paraliticus iacuerat."

fashion (Mark 1:40-42; Luke 5:12-13), as was the cure of the paralytic (Mark 2:3-12; Luke 5:17-26). Immediately on Christ's command, he took up his bed and went home: "Mira divinae potentiae virtus ubi nulla temporis interveniente morula iussa salvatoris salus festina comitatur."[40] When Christ came to Bethsaida, he chose to cure the blind man he met there only in stages (Mark 8:22-26). He spat upon his eyes and imposed his hands upon them, which resulted in improved but still obscure vision. Full clarity was restored only after a second laying on of hands. In Bede's judgment, however, this represents no real exception. Christ could have cured the man immediately with a single word had he so desired. He chose not to do so to teach us something about the spiritual blindness we suffer. Its magnitude is such that only gradually and in distinct stages can we be brought to the light of the divine vision.[41]

As Bede's comments on the healing of Peter's mother-in-law indicate, the suddenness with which Christ's cures were effected differed markedly from normal expectations. This was what made them particularly noteworthy as manifestations of distinctly divine power. It was not the suddenness *per se* that qualified them as miracles, but the contrast with the ordinary course of events, generally evident in other ways as well. When Christ healed the leper, in addition to commanding him to be clean he also touched him, a gesture, says Bede, both unnecessary and forbidden. Its point was to demonstrate the Saviour's superiority to the law, as well as to show that, unlike other men, he did not fear the consequences that could normally be expected from such contact.[42] Touching a leper usually results in contagion; here it was an instrument of healing. The cure was a miracle, therefore, because it was contrary to the regular order of nature, and was explicable only in terms of a special exercise of divine power. The same can be said of the other miracles of Christ, and of the miracles of the Old Testament as well. They were miracles because they transpired *praeter usitatum naturae*

---

40 On Peter's mother-in-law, see *In Marc.* 1, CCL 120:449; *In Luc.* 2, CCL 120:111. On the leper, see *In Marc.* 1, CCL 120:450-451; *In Luc.* 2, CCL 120:117: "Et extendens manum tetigit illum dicens: Volo, mundare. Et confestim lepra discessit ab illo. Nihil medium est inter opus Dei atque praeceptum quia in praecepto est opus." On the paralytic, see *In Luc.* 2, CCL 120:122; cf. *In Marc.* 1, CCL 120:457.

41 *In Marc.* 2, CCL 120:534-535.

42 Ibid. 1, CCL 120:450-451; *In Luc.* 2, CCL 117:120.

cursum.[43] The distinction can be seen clearly in the contrasting births of Ishmael and Isaac:

Ishmael was born like other men, by the commingling of the sexes according to the customary law of nature. Hence he is said to have been born "according to the flesh." ... It was not according to the flesh that Isaac was born to Abraham, but through promise, not because Abraham had not fathered him in the flesh, but because he had begotten him from the depths of despair. Had it not been for the divine promise, the old man would not have dared hope for any posterity from the womb of his aged wife.[44]

43 *In Gen.* 3, CCL 118A:153. On the Virgin Birth, for example, see *In Luc.* 1, CCL 120:34, where Bede comments on Luke 1:36-37: "Ne virgo se parere posse diffidat accipit exemplum sterilis anus pariturae ut discat omnia Deo possibilia etiam quae naturae ordine videntur esse contraria." On the miracle at Cana, see *Hom. Evan.* 1.14, CCL 122:103: "Manifestavit hoc signo quia ipse esset rex gloriae et ideo sponsus ecclesiae qui ut homo communis veniret ad nuptias sed quasi dominus caeli et terrae elementa prout voluisset converteret." On Christ's walking on the water, see *In Marc.* 2, CCL 120:518, where he borrows indirectly from Pseudo-Dionysius: "Ignoramus enim qualiter de virgineis sanguinibus alia lege praeter naturalem formabatur et qualiter non infusis pedibus corporale pondus habentibus et materiale onus deambulabat in umidam et instabilem substantiam." Cf. *De divinis nominibus* 2.9, PG 3:647. Bede's source here, as Laistner, "Library of the Venerable Bede," p. 259n, points out, was the Latin version of the Acts of the Lateran Council of 649. See also *Exp. Act. Apost.* 2.19, CCL 121:19, where, in the context of Acts 2:19, Bede comments on the blood that flowed from the Saviour's side: "nam et sanguinem de mortua carne vivaci rivo profluere, quia contra naturam nostrorum est corporum, signi loco factum credere restat." He returns to the passage in *Retr.* 2.19, CCL 121:112, referring to the "sweat ... like great drops of blood" of Luke 22:44 as well, and maintaining: "inter signa divinitus gesta numeratur quia in consuetudine naturae nequaquam invenire probatur humanae." For an Old Testament example, see *In 1 Sam.* 2, CCL 119:99, where Bede explains what was miraculous about the rain and thunder produced by Samuel in 1 Sam. 12:16-18: "Signum quoque praevaricatoris et duri cordis populi non minimum et eo magis terribile quo illis regionibus inusitatum exhibuit voces scilicet et pluviam tempore messis triticeae quae toto aestatis tempore in terra repromissionis nisi magno miraculo venire non solent."

44 *In Gen.* 4, CCL 118A:239: "Natus est enim Ismahel sicut nascuntur homines permixtione sexus utriusque usitata lege naturae. Ideo dictum est 'secundum carnem' [cf. Gal. 4:22-23]. ... Non ergo secundum carnem natus est Isaac Abrahae, sed ex promissione, non quia eum carne non erat operatus, sed quia de summa desperatione susceperat, et nisi adesset promittens Deus, nihil iam senex de visceribus aniculae coniugis sperare audebat posteritatis." Cf. ibid. p. 207: "ubi ... evidens opus Dei est, vitiata et cessante natura, ibi evidentius intelligitur gratia"; and

Bede's concept of miracle was identical to Gregory's, and was shared by other early medieval hagiographers as well.[45] It posits a regular course of nature according to which, at least in principle, events can be explained in rational, scientific terms. But it also acknowledges the possibility of events that defy the natural order, and that require for their explanation an extraordinary divine initiative.

On first glance at least, several of Bede's works contain passages that might suggest a rather different conception of the natural order and God's relationship to it. At one point in the *Ecclesiastical History*, for example, he tells us that Bishop Chad used to see the hand of God in simple storms:

> If he happened to be reading or doing something else and suddenly a high wind arose, he would at once invoke the mercy of the Lord and beg Him to have pity upon the human race. If the wind increased in violence he would shut his book, fall on his face, and devote himself still more earnestly to prayer. But if there were a violent storm of wind and rain or if lightning and thunder brought terror to earth and sky, he would enter the church and, with still deeper concentration, earnestly devote himself to prayers and psalms until the sky cleared. When his people asked him why he did it he replied, "Have you not read, 'The Lord also thundered in the heavens and the Highest gave His voice? ...' For the Lord moves the air, raises the winds, hurls the lightnings, and thunders forth from heaven so as to rouse the inhabitants of the world to fear Him, [and] to call them to remember the future judgment."[46]

Of course, it is Chad's view that Bede offers here, and not his own. But as Plummer points out, his comments on Ezra 10:9 suggest that his own view was not substantially different. There Bede presents tempests, blizzards, drought and other manifestations of a disturbance of the elements not as products of an inherently natural process but as indications of divine displeasure and intimations of the judgment to come. They are

p. 236: "Visitare dicitur Saram Deus quasi languentem et ab omni sobolis fructu iam desperatam, ut quod natura negare videbatur, divinae praesentia gratiae conferret."

45 See, for example, Adomnan, *Vita S. Columbae* 1.1 & 2.33, ed. & trans. Alan Orr Anderson & Marjorie Ogilvie Anderson (London, 1961), pp. 196, 402; and Eddius Stephanus, *Vita S. Wilfrithi*, chap. 67, ed. & trans. Bertram Colgrave (Cambridge, 1927), p. 144, where miracles are described as happening "contrary to nature." On Gregory the Great, see *Signs of Sanctity*, p. 221ff.

46 *HE* 4.3, p. 343.

visited upon us because of our sins, he says, and so they are to be taken as opportunities for self-examination and amendment rather than as natural adversities to be avoided or overcome.[47]

Elsewhere, in a rather lengthy analysis, Bede tells us that illness is divinely produced as well, and for a variety of reasons.[48] The just are so afflicted either to prevent their merits from being undermined by pride, as was the case with St. Paul (cf. 2 Cor. 12:7), or to enable them, like Job and Tobias, to augment their virtues by patience.[49] Sinners, on the other hand, are punished with illness to bring them to repentance. Hence Miriam, the sister of Aaron, was stricken with leprosy because of her pride and temerity (Num. 12:10); and when Christ healed the paralytic, he first forgave the sins that were responsible for his affliction (Mark 2:3-12; Luke 5:18-26). Sometimes, when there is no possibility of repentence, the suffering of present illness is to be interpreted as a foretaste of the eternal torment that awaits. Sometimes, however, it has nothing to do with the spiritual state of the sick: Christ explained to his disciples that it was not because of his own sin or that of his parents that the man born blind had been deprived of sight, "but that the works of God might be made manifest in him" (John 9:3). Similarly he informed the sisters of Lazarus that their brother's illness was not unto death but was "for the glory of God, so that the Son of God may be glorified by means of it" (John 11:4). Conspicuous by its absence from Bede's

---

47 *In Ezram et Neemiam* 2, CCL 119A:332. Cf. Plummer, *Opera Historica* 2:209. For a somewhat different perspective, see *HE* 1.17, pp. 54-56, where Bede tells us that it was demons who were responsible for the storms that impeded bishops Germanus of Auxerre and Lupus of Troyes in their crossing of the Channel. Enraged at the prospect of such men coming to restore salvation to the people, they raised a fury of wind and rain until they were finally overcome by the prayers of St Germanus and his companions. Although it was common in early medieval hagiography for storms to be interpreted in this manner, to Bede the providential perspective seems to have come more naturally. Here, however, Bede's presentation is governed by that of his source, Constantius of Lyons, *Vita S. Germani* 3.13, SC 112:144-148, from whom he borrows extensively.

48 *In Marc.* 1, CCL 120:455-456; cf. *Hom. Evan.* 1.23, CCL 122:165-166.

49 Cf. *HE* 4.23, p. 410, where Bede says of the Abbess Hild of Whitby: "Verum illa cum multis annis huic monasterio praeesset, placuit pio provisori salutis nostrae sanctam eius animam longa etiam infirmitate carnis examinari, ut iuxta exemplum apostoli virtus eius in infirmitate perficeretur"; and *Historia abbatum* 1.13, Plummer, *Opera Historica* 1:376, where he says of the illnesses that afflicted both Benedict Biscop and Abbot Sigefrith shortly before their deaths: "namque eos affecit infirmitas carnis, ut perficeretur in eis virtus Christi."

extensive discussion is any sense that illness can be produced by natural causes, and can sometimes at least be alleviated by natural remedies. In the case of sickness and all the other temporal adversities that we suffer, Bede says, we ought humbly to give thanks to God for the blessings we have received, and, conscious of our mortal weakness, rejoice at the remedies available to us. We ought to review all our deeds and thoughts with care, and purge away whatever sins we uncover through appropriate acts of contrition.

Passages like this might well suggest that Bede really had no conception of an objective, coherent natural order, but rather subjected nature directly to the governance of God. Such a view continues to be attributed to other early medieval thinkers, to both Gregory the Great and Gregory of Tours, for example, and it is not inconceivable that Bede should be included in their number.[50] In Bede's case, however, such an assessment would be as incorrect as it is in Gregory the Great's. If in his *Ecclesiastical History* and his commentary on Ezra Bede sees storms and other disturbances of the elements from a providential point of view, the perspective he adopts in his scientific works is quite different. In *De natura rerum* storms are described as arising from a number of purely natural causes: clouds colliding with one another, vapours exploding inside clouds, and aqueous particles coming into contact with igneous particles. The possibility of supernatural causation, either divine or demonic, is not even mentioned.[51]

The likelihood of Bede simply contradicting himself, adopting mutually exclusive points of view in works of different genres, is not great. Further on in *De natura rerum* he claims that storms out of season can function as signs, thus suggesting that the naturalistic and providen-

---

50 For recent statements on Gregory the Great and Gregory of Tours respectively, see Carole Straw, *Gregory the Great: Perfection in Imperfection* (Berkeley, 1988), p. 10; and Walter Goffart, *The Narrators of Barbarian History* (Princeton NJ, 1988), esp. pp. 132-134, 188-189. De Nie, *Views from a Many-Windowed Tower*, p. 56, offers a different view: "From his [Gregory of Tours'] not inconsiderable knowledge of what 'usually' happens in nature and also from the factual, analytic description he sometimes gives, it is clear that there is for him an accustomed and recognizable order in nature, which appears to work autonomously and whose processes can be analyzed." Goffart, p. 188n, insists that this is mistaken: "The 'accustomed order' is, in Gregory's view, arbitrary and subject to being effortlessly changed by the Creator."

51 *De natura rerum* 28-29, CSEL 123A:219-220. Cf. Eckenrode, "Growth of a Scientific Mind," pp. 209-210.

tial viewpoints do not preclude one another. Pestilence as well, it would seem, can be seen from both points of view. In each case we are dealing with phenomena that are both natural events and acts of Providence. They arise out of natural causes, but are also used by God, the lord of nature, for our moral and spiritual edification.[52] They have an analogue in eclipses, which function on two different levels as well. Although he sometimes seems to treat them as events of independent significance, to be reported on their own right,[53] like most medieval scholars Bede understood eclipses to be portents, even if their connection with what they presaged could be difficult to determine.[54] At the same time, however, he clearly regarded them as natural events that were amenable to scientific explanation. Indeed, he had a good understanding of the causes of both solar and lunar eclipses, and of the factors governing the frequency of their occurrence.[55]

52 *De natura rerum* 37, CCL 123A:223: "Pestilentia nascitur aere vel siccitatis vel pluviarum intemperantia pro meritis hominum corrupto, qui spirando vel edendo perceptus luem mortemque generat. Unde saepius omne tempus aestatis in procellas turbinesque brumales verti conspicimus. Sed haec cum suo tempore venerint, tempestates; cum vero alias, prodigia vel signa dicuntur." De Nie, *Views from a Many-Windowed Tower*, comes to similar conclusions concerning illness and disease in Gregory of Tours. "Natural and supernatural causes run parallel, overlap" (p. 38). "Though divinely sent, ... diseases were seen by Gregory as phenomena that could be observed, evaded, and possibly cured by concrete practical measures" (p. 40).

53 *HE* 5.24, pp. 562-563.

54 See, for example, ibid. 3.27, pp. 310-312; & 5.24, pp. 564-565: "664. There was an eclipse. King Eorcenberht of Kent died and Colman and his Irish returned to their own people. There was a visitation of the pestilence. Chad and Wilfrid were consecrated bishops of the Northumbrians."

55 See Creider, "Bede's Understanding of the Miraculous," pp. 87-88. Cf. de Nie, *Views from a Many-Windowed Tower*, p. 48; and Umberto Dall'Olmo, "*Eclypsis naturalis* ed *eclypsis prodigialis* nelle cronache medioevali," *Bullettino dell'Istituto storico italiano per il medio evo e Archivio Muratoriano* 87 (1978): 154-172. Dall'Olmo seems to conceive of the two kinds of eclipse mentioned in his title as natural and divinely produced respectively, and to regard them as being, in theory at least, mutually exclusive. He also says, however, that the fact that an eclipse could be predicted, even acurately predicted, did not necessarily eliminate the possibility of its being regarded as a portent.
    Bede, as Creider goes on to say (pp. 88-89), was rather more interested in the portentous dimension of comets, a role for which their irregular behaviour may have made them particularly well suited. Although their status is not entirely clear, the relevant chapter of *De natura rerum*, drawn from Pliny, seems to suggest that they too are natural phenomena bearing special prognostic significance. At least

The kind of dual perspective that we have been considering here appears in Bede's account of human events as well, and enables him to reconcile the different points of view that he could bring to bear on the same set of circumstances as historian and as theologian. The Britons' decision to invite the Saxons across the Channel resulted from a process of consultation in which all, including their king, Vortigern, ultimately agreed. However, Bede also claims that it was ordained by the divine will; and in the next chapter he observes that "the fire kindled by the hands of the heathen executed the just vengeance of God on the nation for its crimes."[56] Both the victory of the Britons over the combined forces of Saxons and Picts and the crushing defeat that the latter inflicted on King Ecgfrith of Northumbria were the result of superior military tactics. In the first case, the famous Alleluia victory, the Britons, under the leadership of Bishop Germanus of Auxerre, executed a skillfully

---

there is nothing to suggest that they are supernaturally caused. See *De natura rerum* 24, CCL 123A:216: "Cometae sunt stellae flammis crinitae, repente nascentes, regni mutationem aut pestilentiam aut bella, vel ventos aestusve, portendentes." In their case as well the precise focus of the portent seems to have been difficult to determine. See, for example, the accounts of the comets of 678 and 729 in *HE* 4.12, pp. 370-371; & 5.23, pp. 556-557 respectively. In the latter case Bede reports: "In the year of our Lord 729 two comets appeared around the sun, striking great terror into all beholders. One of them preceded the sun as it rose in the morning and the other followed it as it set at night, seeming to portend dire disaster to east and west alike. One comet was the forerunner of the day and the other of the night, to indicate that mankind was threatened by calamities both by day and by night. ... At this time a terrible plague of Saracens ravaged Gaul with cruel bloodshed and not long afterwards they received the due reward of their treachery in the same kingdom." The last sentence of this passage has received a good deal of scholarly attention, especially the Saracens' "due reward." Colgrave, *HE*, p. 357n, suggests that it is a reference to Charles Martel's victory at Tours in 732, and that the passage therefore must be a late insertion, given that the *Ecclesiastical History* was completed in 731. More recently, Wallace-Hadrill, *Bede's Ecclesiastical History*, p. 199, has suggested the victory of Odo, Duke of Aquitaine, over the Saracens in 721, a possibility earlier rejected by Plummer, *Opera Historica* 2:338-339, because it jeopardizes the connection with the comets of 729. Whatever the case, the Saracen ravages in Gaul do not seem to capture the significance Bede sees in the portent, and the other events he goes on to mention—the death of the holy man Egbert, and the death of King Osric of Northumbria—seem even less apt. Perhaps at Bede's time of writing the disaster affecting east and west alike was yet to occur.

56 *HE* 1.14 & 15, pp. 48 & 53.

conceived ambush that panicked enemy forces.[57] In the second "the enemy feigned flight and lured the king into some narrow passes in the midst of inaccessible mountains; there he was killed with the greater part of the forces he had taken with him." The victory of the Britons, however, was also a "heaven-sent triumph" in which the bishops (Germanus of Auxerre and Lupus of Troyes) "overcame the enemy without the shedding of blood," a victory obtained "by faith and not by might."[58] Conversely Ecgfrith's defeat was a divine judgment on the savagery that his own forces had displayed against the Irish a year earlier: "he had refused to listen to the holy father Egbert, who had urged him not to attack the Irish who had done him no harm; and the punishment for his sin was that he would not now listen to those who sought to save him from his own destruction."[59]

Schoebe has argued that Bede learned to write history from the Old Testament, and therefore that he possessed the same theocentric view that one finds in the Books of Chronicles. History is not a human drama, but one scripted by God, who measures out success and failure in response to human merits.[60] That Bede's view of history was shaped by the Bible, particularly the historical books of the Old Testament, is indisputable;[61] and earlier Christian historians known to Bede had

---

57   Cf. Michael E. Jones, "The Historicity of the Alleluja Victory," *Albion* 18 (1986): 363-373, esp. 369: "Viewed in the context of Roman military practice the Alleluja victory is not a miracle, but the successful application of conventional Roman tactics to a familiar military problem."

58   *HE* 1.20, p. 65; cf. *Chronica Maiora* = *De temp. ratione* 66.491, CCL 123B:518. It was the season of Lent, and vast numbers of the army had been moved to baptism by the preaching of the bishops. As Bede himself tells us (*HE* 1.20, pp. 62-63), this did much to establish an expectant atmosphere: "The people's faith was fervent and putting no trust in their arms they expectantly awaited the help of God" (*fides fervet in populo, et conterrito armorum praesidio divinitatis exspectatur auxilium*). Colgrave's translation substitutes *contempto* (from the *Vita S. Germani*, which Bede was following closely at this point) for *conterrito*. Cf. Constantius of Lyons, *Vita S. Germani* 3.17, SC 112:156.

59   *HE* 4.26, pp. 427-429.

60   Gerhard Schoebe, "Was gilt im frühen Mittelalter als Geschichtliche Wirklichkeit? Ein Versuch zur 'Kirchengeschichte' des Baeda Venerabilis," in *Festschrift Hermann Aubin zum 80. Geburtstag,* ed. O. Brunner et al. (Wiesbaden, 1965), 2:625-651 at 639. Cf. p. 634: "Geschichte ist kein weltimmanentes und nach irdischnatürlicher Kausalität determiniertes Geschehen: Gott als die übernatürliche Macht grieft in die Geschichte ein."

61   See below, pp. 206-207.

indeed been willing to endorse a strictly theocentric point of view. Orosius was one of them. His view was simple: "insofar as the world exists tranquilly, it is so because of those who believe; insofar as it is perniciously disturbed, it is so as punishment for those who blaspheme." Divine action, therefore, eclipses human causation, and an event like Alaric's sack of Rome is said to have occurred "because of the wrath of God rather than because of the bravery of the enemy" (*magis ... indignatione Dei ... quam hostis fortitudine*).[62] Although Bede too possesses a strong sense of immanent justice, his view of the historical process is fundamentally different. He humanizes the face of Providence, and sees the divine judgment operating in events that are also intelligible in this-worldly terms.[63] Divine intervention does not replace the work of human agents, but runs parallel to and complements it, and presumably, therefore, is discernible only to those who perceive the events in question through the eyes of faith. The coexistence of factors human and divine can be see clearly in one further example: the fire that destroyed the monastic community at Coldingham. The monastery, Bede explains,

was burned down through carelessness (*per culpam incuriae flammis absumtum est*). However, all who knew the truth were easily able to judge that it happened because of the wickedness of those who dwelt there, and especially of those who were supposed to be its leaders. ... God in His mercy did not fail to give warning of approaching punishment so that they might have been led to amend their ways and, by fasting, tears, and prayers, to have averted the wrath of the just Judge from themselves as did the people of Nineveh.[64]

62 Paulus Orosius, *Historiarum adversum paganos libri VII* 7.3 & 7.39, CSEL 5:438 & 545, trans. Roy J. Deferrari (Washington, 1964), pp. 288 & 353. The translation of the latter of the two passages tends perhaps to heighten the antithesis.

63 Cf. Giosué Musca, *Il Venerabile Beda, storico dell'Alto Medioevo* (Bari, 1973), p. 271; and Antonia Gransden, *Historical Writing in England* 1: c. *550 to c. 1370* (Ithaca, 1974), p. 21.

64 *HE* 4.25, pp. 420-423. For a parallel in Gregory of Tours, see de Nie, *Views from a Many-Windowed Tower*, pp. 142-143, who speaks of two versions of the same physical event: "one as it took place on the visible plane and one as it took place on the spiritual plane." Judging from Marc Van Uytfanghe's description, the coexistence of providential and this-worldly perspectives seems to have been characteristic of Merovingian hagiography more generally, although Van Uytfanghe himself seems puzzled by it. See his *Stylisation biblique et condition humaine dans l'hagiographie mérovingienne [600-750]* (Brussels, 1987), pp. 66-71.

Carelessness explains how the fire occurred; the divine judgment explains why.

In view of examples like the latter, it seems clear that, like Gregory the Great before him, Bede was prone to perceive the world through theological lenses, to see the divine presence as much as if not more than the natural process. This was not without consequence for his openness to miracles. Not only did it make it easier for Bede to accept the possibility of divinely produced breaches in the natural order, it resulted in him seeing miracles where no such interpretation was required, and where most twentieth-century readers of his *Ecclesiastical History* or his *Vita Cuthberti* would not independently have seen them. Plummer was not the last to have commented on a phenomenon present in the *Dialogues* of Gregory the Great and other early medieval works as well, although perhaps not with the same frequency: the fact that many of the miracles reported by Bede are nothing more than "coincidences brought about by perfectly natural means, though a devout mind will gladly believe that they have been divinely ordered."[65]

An example that has attracted frequent comment occurs early in the *Vita Cuthberti*, where the young St Cuthbert is healed of a painful ailment of the knee that had virtually incapacitated him. One day, after he had been carried outside by servants, he noticed the approach of a mysterious horseman dressed in white robes:

> The stranger jumped from his horse and examined the afflicted knee very carefully. Then he said: "Boil some wheaten flour in milk, spread this poultice while hot upon the swelling, and you will be healed." With these words he mounted his horse and departed. Cuthbert followed his commands and in a few days was healed. He recognized that he who had given him this advice was an angel, sent by One who once deigned to send the archangel Raphael to cure the eyes of Tobias.[66]

Colgrave's diagnosis is that Cuthbert was suffering from synovitis, the result perhaps of an injury, although he also considers the possibility of a more serious ailment. More recently Rubin has rejected this diagnosis, suggesting instead an acute abscess.[67] Whatever the case, both agree

---

65 Plummer, *Opera Historica* 1:lxiv; cf. Colgrave, "Bede's Miracle Stories," p. 227.
66 *VCP*, chap. 2, pp. 159-161. Cf. Tobias 11.
67 Cf. Bertram Colgrave, *Two Lives of St Cuthbert* (Cambridge, 1940), pp. 312n and 355n; "Bede's Miracle Stories," p. 227; and Stanley Rubin, "St Cuthbert of Lindisfarne: A Medical Reconstruction," *Transactions of the Architectural and Archaeological Society of Durham and Northumberland* n.s. 4 (1978): 101-103 at 102.

that the remedy prescribed was appropriate, and therefore that there was nothing extraordinary about Cuthbert's cure. Cuthbert himself, however, saw it as a miracle; and thereafter, it would seem, this had been the interpretation favoured by the community at Lindisfarne. It was the tradition that Bede inherited from the author of the anonymous life, and he would have been powerless to change it had he wanted to do so.[68] Just as Raphael was sent to remove the film from the eyes of the blind Tobias, so was some unidentified angel sent to alleviate Cuthbert's suffering by prescribing a bread poultice.

In several miracles of this sort fire figures prominently, a symptom perhaps of the sense of helplessness and futility that accompanied its destructive course, and of the feelings of relief and gratitude that welled up when all was not lost. Seeing the hand of God in such events would not have been difficult. An example arises early in the *Ecclesiastical History*, when Bede informs us that the house where Bishop Germanus of Auxerre lay recuperating from an injury emerged unscathed from a major conflagration. Having started in a neighbouring cottage, the fire quickly spread to the thatched roofs of surrounding buildings, and soon it threatened the entire community. Although the efforts of the crowd to control the blaze were all in vain, the presence of St Germanus, says Bede, "proved a sure defence. The saint's dwelling was wide open, yet the flames avoided and leapt over it though they raged hither and thither; and amid the masses of blazing fire, his shelter remained unharmed, preserved by the man who lay within."[69]

In similar circumstances the prayers of other saints were also effective, among them St Cuthbert. Once a fire that had started on the other side of town had been whipped up by strong winds and had spread throughout the entire village. Immediately upon his intercession being requested, Cuthbert went outside and cast himself upon the ground; "and while he was still praying, the winds changed and, blowing from the west, removed all danger of the fire attacking the house which the man of God had entered."[70] The miracle that Cuthbert performed in this unidentified village was duplicated by bishops Mellitus and Aidan to the advantage of Canterbury and Bamburgh respectively. In Canterbury the fire was a product of carelessness; it Bamburgh it had been deliberately set by Penda, the Mercian king. In each case, however, the saint's

68   Cf. *VCA* 1.4, pp. 66-68.
69   *HE* 1.19, p. 61.
70   *VCP*, chap. 14, p. 201; cf. *VCA* 2.7, pp. 88-90.

power was more than equal to the challenge, and brooked no delay. Aidan, for example, had no sooner called upon the Lord than "the winds veered away from the city and carried the flames in the direction of those who had kindled them, so that, as some of them were hurt and all of them terrified, they ceased to make any further attempt on the city, realizing that it was divinely protected."[71]

Bede realized that a sudden change in the direction of the wind could be produced by purely natural causes. But in each of these cases it followed immediately upon the prayers of a known holy man, and that sufficed to assure him that it was an event of a different order, a conviction that his analogical imagination, always on the lookout for the deeper significance beneath the surface of events, was quick to reinforce. Kendall has argued that the basic structure of the universe as Bede conceived it was verbal.[72] "In the beginning was the Word, and the Word was with God, and the Word was God" [John 1:1]. Like words, things were invested with meaning; they were signs by which God could communicate with man, the bearers of religious significance. The case of the fire in Canterbury provides an example. As Bede explains: "So brightly did the man of God burn with the fire of divine love, so often had he repelled the stormy powers of the air from harming him and his people by his prayers and exhortations, that it was right for him to be able to prevail over earthly winds and flames and to ensure that they should not injure him or his people."[73] The images here reflect more than physical realities. They are divinely conceived metaphors that point to realities beyond themselves, and in so doing assure us that more was at issue in the quenching of the flames than a fortuitous change of the wind.

Far from being unique to Bede, analogical thinking of this kind was characteristic of much of the Middle Ages. It was a view of reality that Bede shared with both Gregory the Great and Gregory of Tours. Despite his belief that nature consists of an ordered system of causes, says de Nie, Gregory of Tours "looks for coherence not in causal connections or development in time, but in the ethico-religious meaning of events, which he recognizes in their form." His is a "figural" style of thinking

---

71 *HE* 3.16, p. 263. For the episode involving Mellitus, see ibid. 2.7, pp. 156-158.
72 Calvin B. Kendall, "Bede's *Historia ecclesiastica*: The Rhetoric of Faith," in *Medieval Eloquence: Studies in the Theory and Practice of Medieval Rhetoric*, ed. James J. Murphy (Berkeley, 1978), pp. 145-172 at 162-163.
73 *HE* 2.7, p. 159.

very different from our own, "an 'archaic' and truly poetic view of reality, structured more by images and dreams than by concepts and logic." It is a view of the world in which metaphors are perceived as independent realities.[74] Much the same can be said of Bede. Hence, after telling us of Cuthbert's triumph over the flames, and comparing it to a similar wonder that Gregory the Great attributes to Bishop Marcellinus of Ancona, Bede declares:

It is not to be wondered at that such perfect men who served God faithfully received great power against the strength of flames, when, by daily practice of virtue, they learned both to overcome the lusts of the flesh and "to quench all the fiery darts of the wicked one" [Eph. 6:16]. Them indeed this prophecy most aptly fits: "When thou walkest through the fire thou shalt not be burned neither shall the flame kindle upon thee" [Is. 43:2]. But I and those like me, conscious of our weakness and helplessness, are certain that we dare take no such measures against material fire; we are also uncertain whether we can escape unharmed from that inextinguishable fire of future punishment. But the loving-kindness of our Saviour is mighty and abundant; and He will use the grace of His protection even now to extinguish the flames of vices in us, unworthy though we be, and to enable us to escape the flames of punishment in the time to come.[75]

In a modern text this would verge on free association. Bede's mind moves from physical flames to the fiery darts of temptation, the flames of vice, and finally the unquenchable fires of Hell. The metaphorical potential of the imagery allows "objective spiritual reality ... to materialize into visible phenomena and events,"[76] and in so doing grace them with a touch of the transcendent.

Unsurprisingly, a striking image can clarify the meaning of a miracle. When a woman is cured of blindness while praying in the cemetery of the nuns of Barking, Bede explains: "It seemed as if she had lost the light of this world in order to show by her recovery how bright is the light and how great the grace of healing with which the saints of Christ in heaven are endowed."[77] If it is rich enough in metaphorical potential,

74   De Nie, Views from a Many-Windowed Tower, pp. 24, 65; cf. p. 131.
75   VCP, chap. 14, p. 203 (translation slightly revised).
76   De Nie, Views from a Many-Windowed Tower, p. 128.
77   HE 4.10, p. 365. Cf. Donald K. Fry, "Bede Fortunate in His Translator: The Barking Nuns," in Studies in Earlier Old English Prose, ed. Paul E. Szarmach (Albany, 1986), pp. 345-362, esp. 353-354. Fry comments on the recurring imagery of light in the series of miracles to which this episode belongs.

as we have already seen, vivid imagery can also transform the coinciden-
tal into the providential. It can enable us to see the hand of God at work
where it might not otherwise be visible. An additional example occurs
in the last book of the *Ecclesiastical History*, where Bede reports the
miracle that accompanied Bishop Wilfrid's evangelization of Sussex:
"For three years before his coming into the kingdom no rain had fallen
in those parts, so that a most terrible famine assailed the populace and
pitilessly destroyed them. ... But on the very day on which the people
received the baptism of faith, a gentle but ample rain fell; the earth
revived, the fields once more became green, and a happy and fruitful
season followed." The coincidence was so striking that the rainfall had
to be a providentially arranged sign, one whose aptness is measured by
the parallelism between spiritual and physical rejuvenation that it brings
to mind. Says Bede: "Casting off their ancient superstitions and idolatry,
'the heart and flesh of all rejoiced in the living God'; for they realized
that He who is the true God had, by His heavenly grace, endowed them
with both outward and inward blessings."[78]

Had the circumstances been not quite so compelling, Bede might well
have regarded the events just considered as nothing more than simple
coincidences. At one point, for example, he informs us that, while he
was still a young man, Herebald, the future abbot of Tynemouth, was
once thrown from his horse and seriously injured. As Herebald himself
describes it, he had decided impetuously to race with some companions,
despite the express prohibition of Bishop John of Beverley:

> Immediately, as my fiery horse took a great leap over a hollow in the road,
> I fell and at once lost all feeling and power of movement just as if I were
> dead. For in that place there was a stone, level with the ground and covered
> by a thin layer of turf, and no other stone was to be found over the whole
> plain. Thus it happened by chance, or rather by divine intervention in order
> to punish my disobedience (*casuque evenit, vel potius divina provisione ad
> puniendam inobedientiae meae culpam*), that I hit it with my head and with
> the hand which I had put under my head as I fell; so my thumb was broken
> and my skull fractured and, as I said, I lay like a corpse.

Both Herebald himself and Bede interpret the event as having been a
divinely ordained punishment of the disrespect Herebald showed to the
bishop, and so it is appropriate that the bishop's prayers were instrumental in his recovery. But that, it would seem, became clear only in

78   *HE* 4.13, pp. 373-375. Cf. Ps. 83(84):3.

retrospect. Herebald's first reaction, also reported by Bede, was to consider the event a simple riding accident.[79]

Reporting chance events is not part of Bede's mandate, of course, and so the foregoing story is an isolated episode without close parallels elsewhere in his work. Bede does, however, record other episodes in which, without its being mentioned explicitly, chance might well at some level have been considered as a possible explanation, even if ultimately it was rejected. After Bishop Cedd had died of plague and been buried at his monastery in Northumbria, a number of the monks from his monastery in Essex, about thirty in total, came to join their Northumbrian brethren. They wished to live near the body of their father, or, if it was the Lord's will, to die and be buried there:

> They were gladly received by their brothers and fellow soldiers in Christ, but another attack of the pestilence came upon them and they all died, with the exception of one small boy who was preserved from death by the intercession of Cedd his father. After a long time devoted to the reading of the scriptures, a moment came when he realized that he had not been baptized. He was speedily washed in the waters of the font of salvation and afterwards admitted to priest's orders, rendering useful service to many in the church. I do not doubt (*De quo dubitandum non crediderim*) that he was delivered from the jaws of death by the intercession of his father Cedd, to whose tomb he had come out of love for him, so that he himself might escape eternal death and, by his teaching, exercise a ministry of life and salvation for others.[80]

Bede's protestation of certainty disguises a weak case. If Cedd had a role in saving the young boy, it was clear only in light of the purpose served by his subsequent baptism and ordination, events that unfolded many years later.

A miracle credited to Oethelwald, the anchorite of Farne Island, provides a parallel case. By means of prayer, Bede tells us, Oethelwald

---

79 *HE* 5.6, pp. 466-467. Cf. *In Gen.* 3, CCL 118A:173-174, and *In 1 Sam.* 2, CCL 119:132, where events recorded in Scripture are described as having taken place not by chance but by divine Providence. Although Bede here can conceive of chance as a possible explanation, he rejects it.

80 *HE* 3.23, pp. 288-289 (translation revised). The last sentence reads: "De quo dubitandum non crediderim, quin intercessionibus, ut dixi, sui patris, ad cuius corpus dilectionis ipsius gratia venerat, sit ab articulo mortis retentus, ut et ipse sic mortem evaderet aeternam et aliis quoque fratribus ministerium vitae ac salutis docendo exhiberet."

once stilled the stormy seas threatening some monks who had visited and were returning to the mainland. The words are those of Guthfrith, abbot of Lindisfarne, Bede's informant:

> No sooner was his prayer ended than he had calmed the swelling main; so that the fierce tempest ceased on all sides and favourable winds carried us over a smooth sea to land. As soon as we had landed and carried our little vessel up from the sea, the tempest, which had been calmed for our sakes for a short time, returned and continued to rage furiously all that day; so it was plain to see (*ut palam daretur intellegi*) that the short interval of calm which had occurred was granted by heaven for our escape, in answer to the prayers of the man of God.[81]

Elsewhere Bede reports a miracle of St Cuthbert, who once, by his intercession, rescued from like peril some monks from the monastery at Tynemouth. Strong winds threatened to carry them out to sea to their certain death, but Cuthbert prevailed through the power of prayer: "immediately the violent wind turned about and bore the rafts safe and sound to land, amid the rejoicings of those who were guiding them, and left them in a convenient place near the monastery itself." Living right on the coast, Bede certainly knew that at sea storms could come and go quite suddenly entirely of their own accord. Here, however, the prayers of the holy man capture his attention, especially the immediacy of their effect, and he comes to a different judgment.[82] As Mayr-Harting observes, what is at issue in cases of this sort is not so much credulity as a focus of attention different from our own.[83] In Oethelwald's case Bede insists that the divine intervention was "plain to see," but his insistence conveys a lesson. Had the storm not stopped only long enough to see the brethren safely to shore, the story might never have found its way into the *Ecclesiastical History*.

One of the miracle stories that Bede's *Vita Cuthberti* shares with the anonymous account concerns food that was miraculously made available

---

81   Ibid. 5.1, pp. 454-457.
82   *VCP*, chap. 3, p. 165. In the immediacy of their effect, Cuthbert's prayers also contrasted with those of the monks on the other shore. By divine Providence "the answer to their prayers was long delayed, ... in order that it might be made plain how much virtue there was in Cuthbert's prayers" (ibid., p. 163).
83   Henry Mayr-Harting, *The Coming of Christianity to England* (New York, 1972), pp. 48-49.

for the saint.[84] According to the anonymous author's version, Cuthbert, forced to seek shelter from a storm, once took refuge in a hut that had temporarily been abandoned for the winter season. He unsaddled his horse and secured it to the wall, resolved simply to await fairer weather. As he was praying, however, his horse raised its head and greedily pulled on the thatch above it, out of which there fell a warm loaf of bread and some meat carefully wrapped up in a piece of linen. Cuthbert thanked God for anticipating and miraculously providing for his need, and after being refreshed and strengthened by the food was able to resume his journey. In his much longer account Bede is able to add several details that he has learned from Ingwald, a monk of Wearmouth who, he tells us, heard the story directly from Cuthbert himself. The hut, we learn, was a shepherd's hut (*tugurium*) that had hastily been thrown together the preceding summer. Having served its purpose, it had since been deserted, and the elements had already begun to take a toll upon it. Wind had attacked the roof, and detached a bundle of straw which Cuthbert fed to his horse before turning to his prayers. As Stranks observes, the food the horse's nose detected had undoubtedly been hidden in the thatch by one of the shepherds who occasionally used the place, and then forgotten. However, once the story had won for itself a place among the miracles of Cuthbert, the bread had come to be described as warm and new to preclude the possibility of a simple explanation.[85] This was the state of the tradition as Bede received it from his anonymous predecessor.

Although Bede endorsed that tradition, he also saw the potential for a more straightforward explanation. Hence, to justify treating it as a miracle, he draws on the supplementary information provided by Ingwald to reinforce the miraculous elements in the story. The loaf Cuthbert discovers becomes a half-loaf, and the bread and meat together turn out to be "sufficient for one meal for himself" (*dimidium panis calidi et carnem, quae ad unam sibi refectionem sufficere possent*). These details function to underline how, extraordinary as it may seem, Cuthbert's precise needs were addressed. Even more significant is the larger context in which Bede situates the story. Earlier the same day, at the third hour, he tells us, Cuthbert had turned into a village in order to find a place to rest and something to feed his horse. He was received kindly by a religious

---

84   Cf. *VCA* 1.6, pp. 70-71; *VCP*, chap. 5, pp. 168-171.
85   C.J. Stranks, *The Life and Death of St Cuthbert* (London, 1964), p. 9.

housewife, who urged him to take some refreshment himself as well; but Cuthbert refused because it was Friday, a day on which it was customary to fast until the ninth hour. The woman pressed him to reconsider, for he would find no other villages on the road he was travelling, and he could not possibly complete his journey before sunset. However, Cuthbert remained firm in his resolve—"his love of religion overcame the urgency of her entreaty"—and he set out on his journey once again until, evening having descended, he was forced to take shelter where he could find it.[86] In view of Cuthbert's steadfastness in observing the fast, even if it meant going hungry until the next day, the subsequent discovery of food looks less like a fortuitous event and more like a reward of Providence. Indeed, Bede is able to derive a spiritual lesson from it, one reinforced by an appropriate biblical parallel. From that day on, he tells us,

> [Cuthbert] became readier than ever to fast, because indeed he understood clearly that this food had been provided for him in a solitary place, by the gift of Him who once for many days fed Elijah in solitude, with food of the same kind, through the ministrations of birds [1 Kings 17:6], there being no man there to minister to him.

Although Bede regards the episode as a miracle, he also clearly felt that this interpretation needed reinforcement. Despite the frequency of miracles in his account, and his disposition to note them where we would not, he did not see miracles everywhere. They were exceptional occurrences, even those that we might more readily identify as coincidences; and they were seen against a backdrop of normalcy in which events unfolded in their customary pattern. Among the miracles of Bishop John of Beverley is the cure of a youth who was dumb (but apparently not deaf), and who had frequently received alms from the bishop.[87] He also, Bede tells us, "had so much scabbiness and scurf on his head that no hair could grow on the crown save for a few rough hairs which stuck out around it." The bishop took him by the chin, made the sign of the cross on his tongue, and then taught him to say, first of all letters, and then, in due order, syllables, words and entire sentences. On first reading, the story sounds more like an example of effective speech therapy than anything else. As Wallace-Hadrill observes, the bishop did nothing extraordinary, but simply followed the method outlined in Quintilian's

---

86 In Bede's account it is nightfall rather than wind and rain that brings an end to his travels for the day.

87 *HE* 5.2, pp. 457-459.

Institutio oratoria and endorsed by Bede himself in *De orthographia* and *De arte metrica*.[88] Perhaps this cure should be added to our list—by no means exhaustive in any case—of miracles that otherwise admit of natural explanations, its status as a miracle depending on nothing more substantive than the reputation of the bishop that performed it and his having begun the process by making the sign of the cross.

Certainty is elusive in these matters, of course, but what makes the cure a miracle, I think, is the implication that it was completed in the course of one day. After the young man was cured, Bede says,

> those who were present relate that he never ceased all that day and night (*tota die illa et nocte sequente*), as long as he could keep awake, to talk and to reveal the secrets of his thoughts and wishes to others, which he could never do before. He was like the man who had long been lame, who, when healed by the apostles Peter and John, stood up, leapt and walked, entering the Temple with them, walking and leaping and praising God, rejoicing to have the use of his feet of which he had so long been deprived.

His cure was as sudden and as unexpected as that of the lame man whom the apostles found lying at the gate of the temple begging alms, and he was as irrepressible in his use of his tongue as the beneficiary of the apostles' power was in his newly strengthened limbs. Wallace-Hadrill wonders why Bede would not have cited Mark 7:32-37: I suspect it was the joyous reaction of the man that made Acts 3:2-8 a more appropriate parallel. What is surprising in view of the bishop's miraculous powers, however, is that, having loosed the youth's tongue, he did nothing for his scabby head, but rather ordered his physician to take the matter in hand. The physician did so, Bede reports, and was successful: "with the help of the bishop's blessing and prayers, his skin was healed and he grew a beautiful head of hair."

An analogous situation arises in the cure of Herebald by the same Bishop John of Beverley.[89] After his fall, he "lay like a corpse." He spent the better part of a day and a night in a comatose state, vomiting blood as well because of internal injury. His condition clearly was grave, and the bishop devoted the entire night to a prayer vigil for his recovery. The bishop's efforts were not without effect. Herebald explains:

---

88 Wallace-Hadrill, *Bede's Ecclesiastical History*, pp. 175-176. For a different view, cf. Dietfried Gewalt, "Der entstummte Bettler. Zu Beda Venerabilis, Historia Ecclesiastica Gentis Anglorum V, 2," *Linguistica Biblica* 54 (1983): 53-60.
89 *HE* 5.6, pp. 465-469. See above, pp. 36-37.

In the early morning he came in to me, said a prayer over me, and called me by name. I awoke as though from a heavy sleep and he asked me if I knew who it was who was talking to me. I opened my eyes and said, "Yes, you are my beloved bishop." He answered, "Can you live?" I said, "I can, with the help of your prayers, if it is the Lord's will." Then, placing his hand on my head with words of blessing, he returned to his prayers; when he came back very soon afterwards, he found me sitting up and able to speak.

Whether this should be considered a miracle, however, is another matter. The recovery that followed upon the bishop's prayers was neither sudden nor complete. Despite his reputation for miracles, once again John of Beverley summoned a physician, this time to set and bind Herebald's fractured skull, a fact that Bede reports with complete equanimity.[90] As Rosenthal puts it, "even the most spiritual had material needs, and they first tried to conform to the law of the natural universe."[91]

The same can be said for the humbler members of the population, as becomes clear from a miracle reported by both the Lindisfarne Anonymous and Bede towards the end of their accounts.[92] It concerns a young monk who was suffering from complete paralysis of the limbs, and who was sent to the monastery of Lindisfarne precisely because of the learned physicians known to be there. They applied all the skill that they could summon, but without effect; his disease only worsened, his limited strength gradually ebbing away. Bede and the Anonymous agree: it was only after all hope of a cure had been abandoned that recourse was had to St Cuthbert. As Bede puts it, "when he lay despaired of and deserted by the carnal physicians who had long laboured in vain, he fled to the divine aid of the heavenly Physician," and ultimately was healed through Cuthbert's relics. Undoubtedly, both Bede and the Anonymous

---

90 Plummer, *Opera Historica* 2:777, observes that in his life of John of Beverley Folcard heightened the miracle by suppressing the detail concerning the physician. As Bede tells it, however, "there is nothing distinctly miraculous" in the story. Wallace-Hadrill, *Bede's Ecclesiastical History*, pp. 177-178, offers a different point of view: "It was not the physician but the bishop himself who brought about the recovery by prayers and benediction; and the recovery was spiritual as well as physical."

91 Joel T. Rosenthal, "Bede's Ecclesiastical History and the Material Conditions of Anglo-Saxon Life," *Journal of British Studies* 19.1 (1979): 1-17 at 15. Rosenthal points out that "when Cuthbert had to rely on a miracle to give him enough corn to get through the winter [*HE* 4.28, p. 426], it was only after he had first followed good agronomic practice: starting with wheat and then quickly switching to barley when the former failed."

92 Cf. *VCA* 4.17, pp. 136-138; *VCP*, chap. 45, pp. 298-301.

relate this story to highlight the powers of Cuthbert, to show that he could be successful where the most accomplished physicians had failed. At the same time, however, it tells us that miracles were far from routine events. Not even at Lindisfarne, where the power of Cuthbert should have been particularly effective, was there expectation of a miraculous cure. In the first instance at least, faith was placed, not in the relics of the saint, but in the skill of the physicians. In his reporting of the incident, Bede's own point of view becomes clear. It was a providential perspective that would see miracles where many, perhaps even many of his contemporaries, would not. But it clearly did not perceive them as the norm. Far from stripping nature of any and all consistency of its own, miracles were remarkable precisely because they remained those rare occurrences in which nature was required to yield to the divine, normal human expectations being suspended by the breakthrough of the transcendent.

2

Scepticism, Credulity and Belief

Twentieth-century historians have sometimes tended to see in Bede a kindred spirit, particularly valuing the critical judgment evident in his work. Although few modern commentators would choose to follow Jones in explicitly questioning his belief in miracles, several have been prepared to credit him with being more sober and cautious in his acceptance of miracle stories than most of his contemporaries.[1] Colgrave, for example, while never doubting Bede's belief in miracles, argues that his works contain "comparatively few examples ... of what one could call mere fairy-tale wonders." "Comparatively few" does not mean "none at all," however, and Colgrave himself goes on to provide some examples.[2] One is the extraordinary story of Imma, a thegn of King Ecgfrith who had been captured in battle, but could not be kept fettered like any other prisoner. His brother, Tunna, who was a priest, believed him dead; and every time he offered masses for Imma's soul, his bonds were wondrously loosed. Another is the "fantastic tale" in which Archbishop Laurence is violently beaten by St Peter in his church in Canterbury. Laurence ordered a bed to be prepared for him in the church so that he might spend the night there prayerfully, and while he slept the prince of the apostles visited and "scourged him hard and long." The next morning Laurence was able to show his wounds to the king, who was moved enough by the sight of them to convert to the Christian faith and be baptized.[3]

1 See, for example, Loomis, "Miracle Traditions," pp. 404-405; Musca, *Venerabile Beda*, pp. 60-61, 144-145, 167, 200-201; Alberic Stacpoole, "St Bede the Venerable, Monk of Jarrow," in *Benedict's Disciples*, ed. D.H. Farmer (Leominster, 1980), pp. 86-104 at 92-93. Cf. Charles W. Jones, *Saints' Lives and Chronicles in Early England* (Ithaca, 1947), esp. p. 83, where he outlines "the central theme of this volume, that Bede's words are not intended for material interpretation."
2 Colgrave, "Bede's Miracle Stories," pp. 222-223; *HE*, p. xxxv.
3 *HE* 4.22 & 2.6, pp. 400-404, 154-155. For a recent discussion of the story of Imma, see Seth Lerer, *Literacy and Power in Anglo-Saxon Literature* (Lincoln NE, 1991), pp. 30-48. Lerer reads this chapter of the *Ecclesiastical History* as a "kind of parable of the mythologies of writing in a newly Christian Anglo-Saxon England" (p. 31).

Both stories had precedents that would have made their acceptance easier. In his *Dialogues* Gregory the Great provides a close cognate for the tale of Imma; and in his famous letter to Eustochium Jerome tells us that, like Laurence, he too once was scourged in a vision, in his case for an unhealthy devotion to classical literature. Jerome could still feel the blows after awakening, and his shoulders were black and blue.[4] Not only was Bede unable to disbelieve what was reported by such venerable authorities, he was inclined to take their statements literally. He read the *Dialogues*, not, like some modern commentators, as an extended allegory, but as a factual account. Even the dialogue form itself, purely a matter of literary convention on Gregory's part, was taken at face value as the record of an actual conversation.[5] His reading of Jerome was similarly literal. We have already noted in Chapter 1 that he accepted Jerome's account of his vision as the record of an actual experience. To this we can add that he was inclined to read Jerome's hagiographical work in a like manner. The life of St Hilarion runs to romance and contains obvious fantasies, but Bede includes an entry in his *Martyrology* on the strength of it.[6]

---

4   Gregory the Great, *Dial.* 4.59, SC 265:196; Jerome, *Ep.* 22.30, CSEL 54:190-191. As Plummer (*Opera Historica* 2:89) points out, both the false bishop, Natalius, and St Columba were visited during the night by angels and beaten. Natalius was able to show his wounds the next morning to Bishop Zephyrinus, and Columba bore a scar on his side for the rest of his life. See Eusebius, *Historia ecclesiastica* 5.28, ed. Theodor Mommsen, *Eusebius Werke* 2.1 (Leipzig, 1903), pp. 503-505; Adomnan, *Vita S. Columbae* 3.5, ed. & trans. Anderson & Anderson, p. 472.

5   See *HE* 2.1, p. 124, where, in his short biography of Gregory, Bede refers to and quotes from the conversation that opens the *Dialogues*: "Denique tempore quodam, secreto cum diacono suo Petro conloquens, enumeratis animi sui virtutibus priscis mox dolendo subiunxit: 'At nunc ex occasione curae pastoralis saecularium hominum negotia patitur, et post tam pulchram quietis suae speciem terreni actus pulvere fedatur, cumque se pro condiscensione multorum ad exteriora sparserit, etiam cum interiora appetit, ad haec procul dubio minor redit. Perpendo itaque quid tolero, perpendo quid amisi, dumque intueor illud quod perdidi, fit hoc gravius quod porto.'" Cf. *Dial.* 1 Prol. 4, SC 260:12. On the *Dialogues* as an extended allegory, see, for example, Bolton, "Supra-Historical Sense in the Dialogues of Gregory I."

6   Cf. Henri Quentin, *Les martyrologes historiques du moyen âge. Etude sur la formation du Martyrologe Romain* (1908; repr. Darmstadt, 1969), p. 99; Jacques Dubois & Geneviève Renaud, *Edition pratique des martyrologes de Bède, de l'Anonyme lyonnais et de Florus* (Paris, 1976), p. 191. The entry for Oct. 21 reads: "Sancti patris nostri Hilarionis, cuius Vitam Hieronymus virtutibus plenam scripsit." An entry for Jan. 10 (Quentin, p. 99, Dubois & Renaud, p. 11) draws on Jerome's life

His reputation for restraint notwithstanding, one of the most interesting examples of what could fairly be described as a tendency to credulity on Bede's part occurs at the outset of the *Ecclesiastical History*, where he sets the stage for his narrative by offering brief descriptions of Britain and Ireland. He tells us that "Ireland is broader than Britain, is healthier and has a much milder climate, so that snow rarely lasts there for more than three days. Hay," he goes on to say, "is never cut in summer for winter use nor are stables built for their beasts." He then includes the following curious piece of natural history:

> No reptile is found there nor could a serpent survive; for although serpents have often been brought from Britain, as soon as the ship approaches land they are affected by the scent of the air and quickly perish. In fact almost everything that the island produces is efficacious against poison. For instance we have seen how, in the case of people suffering from snake-bite, the leaves of manuscripts from Ireland were scraped, and the scrapings put in water and given to the sufferer to drink. These scrapings at once absorbed the whole violence of the spreading poison and assuaged the swelling.[7]

Mayr-Harting has argued that Bede cannot be taken seriously: he is simply poking fun at Isidore of Seville. In his *Etymologies* Isidore observes that Ireland has no snakes, only a few birds and no bees, and then goes on to claim that when dust or pebbles from Ireland are put in a bee hive, the swarm will abandon it. Bede's story, says Mayr-Harting, is "a witty parody of this sort of nonsense." It is also, he suggests, a bit of a joke on the Irish: "Admirable as the best Irish scholarship was, the Irish were filling rather too many leaves of parchment with learning, not all of it entirely free from pedantry or wild fantasy. ... What better use, then, for

---

of St Paul the Hermit, which, if anything, is even more fantastic. However, Dubois & Renaud attribute it to Florus rather than Bede. On Jerome's efforts at saintly biography, see Manfred Fuhrmann, "Die Mönchsgeschichten des Hieronymus: Formexperimente in erzählender Literatur," in *Christianisme et formes littéraires de l'antiquité tardive en Occident* (Genève, 1977), pp. 41-89.

Benedicta Ward, *The Venerable Bede* (Harrisburg, 1990), p. 95, points to a case that parallels Bede's reading of the *Vita Hilarionis*: his handling of the passion of St Thecla. One of the saintly women praised in Bede's poem on Aethelthryth is the same Thecla, "the legendary companion of Paul, whose highly-coloured story Bede, surprisingly, seems to have accepted in spite of the doubts of both Tertullian and Jerome." See *HE* 4.20, p. 398. Thecla also is mentioned in the martyrology. See Quentin, p. 93, Dubois & Renaud, p. 176.

7   *HE* 1.1, pp. 18-21.

some of these leaves, than that they should be applied to snake-bites?" Unfortunately, however, there is nothing in either the context or the tone of Bede's remarks to suggest that they should not be taken at face value. He does indeed follow Isidore, who, it is sometimes claimed, was not one of his most highly esteemed authorities. But, as Meyvaert points out, any disagreement would probably have been expressed much more directly, as was Bede's usual style.[8] If a joke on the Irish remains possible, on balance that is not very likely either. The remedy for snake bite here envisaged is not dissimilar to cures mentioned elsewhere in the *Ecclesiastical History*, and Bede tells us that he saw it work with his own eyes.[9]

In a significantly different approach, Kendall argues that the passage is to be read for its allegorical rather than its literal significance. According to this view, the *Ecclesiastical History* was written in conscious imitation of Sacred Scripture, the descriptions of Britain and Ireland at the beginning of book one functioning as the equivalent of a creation scene. Interestingly enough, both are written in the present tense, which seems slightly odd if Bede intends to allude to the bygone Paradise of Eden. Conceivably, therefore, one might prefer to see nothing more profound in Bede's description of the two lands than his endorsement of a standard historiographical practice, one that he could have

8   Mayr-Harting, *Coming of Christianity to England*, p. 50; Meyvaert, "Bede the Scholar," p. 66n. See also Isidore of Seville, *Etymol.* 14.6.6, ed. W.M. Lindsay (Oxford, 1911), n.p.; and Solinus, *Collect.* 22.4(6), ed. Theodor Mommsen (Berolini, 1895), p. 100, on whom Isidore himself was dependent. Although Bede could have drawn on either, Isidore is more likely. Both go on to inform us that Thanet (not Ireland) has soil that is efficacious against snakes: "Dicta autem Tanatos a morte serpentum, quos dum ipsa nesciat, asportata inde terra quoque gentium vecta sit, angues ilico perimit" (*Etymol.* 14.6.3); cf. *Collect.* 22.8(10), Mommsen 101. Robert Wildhaber, "Beda Venerabilis and the Snakes," in *Folklore Today: A Festschrift for Richard M. Dorson*, ed. Linda Dégh, Henry Glassie & Felix J. Oinas (Bloomington, 1976), pp. 497-506 at 497, mentions both possibilities, but prefers folklore to a scholarly, literary source. On Bede's alleged dislike of Isidore, see above, pp. 3-4.

9   See, for example, *HE* 3.2, pp. 214-216; 3.9, p. 242; 3.13, p. 254; 3.17, p. 264; 4.3, p. 346; 5.18, p. 514. Plummer (*Opera Historica* 2:11) points to the similarity. In each case, dust or soil or wood mixed with water becomes the agent of a miraculous cure. In *HE* 1.1, however, the remedy witnessed by Bede seems not to have been miraculous but rather a product of the natural properties of things Irish.

learned from Orosius or Gregory of Tours.[10] Kendall's choice, however, is to see hidden spiritual depths in the passage, and to use them to elucidate Bede's decision to include the curious legend about the snakes:

> The respective physical descriptions of Britain and Ireland are built on comparison: the *copia* of Britain deliberately recalls the absolute goodness of earth before the fall of man, but Ireland is better. It is the Promised Land which prefigures the redemption of the world. ... An island abounding with milk and honey is meant to evoke the land God promised to the people of Moses. ... Since a serpent caused man's (spiritual) death (Gen. iii), it is fitting that there are no snakes or reptiles in the land that prefigures the promise of eternal life; indeed, that almost anything from the island is a remedy for poison, which is one of the basic symbols in [the *Ecclesiastical History*] for the evils of the fallen world.[11]

One can readily acknowledge the biblical reminiscences and allusions in the *Ecclesiastical History*, and that they are present in the descriptions of Britain and Ireland as well. That much is beyond dispute. A creation scene, however, is another matter. In advancing such an interpretation, Kendall has to get around the awkward fact that there are descriptions for two lands. Taking them as a joint evocation of Paradise fails ultimately to do justice to their duality. The solution, therefore, is to consider them sequentially, and to see in Britain an image of the Paradise of Eden, and in Ireland a representation of the Promised Land. The latter in turn prefigures the redemption of mankind. If this were the case, however, presumably the Promised Land, like Ireland, would be without snakes as well, which, of course, it is not, either literally or allegorically. It is only at the third stage, "the redemption of mankind," that the absence of snakes in Ireland receives some kind of allegorical fulfillment. This is incoherent allegorizing that is unworthy of Bede.

In Kendall's view, the imitation of the Bible in the *Ecclesiastical History* actually proceeds on two levels. On the first, particularly evident in book one, Bede's account imitates the Acts of the Apostles and the Pauline Epistles. On the second, as we have just seen, it imitates the whole body of Sacred Scripture. Indeed, Kendall briefly mentions a third

---

10   See R.A. Markus, *Bede and the Tradition of Ecclesiastical Historiography* (Jarrow, 1975), p. 4, who points out that Isidore of Seville also prefaced his history of the Goths with a "geographical encomium" of Spain.

11   Calvin B. Kendall, "Imitation and the Venerable Bede's *Historia ecclesiastica*," in *Saints, Scholars and Heroes* 1:161-190 at 181-182.

level as well, but does not pursue the idea. On this level Bede divided his history into five books in deliberate imitation of the five books of Moses.[12] One might reasonably ask how many levels of allegory it is tolerable to propose for Bede's text. In the final analysis one suspects none at all, especially if, as Kendall also suggests, the *Ecclesiastical History* was directed at a popular audience. Presumably Bede would have seen very little point in burdening his text with mysteries beyond the capacity of the audience he wished to address.[13] The principal weak-

---

12 Ibid., pp. 174 & 176.
13 Kendall, "Imitation," p. 182, argues that, "if Bede had been writing a commentary on the meaning of the history of the sixth age for a learned, monastic audience, he might have elucidated the allegorical significance of these 'signs,' as he did in his commentaries on the Scriptures. But [the *Ecclesiastical History*] like the Bible was written for a more popular audience. Therefore like the Bible it is primarily a record of the literal truths of history which are fit for all levels of understanding." On this analysis, the hidden allegory is without point, except perhaps to the more educated minority in Bede's audience. Kendall goes on to allude to this possibility: "To uncover spiritual truths which the 'letter' sometimes conceals, whether in the Bible or in his narrative of the sixth age in Britain, is part of the exercise of Christian discipline which Bede could expect the learned members of his audience to engage in." However, given that Bede spent most of his career expounding the hidden spiritual sense of Scripture so that his more educated contemporaries would be able to grasp it, one doubts that he would have left them without a guide to the hidden mysteries embedded in his own text. Although Bede probably did conceive of the *Ecclesiastical History* as a continuation in some sense of Sacred Scripture (see below, p. 78), Scripture remained unique. See Arthur G. Holder, "Allegory and History in Bede's Interpretation of Sacred Architecture," *American Benedictine Review* 40 (1989): 115-131 at p. 131: "For Bede (at least for the mature Bede), an allegory in the sense of a figure containing hidden spiritual meaning was a trope found in Scripture, and there alone."
On the issue of the audience of the *Ecclesiastical History*, Kendall probably misplaces the emphasis. At one point Bede refers those desiring additional information to a written life of Fursa: "siqui plenius scire vult, ... legat ipsum de quo dixi libellum vitae eius, et multum ex illo, ut reor, profectus spiritalis accipiet" (*HE* 3.19, p. 270). Wallace-Hadrill, *Bede's Ecclesiastical History*, p. 113, observes: "Bede envisages no 'popular' audience ... ; there will be readers to whom the text of the *libellus* will be available in a (presumably) monastic library." However, Bede's casual reference later on to the readers or hearers of his account—"Hanc historiam ... simpliciter ob salutem legentium sive audientium narrandam esse putavi" (*HE* 5.13, p. 502)—requires some qualification of this assessment. As Plummer (*Opera Historica* 2:299) points out, "Bede evidently contemplates the possibility of his work being read aloud for purposes of edification, as was in fact done." Bede's primary audience was undoubtedly a literate one of monks, other clerics and

ness of this kind of interpretation, however, is the lack of compelling evidence. Kendall points to the poem in praise of Queen Aethelthryth inserted in the fourth book of the history, and to the comments with which Bede prefaces it:

It seems fitting to insert in this history a hymn on the subject of virginity which I composed many years ago in elegiac metre in honour of this queen and bride of Christ, and therefore truly a queen because the bride of Christ; imitating the method of holy Scripture in which many songs are inserted into the history and, as is well known, these are composed in metre and verse.[14]

That Bede was imitating Scripture in this one instance, however, does not prove the kind of large-scale imitation that Kendall has in mind. At the outset of his *Dialogues* Gregory the Great claims that, in writing what he has learned on the authority of others, he is simply following the practice of Mark and Luke.[15] On this basis, however, it would be perilous to argue that the *Dialogues* constitute an extended imitation of the Gospels.[16]

---

possibly educated laymen. However, he also seems to have intended the *Ecclesiastical History*—the only work he ever dedicated to a layman, King Ceolwulf of Northumbria—to reach a more popular audience, possibly through the sermons of some of his readers. This was not an unprecedented literary strategy: cf. *Signs of Sanctity*, pp. 47-57; and Marc Van Uytfanghe, "L'hagiographie et son public à l'époque mérovingienne," *Studia Patristica* 16.2 (1985): 54-62.

14 *HE* 4.20, p. 397; Kendall, "Imitation," pp. 176-177.
15 *Dial.* 1 Prol. 10, sc 260:16.
16 For other attempts to find allegorical meaning in Bede's history, see J.N. Stephens, "Bede's Ecclesiastical History," *History* 62 (1977): 1-14, esp. 13; Nicholas Howe, *Migration and Mythmaking in Anglo-Saxon England* (New Haven, 1989), esp. pp. 116-117; and Ward, *Venerable Bede*, pp. 114-115ff. Whereas Howe argues that Bede conceived the history of his people, particularly their migration, as a reenactment of the Israelite past, Ward maintains that it represents "a world history in miniature." With more or less plausibility, hidden meanings have been uncovered in the *Vita Cuthberti* as well. See, for example, Benedicta Ward, "The Spirituality of St Cuthbert," and Walter Berschin, "*Opus deliberatum ac perfectum*: Why Did the Venerable Bede Write a Second Prose Life of St Cuthbert?" in *St Cuthbert, His Cult and His Community to AD 1200*, ed. Gerald Bonner, David Rollason & Clare Stancliffe (Woodbridge, Suffolk, 1989), pp. 65-76 and 95-102 (esp. 101) respectively. See also Berschin, *Biographie und Epochenstil im lateinischen Mittelalter* (Stuttgart, 1986-1991), 2:274.

If the description of Ireland and the other examples considered hitherto suggest that Bede's alleged reserve vis-à-vis the miraculous should not be overstated, it has been argued more than once that we need to be careful to respect the distinctions among his various works. Given the nature of the genre, it is argued, it was only natural that miracles should abound in a hagiographical work like the *Vita Cuthberti*. Elsewhere, where expectations were not the same, they are much less prominent, and we get a better reading on the kind of critical judgment Bede was capable of employing. In the *Historia abbatum*, the most modern of his works because of the extent to which it anticipates the rational, scientific reconstruction and interpretation of human action, they are completely absent.[17] If they have a major presence in the *Ecclesiastical History*, the explanation is to be found, at least in part, we are told, in the broad popular audience Bede wished to address, an audience that would have been as disoriented by the absence of miracles as modern readers are by their presence. Of even greater importance, however, was their spiritual value as Bede saw it. Bede knew that miracles were in principle questionable, the argument goes, but he felt a responsibility to include them because of the spiritual significance they could be shown to have. This, says Musca, suggests that he had a much more heightened critical sense than the other hagiographers of his time, and even than Gregory the Great: "non c'è in lui credulità ingenua e superstiziosa, ma fede consapevole e matura."[18]

Although the absence of miracles in the *History abbatum* has been affirmed often enough to become common knowledge, in reality the situation is not that clear. After describing Abbot Eastorwine's sanctity, Bede alludes to a grace of foreknowledge similar to St Benedict's. Eastorwine, he tells us, was able to foresee his own death by two days.[19]

17 See, for example, Musca, *Venerabile Beda*, pp. 121 & 202.
18 Ibid. p. 207 & esp. p. 204. Cf. Meyvaert, "Bede the Scholar," esp. p. 51, where this line of argument is identified and criticized. For a recent variant, see Ruth Morse, *Truth and Convention in the Middle Ages: Rhetoric, Representation, and Reality* (Cambridge, 1991), pp. 153-154. Morse argues that the miracles of St Cuthbert are out of place in the *Ecclesiastical History* and constitute a digression, but were inserted to bring the *Vita Cuthberti* up to date. As if the miracles in the *Ecclesiastical History* were limited to St Cuthbert!
19 *Historia abbatum* 1.8, Plummer, *Opera Historica* 1:372: "Eodem quo fratres ceteri cibo, semper eadem vescebatur in domo, ipso quo priusquam abbas esset communi dormiebat in loco, adeo ut etiam morbo correptus, et obitus sui certis ex signis iam praescius, duos adhuc dies in dormitorio fratrum quiesceret."

Conceivably, however, Eastorwine was simply drawing the obvious conclusion from the illness afflicting him. More significant, therefore, is the sign that accompanied the death of Benedict Biscop, the fact that he passed away at the precise moment the brethren began to sing the eighty-second Psalm. Bede explains its theme: that although the earthly and spiritual enemies of Christ may strive to confound the faithful, ultimately it is they who will be routed and who will perish forever. Hence, he tells us, it was quite properly regarded as a disposition of heaven that such a Psalm should be recited at the very moment when Benedict's soul, which no spiritual enemy conceivably could ever overcome, was taking flight from its body.[20] It was so fitting that Bede was incapable of seeing it as a mere coincidence. The hand of Providence was discernible in the event, and that sufficed to elevate it to a different order. But compared to the wonders recorded in the *Vita Cuthberti* or in the *Ecclesiastical History*, this is a modest miracle indeed; and so one might legitimately wonder at the relative absence of miracles in the *Historia abbatum*. Meyvaert advises us to remember that Bede was speaking from immediate and personal experience. If he includes no miracles, presumably it was because he had none to tell.[21] But this explanation, although essentially correct, is less than completely satisfying, for there was at least one miracle that Bede clearly knew about but chose to omit from his account.

One of the sources available to Bede when he set out to write his history of the abbots was the life of the abbot Ceolfrith, Benedict Biscop's successor. This had been written by some anonymous monk of Wearmouth or Jarrow, probably shortly after Ceolfrith's death in 716.[22] Although the anonymous author clearly conceives of Ceolfrith as a saint,[23] like Bede in his *Historia abbatum* he provides an account that is largely devoid of miracles. At the very end, however, he tells us that Ceolfrith's pilgrimage to Rome was interrupted by his death at Langres, and then goes on to report the following:

20 *Historia abbatum* 2.14, Plummer, *Opera Historica* 1:378.
21 Meyvaert, "Bede the Scholar," p. 54.
22 This is the generally accepted view. However, Judith McClure, "Bede and the Life of Ceolfrid," *Peritia* 3 (1984): 71-84, argues that the *Vita Ceolfridi* was written by Bede himself. She sees evidence for Bede's authorship in the circumstances of its composition, in its style and in the historical method employed.
23 See *Vita Ceolfridi* 19 (Plummer, *Opera Historica* 1:394), where he outlines the virtues with which Ceolfrith presided over the joint monasteries for twenty-seven years.

The companions of our father, loved of God, who returned to us, used to tell us that in the night after his venerable body had been committed to the tomb, while three guards of the same church [at Langres] were keeping the night watches, according to custom, the fragrance of a wonderful odour filled the whole church; and it was followed by a light, which remained no little time, and finally rose to the roof of the church. They went out quickly, and gazing they saw the same light rapidly rise to the skies, so that all places round about seemed to be illuminated by its glow, as if it were day-time; so that it was clearly given them to understand that ministers of eternal light and perpetual sweetness had been present and had consecrated by their visitation the resting-place of the holy body. Hence a custom spread among the natives of that place that throughout the various hours of daily and nightly prayer, when the canonical rite of psalmody was ended, all the men should bend their knees in supplication at his tomb. And also report spread abroad that other signs and cures were done there, by the grace of him who is wont both to aid his saints as they strive in this present life and to crown them victors in the future life.[24]

Bede's omission of the same miracle in his *Historia abbatum* must have resulted from a conscious decision, for he clearly knew about it. Not only does he endorse the image of Ceolfrith's saintly character that is found in the anonymous life, he also appropriates some of the anonymous author's language.[25]

In one of its central features, the motif of light, the miracle associated with Ceolfrith is reminiscent of the story of Benedict's vision as recorded in Gregory's *Dialogues*, a factor that could only have recommended it to Bede.[26] However, whereas Benedict sees the soul of Germanus of Capua ascend to heaven, the guards at the tomb of Ceolfrith witness something quite different: the evidence of heavenly visitors having

---

24 Ibid. 40, Plummer, *Opera Historica* 1:403-404; trans. EHD 1:770.

25 See, for example, *Historia abbatum* 2.15, Plummer, *Opera Historica* 1:379: "Qui et ipse tertius, id est, *Ceolfridus* industrius per omnia *vir*, acutus *ingenio*, *actu* inpiger, maturus animo, religionis *zelo fervens*, prius, sicut et supra meminimus, iubente pariter et iuvante Benedicto, monasterium beati Pauli apostoli VII[tem] annis, fundavit, perfecit, rexit; ac deinde *utrique monasterio*, vel sicut rectius dicere possumus, *in duobus locis* posito *uni monasterio*, beatorum apostolorum Petri et Pauli, *viginti* et octo annos *sollerti* regimine praefuit; et cuncta quae suus prodecessor [*sic*] aegregia virtutum opera caepit [*sic*], ipse non segnius perficere curavit."

26 See Gregory the Great, *Dial.* 2.35.3-4, SC 260:238. Wilhelm Levison, "Bede as Historian," in *Bede: His Life, Times, and Writings*, pp. 111-151 at 130n, detects a few phrases from book four of the *Dialogues*.

descended to honour the saint's mortal remains. The main purpose of the latter miracle is to consecrate the site of Ceolfrith's tomb, and so it is followed by a reference to other signs and cures pointing to the efficacy of his relics. In its main *raison d'être* it is fundamentally different from the miracles of the *Dialogues*, which tend, although not exclusively, to be performed by living saints, and to emphasize their moral and spiritual qualities.[27] Elsewhere Bede does not shrink from recording miracles that occurred at saintly tombs.[28] It seems unlikely, therefore, that he was uncomfortable with this miracle, or with the interpretation that had been placed upon it, although the fact that the holy site being commended was in a distant land, and that its connection with his own monastery was only accidental, would certainly have made it easier to disregard. Whatever the case, however, it would clearly be unjustified to see his omission of this one wonder as evidence of a more sceptical, critical attitude than the balance of his works would suggest. Having no miracles to record of the other abbots, he may simply have thought it inappropriate to single out Ceolfrith alone in a work intended to honour them all.

If we are properly to appreciate the degree of scepticism or credulity with which Bede approached miracles, we need to be attentive to Bede's own comments about them, particularly about the miracles of Scripture. As others have observed, there is nothing in his remarks to suggest any doubt on Bede's part. On the contrary, what Scripture presents as fact is to be accepted without question as a truthful and accurate report of events that actually transpired.[29] If anything, Bede tends to highlight the miraculous elements in the biblical narrative. This is the effect of what he has to say concerning Christ's walking on water, for example (Mark 6:45-52). Like the disciples who initially thought that it was a ghost they had seen, even today, says Bede, there are heretics who believe that a mere phantasm without weight and substance appeared on the sea. The catholic faith, however, acknowledges both Christ's human nature and the full reality of the miracle: "fides catholica et pondus secundum carnem habere eum praedicat et onus corporeum et cum pondere atque onere corporali incedere super aquas non infusis pedibus."[30]

---

27 See *Signs of Sanctity*, Chap. 4.
28 See below, pp. 75-76.
29 See, for example, Meyvaert, "Bede the Scholar," p. 52; and Creider, "Bede's Understanding of the Miraculous," pp. 124-125.
30 *In Marc.* 2, CCL 120:517-518.

Frequently Bede draws attention to some significant detail that underlines the reality of the wonder, or that emphasizes its magnitude. In the feeding of the five thousand, for example, Christ first asked the apostles to provide the multitude with something to eat (Mark 6:37; Luke 9:13). His intention, says Bede, was to highlight the greatness of the miracle that follows: "Provocat apostolos ad fractionem panis ut illis se non habere testantibus magnitudo signi notior fiat."[31] After raising the daughter of Jairus from the dead, once again Christ instructed that she be given food to eat (Mark 5:43; Luke 8:55). Here, Bede explains, his purpose was to demonstrate that the revived young girl was more than an apparition, and that an actual, physical resurrection had taken place.[32] When commenting on the rain and thunder summoned up by Samuel and recorded in 1 Sam. 12:16-18, Bede focuses on the reference to the wheat harvest. This, he claims, is a detail that clearly elevates the storm beyond the realm of the ordinary, for such a thing would have been a striking and unusual occurrence in the summer season.[33] In his commentary on the miraculous birth of Isaac to Abraham and Sarah, he points to the physiological details given in Gen. 18:11 and to the way they serve to enhance the miracle (*ad faciendam auxesin potentiae celestis*). There we read that, in addition to being infertile, Sarah had actually experienced menopause. Moreover, says Bede, Scripture informs us that both she and Abraham were advanced in years. Provided that menstruation hasn't ceased, he explains, it is possible for an old woman to bear a child, but only to a young man. Similarly, an old man may father a child, as Abraham himself did with Keturah after Sarah's death, but only to a young woman. That an old man and an old woman should be able to have children is absolutely impossible, and would require, as was the case here, a special and divine intervention in the normal course of nature.[34]

---

31 *In Luc.* 3, CCL 120:199; cf. *In Marc.* 2, CCL 120:512.

32 *In Marc.* 2, CCL 120:500; *In Luc.* 3, CCL 120:193.

33 *In 1 Sam.* 2, CCL 119:99: "Signum quoque praevaricatoris et duri cordis populi non minimum et eo magis terribile quo illis regionibus inusitatum exhibuit voces scilicet et pluviam tempore messis triticeae quae toto aestatis tempore in terra repromissionis nisi magno miraculo venire non solent."

34 *In Gen.* 4, CCL 118A:216. Bede quotes Augustine, *De civitate Dei* 16.28, CCL 48:533, who also goes on to explain that "centenarius quidem senex, sed temporis nostri, de nulla potest femina gignere; non tunc, quando adhuc tamdiu vivebant, ut centum anni nondum facerent hominem decrepitae senectutis."

More generally, Bede often refers to the striking, astonishing nature of the miracles recorded in Scripture, and to the wonder they produced among those privileged to witness them. When Peter and John healed the man lame from birth, the people, accustomed to seeing him lie begging at the gate of the temple, "were filled with wonder and amazement." Many, Bede points out, both Jews and Gentiles, were so moved by what they had witnessed as to place their faith in Christ.[35] He also acknowledges, however, that the reaction of the Jewish leadership was quite different. Whereas the crowd, which was less learned, was amazed by the wonders of Christ and the apostles, the scribes were unmoved. Either they denied the same wonders, or they subjected them to an evil interpretation. "He is possessed by Beelzebul," they said, "and by the prince of demons he casts out the demons."[36] At one level, of course, Bede realized that the miracles of the New Testament were not such as to compel belief; they required a response of faith. At another, however, he was so impressed by their striking and astonishing nature that he could scarcely fathom the possibility of unbelief, and this is the perspective that tends to dominate. Indeed, he regards disbelief in the face of such wonders as irrational, and does not shrink from likening the disbelievers themselves to beasts more than humans.[37]

Although Bede tends to give more systematic attention to the literal, historical sense of Scripture than either Augustine or Gregory, he did share with his predecessors the conviction that the literal meaning was only the most obvious one, and that beneath its surface there were spiritual depths that it was his responsibility to plumb.[38] When the exegete successfully penetrates the *litterae superficiem*, says Bede, even

35 Acts 3:10; *In Abacuc*, CCL 119B:400.
36 Mark 2:22; *In Marc.* 1, CCL 120:474-475.
37 *In Abacuc*, CCL 119B:401. Here he discusses the twofold reaction to the promulgation of the Gospel: "dispersis in mundum praeconibus verbi, turbata sunt gentium corda, alia ad credendum ac suscipiendum sacramentum Dei, alia vero ad contradicendum sive etiam persequendos praecones eiusdem fidei." Disbelievers are described as follows: "ab humana ratione alienati, conparati sunt iumentis insipientibus et similes facti sunt illis. Tales etsi sanctorum virtutibus conturbati sunt et commoti, nec deum tamen timere nec eius facta adnuntiare vel intellegere voluerunt."
38 Bede conceives of the literal text of Scripture as a covering, beneath which additional riches of meaning lie concealed. See, for example, *In Ezram et Neemiam* 2, CCL 119A:312, where he refers to the "archana spiritalia intra tegmen litterae"; or *In Prov.* 2, CCL 119B:121, where he maintains that "subducto litterae velamine suavitas sensus spiritalis aliquanto cum labore vel mora percipitur."

incidental details of the scriptural account are shown to be full of spiritual significance.[39] In his more theoretical pronouncements Bede speaks of Scripture possessing numerous senses, levels of meaning whose number and mutual relationships are described in a variety of ways.[40] In practice he generally limits himself, like Gregory the Great, to two: a literal or historical sense conveying a record of words spoken or deeds done, and a deeper figurative sense in which important teaching about Christian faith or morals is conveyed. The alternative approach, that of the Antiochene school, was not unknown in the West, particularly in the British Isles. Its influence is discernible in Irish exegesis, and it was characteristic as well of the school of Canterbury, where "the scientific explanation of the Bible occupied the central position in Theodore's and Hadrian's scholarly activity." The main focus of Bede's interest, however,

---

39 See, for example, *In Marc.* 1, CCL 120:479; & 4, CCL 120:614: "non solum dicta vel opera nostri salvatoris verum etiam loca et tempora in quibus operatur et loquitur mysticis ut saepe dictum est sunt plena figuris." Cf. *De tabernaculo* 1, CCL 119A:5. For *litterae superficiem*, see *In 1 Sam.* 2, CCL 119:87; *In Prov.* 3, CCL 119B:125.

40 In *De schematibus et tropis* 2, CCL 123A:164-165, Bede distinguishes between two kinds of allegory, factual and verbal; and then goes on (pp. 166-169) to argue that, through the one form of allegory or the other, there are four different senses that Scripture can convey: historical, allegorical, tropological or moral, and anagogic. When one adds the literal sense, the result would seem to be a total of five. By the end of the passage, however, Bede has clearly focused on four senses, explaining that sometimes (*nonnumquam*, p. 169) they are all to be found in the same text. Hence he quotes Ps. 147:12: "Lauda, Ierusalem, Dominum," and explains: "De civibus terrenae Hierusalem, de ecclesia Christi, de anima quaque electa, de patria caelesti, iuxta historiam, iuxta allegoriam, iuxta tropologiam, iuxta anagogen recte potest accipi" (p. 169). In *De tabernaculo* 1, CCL 119A:25, it is the same four senses of Scripture that Bede expounds. Whereas the historical sense is a straight-forward (*plano sermone*) factual record, the allegorical sense is conveyed *verbis sive rebus mysticis*, the tropological *apertis seu figuratis sermonibus*, and the anagogic *mysticis seu apertis sermonibus*. In *In Cant.* 3, CCL 119B:260, they appear again (although Bede speaks of the literal sense rather than the historical), and once again Bede illustrates how all four can be found in the same text. Cf. *In 1 Sam.* 3, CCL 119:157. Elsewhere, however, he speaks of three senses. In *De tabernaculo* 2, CCL 119A:91, it is the anagogic sense that he omits; in *In Gen.* 4, CCL 118A:213-214, and in *In 1 Sam.* 2, CCL 119:87, it is the moral, or tropological, although slightly further on in the latter text (p. 89) he mentions both allegorical and tropological senses, and distinguishes between them. On the ambiguities in Bede's treatment, particularly with regard to the distinction between verbal and factual allegory, cf. Armand Strubel, "«Allegoria in factis» et «Allegoria in verbis»," *Poétique* 23 (1975): 342-357.

lay elsewhere. "Seen against the background of the image of the school of Canterbury which we now have, the writings of Bede signify principally a decisive return to the tradition of the old Latin exegesis."[41]

Like Augustine and Gregory, although perhaps not to the same extent, Bede frequently either ignores the literal sense entirely or gives it only very cursory treatment before passing on to the much more challenging and rewarding task of spiritual interpretation. In this respect miracles are treated no differently than other elements of the biblical narrative. In Bede's view, we should not allow our attention to be captured by the external features of Christ's miracles, astonishing though they may be, but should focus instead on their hidden spiritual import.[42] Indeed, from his occasional comments—his reference to the *vilitas litterae*, for example[43]—one might conclude that he valued the literal sense lightly, that he considered it scarcely worth consideration in comparison to the allegorical riches it concealed. Did Solomon have 3,300 overseers for the workers on the temple or 3,600? Although Scripture records both numbers (1 Kings 5:16; 2 Chron. 2:2, 18), in *De templo* Bede seems unconcerned about reconciling them, for the spiritual significance is the same in each case.[44]

In fact, however, such passages are not really representative. Like Augustine and Gregory, Bede believed that the literal sense was the essential foundation on which everything else depended. Despite the example given above, therefore, his general practice in *De templo* is to subject even the most minute historical details to close examination, appealing to authorities like Josephus to assist in the process, for the

---

41 Bernhard Bischoff, "Turning-Points in the History of Latin Exegesis in the Early Middle Ages," in *Biblical Studies: The Medieval Irish Contribution*, ed. Martin McNamara (Dublin, 1976), pp. 73-160 at 77. Cf. Willmes, "Bedas Bibelauslegung," p. 291.

42 *Hom. Evan.* 2.2, CCL 122:193: "Qui signa et miracula domini ac salvatoris recte cum legunt vel audiunt accipiunt non tam in his quid foris stupeant adtendunt quam quid horum exemplo ipsi intus agere quid in his mysticum perpendere debeant inspiciunt."

43 *In Luc.* 6, CCL 120:388; *In Prov.* 3, CCL 119B:125. Cf. *In Luc.* 2, CCL 120:120: "sub contemptibili litterarum velamine, si adsit qui reseret doctor, divina spiritalis gratiae virtus invenietur."

44 *De templo* 1, CCL 119A:153.

cogency of the allegory depends on it.[45] As Meyvaert puts it, "Bede was not by nature given to flights of fancy; his feet were always on the ground."[46] Although spiritual interpretation is his primary interest, it is not allowed to run roughshod over the literal sense, not even in a text like the Apocalypse, where allegories abound. Nor does it prevent him elsewhere, principally in his commentary on the Acts of the Apostles and his *Retractions*, from turning his attention to exegesis that is essentially historical in orientation.[47] Hence, whenever he passes quickly over the literal sense, it is only because he thinks it straightforward. By no means can his silence about the literal meaning of some miracle story be taken to imply doubts about it.[48] To Bede's mind, the miracles recorded in Scripture are both events that happened and the vehicles of a greater spiritual significance. The allegory of Scripture is an allegory written into the fabric of a narrative that is to be taken as factually true.

The point is well illustrated by his comments on the fortunes of Lot's wife. Startled and frightened by the destruction being visited upon the city of Sodom and by the howls of its doomed inhabitants, she made the fatal error of looking behind her. In this she can be taken to represent those who forsake their monastic vows. Having once decided to renounce the world and set out on the more demanding path of virtue, suddenly they return to the things that were to have been left behind. To Bede's mind, therefore, the passage contains a lesson about the importance of constancy in the monastic vocation, and this is what he is primarily interested in impressing upon his readers. In this particular case, however, perhaps because the events related are especially astonishing, he begins

45 Henri de Lubac, *Exégèse médiévale. Les quatre sens de l'Ecriture* 2.1 (Paris, 1961), p. 418; Meyvaert, "Bede the Scholar," p. 61. The same can be said of his commentary on Samuel. See, for example, Jonathan Black, "*De Civitate Dei* and the Commentaries of Gregory the Great, Isidore, Bede, and Hrabanus Maurus on the Book of Samuel," *Augustinian Studies* 15 (1984): 114-127 at 126; Simonetti, "Technica esegetica di Beda nel *Commento a 1 Samuele*," pp. 105, 109-110.

46 Meyvaert, "Bede the Scholar," p. 61. Cf. Ray, "Bede's Commentaries," p. 20: "the *Historia Ecclesiastica* is but one measure of his power as a historian; the commentaries are another."

47 See Gerald Bonner, *Saint Bede in the Tradition of Western Apocalyptic Commentary* (Jarrow, 1966), who points to Bede's insistence, against Tyconius, that Rev. 20:13 be allowed to retain its literal meaning; and Glenn W. Olsen, "Bede as Historian: The Evidence from his Observations on the Life of the First Christian Community at Jerusalem," *Journal of Ecclesiastical History* 33 (1982): 519-530.

48 Cf. Creider, "Bede's Understanding of the Miraculous," pp. 247-248.

by assuring his readers that the story is to be accepted as literally true: "Hoc vere iuxta litteram factum esse credendum est." Lot's wife really was turned into a pillar of salt. In fact, he tells us, Josephus claims that in his day it could still be seen.[49] Far from replacing the literal sense, allegory complements it. On occasion, in fact, it even reinforces it. We ought not to be surprised, says Bede, that when Christ appeared to the storm-tossed disciples on the sea of Galilee, the winds ceased as soon as he joined them in the boat. For all the raging of vice and all the strife of evil spirits is immediately suppressed and laid to rest in any heart where he is present by the grace of his love.[50]

Despite the prevalence of allegorical exposition, therefore, Bede's consistent approach to the miracles of Scripture is to accept them as reported. If this means that they are never questioned, it also has the consequence that very seldom is anything other than the spiritual sense ever explained. A rare exception is provided by his enquiry into how the miracle of Pentecost transpired. Did the apostles actually speak in each of the many languages of those present? Or did the miracle rather not consist in the fact that each listener heard the words as if they had been uttered in his or her own tongue? Bede's preference for the latter alternative is clear.[51] A similar curiosity is revealed in his commentary on Gen. 18:1-15. Here Abraham greets the three angels that appeared to him by the oaks of Mamre, treats them like travellers, and has a meal prepared for them. Bede informs us that the incident is to be read as a figure of the Incarnation of the Lord, but he also considers the question of how angels could possibly have consumed food. Unlike men, angels are sustained by invisible nourishment, the feast of the divine presence that they constantly enjoy, even when temporarily absent from heaven and serving as God's emissaries to others. If they appeared to consume

---

49   *In Gen.* 4, CCL 118A:227. Cf. Josephus, *Jewish Antiquities* 1.11.4(203), Loeb Classical Library (London, 1930), p. 101; ed. Franz Blatt, *The Latin Josephus* 1: *Introduction and Text* (Aarhus, 1958), p. 150.
50   *In Marc.* 2, CCL 120:518.
51   *Exp. Act. Apost.* 2.6, CCL 121:17; *Retr.* 2.6, CCL 121:110-111. In the latter text Bede tells us that he was criticized by some for raising the issue, but that he had said nothing that could not be found in the words of Gregory Nazianzen, *irreprehensibilis per omnia magister.* He also assures us that the reality of the ' miracle itself is not in doubt: "constat quod repleti spiritu sancto apostoli linguis omnibus loquebantur neque de hoc ulli dubitare fidelium licet. Sed quomodo loquerentur merito queritur."

food in this particular case, Bede suggests, it was immediately vaporized, like water by a flame, as soon as it came in contact with their spiritual bodies.[52] It was unusual, however, for Bede to allow himself to be drawn into this kind of discussion, as it had been for Gregory the Great before him. His customary practice is to resist any temptation to enquire how a wonder may have taken place, especially if the effect could be to reduce it to the status of an ordinary event. Whenever presented with the opportunity of a rationalizing explanation that would eliminate the miracle, Bede summarily rejects it.

In *De temporum ratione* Bede follows Jerome in dismissing a natural explanation of the darkness that descended at the time of the crucifixion. It was no miracle, it had been argued; it was a simple eclipse of the sun. In rejecting this view, however, Bede argues from scientific grounds: in the normal course of events an eclipse of the sun cannot occur when the moon is full, as must have been the case at Passover.[53] More interesting, therefore, is his rejection of an explanation that would have taken some of the wonder out of the story of the Ark. Quoting Augustine, he tells us that doubts had arisen concerning the size of the Ark, and whether it would have been large enough for all the animals it had to accommodate. Origen, he goes on to say, had suggested that the dimensions given by Moses were in geometric cubits, a standard of measurement he had learned from the Egyptians. Since the geometric cubit was six times the length of the standard cubit, this would have made the Ark very much larger than had been thought. Although Augustine liked this solution, Bede rejects it categorically. Moses may have known about geometric cubits, but the people for whom he was writing did not, and could only have been misled by any reference to cubits other than those with which they were familiar. Furthermore, Moses gives the dimensions of the tabernacle in cubits as well, presumably the same cubits he has in mind elsewhere; and they cannot have been geometrical cubits unless the tabernacle was absurdly large. Indeed, it would have dwarfed the temple of Solomon. In Bede's view, the Ark is a subject of many mysteries, all of them defying comprehension. How, for example, could eight people possibly have tended to the daily needs of so many creatures? Why did the hull not rot through from the filth that collected in the bilge? How were man and beast alike able to

---

52 *In Gen.* 4, CCL 118A:215-216.
53 *De temp. ratione* 27, CCL 123B:363; Jerome, *In Matth.* 4, CCL 77:273.

endure the inevitable stench? In the face of these and other wonders, the search for rational explanations is misguided: "omnia quae in ea vel erga eam gesta sunt divinae virtutis erant plena miraculis."[54] Even more revealing are the remarks that he directed to his friend, Nothhelm, who had asked for assistance with the interpretation of the apostle's words in 2 Cor. 11:25. There, after mentioning that he has

54 *In Gen.* 2, CCL 118A:111-113. Cf. Augustine, *Quaest. in Hept.* 1.4, CCL 33:3; *De civitate Dei* 15.27, CCL 48:495-496. Although it is not the first thing that comes to his mind, slightly further on (p. 120) Bede does allow a natural or quasi-natural explanation for an occurrence near the end of the story. However, the event in question still remains a miracle for him. Commenting on Gen. 8:1: "adduxit [Deus] spiritum super terram et imminutae sunt aquae," he says: "Potest in nomine 'spiritus' ipse vivificator Dei Spiritus accipi, de quo in principio dictum est, *Et Spiritus Dei ferebatur super aquas.* De quo dubium non est quia sicut tunc, congregatis aquis, in locum unum arefecit terram, ita etiam nunc, ablatis de medio aquis diluvii, denuo faciem terrae revelavit. Potest et ventus iste aerius nomine 'spiritus' appellari, iuxta illud psalmistae, *Dixit et stetit spiritus procellae* [Ps. 106(107):25], cuius flatibus crebris plerumque solent aquae minui vel de loco moveri."

For an approach offering a sharp contrast to Bede's, cf. Augustinus Hibernicus, *De mirabilibus Sacrae Scripturae* 1.4-9, PL 35:2149-2200 at 2155-2160. The fundamental premise of the work is stated in the Prologue: "Cuncti vero laboris hoc magnopere intentio procurat, ut in omnibus rebus, in quibus extra quotidianam administrationem aliquid factum videtur, non novam ibi Deum facere naturam, sed ipsam quam in principio condidit, gubernare ostendat" (col. 2151). In application, this approach tends to have a rationalizing effect, as is the case in the treatment of the Flood specifically. Augustinus asks a series of questions, addressing each in rational terms. While he recognizes that there are limits to our knowledge, and that some things will be known only in the hereafter, the approach taken still functions to remove the mystery from the Flood as much as possible. For a general introduction to the ideas and arguments of the *De mirabilibus,* see Manlio Simonetti, "*De mirabilibus sacrae scripturae.* Un trattato irlandese sui miracoli della Sacra Scrittura," *Romanobarbarica* 4 (1979): 225-231; and Carol Susan Anderson, "Divine Governance, Miracles and Laws of Nature in the Early Middle Ages" (Ph.D. dissertation, University of California, Los Angeles, 1982). Any influence it had on Bede was strictly limited and probably second-hand. Bede's treatment of the Flood provides no indication that he was familiar with the *De mirabilibus* at all. Eckenrode, "Growth of a Scientific Mind," p. 198, has suggested that Bede owes to it the technical vocabulary of *malinae et ledones,* spring and neap tides, found in his *De natura rerum.* If so, his dependence is not verbal; the source Bede quotes is Pseudo-Isidore. Cf. Bede, *De natura rerum* 39, CCL 123A:224-225; Pseudo-Isidore, *De ordine creaturarum* 9.4-7, ed. Manuel C. Díaz y Díaz (Santiago de Compostela, 1972), pp. 148-150; Augustinus Hibernicus, *De mirabilibus Sacrae Scripturae* 1.7, PL 35:2159.

been beaten, stoned and shipwrecked three times, St Paul states: "A day and a night have I spent in the depths of the sea" (*nocte et die in profundo maris fui*). Bede was aware that Theodore of Canterbury had offered a straightforward and non-miraculous interpretation. St Paul, he had suggested, was referring to a pit in Zizicus that had been dug for the punishment of prisoners; this was where he had been forced to spend a day and a night. However, Bede rejects this view. The Fathers, he tells us, saw nothing in the apostle's words other than their obvious meaning (*nihil in his verbis aliud quam hoc quod sonat intelligere solebant*), and it is the view of the Fathers that he chooses to endorse: the apostle to the Gentiles was once fully submerged for a day and a night before he could be rescued. It was a very great miracle that he was neither suffocated by the waters nor devoured by the beasts of the sea, a miracle that, in the judgment of the Fathers, shows him to have been the full equal of St Peter: "non amplius Petrum super undas ambulantem nec demersum, quam Paulum sub undis retentum nec necatum praedicant esse mirandum."[55]

Although there was some precedent for Bede's view,[56] it was very slight; and the weight of opinion seems clearly to have been against it. Some may think that the apostle actually spent a day and a night immersed in the waters, says Chrysostom, but this is not very likely. St Paul does not present the episode as being especially noteworthy, nor do

---

55 *Aliquot quaestionum liber*, quaestio 3, PL 93:456-457. Cf. Bede's hymn *In natali SS. Petri et Pauli*, CCL 122:428-430 at 428-429. Here, conversely, Paul's powers over the waves, unlike Peter's, seem entirely metaphorical:

> Gressus Cephae per caerula
> Christi iuvantur dextera;
> Christus suos, ne saeculi
> Demergat aequor, erigit.
> ....
> Huius pericla saeculi
> Vinci fide credentium
> Paulus docet iam naufragos
> Salvans ab undis socios.

56 Cf. Sulpicius Severus, *Epist.* 1.6, SC 133:318-320: "Video quidem Petrum, fide potentem, rerum obstante natura mare pedibus supergressum et instabiles aquas corporeo pressisse vestigio. Sed non ideo mihi minor videtur gentium praedicator. ... Atque nescio an paene plus fuerit vixisse in profundo an supra maris profunda transisse"; and Pseudo-Augustine, *Sermo* 203.3, PL 39:2123: "Petrus ambulare super aquas debita soli Deo potestate praesumpsit, ... sed non minor Paulus, qui, sicut ipse de se dicit, nocte et die in profundo maris fuit."

his words suggest a misfortune greater than shipwreck.[57] Other commentators do not pursue the issue in the same detail, but they refer to no miracle either, presumably because, in their view, there was none. In the first book of the *Dialogues*, a text that Bede knew well, Peter asks Gregory the Great why there are no longer saints like those of former times. Gregory replies:

> One cannot conclude that there are no great saints just because no great miracles are worked. The true estimate of life, after all, lies in acts of virtue, not in the display of miracles. There are many, Peter, who without performing miracles, are not at all inferior to those who perform them.

When Peter probes a little further, Gregory offers the example of Saints Peter and Paul:

> You recall ... how Peter walked on the water, whereas Paul was shipwrecked on the high seas. In the very same element, then, where Paul was unable to proceed on board ship, Peter could go on foot. Though these two Apostles did not share equally in the power of performing miracles, it is clear that they have an equal share in the rewards of heaven.[58]

Neither here nor elsewhere does Gregory comment directly on 2 Cor. 11:25, but his view is clear nonetheless. That Bede should persist with the interpretation he does, therefore, is quite revealing. That he should have regarded it as the clear and obvious reading suggests a literal-mindedness on the question of miracles that was not the necessary inheritance of the Fathers.

One further example illustrates Bede's tendency to see miracles where they are not required. According to the Gospel of Mark, the day after the cleansing of the temple Christ and the apostles came upon the fig tree that had earlier been cursed, and noticed that now it was completely withered. When Peter, on behalf of all the apostles, expressed his astonishment, Christ answered: "Have faith in God. Truly, I say to you, whoever says to this mountain, 'Be taken up and cast into the sea,' and does not doubt in his heart, but believes that what he says will come to

57 John Chrysostom, *Hom. in 2 Cor.* 25.1, PG 61:570-571: *"Ter virgis caesus sum, semel lapidatus sum, ter naufragium feci.* Et quid hoc ad evangelium? Quia longas vias, et marinas obivit. *Die ac nocte in profundo maris fui.* Quidam in medio mari fuisse, quidam natavisse dicunt, quod quidem ad similitudinem veri magis accedit. Nam illud ne admiratione quidem dignum est: neque ita positum fuisset, tamquam naufragio maius."
58 *Dial.* 1.12.4-5, Zimmerman 51-52, SC 260:116.

pass, it will be done for him" (Mark 11:22-23). Bede's comments on this passage suggest that it can be taken quite literally. Unbelievers, he says, have been accustomed to taunt Christians for lacking the kind of power here promised. Christ's assurances notwithstanding, they have been unable to cast mountains into the sea, a symptom presumably of the paucity of their faith. However, says Bede, it is mistaken to conclude that events have not happened simply because they have not been recorded. As St John informs us, Christ performed many deeds in addition to those mentioned in his Gospel. Even though we have no record, therefore, a miracle of the sort here envisaged could very well have taken place.[59]

In its central thrust, Bede's comment echoes Chrysostom, who also reads Christ's promise straightforwardly.[60] It is fundamentally dissimilar, however, to anything encountered elsewhere. Although Jerome, for example, also mentions the ridicule of the unbelievers, he answers it in an entirely different manner. Jerome's remarks are occasioned by the parallel text of Matt. 17:19-20. Christ has just cast a demon out of an epileptic boy whom the disciples were unable to cure. When they ask him the reason for their ineffectiveness, he replies: "Because of your little faith. For truly, I say to you, if you have faith as a grain of mustard seed, you will say to this mountain, 'Move hence to yonder place,' and it will move; and nothing will be impossible to you." Jerome charges with foolishness those who would argue that the apostles must all have had little faith indeed, since none of them ever moved a mountain. The text has nothing to do with the physical moving of mountains, but rather with the casting out of demons. Having just driven the demon out of the possessed boy, Christ tells the apostles that they too will be able to expel Satan if they have the faith required.[61]

59 *In Marc.* 3, CCL 120:580; cf. John 21:25.
60 See *Hom. in Matt.* 57(58).3, PG 58:562, where Chrysostom comments on Matt. 17:20: "Quod si dixeris, Ubinam montem transtulerunt? dicam illos multo maiora fecisse, cum mille mortuos suscitarint. Neque paris potestatis est, montem transferre, ac mortem a corpore pellere. Narrant post illos sanctos quosdam illis minores, montes necessitate postulante transtulisse. Unde liqueat illos quoque translaturos fuisse, si id necessitas postulasset. ... Potuit etiam id accidisse, etsi scriptum non fuerit; neque enim omnia quae illi edidere miracula scripta sunt." Cf. his *Hom. in 1 Cor.* 32.4, PG 61:269.
61 Jerome, *In Matth.* 3, CCL 77:153: "Montis translatio non eius significatur quem oculis carnis aspicimus sed illius qui a Domino translatus fuerat ex lunatico. ... Ex quo stultitiae coarguendi qui contendunt apostolos omnesque credentes ne parvam quidem habuisse fidem quia nullus eorum montes transtulerit. Neque enim tantum

In its essentials, the view of Ambrose was identical to Jerome's, as his comments on Luke 17:6 make clear. Here the apostles ask the Lord to increase their faith, and receive the reply: "If you had faith as a grain of mustard see, you could say to this sycamine tree, 'Be rooted up, and be planted in the sea,' and it would obey you." What reason, what profit could there possibly be, asks Ambrose, in doing such a thing? Although conceivably faith could work such a wonder, the real significance of Christ's words is to be found in what the figure of the tree represents. For that we can take our cue from Matt. 17:19: like the mountain mentioned there, the tree in the present text signifies Satan. In each case it is not the ability to work a spectacular but possibly pointless physical wonder that is at issue, but rather the power to control and expel demonic forces.[62] For that, as both Ambrose and Jerome also explain, more than a modest amount of faith is necessary: "Nec exigua haec, sed magna est fides, quae monti possit ut se transferat imperare; neque enim mediocrem fidem dominus exigit ab apostolis, quibus adversus altitudinem extollentem se nequitiae spiritalis scit esse certandum."[63] We should not be misled by initial appearances. It is a perfect faith that is required, as St Paul himself informs us. If it is likened to a grain of mustard seed, so is the Kingdom of Heaven.[64]

Jerome discusses the issue again in the context of Matt. 21:21, the analogue of the verses in Mark 11 that elicit Bede's comment. In Matthew's version, after the cleansing of the temple Christ curses the barren fig tree, and it withers at once. When the disciples marvel, he explains: "Truly, I say to you, if you have faith and never doubt, you

---

prodest montis de alio in alium locum translatio et vana signorum quaerenda ostentatio quantum in utilitatem omnium iste mons transferendus est qui per prophetam corrumpere dicitur omnem terram." Cf. Zach. 4:7; and *In Zach.* 1, CCL 76A:780. For similar readings of Matt. 17:19-20, cf. Origen, *Comm. in Matt.* 13.7, PG 13:1110-1111; idem, *Hom. in Ieremiam* 12.12, PG 13:394, SC 238:41-43; Eusebius, *Comm. in Ps.* 45.4, PG 23:407; Gregory of Nyssa, *Comm. in Cant.*, Hom. 5, PG 44:862.

62 Ambrose, *Expos. Evan. Luc.* 8.28-29, CCL 14:308: "Arborem lego, non tamen arborem credo. Nam quae ratio, qui profectus hic noster, ut arbor, quae laborantibus agricolis ferat fructus, eradicetur et mittatur in mare? Licet hoc pro virtute fidei possibile iudicemus, ut sensibilibus inperiis natura insensibilis obsequatur, quid sibi vult tamen etiam ipsa arboris species?" Cf. *Expl. Ps. 36*, 77.2, CSEL 64:132.

63 Ambrose, *Expos. Evan. Luc.* 7.176, CCL 14:275; cf. *Expl. Ps. 45*, 9.4, CSEL 64:335-336. Cf. Jerome, *In Matth.* 2, CCL 77:108; & 3, CCL 77:153; *In Hiezech.* 13, CCL 75:605-606. Cf. also Origen, *Comm. in Matt.* 13.7, PG 13:1110-1111.

64 1 Cor. 13:2; Matt. 13:31-32; Mark 4:30-32; Luke 13:18-19.

will not only do what has been done to the fig tree, but even if you say to this mountain, 'Be taken up and cast into the sea,' it will be done." Here Jerome seems closer to endorsing a literal reading. Unbelievers rail against us, he says, because the apostles never moved mountains. But since St John tells us that he has not been able to include all the deeds of Christ in his account, so may we believe that Scripture has omitted some of the apostles' miracles as well. Many great miracles have been left unrecorded to deprive unbelievers who have rejected lesser wonders of the opportunity of heaping further damnation on themselves. This seems to have been the text that provided Bede with his main inspiration, and in its own right it seems to leave the way open for the physical moving of mountains. In fact, however, Jerome quickly closes off the possibility, announcing that the mountain at issue is really Satan, the destroying mountain of Jeremiah 51:25. By the faith of the apostles he can be taken up and cast into the sea, driven from the hearts of those he would possess and consigned to some salty and bitter place utterly lacking in the sweetness of the divine presence.[65]

Other authorities known to Bede had seen other possible meanings in these scriptural texts. In this regard Augustine offers some interesting comments in his exegesis of Psalm 45(46):2-3: "God is our refuge and strength, a very present help in trouble. Therefore we will not fear when the earth is changed (*dum turbabitur terra*), and the mountains are transferred into the heart of the sea (*et transferentur montes in cor maris*)." He begins by referring to Matt. 17:19, which he conflates either with Matt. 21:21 or with Mark 11:23: "If you have faith as a grain of mustard seed, you will say to this mountain: 'Be taken up and cast into the sea,' and it will be done." The mountain here is Christ himself, says Augustine, "the mountain of the house of the Lord" of Isaiah 2:2, "established as the highest of the mountains." The other mountains, also referred to in Psalm 45, are, of course, the apostles; while the earth, which is mentioned in the Psalm, and the sea, mentioned in both the Psalm and the New Testament text, represent Israel and the world respectively.

Having established the broad lines of his exegesis, the meaning of both Psalm and New Testament text become clear. The earth was changed and the mountains transferred into the heart of the sea when the apostles shifted the focus of evangelization from Jews to Gentiles. A mountain

---

65 Jerome, *In Matth*. 3, CCL 77:191-192.

was taken up and cast into the sea when, in the face of Jewish rejection, the proclamation of the Gospel of Christ was moved from Israel to the nations of the world.[66] Can the Gospel text be taken literally as well, or is Christ simply using figural language? Augustine's answer seems clear. In his *Quaestiones Evangeliorum* he advances a similar interpretation of Luke 17:5-6. Hence the tree of this text is a figure for the Gospel of Christ, and its being uprooted and planted in the sea represents its being transferred from Jews to Gentiles. More significantly, however, he reads these verses together with the immediately following parable of the Lord and servant (verses 7-10), and draws on his interpretation of them to make sense of the parable. Everything suggests, therefore, that Augustine saw only the figural sense in Christ's words. There was no literal level on which they could also be understood as a promise that faith would be accompanied by miraculous powers.[67]

In his commentary on Matthew's Gospel, Hilary of Poitiers offers yet another interpretation of Matt. 17:19-20, indicating something of the allegorical richness of which the verses were capable. In this view the disciples, who were unable to relieve the suffering of the boy possessed of the demon, represent the scribes and Pharisees, who were even less effective in offering any spiritual assistance to the nation of Israel. That the reference to the disciples is to be taken figuratively, says Hilary, is clear from the context. In calling them a faithless and perverse generation, it is not the disciples themselves but the scribes and Pharisees they represent that Christ wishes to condemn. If these latter had had faith as a grain of mustard seed, that is, if they had had faith in Christ himself, they would have been able to move the mountain of sin and disbelief that had been burdening the Jewish people.[68]

---

66 Augustine, *Enar. in Ps.* 45.6, CCL 38:521. Cf. *Quaest. Evan.* 1.29, CCL 44B:24; *Sermo* 89.2, PL 38:554-555.

67 See *Quaest. Evan.* 2.39.1, 2-4, CCL 44B:93, 95-96. Cf. *Sermo* 89.2, PL 38:555, where he comments on Matt. 21:21: "Legimus Apostolorum miracula, nusquam autem legimus arborem ab his arefactam, aut montem in mare translatum. Quaeramus ergo ubi factum sit. Non enim verba Domini vacare potuerunt. Si attendas istas usitatas et notas arbores et istos montes, non est factum. Si attendas arborem de qua dixit, et montem ipsum Domini de quo propheta dixit, *Erit in novissimis diebus manifestus mons Domini* [Isaiah 2:2]: si haec attendas, si haec intelligas; et factum est, et per ipsos factum est."

68 Hilary of Poitiers, *In Matth.* 17.8, SC 258:68.

Hilary also acknowledges that the mountain can represent Satan, as it does in the interpretations of Jerome and Ambrose discussed above. On this reading, when Christ tells the disciples that with faith like a grain of mustard seed they would be able to move a mountain, the mountain is the Devil, whom they had been unable to dislodge from the boy because of their lack of faith.[69] When he goes on to comment on Matt. 21:21, this is the meaning that Hilary discerns in the image of the mountain. The fig tree represents the synagogue, and its cursing is a figure for the sentence Christ will levy against Israel when the time of grace expires. Hence, when Christ tells the disciples that, if their faith is sufficient, they will be able not only to do the same but even to move the mountain, he is promising that, in addition to their being judges of Israel, even Satan himself will be subject to their authority.[70] Throughout all of this, however, it is clear that, in Hilary's view, Christ is not referring to any physical, real mountain, but only to a figural one. He is not promising a physical miracle and conquest over Satan at a deeper level, but only the latter.

Like his predecessors, Bede was aware of the allegorical potential of these passages of Scripture. Hence in his commentary on Mark 11:22-23 he too points out that the mountain that can be moved by faith is a figure for the Devil.[71] What distinguishes Bede's approach is the suggestion that, in addition to having their allegorical meaning, Christ's words can be taken literally. It was a view with some appeal to hagiographers in search of Scriptural guarantees of the miracles performed by their saintly heroes,[72] but it had little precedent in the theological literature. To confirm his reading, however, Bede goes on to tell us that such a wonder was once performed by Gregory Thaumaturgus, *vir meritis et virtutibus eximius*. Gregory was distressed by the fact that the location that seemed most appropriate for a church he wanted to build was too narrow, being

---

69 Ibid. 17.7, SC 258:66-68.
70 Ibid. 21.6-7, SC 258:130-132.
71 *In Marc.* 3, CCL 120:581.
72 See, for example, *Vita S. Hilarionis* 29.5-6, ed. A.A.R. Bastiaensen, in *Vite dei santi* 4 (Milan, 1975), pp. 69-142 at 132-134, where Jerome takes a quite different tack than in his scriptural commentaries; and Gregory of Tours, *Liber vitae patrum* 3 Prol., MGH, SRM 1.2:222. See also Marc Van Uytfanghe, "Le culte des saints et l'hagiographie face à l'Ecriture: les avatars d'une relation ambiguë," in *Santi e demoni nell'alto medioevo occidentale (secoli V-XI)* (Spoleto, 1989), pp. 155-202 at 168-169.

bound on one side by the seashore and on the other by a mountain. So he came to the place by night, and on bended knee reminded the Lord of his promise in the Gospel. When he returned in the morning, he discovered that the mountain had yielded precisely the space necessary for the builders of the church. By his prayers Gregory had physically moved the mountain; and what was possible for Gregory, says Bede, was possible for others of equal merit as well.[73]

Exegesis of this kind invites the conclusion that, if anything, Bede was even more credulous than many other early medieval thinkers. At the very least, as his hagiographical and historical works suggest, he shared fully their major convictions, as well as their conception of what constituted good scholarly and historical practice. The point is illustrated by one particular feature that his miracle stories share with others from the early medieval period, a feature of especial interest for appraising the openness to miracles characteristic of the time: the tendency to appeal to witnesses who seem to have been valued much more for their moral than their intellectual qualities. As his source for the stories about John of Beverley, Bede identifies "the most reverend and truthful [abbot] Berhthun."[74] To corroborate one of the miracles of St Cuthbert, he appeals to the monk and priest Cynemund, a man "well known far and wide ... on account of his great age and of his manner of life."[75] Qualities of character are adduced to corroborate statements of fact, as if integrity could guarantee accuracy, or honesty reliability. To make matters worse, the sources distinguished by such qualities of soul are not always firsthand observers of the events reported.[76] Bede does not seem to be

---

73 *In Marc.* 3, CCL 120:580-581: "Poterat ergo hic poterat alius quis eiusdem meriti vir, si oportunitas exigisset, impetrare a domino merito fidei ut etiam mons tolleretur et mitteretur in mare." Cf. *Chronica Maiora = De temp. ratione* 66.379, CCL 123B:506: "*Theodorus*, cuius supra meminimus, cognomento *Gregorius*, *Neocaesareae Ponti episcopus*, magna virtutum gloria claret, e quibus unum est quod, ut ecclesiae faciendae locus sufficeret montem praecibus movit." Rufinus, whom Bede does not quote precisely, reports the same miracle: see *Eusebius Werke* 2.2 (Leipzig, 1908), p. 954. Gregory the Great alludes to it at *Dial.* 1.7.3, SC 260:68.

74 *HE* 5.2, pp. 456-457: "vir reverentissimus ac veracissimus Bercthun." Cf. ibid 3.27, pp. 312-313, where another witness to a miracle story is described as "quidam veracissimus et venerandae canitiei presbyter."

75 *VCP*, chap. 36, p. 271.

76 See, for example, *HE* 3.15, pp. 260-261, where we learn that Cynemund, the "most trustworthy (*fidelissimus*) priest" who was Bede's source for the story of Aidan's calming of the sea, had himself learned of the miracle only second-hand from the

disturbed by such a state of affairs. In book four of the *Ecclesiastical History* he tells us that "the most reverend father (*reverentissimus pater*) Egbert" is reported to have said: "'I know a man in this island, still in the flesh, who saw the soul of Chad's brother Cedd descend from the sky with a host of angels and return to the heavenly kingdom, taking Chad's soul with him.'" Whether Bede actually heard these words from Egbert himself is unclear. It scarcely seems to matter. Bede explains: "Whether he was speaking of himself or of another is uncertain, but what cannot be uncertain is that whatever such a man said must be true."[77]

The tendency to defer to honest and trustworthy witnesses and to take their evidence at face value was characteristic of both medieval hagiography and medieval historiography as a whole. As late as the twelfth century moral criteria prevailed in the assessment of sources, and were fundamental in shaping criteria of probability as well.[78] Hence we should probably not be especially puzzled to see the same predisposition at work in Bede's thought. Perplexing though it may be, at least Bede was not uniquely bizarre. Ultimately, however, the suggestion that medieval scholars were simply incapable of distinguishing between trustworthiness and accuracy is less than satisfying, and itself cries out for explanation. While a complete accounting is undoubtedly beyond us, in Bede's case specifically one of Jones's observations casts at least some light on the mystery. When Bede appeals to witnesses, Jones points out, it is always in support of miracle stories.[79] To Bede's mind, more ordinary political or military events evidently did not require such corroboration. Jones concludes that miracle stories were distinguished in this way because they were statements that pertained to the moral rather than the factual order, and were not intended to be taken literally. This is an issue to which we must return in due course.[80] In the meantime,

---

priest Utta. Cf. *VCP*, chap. 3, pp. 164-165: "In fact a very worthy brother (*frater probatissimus*) of our monastery, from whose lips I heard the story, declared that he himself had often heard these things related in the presence of many by one of these same people [who had witnessed the miracle], a man of rustic simplicity and absolutely incapable of inventing an untruth (*rusticae simplicitatis vir et simulandi prorsus ignarus*)."

77 *HE* 4.3, pp. 344-345. Cf. Berlin, "Bede's Miracle Stories," pp. 440-443, who points to parallels with similar kinds of evidence in Anglo-Saxon courts.

78 *Signs of Sanctity*, pp. 197-198.

79 Jones, *Saints' Lives and Chronicles*, pp. 75-76.

80 See below, pp. 197-198.

however, a simpler explanation would see the basis for the distinctive treatment of miracles in their extraordinary nature. Miracles defied normal experience; reports of them might well be greeted with scepticism. Along with the occasional written source, therefore, Bede adduces witnesses to reassure us that, despite any doubts we may feel, the stories he reports are worthy of belief.[81] The fact that in these circumstances it is the moral qualities of the witnesses that he chooses to highlight is significant. It suggests that for both Bede and his intended audience unbelief was an ethical issue, not an intellectual one. It was the product of moral failure, evidence of a deformed or defective will lacking the courage of its deepest convictions; and so it is to be countered with a moral rather than a scientific challenge.[82]

With regard to the miracles of Sacred Scripture one can readily understand why this should have been the case. In view of its status as a divinely inspired account, doubt about the miracles there recorded was unthinkable. Not quite so obvious at first is the fact that the consensus of the community could credit the miracles of the more celebrated of the post-biblical saints with almost identical standing. Heffernan has recently described the limited licence granted to the author of cultic biography in the Middle Ages.[83] His primary audience was generally the community that had taken up the cause of the saint in question and was committed to his or her veneration. Rather than aiming for a more accurate account of the saint's life and virtues, the purpose was to confirm what was already known. The hagiographer's mandate called for the adoption of a collective narrative voice, not the articulation of any personal, idiosyncratic view. Since his readers and hearers already possessed the definitive view of the saint in question, it was not their expectation to be

---

81 Cf. Schoebe, "Was gilt im frühen Mittelalter als Geschichtliche Wirklichkeit?" p. 647; Musca, *Venerabile Beda*, pp. 166-167, 207-208. Bertram Colgrave, "The Earliest Saints' Lives Written in England," *Proceedings of the British Academy* 44 (1958): 35-60 at 46, suggests that a comment inserted in the Preface to Bede's *Ecclesiastical History* may have been intended as a defence against critics sceptical of St Cuthbert's miracles. In addition to referring to "the trustworthy testimony of reliable witnesses," Bede tells us of the use he made—"accepting the story I read in simple faith"—of the earlier anonymous life (*HE*, Praef., p. 7).

82 The idea was suggested by the comments of Carol Zaleski, *Otherworld Journeys: Accounts of Near-Death Experience in Medieval and Modern Times* (New York, 1987), p. 88.

83 Thomas J. Heffernan, *Sacred Biography: Saints and Their Biographers in the Middle Ages* (New York, 1988), pp. 19-22.

informed. Their role was to act, first as a resource, and then as judge and jury of the hagiographer's effort. In circumstances like these any expression of doubt on the hagiographer's part would have been regarded as tantamount to betrayal of the community's trust.

That Bede was not immune to such considerations, and to the moral pressure to belief that they entailed, is clear from his treatment of St Cuthbert. In the prologue to his prose life, dedicated to Cuthbert's brethren, the community of monks at Lindisfarne, he emphasizes his commitment to provide a truthful account: "I have not presumed," he says, "to write down anything concerning so great a man without the most rigorous investigation of the facts nor, at the end, to hand on what I had written to be copied for general use, without the scrupulous examination of credible witnesses." The extent to which Bede here commits himself to a factually accurate account is an issue to which we must return.[84] Shortly thereafter, however, he goes on to speak of his decision to submit his account to the scrutiny of the brethren, "in order that it might be corrected if false, or, if true, approved by the authority of your judgment." He is pleased to report that after two days' examination "no word of any sort was found which had to be changed, but everything that was written was pronounced by common consent to be, without any question, worthy of being read, and of being delivered to those whose pious zeal moved them to copy it" (*absque ulla ambiguitate legenda, et his qui religionis studio vellent ad transcribendum ... trahenda*).[85]

Bede begins by appealing to the brethren as judges of the factual accuracy of his account, which seems reasonable enough. Along with the anonymous *vita*, the collective memory of the monks of Lindisfarne was an important source for the essential facts of Cuthbert's life and career. Toward the end, however, Bede suggests that it was not simply a judgment on the facts that the brethren rendered. Although presumably fully consistent with the facts as Bede saw them, it also carried moral weight. Indeed, the process Bede describes would probably have been most effective in separating, not the true from the false, but the appropriate from the inappropriate. The sentence of the brethren indicated that Bede's account had met the community standard, and presumably, therefore, deserved to be read with the same reverence as the earlier

---

84 See below, pp. 199-201.
85 *VCP*, Prol., pp. 142-145.

anonymous version of the life of St Cuthbert produced at Lindisfarne itself. In his *Ecclesiastical History* Bede tells us that he was prepared to endorse that earlier life without question, accepting the story he read there in simple faith (*simpliciter fidem historiae quam legebam accommodans*).[86] In the environment in which he was working, any other course would have been scarcely conceivable.

---

86 *HE*, Praef., p. 6. Cf. Colgrave, "Bede's Miracle Stories," p. 225: "It would almost have been an act of heresy if he had refused to believed these stories [of St Cuthbert]. And Bede was, as we know, particularly sensitive to any aspersion of this kind."

3

The Age of Miracles

One of the more intriguing features of the *Ecclesiastical History* is the large number of references it contains to contemporary miracles. Although it is chiefly a work of historical scholarship, and unlike Gregory the Great's *Dialogues* was not conceived as a record of recent wonders, Bede's approach to his task was still flexible enough to allow at least mention of the most significant current events, including current miracles. Hence in the very first book of the *History*, having informed us of the death of St Alban and of the construction of "a church of wonderful workmanship" in his memory, Bede goes on to speak of his continuing power: "To this day sick people are healed in this place and the working of frequent miracles continues to bring it renown."[1] He speaks of the enduring miraculous power of several other saints as well, among them Paulinus and Chad. The *locus* of Paulinus's *virtus* was the stone church that he had had built in Lincoln: "its roof has now fallen either through long neglect or by the hand of the enemy," says Bede, "but its walls are still standing, and every year miracles of healing are performed in this place for the benefit of those who seek them in faith."[2] For his part, Chad seems to have benefited from an elaborate tomb:

> The place of his burial is covered with a wooden shrine made in the shape of a little house, having a hole in its side through which those who go thither out of devotion may insert their hands and take some of the dust. When it is put in water and given either to cattle or men who are ailing, they are at once freed from their ailments and restored to the joys of desired good health.[3]

---

1   *HE* 1.7, p. 35. Cf. Rollason, *Saints and Relics*, pp. 12-14.
2   *HE* 2.16, p. 193 (punctuation amended).
3   Ibid. 4.3, pp. 346-347: "Est autem locus idem sepulchri tumba lignea in modum domunculi facta coopertus, habente foramen in pariete, per quod solent hi qui causa devotionis illo adveniunt manum suam inmittere ac partem pulveris inde adsumere; quam cum in aquas miserint atque has infirmantibus iumentis sive hominibus gustandas dederint, mox infirmitatis ablata molestia cupitae sospitatis gaudia redibunt." The translation has been amended in the light of the one supplied by Charles Thomas, *The Early Christian Archaeology of North Britain* (London, 1971), p. 147; idem, *Bede, Archaeology, and the Cult of Relics* (Jarrow, 1973), p. 10. Both

In the case of Eorcenwald, bishop of London, it was not his tomb but rather the litter on which he used to be carried that provided the focus for his continuing miraculous power. Its health-restoring virtue persists to this day, says Bede. "Not only are ill people cured who are placed in or near the litter, but splinters cut from it and taken to the sick are wont to bring them speedy relief."[4] Splinters feature in the continuing miracles of King Oswald as well, fragments of the cross he set up at Heavenfield, the site of one of his great victories. "Even to this day," Bede claims, "many people are in the habit of … putting them in water, which they then give to sick men or beasts to drink, or else they sprinkle them with it; and they are quickly restored to health."[5] The place where Oswald fell in battle was also renowned for its miracles, again both men and beasts being among the beneficiaries. In this case the miraculous virtue seems to have been vested in the very soil itself, which people mixed with water for the relief of the sick.[6] Of no less importance, however, was the continuing efficacy of St Cuthbert's intercession. "Even now," says Bede, "signs and miracles are not wanting, if an importunate faith seeks for them. Even the garments which covered his most holy body, whether in life or death, do not lack the grace of healing."[7]

The key to Bede's belief in contemporary miracles is undoubtedly to be found in his conception of history, especially the relationship between

---

Thomas and Colgrave conceive the *tumba lignea* mentioned at the outset as a "wooden coffin." In Thomas's case this reinforces the conclusion that the shrine at Lichfield was an open grave covered only by a wooden structure. Wallace-Hadrill, *Bede's Ecclesiastical History*, p. 141, endorses this view. Rollason, *Saints and Relics*, p. 44, prefers to think in terms of "a coffin-reliquary in the form of a house, a larger version of the house-shaped caskets for minor relics." On his view as well, however, Chad's bones would have been directly accessible to pilgrims putting their hands through the aperture, an improbable arrangement.

4   *HE* 4.6, pp. 354-355 (translation amended): "Non solum autem subpositi eidem feretro vel adpositi curantur egroti, sed et astulae de illo abscissae atque ad infirmos adlatae citam illis solent adferre medellam."

5   Ibid. 3.2, pp. 215-217 (punctuation amended). Slightly further on (pp. 217-219) we learn that Bothelm, a brother of the church of Hexham and still living, was miraculously cured of a broken arm by means of some of the moss that covered the wood of the cross.

6   Ibid. 3.9, p. 243.

7   *VCP*, chap. 43, p. 297. Cf. *VCM, Epist. ad Johannem*, p. 57; and *VCM* 44, p. 127:
     Nec sanctum aetherio vacuatur munere tectum,
     Quo sacer astra petens corpus exsangue reliquit,
     Nunc quoque sed solitam partitur ubique medelam.

his own age and biblical times. Michael Hunter has argued that the Anglo-Saxon understanding of the past was characterized by a "confusion of different periods and cultures," and by an imperfect at best awareness of any difference between past and present. Not surprisingly, some of the same weaknesses have been seen in Bede. However, whereas Hunter speaks of a tendency to conceive of the past as an idealized version of the present, Schoebe has argued that the true state of affairs was really the reverse. Bede, like most of his contemporaries, saw his own epoch in essentially Old Testament terms. An expert in chronology, he did, of course, have some awareness of the passage of time, but one unaccompanied by any sense of historical process: "er betrachtet Geschichte, sit venia verbo, als zeitloses Geschehen, als Geschehen, das gar nicht von Zeitverlauf und Zeitfolge affiziert ist." He had no awareness of any historical development that could have served to distinguish the period of the patriarchs from his own.[8]

In the light of more recent scholarship it seems clear that Schoebe's assessment requires qualification. While acknowledging that both in Bede and in medieval historiography as a whole the Christian conception of history entailed some of the consequences that Schoebe identifies, Davidse argues that this is not the whole story. "History is the history of redemption," he admits, "and is so greatly imbued with the continuity which connects it to a future in which God's aims are to become reality that every awareness of the difference between the present and the past disappears." However, he also points to the presence of a strong countertendency demanding that human events be grasped precisely in their historical dimension, for it was God himself who created the temporal order and ordained it as the framework in which man was to live out his relationship with the divine. The result, says Davidse, was that Bede had a clear awareness of the importance of temporal succession, and of the distinctions to be drawn between earlier and later. Given the nature of Bede's analysis of early Christian life at Jerusalem, Olsen goes further, suggesting that he had a much greater sense of time, place and development than any of his contemporaries. He was not entirely

8   Cf. Michael Hunter, "Germanic and Roman Antiquity and the Sense of the Past in Anglo-Saxon England," *Anglo-Saxon England* 3 (1974): 29-50, esp. 46-47; and Schoebe, "Was gilt im frühen Mittelalter als Geschichtliche Wirklichkeit?," p. 642. On the influence of the Old Testament on Bede's perspective, see below, pp. 206-207. See also Van Uytfanghe, *Stylisation biblique et condition humaine*, pp. 205-216, for a discussion of the Old Testament ambience of Merovingian hagiography.

immune to the traditional and anachronistic view, which saw in the Jerusalem community a model of cenobitism against which the monastic practices of succeeding centuries could be measured. But Bede's historical investigations did much to qualify this image of original perfection. Most importantly, he was able to understand that there had been development and change in the early church, and that the initial dominance of Jewish influences had gradually given place to more distinctively Christian teachings and practices.[9]

Important as these qualifications are, however, the central point remains unimpaired. Like Gregory the Great Bede saw no fundamental cleavage separating biblical times from his own. On the contrary, the history of the church, prefigured in the Old Testament and inaugurated in the New, was a continuous and continuing story, one to which the *Ecclesiastical History* itself added a few pages. As Tugène puts it, "l'histoire de l'Eglise anglo-saxonne se situe dans le prolongement direct d'une ligne historique issue de la Bible. Elle participe de l'accomplissement néo-testamentaire des promesses de l'Ancien Testament."[10] Bede believed in modern miracles, therefore, because he believed in the miracles of the Bible, and saw no reason why God should operate any differently in the present than he did in the past. In the *Vita Cuthberti*, as we have already noted, he tells us that the ministrations of an angel who had approached on horseback once relieved the pain in Cuthbert's badly swollen knee, a miracle reminiscent of the sending of the archangel Raphael to cure the eyes of Tobias. Bede adds: "if it should seem incredible to anyone that an angel appeared on horseback, let him read the history of the Maccabees in which angels on horseback are said to have appeared to defend Judas Maccabaeus and the temple itself."[11] When he was still a child, says Bede, Cuthbert was once chastised by another very young boy for his childish ways: "'Why, O Cuthbert, most holy bishop and priest, do you do these things so contrary to your nature

9   Jan Davidse, "The Sense of History in the Works of the Venerable Bede," *Studi Medievali* 3rd ser. 23 (1982): 647-695, esp. 652-654; Olsen, "Bede as Historian," pp. 529-530. Cf. idem, "From Bede to the Anglo-Saxon Presence in the Carolingian Empire," in *Angli e Sassoni al di qua e al di là del mare* (Spoleto, 1986), pp. 305-382 at 371.

10 Georges Tugène, "L'histoire 'ecclésiastique' du peuple anglais. Réflexions sur le particularisme et l'universalisme chez Bède," *Recherches augustiniennes* 17 (1982): 129-172 at 162.

11 *VCP*, chap. 2, p. 161; cf. Tobias 11, 2 Mach. 11:6-8.

and your rank? It is not fitting for you to play among children when the Lord has consecrated you to be a teacher of virtue even to your elders.'" Bede tells us that Cuthbert accepted the reproof with good grace: "That Spirit assuredly instructed his heart from within, which had sounded in his ears from without through the mouth of an infant. Nor need anyone wonder that the wantonness of a child should be checked through a child by the Lord who, when He wished, placed rational words in the mouth of a dumb beast of burden to check the madness of a prophet."[12]

12 VCP, chap. 1, pp. 156-159; cf. 2 Pet. 2:16. Colgrave, "Bede's Miracle Stories," esp. pp. 207-211, points to the fact that in both the *Vita Cuthberti* and the *Ecclesiastical History* "a large proportion" of Bede's miracle stories are "obviously based upon scriptural precedents" (p. 207). The saints are able to calm storms, produce water from rock, or turn water into wine. This was a common feature of medieval hagiography. More noteworthy, perhaps, is the fact that only relatively rarely does Bede acknowledge and draw attention to the biblical parallels. Indeed, at several points in the *Life of St Cuthbert* he avoids mentioning parallels already identified by the Lindisfarne Anonymous. Cf., for example, VCA 2.3, p. 82; 2.4, p. 84; 3.3, p. 98; and VCP, chap. 10, p. 190; chap. 11, pp. 192-194; chap. 18, pp. 216-218. The Anonymous does not include the episode in which Cuthbert changes water into wine (although he does mention it briefly at VCA 4.18, p. 138). Had he done so, one suspects that he would not, like Bede, have avoided all mention of the miracle at Cana (VCP, chap. 35, pp. 264-266).
   Presumably Bede wished to avoid dwelling on the obvious, or simply echoing what the Anonymous had already said, for there are some counter instances. Both Bede and the Anonymous mention the parallel between the healing of the wife of the *gesith* and the cure of Peter's mother-in-law (VCA 4.3, p. 114; VCP, chap. 29, p. 254); and when Cuthbert's horse uncovers a package of food in the thatch of a hut in which Cuthbert has taken refuge for the night, it is Bede alone who detects the biblical cognate (VCA 1.6, p. 70; VCP, chap. 5, p. 170). Bede also is much more effective at bringing out the point of such parallels: there is nothing in the anonymous account comparable to the comments Bede provides in the two examples given above. For whatever reason, however, Bede is much less inclined than the Anonymous to mention the biblical parallel in the first place. What does capture his attention, much more than that of the Anonymous, is any post-biblical precedent established by another saint. It is Bede alone who mentions parallels between St Cuthbert and St Anthony (VCP, chap. 19, p. 222) and between St Cuthbert and St Augustine (VCP, chap. 38, pp. 280-282); and on three occasions it is Bede alone who draws attention to parallels between St Cuthbert and St Benedict (VCP, chap. 14, pp. 200-202; chap. 19, p. 222; chap. 20, p. 222). The fact that on the first of these latter occasions he also mentions Cuthbert imitating a miracle of Bishop Marcellinus of Ancona lends weight to the thesis of Loomis, "Miracle Traditions," who argues that, to help him sort out the spurious from the genuine, Bede regarded the *Dialogues* of Gregory the Great and the miracles there reported as a standard of authenticity.

Perhaps the clearest example of the logic that applied is provided by Bede's comments on the saintly Queen Aethelthryth, the wife of King Ecgfrith of Northumbria. Although she lived with her husband for twelve years, Aethelthryth managed to preserve the glory of her virginity intact, a fact that was confirmed after her death by the miracle of her uncorrupted body. "There is no doubt," says Bede, "that what often happened in days gone by, as we learn from trustworthy accounts, could happen in our time too through the help of the Lord, who has promised to be with us even to the end of the age."[13] In view of this kind of statement, both the occurrence of modern miracles and the central reason for them are beyond dispute. In Bede's judgment, they remained a fixture of the spiritual life of the church as he knew it, for as God acted in former times, so could he act even in the eighth century. Against this background, therefore, the perspective that he adopts in his theological works can only strike us as puzzling. Whereas modern miracles are proclaimed in both the *Ecclesiastical History* and the lives of St Cuthbert, at first glance at least the thesis of Bede's sermons and scriptural commentaries is that the age of miracles is over. Miracles were most appropriate only to a church in its infancy; in the contemporary world, he seems to say, they have lost their *raison d'être*.

One noteworthy feature of such pronouncements is the fact that Bede frequently follows in the footsteps of Gregory the Great or Jerome, often simply quoting verbatim. Occasionally, therefore, one wonders about the degree to which he has made their thoughts his own. His comments on Luke 9:1-2 can be taken as a case in point:

> *Having called together the twelve apostles, [Christ] gave them power and authority over all demons and to cure diseases, and he sent them out to preach the kingdom of God and to heal the sick.* The power of miracles having first been granted, he sent them out to preach the kingdom of God. The greatness of their works would bear witness to the greatness of their promises; *manifest virtue would inspire faith in their words; those who were preaching a new Gospel would perform new deeds.* Hence now that the number of the faithful has increased, there are many within Holy Church who lead a life of virtue without possessing the signs of virtue, because in vain is a miracle displayed on the outside if the inner purpose which it

---

13 *HE* 4.19, pp. 392-393 (translation revised): "Nec diffidendum est nostra etiam aetate fieri potuisse, quod aevo praecedente aliquoties factum fideles historiae narrant, donante uno eodemque Domino, qui se nobiscum usque in finem saeculi manere pollicetur." Cf. Matt. 28:20.

serves is lacking. According to the apostle to the Gentiles, "tongues are a sign not for believers but for unbelievers" [1 Cor. 14:22].[14]

Bede's primary concern is to clarify the relationship, left vague in the text of Scripture itself, between the preaching of the apostles and their miracles. He does so by explaining that the wonders they performed had a supportive role, that they were intended to secure an audience for the apostles by corroborating the truth of the Gospel they proclaimed; and to reinforce his argument he quotes from Gregory the Great's *Homilies on the Gospels*. In the Gregorian text this point leads immediately to a second one: that miracles are not now as frequent as they once were. Now that the Christian faith has been firmly established, there is no longer the same need for them. However, it is Gregory who makes this point, not Bede; and although Bede quotes Gregory with apparent full approval, at this juncture Gregory's comments are incidental to his main concern. Bede appeals to Gregory to support the notion that New Testament miracles served essentially apologetic purposes, a point that Gregory makes at the beginning of the excerpt from his *Homilies on the Gospels*, and a point that he reinforces with the reference to St Paul at the end. His comments about the relative scarcity of miracles in the modern world have the force of a parenthetical aside to which Bede may not have wished fully to commit himself, given the fact that his attention was focused elsewhere.

A similar situation in the sixth book of his commentary on the Canticle of Canticles gives rise to similar doubts. Here once again we have a quotation from Gregory the Great, an excerpt from his *Homilies on Ezechiel* in which he argues that the miracles the biblical saints performed are beyond our power.[15] Bede borrows extensively from Gregory, and

---

14 *In Luc.* 3, CCL 120:194: "*Convocatis autem duodecim apostolis dedit illis virtutem et potestatem super omnia daemonia et ut languores curarent et misit illos praedicare regnum Dei et sanare infirmos.* Concessa primum potestate signorum misit praedicare regnum Dei ut promissorum magnitudini attestaretur etiam magnitudo factorum *fidemque verbis daret virtus ostensa et nova facerent qui nova praedicarent. Unde nunc quoque cum fidelium numerositas excrevit intra sanctam ecclesiam multi sunt qui vitam virtutum tenent et signa virtutum non habent quia frustra miraculum foras ostenditur, si deest quod intus operetur. Nam iuxta magistri gentium vocem linguae in signum sunt non fidelibus sed infidelibus.*" Cf. Gregory the Great, *Hom. in Evan.* 1.4.3, PL 76:1090-1091. See also Bede's comments on Mark 3:14-15: *In Marc.* 1, CCL 120:470.

15 *In Cant.* 6, CCL 119B:368. Cf. Gregory the Great, *Hom. in Ezech.* 2.3.23, CCL 142:254-255.

without demur; but in this case as well the degree to which he would endorse Gregory's comments remains unclear. Rather than personal exegesis reinforced by selective quotation, book six of the commentary on the Canticle of Canticles is a simple pastiche of borrowings. It is made up exclusively of quotations from Gregory, passages that are allowed to stand on their own without being worked into the fabric of Bede's own thought. Clearly, Bede regarded the excerpts he selected as worthy of note, but it would be perilous to treat them as primary evidence for his own personal opinions.[16] Indeed, in this particular case it is also doubtful whether even Gregory intended a comment on the relative frequency of miracles in the contemporary world, and whether Bede would have interpreted him in that vein. In all probability, in fact, Gregory's point was to contrast the relative weakness of simple believers with the power of the saints: *we* may not be able to perform miracles, but *the saints* can.[17]

If these texts are problematic, however, elsewhere the relationship between Bede and the authorities he quotes seems clearer, and the suggestion more easily justifiable that he would have endorsed their views. Hence his comments on Luke 11:14, for example, do seem to posit an important difference between New Testament and modern times:

> Now [Christ] was casting out a demon, and that demon was dumb. And when he had cast out the demon, the dumb man spoke, and the crowds marvelled. According to Matthew, this demoniac was not only dumb but also blind, and he was cured by the Lord so that he could both speak and see [Matt. 12:22]. *Three miracles, therefore, were accomplished in one man at the same time: a blind man saw; a dumb man spoke; a man possessed was freed from a demon. At that time these things took place in a physical manner, but they also occur daily in the conversion of believers. First the*

16 Despite his very high regard for Gregory, Bede is still able to distinguish between Gregory's views and his own. See *In Cant.* 6, CCL 119B:359, where Bede introduces the last book of his commentary as follows: "Cudatur ergo septimus [*sic*] in cantica canticorum liber nostro quidem labore collectus sed beati Gregorii sermonibus et sensu compositus ut si quis forte sit qui nostra opuscula iure spernenda aestimet habeat in promptu legenda eius dicta qui constat nullatenus esse spernendus. Si quis vero haec quoque nostra si quis captus amore legat sit ut marmoreis nostrae parvitatis aedificiis aureum tantus architectus culmen imponat." Bede refers to book seven because he considers the critique of Julian of Eclanum with which he prefaces his commentary to be book one.

17 *Signs of Sanctity*, p. 21.

demon is driven out so that they can see the light of faith; then mouths hitherto bound in silence are loosened to proclaim God's praises.[18]

Here the substance of Bede's comment is borrowed verbally from Jerome, but in such a way that Jerome's words are integral to the structure of Bede's own argument. Indeed, Bede shifts the example from Luke 11 to Matthew 12 to ensure a proper context for Jerome's remarks. There is no reason for suspecting he does not fully endorse what Jerome is suggesting: that the physical miracles performed by Christ and the apostles have now been replaced by spiritual cognates.

The same point is made in Bede's discussion of Mark 16:17-18. Immediately after commissioning the apostles to go out into the world to preach the Gospel to the whole creation, here Christ promises the miraculous power that will accompany those who believe: "in my name they will cast out demons; they will speak in new tongues; they will pick up serpents, and if they drink any deadly thing, it will not hurt them; they will lay their hands on the sick, and they will recover." Bede explains that these powers were necessary in the early church as an aid in the process of evangelization. When we plant a vineyard, we carefully water the young plants until they have taken root and are capable of surviving on their own. In a similar way the primitive church needed to be watered with the grace of miracles until the roots of the new faith had been firmly anchored. Now, however, that the period of tender beginnings has passed, the church regularly performs in a spiritual fashion the miracles that the apostles accomplished in a physical or material way. The priest casts out demons whenever he performs the sacrament of exorcism. The faithful speak in new tongues when they proclaim the sacred mysteries and sing the praises of the Creator. To expel by exhortation the evil from the hearts of others is to pick up serpents; to receive evil counsel yet resist being drawn into evil actions is to imbibe poison without being harmed; to strengthen those not yet securely established in good works is to lay hands on the sick and speed

---

18 *In Luc.* 4, CCL 120:231-232: "*Et erat eiciens daemonium, et illud erat mutum. Et cum eiecisset daemonium locutus est mutus, et ammiratae sunt turbae.* Daemoniacus iste apud Matheum non solum mutus sed et caecus fuisse narratur curatusque dicitur a domino ita ut loqueretur et videret. *Tria ergo signa simul in uno homine perpetrata sunt, caecus videt, mutus loquitur, possessus daemone liberatur. Quod et tunc quidem carnaliter factum est sed et cotidie completur in conversione credentium ut expulso primum daemone fidei lumen aspiciant deinde ad laudes Dei tacentia prius ora laxentur.*" Cf. Jerome, *In Matth.* 2, CCL 77:91-92.

their recovery. These modern miracles are all the greater than those of former times for being spiritual in nature. The apostles healed sick bodies; modern wonders restore souls to life.

Once again Bede draws on others to convey his thoughts, in this case Gregory the Great.[19] But here the borrowing is extensive, and it is confirmed by Bede's comments elsewhere. One significant passage is his explication of Christ's statement in Luke 13:32: "Behold, I cast out demons and perform cures today and tomorrow, and the third day I finish my course." Bede explains that Christ's words are to be taken allegorically. Even though spoken in his own person, they actually refer to his body, the church. "Demons are cast out when, having abandoned ancestral superstition, the nations of the world believe in him. Cures are performed when, having renounced the Devil and this world, they live according to his precepts."[20] The wonders to be performed in the church, it would seem, are not the physical wonders recorded in Scripture but their spiritual analogues. In his commentary on the first Epistle of St John Bede confirms this assessment, informing us that the gift of the Holy Spirit is not made manifest by external signs, as in the days of the early church, but rather by the charity in the heart of the believer.[21] All things considered, therefore, the perspective on contemporary miracles provided by Bede's homilies and scriptural commentaries seems

19 *In Marc.* 4, CCL 120:645-646. Cf. Gregory the Great, *Hom. in Evan.* 2.29.4, PL 76:1215-1216.

20 *In Luc.* 4, CCL 120:273: "Expelluntur enim daemonia cum relictis paternis superstitionibus credunt in eum gentes, et perficiuntur sanitates cum secundum eius praecepta vivitur posteaquam fuerit diabolo et huic saeculo renuntiatum."

21 *In epist. 1 Ioh.* 3.24, CCL 121:310: "Primis temporibus cadebat super credentes spiritus sanctus et loquebantur linguis quas non didicerant; nunc autem quia exterioribus signis sancta ecclesia non indiget, quicumque credens in nomine Iesu Christi fraternam habuerit caritatem spiritui sancto in se manenti testimonium perhibet." Cf. *In Luc.* 1, CCL 120:48: "usque hodie et usque ad consummationem saeculi dominus in Nazareth concipi nasci in Bethleem non desinit cum quilibet audientium verbi flore suscepto domum se aeterni panis efficit. Cotidie in utero virginali, hoc est in animo credentium per fidem concipitur per baptisma gignitur." See also *Hom. Evan.* 2.8, CCL 122:237-238, where Bede points out that the Evangelists record ten occasions on which Christ appeared to his disciples after his resurrection. To all of these there correspond occasions on which he will be present to us as well, but in a more spiritual way: "Hac ergo frequentia corporalis suae manifestationis ostendere voluit dominus ut diximus in omni loco se bonorum desideriis divinitus esse praesentem. Apparuit namque ad monumentum lugentibus; aderit et nobis absentiae eius recordatione salubriter contristatis."

fairly clear, although paradoxical. At first glance at least it is scarcely consistent with the many reported modern miracles found in the *Ecclesiastical History* and elsewhere.

It has sometimes been suggested that the tension in Bede's thought was a traditional one, and that the same inconsistency is present in the Church Fathers. In his apparent entertaining at one and the same time of two mutually exclusive views on the issue of contemporary miracles, one to the effect that God continues to demonstrate his miraculous power through the agency of his saints, and another to the effect that the age of miracles ended with the consolidation of the post-apostolic church, Bede was simply endorsing "an authoritative tradition of apparent self-contradiction."[22] Intuitively this is not a very satisfying explanation, and indeed we ought not to be satisfied with it. Although the accusation of confusion or contradiction has been directed more frequently and with greater insistence against Gregory the Great than anyone else, in point of fact the tension that scholars have noted between the *Dialogues* and Gregory's other works is more apparent than real. Gregory refers to contemporary miracles in many of the same works that appear to deny them. What he is saying, therefore, is not that the age of miracles has ended, but simply that miracles are not as frequent or as spectacular now as they once may have been.[23]

A careful review of his exegetical works and sermons would suggest that Bede's view was essentially the same.[24] Like Gregory's more strictly theological works, Bede's commentaries and homilies are not devoid of references to contemporary miracles. A clear example is found in the second book of the *Homilies on the Gospels*, where Bede provides a gloss for Christ's promise in John 16:13: "When the Spirit of truth comes, ... he will declare to you the things that are to come":

> It is well known that through the gift of the Holy Spirit many of the faithful have had advance knowledge of and have been able to foretell the future. However, there are several who, filled by the grace of the Spirit, heal the sick, raise the dead, command demons, indeed shine with many virtues and

22 Rosemary Woolf, "Saints' Lives," in *Continuations and Beginnings: Studies in Old English Literature*, ed. Eric Gerald Stanley (London, 1966), pp. 37-66 at 42. Cf. Colgrave, "Bede's Miracle Stories," pp. 227-229; "Earliest Saints' Lives Written in England," p. 41.
23 See *Signs of Sanctity*, Chap. 1.
24 Cf. Creider, "Bede's Understanding of the Miraculous," pp. 277-278, 280-281, 291.

live angelic lives on earth, and yet have no knowledge of the future through the revelation of the same Spirit. Hence the Lord's statement here can also be taken to mean that the Spirit arrives and announces what is to come to us when he makes us mindful of the joys of heaven.[25]

Unless it is the historical present that Bede employs in the second sentence, his choice of tense is significant. It implies, although it is not his primary point, that the saints of his own day continue to possess miraculous power. If one pursues the comparison with Gregory the Great a little further, however, one is struck by the paucity of such passages. One additional example, inconclusive at that, completes the list.[26] Even more striking is the virtual absence of modern miracle stories from Bede's sermons and scriptural commentaries. In this regard the contrast with Gregory the Great could hardly be greater. Despite the presence of passages that have been taken to signal the end of the age of miracles, Gregory's *Homilies on the Gospels* contain no less than thirteen modern miracle stories (fourteen in total, since one is a duplicate), many of which are repeated almost verbatim in his *Dialogues*.[27] Bede's *Homilies on the Gospels* contain no such stories. Indeed, the entire corpus of his exegetical and homiletical works contains only two possible examples. One is the not

---

25 *Hom. Evan.* 2.11, CCL 122:257: "Constat innumeros fidelium per donum spiritus sancti praenosse ac praedixisse ventura. Sed quia sunt non nulli qui spiritus gratia pleni infirmos curant mortuos suscitant daemonibus imperant multis virtutibus coruscant ipsi angelicam in terris vitam gerunt nec tamen quae ibi sint ventura spiritus eiusdem relevatione agnoscunt potest hic domini sermo etiam sic accipi quia spiritus adveniens quae ventura sunt adnuntiat nobis cum gaudia nobis patriae caelestis ad memoriam reducit."

26 See *In Cant.* 2, CCL 119B:248, where, referring to the church, Bede says: "nitorem quoque carismatum quibus infirmos curat mortuos suscitat leprosos mundat daemones eicit et cetera huiusmodi possunt infideles cum fidelibus intueri possunt etiam mirari." Cf. *In Cant.* 6, CCL 119B:372: "In omelia Hiezechielis IIII parte secunda. *Sicut cortex mali punici genae tuae absque occultis tuis* [Cant 6:6]. *Genae sunt sanctae ecclesiae spiritales patres qui nunc in ea miraculis coruscant et velut in eius facie venerabiles apparent. Cum enim videmus multos mira agere ventura prophetare mundum perfecte relinquere caelestibus desideriis ardere sicut cortex mali punici sanctae ecclesiae genae rubent.*" The italicized passage, however, is simply an excerpt from Gregory's *Hom. in Ezech.* 2.4.8, CCL 142:264. For reasons already discussed, its significance is limited. Moreover, despite the present tense and the use of *nunc*, the context suggests that the *spiritales patres* Gregory has in mind are the Fathers of the Old and New Testaments.

27 See Adalbert de Vogüé, *Grégoire le Grand, Dialogues* 1: *Introduction, bibliographie et cartes* (Paris, 1978), p. 29 with n. 15.

particularly remarkable story of a holy woman's delivery from a demon. The other, more clearly a miracle story, is scarcely modern. It is the story of the third-century saint Gregory Thaumaturgus, whose faith was strong enough once literally to have moved a mountain.[28]

Conceivably the tension in Bede's thought would be lessened if, as has been suggested, one could posit a clear distinction between Bede the historian and Bede the hagiographer. As Woolf explains: "A Christian historian will accept a miraculous interpretation of an event only if no other seems possible; the hagiographer will prefer a miraculous interpretation unless a naturalistic explanation is inescapable." Colgrave argues that Bede was actually three men in one: a hagiographer, an historian and a theologian. Whereas Bede the hagiographer would have had no difficulty with the notion that God could continue to work miracles through his saints, both Bede the historian and Bede the theologian would have had reservations.[29] Undoubtedly Bede's works can be considered more or less hagiographical, or more or less historical, depending on the degree to which they conform to our models of the two genres. From this point of view the hagiographical character of the *Vita Cuthberti* seems clear, as does the very different, more historiographical character of the *Historia abbatum*. In the former the references to date and place that would localize the narrative in space and time are for the most part lacking; in the latter they figure prominently. In the *Life of Cuthbert* the miracles of the saint are highlighted; in the *History of the Abbots* miracles are virtually if not completely absent.[30] We should resist, however, the temptation to allow such comparative judgments to harden into absolutes. In this regard the case of Bede's master work, the *Ecclesiastical History*, is quite instructive. Here the prominence of both hagiographical and historiographical elements results in a work much more highly resistant to simple classification.

Markus has attempted to solve the problem by arguing that, in the *Ecclesiastical History*, hagiography ultimately is absorbed into history. Although Bede utilized "a mass of hagiographical material" in the

---

28 *In Luc.* 3, CCL 120:184-185; *In Marc.* 3, CCL 120:580-581.

29 Woolf, "Saints' Lives," pp. 42-43; Colgrave, "Bede's Miracle Stories," pp. 228-229.

30 Cf. Karen A. Winstead, "The Transformation of the Miracle Story in the *Libri Historiarum* of Gregory of Tours," *Medium Aevum* 59 (1990): 1-15. Winstead argues that a comparison of episodes common to the *Libri Historiarum* and the *Liber in gloria confessorum* reveals a "conscious or subconscious awareness of genres" (p. 2) on Gregory's part.

making of the history, "most of it," he suggests, "has been transformed into the substance of history in the course of the process." Since large stretches of Bede's account retain their hagiographical character, the result of such an analysis is unfortunate. An episode as prominent as the vision of Fursa becomes a bit of "hagiographical residue" that "resists integration into the historical narrative."[31] A more profitable approach would acknowledge the limitations of what are essentially modern distinctions, and recognize that medieval scholars may well have seen things differently. As Goffart puts it: "Saints were historical personages, their miracles and the adventures of their relics were historical events. Hagiography has as much claim to be integrated in a medieval historian's output as biography in a modern one's."[32]

When Bede himself is consulted on the matter, the evidence suggests that the tensions in his thought are not to be relieved by making distinctions of genre. In the list that he appends to the *Ecclesiastical History*, the lives of Felix, Anastasius and Cuthbert are referred to as "histories of the saints," and are listed right alongside his "history of the abbots" and his "Ecclesiastical History" of the English people. To Bede's mind hagiography, like modern biography, is a branch of history; basically he acknowledges only one fundamental category, and he identifies it as history.[33] Moreover, all of this work, historiographical or hagiographical, together with his commentaries and his homilies, seems to be unified in Bede's mind in essentially theological terms. From the age of seven, he tells us, when his kinsmen first committed him to the charge of Benedict Biscop and then of Ceolfrith to be educated, his exclusive concern has been the study of Sacred Scripture.[34] We are still left, however, with the puzzling fact of contrasts and tensions in Bede's works that are not easily resolved. In particular, there is a greater contrast between the *Ecclesiastical History* and Bede's more strictly theological works than there is between the *Dialogues* and Gregory the Great's other works. In his homilies and commentaries Bede rarely if

---

31 Markus, *Bede and the Tradition of Ecclesiastical Historiography*, pp. 7-8.
32 Goffart, *Narrators of Barbarian History*, p. 245. Cf. Jean-Michel Picard, "Bede, Adomnán, and the Writing of History," *Peritia* 3 (1984): 50-70.
33 Cf. Meyvaert, "Bede the Scholar," p. 53. For a different view, see W.F. Bolton, *A History of Anglo-Latin Literature, 597-1066* (Princeton, 1967), 1:133-134. On the basis of the same evidence Bolton argues·that Bede conceives of three different genres: hagiography, biography and history.
34 *HE* 5.24, pp. 566-570.

ever considers modern miracles; his focus is almost exclusively on the miracles of Scripture. Where modern miracles do emerge, they do so in a virtual theological vacuum. The primacy of Bede's focus on Scripture notwithstanding, the treatment he accords modern miracles lacks the context that a consideration of the miracles of Scripture would have provided. This suggests that Bede distinguished between scriptural and modern miracles in a way that Gregory did not, and probably conceived of them having different rationales and purposes.

He also conceived of the context of modern miracles very differently than did Gregory the Great. In Gregory's case, part of the rationale for the continuation of miracles into his own time is the quickly approaching consummation of the age. In the *Dialogues* this is the explanation that he provides for a relative increase in visions of the hereafter. Comparing this world to the darkness of night, and the world to come to the light of approaching day, he states:

> In the transitional hour before sunrise, when the night comes to an end and the new day is about to begin, darkness is somehow blended with light until the remaining shadows of the night are perfectly absorbed in the brightness of the coming day. In this way the end of the world merges with the beginnings of eternal life. Earth's remaining shadows begin to fade as the beams of spiritual light filter through them. We can, therefore, discern many truths about the future life, but we still see them imperfectly, because the light in which we see is still dim and pale, like the light of the sun in the early hours of the day just before dawn.[35]

Although there are nuances of scholarly judgment that preclude unanimity on the issue, the prevailing view is that Bede as well shared the expectation of the end that was to haunt much of the Middle Ages. On this issue as on many others, it is said, Gregory's was the decisive influence.[36] When it is examined more closely, however, this view of the relationship between Gregory and Bede is difficult to sustain.

---

35 *Dial.* 4.43.2, Zimmerman 251, SC 265:154.
36 Bonner, *Saint Bede in the Tradition of Western Apocalyptic Commentary*, p. 5. Cf. Plummer, *Opera Historica* 2:62; J.M. Wallace-Hadrill, *Bede's Europe* (Jarrow, 1962), reprinted in his *Early Medieval History* (Oxford, 1975), pp. 60-75 at 71-72; Mayr-Harting, *Coming of Christianity to England*, p. 217; and Markus, *Bede and the Tradition of Ecclesiastical Historiography*, p. 14. For a different emphasis, see Creider, "Bede's Understanding of the Miraculous," p. 159; Rosenthal, "Bede's Ecclesiastical History," pp. 15-16; and Davidse, "Sense of History," pp. 665-666.

In *De die iudicii* Bede issues a call to repentance before the Judgment that will follow on Christ's return.[37] In book one of the *Ecclesiastical History* he reproduces Gregory's famous letter of June 601 to King Aethelbert of Kent, apparently endorsing Gregory's claim that the end of the world is "at hand" (*praesentis mundi iam terminus iuxta est*).[38] Taken in isolation, such texts might well be seen as evidence that he thought the Day of Judgment to be imminent. In point of fact, however, the situation is not quite so straightforward. The letter to Aethelbert is one of the more nuanced of Gregory's pronouncements on this issue, as is clear from the text that Bede quotes. Says Gregory:

> As the end of the world approaches, many things threaten which have never happened before; these are changes in the sky and terrors from the heavens, unseasonable tempests, wars, famine, pestilence, and earthquakes in divers places. Not all these things will come about in our days, but they will all follow after our days. So if you see any of these things happening in your land, do not be troubled in mind; for these signs of the end of the world are sent in advance to make us heedful about our souls, watching for the hour of death, so that when the Judge comes we may, through our good works, be found prepared.

His expectant tone notwithstanding, Gregory suggests that the consummation of the age is not to occur in his own days but at some point in the indeterminate future. Moreover, although they are identified as harbingers of the last days, the signs for which Aethelbert is encouraged to be watchful serve primarily to focus his attention on the hour of death, not the end of the world. As a representative expression of Gregory's thought, this letter would not be well chosen. As a typical example of Bede's, however, it serves much better. In the final analysis Bede shares very little of Gregory's eschatological perspective.

Given the overwhelmingly biblical imprint of Bede's thought, it would be most surprising to find the eschatological dimension completely

---

37 *De die iudicii*, CCL 122:439-444 at 440-441:
     Cur, rogo, mens, tardas medico te pandere totam?
     Vel cur, lingua, taces, veniae dum tempus habebis?
     Auribus Omnipotens te nunc exaudit apertis.
     Ille dies veniet, iudex dum venerit orbis,
     Debebis qua tu rationem reddere de te.
     Suadeo praevenias lacrimis modo iudicis iram.

38 *HE* 1.32, pp. 112-115. Cf. Gregory the Great, *Epist.* 11.37, CCL 140A:929-932 at 931.

lacking; and we do not.[39] There were, of course, certain passages of Scripture that required careful interpretation in light of the much-delayed *Parousia*, Christ's pronouncement in Luke 9:27, for example: "there are some standing here who will not taste death before they see the kingdom of God";[40] or his statement in Luke 21:32, where, after referring to the signs of the end time, he proclaims: "Truly, I say to you, this generation will not pass away till all has taken place."[41] These texts simply could not be allowed to mean what a quick and literal reading would suggest. Hence Bede informs us that the "generation" that will not pass away must be the human race, or the Jewish people;[42] and that, as Gregory the Great himself explains, the "kingdom of God" of Luke 9 must be a reference to the present church. Rather than suggesting that they will survive until his second coming, what Christ is promising is simply that some of the disciples will live to see the church militant firmly established. Somewhat more plausibly, Bede goes on to suggest that, if we wish to see in "the kingdom of God" a reference to the heavenly kingdom, then some of the disciples had a foretaste even of that by being witnesses to the Transfiguration. Although this still strains the context, at least the Transfiguration follows immediately after the verses in question in the Gospel.[43] We can sympathize with Bede's problem: apparent predictions on Christ's part that his return would occur within the lifetime of some of his followers presented obvious difficulties of interpretation. Elsewhere, however, where there was no threat of its being falsified by experience, the eschatological dimension of Scripture could be openly acknowledged, as it was by virtually all medieval thinkers.

At times Bede surprises us by missing what seems to be the clear import of the passage under consideration. A case in point is provided by his remarks on Luke 12:40: "the Son of Man is coming at an hour you do not expect." Although this seems to invite comments on Christ's

---

39 "Eschatology" is here used in its general or collective sense, according to which it has to do with the second coming, the resurrection of the dead, the Last Judgment and the end of the world. In its individual sense it deals with death, particular judgment, purgatory, heaven and hell.

40 Cf. Mark 8:39(9:1).

41 Cf. Mark 13:30.

42 *In Luc.* 6, CCL 120:370; *In Marc.* 4, CCL 120:602.

43 *In Luc.* 3, CCL 120:203-204; cf. *In Marc.* 2, CCL 120:540-541; *Hom. Evan.* 1.24, CCL 122:171. Cf. also Gregory the Great, *Hom. in Evan.* 2.32.6, PL 76:1236-1237.

second coming, Bede chooses to interpret it exclusively with regard to the hour of death. In this case, however, our surprise is tempered by the fact that Gregory the Great did not see an allusion to the Lord's return either. Indeed, Bede takes his lead from Gregory, and it is Gregory whom he quotes in fashioning his own comments.[44] Elsewhere, by way of contrast, we are startled to find Bede discovering eschatological import where we might not otherwise have expected it. An example is provided by his treatment of Luke 14:15-24, the parable of the great banquet. The hour of the banquet, we are informed, represents the end of the age: "Quid hora caenae nisi finis est mundi." However, Bede's further thoughts on the passage—once again verbally inspired by Gregory—are such as to remove the edge from any sense of expectancy. If we are now at the end of the world, we have been in this position for some time, as the apostle's comments at 1 Cor. 10:11 clearly indicate: St Paul refers to himself and his contemporaries as people "upon whom the end of the ages has come."[45] If we are standing near the end of time, it is important to realize that, from Bede's perspective, the same could be said of those who witnessed Christ's sacrifice on the Cross.[46] Clearly, eschatological language does not imply any sense that the consummation of the age is imminent.

Representative of Bede's approach are his comments on 1 John 2:18: "Children, it is the last hour," a passage he chooses to interpret in the light of Matt. 20:1-16, the parable of the labourers in the vineyard:

> Those who served the will of their Creator either by teaching or living properly from the beginning of the world cultivated the vineyard of the Lord from the first hour; those who lived from the time of Noah did so from the third hour; those who lived from the time of Abraham did so from the sixth hour; those who lived from the time of the giving of the law did so from the ninth hour; those who obey the heavenly commands from the

---

44 *In Luc.* 4, CCL 120:257. Cf. Gregory the Great, *Hom. in Evan.* 1.13.5-6, PL 76:1126.

45 *In Luc.* 4, CCL 120:278: "*Quid hora caenae nisi finis est mundi in quo nimirum nos sumus sicut iamdudum Paulus testatur dicens nos in quos fines saeculorum devenerunt. Si ergo iam hora caenae est cum vocamur, tanto minus debemus excusare a convivio Dei quanto propinquasse iam cernimus finem saeculi.*" Bede is quoting here from Gregory the Great, *Hom. in Evan.* 2.36.2, PL 76:1267.

46 *In Ezram et Neemiam* 2, CCL 119A:329: "dominus in fine saeculi sacrificium suae carnis et sanguinis obtulit patri ac nobis in pane et vino offerendum praecepit." Cf. *In epist. Judae* 6, CCL 121:336: "Qui enim homo in fine saeculorum ex virgine natus Iesu nomen angelo dictante accepit."

time of the Lord's incarnation to the end of the world do so from the eleventh hour. In this [eleventh] hour, namely, it was foretold by the prediction of the prophets that there would be both the coming of the saviour in the flesh and that there would follow the plague of the antichrist, which would assail the heralds of salvation.

Bede's attitude is reminiscent of Augustine's. Although this is indeed the last hour, says Augustine, we cannot be certain of its length, and it has already proven to be remarkably long.[47] Rather than fueling eschatological expectations, Bede's approach is such as to dampen them down. Instructive in this regard are his remarks on 1 Peter 4:7: "The end of all things is at hand; therefore keep sane and sober for your prayers." Although the end is at hand, Bede also observes that the timing of the Last Judgment is in the indefinite future; and he then switches the focus to the individual judgment each of us will undergo after death. Lest any be tempted to derive comfort from a Last Judgment thought to be far off, we should be mindful that the time allotted for this mortal life is not long.[48]

The notion of an eleventh hour stretching from the Incarnation through the present and off into the indefinite future becomes less incongruous when appraised in the context of the doctrine of the six ages of the world, a conception of history that Bede inherited from Augustine. In Southern's judgment, Augustine's vision was nothing less than "an extraordinary flight of imagination springing from the mysterious depths of biblical truth."[49] The clue to the overall course of historical development was to be found in the first chapter of Genesis, its decipherment being assisted by the genealogies in the Gospel of St Matthew. Just as

---

47 In epist. 1 Ioh. 2.18, CCL 121:295; trans. David Hurst, Bede the Venerable: Commentary on the Seven Catholic Epistles (Kalamazoo, 1985), p. 175. Cf. Augustine, Epist. 199.6.17, CSEL 57:257-258: "neque enim dixit 'novissimum tempus est' aut 'novissimus annus' aut 'mensis' aut 'dies', sed: Novissima hora est. et ecce ista hora quam longa est!"

48 In epist. 1 Pet. 4.7, CCL 121:253. Goffart, Narrators of Barbarian History, p. 187, suggests a similar approach in Gregory of Tours. Any "apocalyptic flavour" in his History of the Franks is "literary color rather than seriously meant." For a different view, however, one emphasizing development in Gregory's thought, see de Nie, Views from a Many-Windowed Tower, pp. 52-56, 68, 295-296.

49 R.W. Southern, "Aspects of the European Tradition of Historical Writing 2: Hugh of St Victor and the Idea of Historical Development," Transactions of the Royal Historical Society 5th ser. 21 (1971): 159-179 at 161.

there are six days of Creation, Augustine explains, so there are six ages of history:

> The first age or day is that from Adam to the flood; the second, from the flood to Abraham. (These two "days" were not identical in length of time, but in each there were ten generations.) Then follow the three ages, each consisting of fourteen generations, as recorded in the Gospel of St Matthew: the first, from Abraham to David; the second, from David to the transmigration to Babylon; the third, from then to Christ's nativity in the flesh. Thus, we have five ages. The sixth is the one in which we now are. It is an age not to be measured by any precise number of generations, since we are told: "It is not for you to know the times or dates which the Father has fixed by his own authority" [Acts 1:7].[50]

Bede discusses this doctrine at various points, drawing attention, like Augustine, to the parallel with the six ages of man as well as with the six days of Creation, and arguing, again like Augustine, that just as the six days on which God created the universe were followed by a seventh on which he rested, so the six ages of the world will be followed by a seventh age of eternal repose.[51] Given the length of the sixth and final age, however, one could readily think in terms of the approaching end of the world without at the same time expecting it to materialize soon.

Although it is clearly a good thing to long for and ardently desire the day of the Lord, Bede's consistent position is that we must avoid imagining that it is close at hand.[52] Two important signs of the end of

50 *De civ. Dei* 22.30, CCL 48:865-866; trans. Gerald G. Walsh and Daniel J. Honan, Fathers of the Church 24 (Washington DC, 1954), p. 510.

51 Cf. *De temporibus* 16, CCL 123C:600-601; *De temp. ratione* 10, CCL 123B:310-312; Paolo Siniscalco, "Le età del mondo in Beda," *Romanobarbarica* 3 (1978): 297-332. Alternatively Bede conceives of the six ages of history being followed by seventh and eighth ages signifying eternal rest before and after the resurrection. The seventh age is the one the blessed enter immediately after their deaths. See *Chronica Maiora = De temp. ratione* 66.1-8, CCL 123B:463-464. See also Bede's *Hymnus ... de opere sex dierum primordialium et de sex aetatibus mundi*, CCL 122:407-411. For the larger context, see Paul Archambault, "The Ages of Man and the Ages of the World: A Study of Two Traditions," *Revue des études augustiniennes* 12 (1966): 193-228; and J.A. Burrow, *The Ages of Man: A Study in Medieval Writing and Thought* (Oxford, 1986).

52 *In Luc.* 5, CCL 120:316: "Huius ergo diei bonum est desiderare praesentiam nec tamen magnitudine desiderii nobis somnia fingere *quasi instet dies domini* [2 Thess. 2:2]." Cf. *Chronica Maiora = De temp. ratione* 68.598, CCL 123B:537, where he says of the Lord's return: "Cuius quidem Adventus horam merito sancti omnes

the age have yet to occur: the conversion of the Jews and the persecution of the Antichrist. Neither can be confused with contemporary events.[53] Bede clearly distinguishes between his own time, when a few Jews are embracing the Christian faith, and the end of time, when all Israel will be saved,[54] just as he differentiates the persecution the church has suffered throughout its history from the trials it will endure when the Antichrist is allowed to rage in all his fury. Sulpicius Severus had confidently announced that the Antichrist was already born. Gregory the Great had proclaimed that, if not the Antichrist himself, at least his precursors were alive and active in the world.[55] Bede was much more guarded. The text of 1 John 4:3 might have tempted him to issue apocalyptic pronouncements. But Bede is content to state that, if the Antichrist is presently active in the world, it is only in the minds of those who, without hope of repentance, battle against the Saviour by their words or their deeds.[56]

In his *Chronica Maiora* Bede explains the connection that he sees between the conversion of the Jews and the advent of Antichrist, the one being a precondition for the other.[57] Before the Antichrist's persecution is unleashed, Enoch and Elijah will return to this earth to preach the Gospel to the Jews. Only after the Jewish people as a whole have been brought to the faith of the church, a process of evangelization lasting three and a half years, will the stage be set for Antichrist's advent.

---

diligunt et citius adesse desiderant; sed periculose satis agunt si qui hanc prope an longe sit putare vel praedicare praesumunt."

53 *Chronica Maiora* = *De temp. ratione* 69.600, CCL 123B:538: "Duo sane certissima necdum instantis diei iudicii habemus indicia, fidem videlicet Israheliticae gentis et regnum persecutionemque Antichristi."

54 *In Reg. Quaest.* 1, CCL 119:297.

55 Gregory the Great, *Mor.* 33.35.59, CCL 143B:1724; Sulpicius Severus, *Dial.* 2.14, CSEL 1:197. Sulpicius reports the view of St Martin: "Non esse autem dubium, quin Antichristus malo spiritu conceptus iam natus esset et iam in annis puerilibus constitutus, aetate legitima sumpturus imperium." Cf. Jos Vaesen, "Sulpice Sévère et la fin des temps," in *The Use and Abuse of Eschatology in the Middle Ages*, ed. Werner Verbeke, Daniel Verhelst & Andries Welkenhuysen (Leuven, 1988), pp. 49-71.

56 *In epist. I Ioh.* 4.3, CCL 121:311: "*Et hic est antichristus de quo audistis quoniam venit et nunc iam in mundo est.* Venit imminente die iudicii nato in mundum homine illo ceteris amplius nefando, filio iniquitatis, et nunc iam in mundo est habitans in mentibus eorum qui Christo vel professione vel opere sine remedio paenitendi repugnant."

57 *Chronica Maiora* = *De temp. ratione* 69.600-603, CCL 123B:538-539.

Enoch and Elijah, now crowned with martyrdom, will become his first victims. Then Antichrist will widen his attention to make both martyrs and apostates in the greater Christian community. The entire process will take a further three and a half years. Thereafter Christ's return and the Last Judgment will take place, but not immediately, lest the timing of the Judgment be evident once Antichrist's persecution gets underway. The clear impression that Bede creates in all of this is that we are dealing with events in the indefinite and possibly remote future.[58] Elsewhere his remarks suggest that he did not expect that the second coming and Last Judgment would occur in his own generation.[59] However, Bede would censure even the most modest conjecture in these matters, for his firmest conviction, like Augustine's, is that it can serve no constructive purpose: the length of the sixth and last age is indeterminate.[60] Christ the Saviour himself proclaimed that "of that day or that hour no one knows, not even the angels in heaven, nor the Son, but only the Father" (Mark 13:32; cf. Matt. 24:36). As he teaches elsewhere: "It is not for you to know times or seasons which the Father has fixed by his own authority" (Acts 1:7). Whether the Lord comes sooner or later, therefore, is unimportant; what is crucial is that he find us properly prepared.[61]

Some had apparently argued that the year of the Lord's return might well be calculated on the premise that a total of six thousand years can be allotted for the entire course of earthly history. Bede does not say so, but presumably they were inspired by the parallelism between the six

---

58 Cf. *De tabernaculo* 1, CCL 119A:33, where the times before and after Christ's earthly ministry are each divided into three periods. Bede conceives of himself as living in the second of the three post-ascension times: "Fuerunt etenim iusti ante legem fuerunt sub lege fuerunt temporibus prophetarum, item post ascensionem dominicam congregata est ecclesia primitiva de Israhel congregatur nunc de gentibus congreganda est in fine mundi de reliquiis Israhel."

59 See, for example, *De templo* 1, CCL 119A:169-170: "Dum enim hi qui nunc praecedentibus erudiuntur magistris rursum ipsi alios erudiunt quasi super invicem positis ordinibus quique lapidum vivorum in domo Dei sic ab aliis fixa constantia portantur ut ad portandos alios et ipsi sufficiant usque *ad ultimos qui in fine mundi nascituri sunt iustos*, qui quasi in summo domus Dei cacumine locati docentur et portantur ab aliis sed quos doceant quorumve fragilitatem tolerent ipsi non habent." Emphasis added.

60 See *De temporibus* 16, CCL 123C:601, where Bede says of the sixth and present age: "Sexta, quae nunc agitur, nulla generationum vel temporum serie certa sed, ut aetas decrepita ipsa, totius saeculi morte finienda."

61 *In Luc.* 5, CCL 120:316; *In epist. II Pet.* 3.3-4, CCL 121:276.

ages of world history and the six days of Creation, and by the fact that "with the Lord one day is as a thousand years, and a thousand years as one day" (2 Peter 3:8). Even worse, Bede says, some have argued that, just as the Lord enjoyed a seventh day of rest after his six days of labour in creating the world, so the saints can anticipate a seventh age after the resurrection, not the eternal repose that Bede usually thinks of in this connection, but an earthly millennium in which the blessed will reign with Christ before the final consummation of all things. Bede roundly condemns such ideas—"heretica sunt et frivola"—pointing out that they are no more true to history than they are to orthodox Christian doctrine. None of the past ages has been a thousand years in length; in fact, no two of them have had the same length. Hence it is perilous to speculate on the time that may be remaining in the final age in which we now find ourselves. Rather than trying to anticipate the timing of the Lord's coming, a vain and futile task at best, we should emulate the servants of Luke 12:35-36, and with loins girded and lamps alit, patiently await the return of the master from the marriage feast.[62]

In his treatment of these matters, as we have seen, Bede frequently expresses his thoughts by drawing on Gregory the Great. The effect, however, is radically different. In Gregory's case many of the same words and phrases are accompanied by a heightened sense of expectancy, primarily because of the degree to which his perspective was shaped by the evils of his time. In his letter of April 593, for example, to the church of Milan, the ravages of war are interpreted as sure indications of the approaching Judgment:

> Behold, all the things of this world, which we heard in Sacred Scripture were to perish, we now see destroyed. Cities have been overturned, encampments uprooted, churches demolished. No tiller of the soil dwells in our land. Among the very few of us who have been left behind for a short time, the human sword rages incessantly with the devastation of a celestial blow. We now see, therefore, the evils of the world which formerly we heard were to come. The very afflictions of the earth have now become as it were the pages of books written for our benefit. ... Look toward the approaching day of the eternal Judge with a careful mind, and

---

62 Cf. *Ep. ad Pleguinam* 14-15, CCL 123C:624-625; *Chronica Maiora* = *De temp. ratione* 67.594-597, CCL 123B:536-537. On the persistence in the western tradition of the notion that the world is destined to last for 6,000 years, see Richard Landes, "Lest the Millennium Be Fulfilled: Apocalyptic Expectations and the Pattern of Western Chronography 100-800 CE," in *Use and Abuse of Eschatology*, pp. 137-211.

anticipate the terror of that day by repenting. Wash away the stains of all your sins with tears. Check the wrath that looms eternal with a temporal lament. For when our righteous Creator comes to judgment, the more he perceives that we have punished our own faults ourselves, the greater will be the grace with which he comforts us.[63]

One searches in vain the entire corpus of Bede's work for anything even remotely comparable.

In Markus's view, "a new urgency" can be detected in Bede's later writings, a sharpening of his apocalyptic sense: "The history of his own days," he suggests, "is drawn into Bede's eschatological perspective."[64] The strongest impression created by the texts themselves, however, is one of consistency throughout Bede's career. One of the most eschatologically charged of Bede's statements is found in a relatively early work, his commentary on the first book of Samuel, written in 716. More and more, says Bede, one of the signs of the last times is becoming evident: as the Saviour predicted, and as the Evangelist recorded in Matt. 24:12, wickedness is being multiplied, and charity is growing cold.[65] In his commentary on Luke, however, also an early work, Bede refers to the same text of Matt. 24:12, clearly acknowledging that the sins of his own generation are to be followed by even worse offenses.[66] In the commentary on Genesis, written in the period 725-731 and hence belonging to the later stage of his career to which Markus refers, Bede's position is much the same. He comments once

---

63 *Epist.* 3.29, CCL 140:174-175 at 175.
64 Markus, *Bede and the Tradition of Ecclesiastical Historiography*, p. 14.
65 *In 1 Sam.* 4, CCL 119:221-222: "videat lector nec sine lacrimis rem lacrimis dignam contempletur quantum ecclesiae status ad peiora cotidie vel ut mitius dicam ad infirmiora gerenda devoluatur. ... Neque haec ita prosecutus sum quasi non et hodie multos existere multos semper extituros perfectos in fide et veritate crediderim sed quod maxima in parte viderim iam iamque instare tempora quae olim praedicta sunt in quibus abundante iniquitate refrigescat caritas multorum."
66 *In Luc.* 5, CCL 120:318-319: "licet mundi terminus olim praefinito sit venturus in tempore frigente tamen circa finem caritate multorum tanta crebrescet humani generis iniquitas ut merito debeat cum ipso quem inhabitat orbe deleri. Nam et nunc quidem innumeros adeo comesationi et ebrietati emptioni et venditioni ceterisque mundi rebus inhaerere videmus ut palam districti iudicis iram eos provocare non lateat sed tamen quod sine gravi maerore sapiens quisque saltim cogitare non valet peiora iam iamque superventura formidamus. Quod enim de una quondam peccatrice gente delenda dictum est, *necdum completa sunt peccata Amorreorum*, de tota procul dubio pravorum massa damnanda constat esse sentiendum."

again on the same Gospel text without giving any impression that events are coming to a climax. The increasing ruin of the world suggests that the Day of Judgment is approaching; even now we can catch a glimpse of the evening of the sixth age. In none of this, however, would Bede's language suggest that the last times are imminent.[67]

On a cursory view at least, some texts dating from Bede's later years could indeed suggest a mind, like Gregory the Great's, dominated by the evils of the age. One is his famous letter of 734, the last year of his life, to Egbert, bishop, afterwards archbishop, of York. Here, in fact, Bede sketches the broad outline of a society deep in the throes of a spiritual crisis. He begins by roundly condemning at least some of the bishops of his time for the company that they keep: "it is rumoured abroad about certain bishops that they serve Christ in such a fashion that they have with them no men of any religion or continence, but rather those who are given to laughter, jests, tales, feasting and drunkenness, and the other attractions of a lax life."[68] Presumably the behaviour of the bishops was no better than that of their attendants. But even more troubling than moral laxity was their failure in their official responsibilities. Quick to insist on the dues to which they were entitled, they were slow to provide, if they provided them at all, the spiritual services that the salvation of Christian people required. Indeed, says Bede, for the inhabitants of remote villages and hamlets, who frequently do not receive even the most elementary instruction in Christian life and doctrine, years can pass without a bishop ever putting in an appearance, although not one such village would ever be excused from the dues that the bishop or his agents demand.

Although it would not have completely solved the problem, Bede argues that, minimally at least, the number of bishops should be increased, and that they should be attached to established monasteries. If

---

67 See *In Gen.* 1, CCL 118A:38-39, where, comparing the six days of Creation to the six ages of the world, Bede says of the sixth day: "Cuius diei vesperam iam nunc adpropinquare cernimus, cum, *abunda*nte per omnia *iniquita*te *refrigescit caritas multorum.* Adveniet autem multo tenebrosior ceteris, cum, apparente homine peccati, filio iniquitatis qui extollitur et elevatur super omne quod dicitur Deus aut quod colitur. Tanta fuerit tribulatio ut in errorem inducantur si fieri potest, etiam electi." Cf. ibid. 2, CCL 118A:98: "Nam et hoc tempore consolatio bonorum est, cum viderint crebrescentibus mundi ruinis adpropinquare diem iudicii, in quo, consumpta universitate pravorum, ipsi cum Domino nova futuri seculi regna possideant."
68 *Epist. ad Ecgbertum* 4, Plummer, *Opera Historica* 1:407; EHD 1:800-801.

additional resources are necessary, says Bede, they could be obtained by attending to another pressing problem, the existence of "places, as we all know, allowed the name of monasteries by a most foolish manner of speaking, but having nothing at all of a monastic way of life." Under the pretext of piety, says Bede, laymen are often allowed to buy lands on which they establish institutions that are monasteries in name only. Setting themselves up as abbots, by bribery they manage to obtain royal edicts establishing their hereditary rights and excusing in perpetuity the services that would otherwise be incumbent on the land. These documents are often confirmed through the active connivance of bishops, abbots and other notable persons. "There are many and large places of this kind," says Bede, "which, as is commonly said, are useful neither to God nor man. ... If anyone should establish an episcopal see in those same places on account of the necessities of the times, he will be proved to incur no guilt of violation of duty, but rather to be doing an act of virtue."[69]

Wormald argues that, harsh as it may seem, Bede's judgment probably constitutes fair comment on the society of his time.[70] If so, as Wormald also acknowledges, it is important to recognize that the letter is not an entirely unbiased account. The remarks about family monasteries need to be read in light of the fact that Bede's only personal experience was that of a very different and competing brand of monasticism.[71] The complaints about bishops failing to meet the spiritual needs of the laity are also those of a competitor, a monk who felt that monasteries shared in the responsibility for this kind of ministry; and their proper appraisal requires acknowledging the difficulties involved in addressing the needs of a scattered rural population.[72] But of the

69   Ibid. 10 & 11, Plummer, *Opera Historica* 1:413-414; EHD 1:804, 804-805.
70   Patrick Wormald, "Bede, 'Beowulf' and the Conversion of the Anglo-Saxon Aristocracy," in *Bede and Anglo-Saxon England*, pp. 32-95 at 51-52.
71   Cf. Henry M.R.E. Mayr-Harting, *The Venerable Bede, the Rule of St. Benedict, and Social Class* (Jarrow, 1976), esp. p. 12; and Patrick Sims-Williams, *Religion and Literature in Western England: 600-800* (Cambridge, 1990), pp. 125-130. Wormald, "Bede, 'Beowulf' and the Conversion," p. 53, suggests a less than complete grasp of the situation on Bede's part: "the foundations he so much disliked were essentially expressions of the understandable sense of kindred in the Anglo-Saxon upper classes."
72   Cf. Sarah Foot, "Parochial Ministry in Early Anglo-Saxon England: The Role of Monastic Communities," *Studies in Church History* 26 (1989): 43-54; and Thomas L. Amos, "Monks and Pastoral Care in the Early Middle Ages," in *Religion, Culture, and Society in the Early Middle Ages: Studies in Honor of Richard E. Sullivan*,

sincerity of Bede's judgment there is no question; and rather than being an aberration, it is reflected in several other of his later works as well.[73] When the *Ecclesiastical History* is read in the light they collectively supply, Bede's concern about society's prospects is undeniable.

To Bede's mind a major turning point in the nation's fortunes seems to have occurred in 685, with King Ecgfrith's defeat by the Picts at Nechtansmere. "From this time," says Bede, "the hopes and strength of the English nation began to 'ebb and fall away.'"[74] In Bede's view, the history of the Anglo-Saxons, like that of the ancient Hebrews, was a tale of a chosen people that had often failed to be worthy of its divine calling. Not infrequently, therefore, the proudest achievements of past generations are held up before Bede's readers as both a measure of current degeneration and a call to reform.[75] This does not mean, however, that Bede saw Anglo-Saxon society as inexorably headed down a path of decline. He does record the appearance in 729 of two comets that terrified all observers: "One of them preceded the sun as it rose in the morning and the other followed it as it set at night, seeming to portend dire disaster to east and west alike." Whether the portent was fulfilled, at least partially, by the Saracen ravages in Gaul to which he refers shortly thereafter is not clear. He also comments on the inauspicious beginning to the reign of the current king of Northumbria, Ceolwulf, who assumed the throne in the same fateful year of 729, and he displays at the same time some anxiety as to what the future might hold: "Both the beginning and the course of his reign have been filled with so many and such serious commotions and setbacks that it is as yet impossible to

---

ed. Thomas F.X. Noble & John J. Contreni (Kalamazoo, 1987), pp. 165-180. The worldliness of early eighth-century bishops, amply demonstrated by the career of Wilfrid, also needs to be placed in context. Wormald, "Bede, 'Beowulf' and the Conversion," p. 55, observes: "as in Frankish Gaul, such secularity is best understood not as backsliding, but as a natural function of the place of bishops in society."

73 See, for example, *De templo* 2, CCL 119A:206-207; and *In Ezram et Neemiam* 2 & 3, CCL 119A:302-303, 359-360, 386. Cf. Thacker, "Bede's Ideal of Reform," pp. 130-153.

74 *HE* 4.26, p. 429.

75 Thacker, "Bede's Ideal of Reform," pp. 142-143. See, for example, *HE* 3.26, p. 310, where Bede praises the piety of Colman and his party, despite their endorsement of Irish practices on the Easter question. The point, even though implicit, is unmistakable. Plummer, *Opera Historica* 2:194, observes: "In the whole of this paragraph Bede is obliquely glancing at the ecclesiastical evils of his own time."

know what to say about them or to guess what the outcome will be."[76]
But any note of pessimism detected here has to be balanced against the
essentially positive picture of English society in the 720s and 730s that
the *Ecclesiastical History* provides. As Rosenthal puts it:

> Instead of a world of pathless desolation, with despair and depression as its
> inevitable psychological hallmarks, we find more than an occasional hint of
> peace, of settled order, of prosperity. ... The new era of faith was not
> going to be just a brief flicker in the dusk, saving men's souls as their
> bodies went under. It was more likely to be a joint step forward, a new and
> more spiritual world in which God's kingdom on earth would achieve a
> level of human order and prosperity that had been beyond the aspirations
> of the preceding generations.[77]

Particularly significant are the concluding thoughts of the *Ecclesiastical
History*, which invite us to look to the future with considerable hope. "In
these favourable times of peace and prosperity," Bede says, "many of
the Northumbrian race, both noble and simple, have laid aside their
weapons and taken the tonsure, preferring that they and their children
should take monastic vows rather than train themselves in the art of war.
What the result will be, a later generation will discover."[78]

In view of the tension with the letter to Egbert, it has been argued
that these latter comments are not to be taken at face value. The clue,
we are told, is in the final sentence, in which Bede points to results as
yet uncertain. The passage is to be read, therefore, as a veiled reference
to the abuses that he would criticize openly only later.[79] As one recent
commentator puts it, "the irony of these lines is not easily grasped without outside assistance." Had we not the letter to Egbert to guide us, the
"fleeting appearance" of pseudo-monasteries in book five of the *Ecclesiastical History* would probably escape detection. Indeed, "we might
easily reach the false conclusion that Bede foresaw an idyllic future
in which all Northumbrians laid down their weapons in order to live as

---

76 *HE* 5.23, pp. 557 & 559. In the continuation to the history Bede informs us, under
    the year 731, that "King Ceolwulf was captured and tonsured and then restored to
    his kingdom" (p. 573). This is the same "most glorious king Ceolwulf" (Praef.,
    p. 3) to whom the *Ecclesiastical History* is dedicated.
77 Rosenthal, "Bede's Ecclesiastical History," pp. 15-16; cf. Davidse, "Sense of
    History," p. 667.
78 *HE* 5.23, p. 561.
79 This has been the view of the editors of the text, from Plummer, *Opera Historica*
    2:343, to Colgrave and Mynors, p. 560n.

monks."[80] The disadvantage of this view, however, is that it requires us to see irony where absolutely nothing prepares us to recognize it. Much more likely, therefore, is the suggestion that would see in Bede's note of uncertainty, not a veiled criticism of monastic vocations, but a simple acknowledgment of the fact that the future is known to God alone. Bede ends his shorter chronicle with such a reference, and a parallel ending to the *Ecclesiastical History* would be entirely appropriate.[81] Both the *Ecclesiastical History* and the letter to Egbert are to be taken seriously, and if they are somewhat in tension it is because they offer us different glimpses of the same complex reality that was eighth-century Northumbria.[82] The result is a more subtle appraisal of the state of society at Bede's time of writing than would otherwise have been possible, one revealed as well in his description—essentially a balanced one—of the circumstances of the year 731, the year in which the *Ecclesiastical History* was completed:

> The Picts now have a treaty of peace with the English and rejoice to share in the catholic peace and truth of the Church universal. The Irish who live in Britain are content with their own territories and devise no plots or treachery against the English. Though, for the most part, the Britons oppose the English through their inbred hatred, and the whole state of the catholic Church by their incorrect Easter and their evil customs, yet being opposed by the power of God and man alike, they cannot obtain what they want in either respect. For although they are partly their own masters, yet they have also been brought partly under the rule of the English.[83]

Although this is a sober assessment, it is not an overwhelmingly negative one. It was clearly not written by a man expecting imminent disaster. It has virtually nothing in common with Gregory's letter to the church of Milan, and it is fully consistent with the reference to "favourable times of peace and prosperity" that follows directly. Despite their common interest in narrating modern, contemporary miracles, therefore, the backdrop against which Bede and Gregory the Great would have us view these wonders is fundamentally different in the two cases. Bede

---

80 Goffart, *Narrators of Barbarian History*, p. 255.
81 Markus, *Bede and the Tradition of Ecclesiastical Historiography*, p. 15; cf. Wallace-Hadrill, *Bede's Ecclesiastical History*, p. 200. Cf. also *Chronica Minora* = *De temporibus* 22, CCL 123C:611: "Reliquum sextae aetatis Deo soli patet."
82 Cf. Davidse, "Sense of History," pp. 667-669; Brown, *Bede the Venerable*, p. 80.
83 *HE* 5.23, p. 561.

does not disguise the problems of his society, nor does he hide from the human failings to which he and his contemporaries were subject. They appear in particularly sharp relief whenever he measures the church of his own day against the standards of the apostolic ideal or of the heroic age of Anglo-Saxon Christianity. But in Bede's mind these problems do not produce a sense of impending doom, nor do they tempt him to think that the end is quickly approaching and that judgment is imminent. The idea never seriously occurs to him.

4

The Purpose of Miracle

The influence of Gregory the Great on the thought of the Venerable Bede is nowhere clearer than in Bede's treatment of the role of miracles in the primitive church. Quoting Gregory extensively, Bede argues that, just as a garden requires special nurturing when first planted, so did the early church need to be watered by the grace of miracles: "ut ... ad fidem cresceret miraculis fuerat nutrienda." Like Gregory before him, Bede focuses on an essentially apologetic purpose for the miracles of the New Testament. Miracles were necessary to establish the faith. Now that it has been placed on a secure foundation, he states, they do not occur with the frequency they enjoyed earlier.[1]

When required by the context to comment on the purpose of Christ's miracles specifically, Bede's most favoured response is that they served to manifest his glory. They demonstrated his divinity, otherwise disguised by the assumption of human form.[2] If, despite this, Satan was still deluded enough to tempt evil men into crucifying the Saviour, it was only because he did not see how Christ's death would lead to his own damnation. It was not because he did not know he was the Christ.[3] Hence the point of the miracle at Cana (John 2:1-11) was to reveal Christ's status as the king of glory, the lord of heaven and earth who could command the very elements of nature; and the purpose of his miraculous cure of the paralytic (Mark 2:3-12), as the text of Scripture itself suggests, was to establish that he possessed the essentially divine power of forgiving sins.[4]

More generally, Bede states that the purpose of Christ's miracles was to substantiate his authority, to stimulate belief in him by confirming the

---

1   *In Marc.* 4, CCL 120:645-646. Cf. Gregory the Great, *Hom. in Evan.* 2.29.4, PL 76:1215-1216.
2   *Hom. Evan.* 1.8, CCL 122:58; *In 1 Sam.* 1, CCL 119:36: "filium pater incarnatum miraculis Deum verum demonstravit." Cf. *Exp. Act. Apost.* 10.36-37, CCL 121:53-54; *In Cant.* 6, CCL 119B:362-363; *In Tob.*, CCL 119B:7. Cf. also *In Abacuc*, CCL 119B:383, where he comments specifically on the miracles that accompanied Christ's Passion.
3   *In Marc.* 1, CCL 120:449.
4   *Hom. Evan.* 1.14, CCL 122:97, 103; *In Marc.* 1, CCL 120:455.

truth of his teaching.[5] Accordingly, immediately after the Sermon on the Mount, Christ proceeded to the healing of the leper, as reported in Matthew 8:1-3: "quae verbis docuit virtutibus credenda esse monstravit." The crowds who had heard his teaching on the mountain had been astonished at his words; as Scripture reports, he taught as one who had authority, not as one of the scribes. To convert astonishment into belief, however, Christ responded sympathetically to the leper who approached him, and cleansed him of his illness by the mere touch of his hand.[6] In Bede's judgment, the miracles performed by the apostles are to be conceived in a similar manner: they too were intended to attest to the truth of their message. Novel wonders authenticated novel teaching; the sick in body were cured to entice the sick in soul to the life-giving way of salvation.[7]

In view of their apologetic purpose, it may seem puzzling that at several points in the Gospels Christ enjoins silence on those who were either beneficiaries of his miracles or witnesses to them. In each case, however, Bede would tell us that puzzlement is alleviated when the circumstances are investigated more carefully. If Christ prohibited the demons he expelled from declaring his status as the Son of God (Mark 3:11-12), it was because of the unseemliness of having the Gospel proclaimed by agents of error. Their mixing of truth and falsehood aims only to further Satan's essentially evil purposes. If the apostles were consigned to silence in the period before the Passion (e.g. Mark 8:30), it was to ensure that the plan of salvation not be impeded. This required

---

5   See, for example, *In epist. 1 Ioh.* 1.2, CCL 121:285; and *In Prov.* 1, CCL 119B:59, where Bede comments on the miracle reported in Luke 7:11ff: "in ipsa etiam porta civitatis Naim mortuum resuscitans exemplo miraculi verba quae docuerat commendabat."

6   *In Cant.* 4, CCL 119B:290. Cf. *In Luc.* 2, CCL 120:110, where Bede comments on the expulsion of the demon in Luke 4:35: "*Et cum proiecisset illum daemonium in medium exiit ab illo nihilque illum nocuit.* Divina permissione liberandus a daemone homo proicitur in medium ut virtus patefacta salvatoris plures ad fidem viamque salutis invitet."

7   *In Cant.* 2, CCL 119B:248-249; cf. *In Abacuc*, CCL 119B:397; *In Luc.* 3, CCL 120:194; *In Marc.* 1, CCL 120:470. Cf. also *Exp. Act. Apost.* 20.9, CCL 121:81, where Bede states that in raising Eutychus from the dead (Acts 20:7-12) St Paul confirmed the truth of his message; and *In Cant.* 6, CCL 119B:368, where he says of the biblical saints in general: "Hi itaque quam vera de Deo dixerint testantur miracula quia talia per illum non facerent nisi de illo vera narrarent." This latter passage is a quotation from Gregory the Great, *Hom. in Ezech.* 2.3.23, CCL 142:255.

not only Christ's coming into the world, but his death as an atoning sacrifice at the hands of evil men unable to recognize him for what he was.[8] Perhaps especially puzzling at first glance is an episode like the one recorded in Mark 1:43-45, where word of Christ's miracle got out despite his prohibition, as if his wishes counted for naught. But Bede informs us that events unfolded in the way they did to convey a particular message, and we must not think that the Saviour was unable to ensure that his will be done. He desired the miracle to be hidden to provide an edifying example to the saints. Individuals possessed of the grace of miracles should wish to avoid the renown they can bring; it constitutes a serious threat to humility. His miracle became known nonetheless to illustrate what the providential scheme requires, all private desires notwithstanding. The larger purpose miracles are intended to achieve would be frustrated if knowledge of them were successfully suppressed.[9]

In addition to their apologetic purpose, of course, Bede also acknowledges and expounds at some length the deeper allegorical significance of the miracles recorded in the New Testament. Scripture itself hints at such significance, and in exploring it further Bede simply follows in the footsteps of the great Latin Fathers from whom he derived much of his inspiration. The key that unlocks the mysteries behind the letter of the text is the kind of figural thinking discussed earlier.[10] Events recorded in Scripture function as signs; they point beyond themselves by providing images of spiritual truth that one grasps by identifying the appropriate analogies. At the literal level the miracle at Cana demonstrates Christ's divine power. At the allegorical level, however, the

---

8 *In Marc.* 1, CCL 120:468-469.
9 Ibid. CCL 120:451-452. Cf. *In Marc.* 2, CCL 120:523, 535-536, where Bede comments on Mark 7:24 and on Mark 8:22-26 respectively. Elsewhere Bede identifies a rather different although not contradictory spiritual message behind similar injunctions to silence. See ibid. CCL 120:500-501, 527. In the first of these passages he considers the raising of Jairus's daughter (Mark 5:21-43) in the context of the other resurrections performed by Christ; in the second he follows Augustine in his treatment of Mark 7:31-37, the cure of the man who was deaf and dumb. In the latter episode we read that, the more Christ enjoined silence on the witnesses to the cure, "the more zealously they proclaimed it." Says Bede: "Si sciebat eos sicut ille qui notas habebat et praesentes et futuras hominum voluntates tanto magis praedicaturos quanto magis ne praedicarent eis praecipiebat, ut quid hoc praecipiebat, nisi quia pigris volebat ostendere quanto studiosius quantoque ferventius eum praedicare debeant quibus iubet ut praedicent quando illi qui prohibebantur tacere non poterant?"
10 See above, pp. 34-36.

changing of water into wine signifies the transformation of the Old Law in the new Christian dispensation. The letter of its provisions has passed away; the deeper spiritual meaning, hitherto veiled, has been revealed.[11] A similar lesson is conveyed by the feeding of the five thousand. The five loaves are the five books of Moses; the two fishes represent the Psalms and the Prophets. Christ blessed and multiplied the loaves and fishes, therefore, because it was in him that all of Scripture achieved its fulfillment.[12]

In general the miracles of physical healing worked by Christ announce on the allegorical level his ability to cure the spiritual ailments that afflict humankind. Hence the deaf mute of Mark 7 represents those with neither ears to hear the word of God nor mouths to speak it; and the blind man of Mark 8 is a figure of those who, spiritually sightless, have stumbled far from the pathway of truth.[13] The three resurrections that Christ performed proclaim—each in its own way—the spiritual regeneration of those dead in sin. His raising of the daughter of Jairus, the ruler of the synagogue, signifies Christ's ability to restore those whose offense is limited to their having consented to sin, and taken delight in the prospect of sinful conduct. The dead girl had not yet been removed for burial when the Saviour restored her to life, but was stretched out in her own home. She represents those who, without actually having committed sinful acts, have sinned in their hearts. The

---

11 *Hom. Evan.* 1.14, CCL 122:97. Cf. *In Cant.* 3, CCL 119B:258-259; *In Ezram et Neemiam* 3, CCL 119A:351.

12 See *In Marc.* 2, CCL 120:513, where Bede comments on Mark 6:30-43. Cf. *In Luc.* 3, CCL 120:199-200; and *Hom. Evan.* 2.2, CCL 122:196, where he comments on the versions of the miracle in Luke 9:10-17 and John 6:1-14 respectively. In the first of these latter passages the allegory is changed somewhat, for the two fishes represent the two Testaments. Its primary meaning, however, remains the same. See also *In Marc.* 2, CCL 120:527, where Bede refers to the cognate miracle, the feeding of the four thousand, and explains: "Hoc vero typice inter hanc refectionem et illam quinque panum ac duorum piscium distat quod ibi littera veteris instrumenti spiritali gratia plena esse signata est hic autem novi veritas ac gratia testamenti fidelibus ministranda monstrata est." Creider, "Bede's Understanding of the Miraculous," pp. 248-249, points out that frequently much of Bede's interpretation of a miracle is based on details incidental to the miracle itself. The present case provides a good illustration of the point.

13 *In Marc.* 2, CCL 120:534; cf. *In Marc.* 2, CCL 120:525. On the healing of the man who was deaf and dumb, see also *Hom. Evan.* 2.6, CCL 122:220. On the healing of the blind, see *In Marc.* 3, CCL 120:567; *In Luc.* 2 & 5, CCL 120:105-106, 331; *In Ezram et Neemiam* 3, CCL 119A:350.

THE PURPOSE OF MIRACLE

son of the widow of Nain, however, depicts a more serious sinner, one who has sinned in act as well as in thought. His body had been displayed to public view, and had been carried outside the city gates. Yet Christ revived the young man, and restored him to his mother's bosom as a repentant sinner is restored to the unity of the church. Lazarus, who was called forth from the tomb, symbolizes the habitual offender, buried under a heap of sins. He had been dead for four days, and was stinking, because heinous sin is customarily accompanied by an evil reputation. However, even the notorious sinner can be restored to spiritual life if pious thoughts, like the devout sisters of Lazarus, are present to intercede with the Redeemer.[14] Bede develops the spiritual meaning of these and other miracles at length. Allegorical interpretation is as central to his approach to the Bible as it is to Gregory's, and it occupies as prominent a position in his exegesis. However, he never presents the allegorical meaning of Christ's miracles as the reason for their occurrence in the first place. Although at a deeper level they are an important source of teaching on both morals and doctrine, it is always their apologetic purpose that Bede offers as their rationale: miracles occurred to substantiate the truth of the Gospel, and to stimulate acceptance of the new faith.

Conceivably, one might argue, a balanced view of the theology of miracles would have to take account of their being a reward for faith as well as a remedy for disbelief, a fact that Bede himself seems to acknowledge at one point in his commentary on Mark.[15] However, the isolated nature of the comment is significant, indicative of a perspective on Christ's earthly ministry quite different than that of some modern scholars. In a recent work Kee has pointed to what he regards as Christ's refusal to corroborate his own authority. Christ resorted to miracles only to alleviate human suffering, says Kee, to heal the sick and free the demon-possessed, never merely to establish his heavenly credentials. In confirmation he refers to the Lord's pronouncement in

14 *In Marc.* 2, CCL 120:500-501; *In Luc.* 3, CCL 120:193. Cf. ibid. 2, CCL 120:157-158. The same general point, that resurrection from the dead is a type of spiritual regeneration, applies to St Peter's raising of Tabitha (Acts 9:36-41) and St Paul's raising of Eutychus (Acts 20:7-12). Hence Eutychus symbolizes the lapsed Christian. See *In Ezram et Neemiam* 1, CCL 119A:275-276; and *Exp. Act. Apost.* 20.9, CCL 121:81.2
15 *In Marc.* 2, CCL 120:523.

Luke 11:29: "This generation is an evil generation; it seeks a sign, but no sign shall be given to it except the sign of Jonah"; and then explains:

Jonah's story concerns the divine summons to a man to declare God's message among non-Israelites, in the city of Nineveh. What constitutes Jonah's "sign", according to Luke, was not a miracle, but a call to repentance—to which the Ninevites responded in faith. Clearly the point is that the message is self-authenticating; miracles are not going to be performed in order to confirm what Jesus is doing. His miracles are enacted in order to meet human need, thereby pointing to the larger, impending reality: the establishment of God's rule in the world, and the calling together of a new covenant people.[16]

To Bede the point was equally clear, but significantly different. Earlier in the chapter, in Luke 11:15-16, we are told that some accused Christ of casting out demons through Beelzebul, while others, seeking to test him, sought a sign from heaven. It is to these latter people, Bede says, that Christ responds in verse 29. Rather than a sign from heaven they would be unworthy to receive, he will show them only the sign of Jonah. Shipwrecked and devoured by the great fish, but ultimately freed from the abyss and the jaws of death, Jonah is a figure of Christ's incarnation, not his divinity, a sign of his passion, not his glorification. To his disciples, however, Christ did indeed give a sign from heaven. He provided them with an image of his eternal glory in the Transfiguration, and later he appeared to them in his glorified body after the resurrection.[17]

As Bede sees it, therefore, the point is not that signs would not be provided in confirmation of Christ's divine status, but rather that they would not be performed on demand for those unworthy to receive them. Indeed, to Bede, as to Augustine and Gregory the Great, the matter seems to have admitted no doubt whatever. The miracles of the New Testament were manifestly designed to substantiate the truth of the Gospel. This was their most obvious feature. More specifically, their role was to shock, to stupefy, to charge with awe, and hence to produce a cast of mind receptive to the Christian message. When Peter and John cured the lame man who lay begging for alms at the gate of the temple, those who witnessed the event "were filled with wonder and amazement"

---

16 Howard Clark Kee, *Medicine, Miracle and Magic in New Testament Times* (Cambridge, 1986), p. 80.
17 *In Luc.* 4, CCL 120:237-238.

(Acts 3:10). Peter capitalized on the opportunity by addressing a sermon to them; and as Scripture subsequently informs us (Acts 4:4), "many of those who heard the word believed."[18] When Christ rebuked the demon and expelled him from the man in the synagogue, the bystanders "were all amazed, so that they questioned among themselves, saying, 'What is this? A new teaching! With authority he commands even the unclean spirits, and they obey him'" (Mark 1:27). Says Bede:

> Having witnessed his miraculous power, they were astonished at the newness of the Lord's teaching. Through what they had seen they were roused to investigate what they had heard. Indeed, it was for this purpose that miracles were performed, whether by the Lord himself in his assumed humanity or by the power that he committed to the disciples. The Gospel of the Kingdom of God that was being proclaimed would more surely be believed when those who promised future heavenly joys to the inhabitants of earth demonstrated on earth itself works both heavenly and divine.[19]

Occasionally Bede seems to suggest that the miracles reported in the New Testament were compelling proof of the claims of the Gospel. Hence at one point the Jews, who refused to acknowledge Christ despite his miracles, are castigated for their blindness;[20] and at another it is suggested that denying assent to the truth to which miracles attested would have been scarcely rational.[21] It is unlikely that such statements reflect Bede's considered opinion. Elsewhere he registers the existence of disbelief much more dispassionately, in partial acknowledgment

18 *In Abacuc*, CCL 119B:400.
19 *In Marc.* 1, CCL 120:448: "Visa virtute miraculi novitatem dominicae ammirantur doctrinae atque ad inquisitionem eorum quae audierant per ea quae viderant excitantur quia nimirum ad hoc fiebant signa quae vel ipse dominus in assumpto homine faciebat vel discipulis facere dedit ut per haec evangelio regni Dei quod praedicabatur certius crederetur dum hi qui caelestia terrigenis gaudia futura promittebant caelestia in terris ac divina opera monstrabant."
20 *In Luc.* 6, CCL 120:407: "Quanta ergo caecitas Iudaeorum qui tot per dominum virtutibus factis tantis in morte eius apparentibus signis credere respuerunt et insensibiliores gentilibus Deum glorificare vel timere contempserunt." Cf. ibid. 5, CCL 120:346, where Bede speaks of the madness of the Pharisees; and *In Marc.* 1, CCL 120:474-475, where the reaction of the scribes before Christ's miracles is characterized as one of willful disbelief.
21 See *In Abacuc*, CCL 119B:401, where he refers to people who, "ab humana ratione alienati, conparati sunt iumentis insipientibus et similes facti sunt illis. Tales etsi sanctorum virtutibus conturbati sunt et commoti, nec deum tamen timere nec eius facta adnuntiare vel intellegere voluerunt."

perhaps of the inherent ambiguity of miracles, and that they could give rise to rival interpretations.[22] Indeed, not even the disciples were able to appreciate the full significance of what they witnessed. In the miracle of the loaves and the fishes, says Bede, Christ demonstrated his creative lordship; in calming the storm he showed his mastery of nature; in walking on the waters he revealed himself to have a body free from the weight of sin. Despite all this, however, the disciples were still not able to grasp that he was God in human form. They were astonished by the wonders he performed, but were not able to see them for what they were: a revelation of his divine majesty.[23]

Although he does not address the matter explicitly, Bede seems to acknowledge that by themselves the miracles performed by Christ and the apostles would have been largely without effect. This had been openly stated by Augustine and by Gregory the Great, for grace was necessary if the veil of error was to be lifted and the truth of the Gospel acknowledged.[24] Even so, however, miracles had an essential role to play in winning converts to the new faith, a role that Bede informs us clearly extended into post-apostolic times. Indeed, says Bede, as a result of the miracles performed by the *doctores sancti*, the entire world has been brought to the faith of Christ.[25] At first glance at least the great persecution seems to have been an unmitigated disaster for the early church. But tragedy was turned to triumph when the miracles of those who had been martyred brought many to the faith.[26] Indeed, the martyrs worked miracles in both life and death, and the effect frequently was to achieve the conversion of unbelievers, often the very persecutors themselves.[27] Hence right at the outset of the *Ecclesiastical History*

---

22   Cf. *Expl. Apoc.* 2.9, PL 93:155, where he acknowledges without comment that some responded to Christ's miracles with belief, others with disbelief; and *In Cant.* 5, CCL 119B:330, where he recognizes a rival, and to his mind simply false, interpretation of the miracle at Pentecost.

23   *In Marc.* 2, CCL 120:518-519.

24   Cf. Creider, "Bede's Understanding of the Miraculous," pp. 268-269.

25   *Hom. Evan.* 2.11, CCL 122:257-258.

26   *In Ezram et Neemiam* 3, CCL 119A:377-378.

27   This is the lesson taught by several of the entries in Bede's *Martyrology*: see Quentin, *Martyrologes historiques du moyen âge*, pp. 17-119; Dubois & Renaud, *Edition pratique des martyrologes*. See especially the entries for St Peter the exorcist and St Marcellinus (June 2), Quentin, p. 82, Dubois & Renaud, p. 100; St Anatholia (July 9), Quentin, pp. 96-97, Dubois & Renaud, p. 122; Sts Fausta and Evilasius (September 20), Quentin, pp. 72-73, Dubois & Renaud, p. 174; and Sts

Bede describes how St Alban's executioner was shaken by one of his miracles: "he threw away his sword which he was carrying ready drawn and cast himself down at the saint's feet, earnestly praying that he might be judged worthy to be put to death either with the martyr whom he himself had been ordered to execute, or else in his place." The man's conversion is clearly implied. Alban's miracles were not without their effect on the executioner's superior either, although whether he actually converted to the Christian faith is not certain.[28]

One clear implication of St Alban's example is that miracles had a role to play in the establishment of the English church, the primary theme of Bede's *Ecclesiastical History*. In his mission to Britain to rid the island of Pelagianism, Bishop Germanus of Auxerre cured a young girl of her blindness. "The parents rejoiced while the people were overawed by the miracle," says Bede. "From that day the evil doctrine was so utterly banished from the minds of them all that they thirsted eagerly after the teaching of the bishops."[29] Later on miracles were equally important in achieving the conversion of the Anglo-Saxons. Hence Bede quotes extensively from Gregory the Great's famous letter of June 601 to Augustine of Canterbury, a letter in which Augustine is admonished lest his miracles, essential for the conversion of the Anglo-Saxon people, become an occasion for vainglory:

> You should rejoice because the souls of the English are drawn by outward miracles to inward grace; but you should fear lest among these signs which are performed the weak mind be raised up by self-esteem, and so the very cause by which it is raised to outward honour lead through vainglory to its inward fall. ... So it remains, most dear brother, that amidst those outward

---

Caesarius and Julian (November 1), Quentin, pp. 64-65, Dubois & Renaud, p. 199. Miracles effecting the conversion of unbelievers are also recorded in the entries for Pope St Clement (November 23), Quentin, pp. 68-69, Dubois & Renaud, p. 212; and for St Victoria (December 23), Quentin, p. 96, Dubois & Renaud, p. 228.

28 *HE* 1.7, pp. 33 & 35.

29 Ibid. 1.18, p. 59. A little further on in the same chapter, having described some additional incidents, at least one of them miraculous in nature, Bede says: "Quibus ita gestis, innumera hominum eodem die ad Dominum turba conversa est" (p. 60). Three chapters later he informs us of the consequences that ensued when Germanus healed the son of Elafius, a local chieftain, of a withered knee: "Inplentur populi stupore miraculi, et in pectoribus omnium fides catholica inculcata firmatur" (*HE* 1.21, p. 66). Cf. *Chronica Maiora = De temp. ratione* 66.491, CCL 123B:518, where Bede says of the combined mission of bishops Germanus of Auxerre and Lupus of Troyes: "Confirmant antistites fidem verbo veritatis simul et miraculorum signis."

deeds which you perform through the Lord's power you should always judge your inner self carefully, and carefully note within yourself what you are and how great is the grace shown to that people for whose conversion you have received the gift of working miracles. ... These gifts have been conferred not on you, but on those for whose salvation they have been granted you.[30]

Although a clearer endorsement of the role of miracles in the conversion of the *Angli* would be hard to imagine, Rosenthal has argued that they are conspicuous by their absence in Bede's narrative itself. The majority of the miracles in the *Historia Ecclesiastica* are to be found in the latter pages of the book, not the early sections where the story of the conversion is related. In Rosenthal's judgment this means that Bede actually rejected an apologetic purpose for miracles in the Anglo-Saxon context: "They were not to *prove* God's dispensation. They were rather to enrich it, to revitalize it for those who had *already* received it." Indeed, he argues that an apologetic role for miracles would have been irreconcilable with conversion as Bede conceived it: "Conversion was for Bede a rational or a spiritual process, whereas miracles were wonders to be savored by those who had *already* joined the elite."[31]

Rosenthal is partly right in this and partly wrong. There are indeed proportionately more miracle stories in books four and five of the *Ecclesiastical History* than there are in books one and two;[32] and Bede clearly does conceive of many of these as having happened for the benefit of people who already were believers. This is an issue to which

30 *HE* 1.31, pp. 109-111 (revised); cf. Gregory the Great, *Epist.* 11.36, CCL 140A: 925-929 at 926-927. In his biography of Gregory the Great Bede quotes from the famous passage of the *Moralia* in which Gregory rejoices in the conversion of the Anglo-Saxons: "'Lo, the mouth of Britain, which once knew only how to gnash its barbarous teeth, has long since begun to sing the praises of God with the alleluia of the Hebrews.'" He then states: "Quibus verbis beatus Gregorius hoc quoque declarat, quia sanctus Augustinus et socii eius non sola praedicatione verborum sed etiam caelestium ostensione signorum gentem Anglorum ad agnitionem veritatis perducebant." *HE* 2.1, pp. 130-131 (translation revised); cf. *Mor.* 27.11.21, CCL 143B:1346.

31 Rosenthal, "Bede's Use of Miracles," pp. 330 & 333. Cf. Claudio Leonardi, "Il Venerabile Beda e la cultura del secolo VIII," in *I problemi dell'occidente nel secolo VIII* (Spoleto, 1973), pp. 603-658 at 638-639; and Lellia Cracco Ruggini, "Il miracolo nella cultura del tardo impero: concetto e funzione," in *Hagiographie, cultures et sociétés, IVe-XIIe siècles* (Paris, 1981), pp. 161-202 at 166.

32 See below, pp. 164-165.

we must return.[33] But it is mistaken to think that he saw no role for miracles in the conversion of his own people. As Rosenthal acknowledges, the most important conversion in the history of the Anglo-Saxon church was that of King Aethelbert of Kent, and here the miracles of Augustine and his companions played a decisive role. "At last the king ... believed and was baptised," says Bede, "being attracted by the pure life of the saints and by their most precious promises, whose truth they confirmed by performing many miracles."[34] Rosenthal argues that "the miracles were in confirmation, i.e., to verify what the missionaries *had already* exemplified; to use the terminology of the social sciences they were no more than a 'dependant variable.'"[35] However, this seems a perverse way of denying miracles efficacy in the conversion process as Bede describes it. Of course miracles were in confirmation; no more conceivably could have been expected of them. A miracle standing alone, independent of any teaching or preaching, might have astonished onlookers and stimulated a desire for conversion. But it would have conveyed no information whatever about the contents of the new faith. Central to the conversion process was the preaching of the Gospel. The role of miracles was to ensure that the message be believed.[36]

Given the information supplied in his prose biography of the saint, it is clear that, as Bede conceives it, the apologetic role of miracles continued at least up to the time of St Cuthbert. In the period before his conversion to the monastic life, Cuthbert's prayers were once efficacious in calming stormy winds that had threatened to carry a party of monks out to sea. The effect on some bystanders was immediate: "When the countryfolk saw this, they were ashamed of their own unbelief, but forthwith they duly praised the faith of the venerable Cuthbert, and thereafter never ceased to praise it."[37] Conceivably Bede would have us understand that the apologetic role of miracles extended into his own

---

33 See below, pp. 140-153.
34 *HE* 1.26, p. 77. Cf. ibid. 2.6, p. 154, where we read of the conversion of Aethelbert's successor, Eadbald. The precipitating cause was a miraculous vision experienced by Archbishop Laurence; see above, p. 44.
35 Rosenthal, "Bede's Use of Miracles," p. 334.
36 Cf. Creider, "Bede's Understanding of the Miraculous," pp. 288-289.
37 *VCP*, chap. 3, p. 165. Later Bede suggests that, by Cuthbert's own admission, his miracles served to confirm the faith: "solebat enim sepe quia laeti vultus et affabilis erat ad confirmandam fidem audientium, aliqua etiam de eis quae ipse credendo optinuerit in medium proferre" (chap. 19, pp. 220-222).

time as well, and was the primary reason for his recording contemporaneous wonders in the *Ecclesiastical History*. Like Gregory the Great, he may have regarded modern miracles as necessary to complete the work of conversion in the Anglo-Saxon church.[38] Stephens has argued that the *Ecclesiastical History* is to be read as a Christian replacement for the epic; the wonders it contains demonstrate that "Christian fame is greater than pagan fame." To Mayr-Harting the point is similar; Bede's contemporary audience would have understood from his miracle stories that "Christian medicine could work as well as pagan magic."[39] In Creider's view, although there were significant differences between them, to Bede's mind the miracles of the early church and the miracles of his own day (in part at least) were united by the same rationale. They were the work of the same Holy Spirit; when necessary, therefore, they could still occur "to ensure the conversion of the heathen."[40] Plausible though it may seem, however, this is a line of argument that cannot survive close scrutiny. It lends a greater degree of coherence to Bede's thought than the texts themselves would warrant.

The *Ecclesiastical History* does not have to be read particularly carefully to reveal that in 731, at Bede's time of writing, the conversion of the Anglo-Saxons was still a recent phenomenon. Bede's own kingdom of Northumbria had embraced the faith a mere century earlier, in 627, when King Edwin, his nobles and a large number of common people had all received holy baptism.[41] Elsewhere the experience was an even fresher memory. The East Saxons were not converted until the 650s,[42] and the kingdom of the South Saxons remained pagan until the 670s or 680s, when Wilfrid evangelized them.[43] Some scattered observations on Bede's part suggest as well that, in addition to being recent, the conversion remained incomplete. Resentment of the newfangled religion could run deep, as further details of the example from the life of the young St Cuthbert referred to above indicate. Although the miracle induced a change of heart, initially the local population had been unmoved by Cuthbert's rebuke and jeered when contrary winds threat-

---

38 See *Signs of Sanctity*, Chap. 2.
39 Stephens, "Bede's Ecclesiastical History," esp. p. 6; Mayr-Harting, *Coming of Christianity to England*, p. 47.
40 Creider, "Bede's Understanding of the Miraculous," p. 291.
41 *HE* 2.14, p. 186.
42 Ibid. 3.22, pp. 280-284.
43 Ibid. 4.13, p. 372.

ened to carry the monks out to sea: "'Let no man pray for them, and may God have no mercy on any one of them, for they have robbed men of their old ways of worship, and how the new worship is to be conducted nobody knows.'"[44] Among many, adherence to the new faith was tenuous at best. Hence while he was prior at Melrose, Bede tells us, Cuthbert had to deal with the problem of paganized Christians who were quick to defect under adverse circumstances:

> Many of them profaned the faith they held by wicked deeds, and some of them also at the time of the plague, forgetting the sacred mystery of the faith into which they had been initiated, took to the delusive cures of idolatry (*erratica idolatriae medicamina*), as though by incantations or amulets or any other mysteries of devilish art, they could ward off a blow sent by God the creator (*quasi missam a Deo conditore plagam per incantationes vel alligaturas, vel alia quaelibet demoniacae artis archana cohibere valerent*).[45]

The plague in question was undoubtedly the epidemic of 664, which, "raging far and wide with cruel devastation," carried off a great many victims, among them Bishop Tuda of Lindisfarne.[46] It also occasioned the apostasy of Sigehere, king of Essex, thereby revealing that the recent conversion of the East Saxons had been superficial at best. Bede tells us that "the king himself and the majority of both commons and nobles loved this present life, seeking no other and not even believing in any future existence; so they began to restore the derelict temples and to worship images, as if they could protect themselves by such means from the plague."[47] Fortunately, Sigehere's colleague and co-ruler, King Sebbi, held constant in this time of trouble. But royal tergiversation, with all the consequences that ensued for the rest of the population, was by no means an isolated phenomenon. An additional example is that of Redwald, king of the East Angles, whose initiation to the Christian faith while he was in Kent turned out to be shortlived:

> On his return home, he was seduced by his wife and by certain evil teachers and perverted from the sincerity of his faith, so that his last state

---

44 *VCP*, chap. 3, p. 165. On this episode see Rosalind Hill, "Bede and the Boors," in *Famulus Christi*, pp. 93-105.

45 *VCP*, chap. 9, pp. 184-185. Cf. *HE* 4.27, p. 432.

46 *HE* 3.27, pp. 310-312. Cf. Clare Stancliffe, "Cuthbert and the Polarity between Pastor and Solitary," in *St Cuthbert, His Cult and His Community*, pp. 21-44 at 30-31.

47 *HE* 3.30, p. 323.

was worse than his first. After the manner of the ancient Samaritans, he seemed to be serving both Christ and the gods whom he had previously served; in the same temple he had one altar for the Christian sacrifice and another small altar on which to offer victims to devils.[48]

As the details indicate, Redwald's case is really one of religious syncretism rather than conversion and apostasy. It is also earlier than the examples given above, dating from the late sixth or early seventh century, and less compelling for that reason.[49] But it does serve to illustrate something of the power of paganism as a religious force, and other sources from the seventh and eighth centuries confirm that that power clearly lasted well into Bede's lifetime. Sacrifice to idols, divination and augury were all forbidden by Theodore's Penitential. In 747 the Council of Clovesho condemned the same *incantationes* and *fylacteria* denounced by Bede.[50] The situation elsewhere was not all that different.[51] Syncretism of the kind practised by Redwald was later encountered by St Boniface in the twin rulers Dettic and Deorulf, although Willibald informs us that Boniface dealt with it effectively.[52] Both in Anglo-Saxon England and on the continent conversion was a

---

48 Ibid. 2.15, p. 191. Cf. Hans-Joachim Diesner, "Inkarnationsjahre, 'Militia Christi' und anglische Königsporträts bei Beda Venerabilis," *Mittellateinisches Jahrbuch* 16 (1981): 17-34, esp. 22. Bede's condemnation of Redwald is harsh, an assessment that Diesner suggests is less than fair.

49 See Colgrave & Mynors, *HE*, p. 176n. The dates of Redwald's life and reign are uncertain, but they extend up to 616 at least.

50 For these and additional examples, see Plummer, *Opera Historica* 2:59-60. See also Colgrave, "Bede's Miracle Stories," pp. 202-203.

51 See, for example, J.M. Wallace-Hadrill, *The Frankish Church* (Oxford, 1983), pp. 17-36. Recently Valerie I.J. Flint, *The Rise of Magic in Early Medieval Europe* (Princeton, 1991), has argued that the practice of pagan magic continued largely unimpaired in the early Middle Ages: "To suggest that we are concerned here mainly, or even partly, with 'pagan survivals' is to put the matter altogether too feebly. This is not a case of faint and lingering traces and last gasps, but of a whole alternative world of intercession" (p. 69). The issue of "pagan survivals" is more complex than it may at first seem. On the shifting boundaries by which judgments can be bedevilled, see R.A. Markus, *The End of Ancient Christianity* (Cambridge, 1990), esp. pp. 8-9.

52 Willibald, *Vita S. Bonifatii*, chap. 6, ed. Wilhelm Levison (1905; repr. Hannover, 1977), p. 26: "eosque a sacrilega idulorum censura, qua sub quodam christianitatis nomine male abusi sunt, evocavit." Further on in the same chapter (pp. 30-31) we learn that, after his second trip to Rome and consecration there as bishop in 722, Boniface had to deal with pagan/Christian syncretism on a large scale among the Hessians.

protracted affair, and both in Bede's time and later pagan survivals and backsliding were common.

Paradoxically, however, these are conclusions to which we are driven despite Bede, not because of him. Bede may provide some of the relevant evidence, but his own point of view is really quite different. Unlike Paul the Deacon or Gregory of Tours, who encourage few illusions about the Christianization of their contemporary societies, Bede chooses to present the conversion of the Anglo-Saxons essentially as a once-for-all phenomenon. As Wormald puts it: "Apart from the famous passage on the tribal origins of the Angles, Saxons and Jutes, a few shards of Kentish tradition, and a snippet of Northumbrian tribal pride concerning the deeds of King Aethelfrith, conversion for Bede is where the story of the Anglo-Saxons begins, and thereafter it is a story of saints, not sinners." The result is that Bede has no option but to treat a case like Redwald's as first of all an isolated instance, and secondly an example of apostasy rather than partial and incomplete adherence to Christianity. His perspective, as Wormald goes on to say, precludes any serious consideration of the "extent to which the Anglo-Saxons remained tied, by custom or memory, to their past."[53]

It has sometimes been observed that Bede seems uninterested in paganism, and chooses to tell us relatively little about it.[54] All things considered, this assessment is probably not too wide of the mark. The chapter of the *Ecclesiastical History* devoted to Edwin's council does convey some interesting and important information. We learn of pagan priests, and of some of the rules by which their conduct was governed. Hence we are told that "a high priest ... was not allowed to carry arms or to ride except on a mare," taboos that Coifi, the chief priest, violated when he opted for Christianity. Of pagan theology we are told next to nothing, although the parable of the hall and the sparrow, related by one of the king's chief men and the most famous part of the chapter, reveals the absence of a concept of the afterlife:

> It [the sparrow] enters in at one door and quickly flies out through the other. For the few moments it is inside, the storm and wintry tempest cannot touch it, but after the briefest moment of calm, it flits from your

---

53 Wormald, "Bede, 'Beowulf' and the Conversion," p. 59.
54 See, for example, Audrey L. Meaney, "Bede and Anglo-Saxon Paganism," *Parergon* n.s. 3 (1985): 1-29. Meaney argues that, although he does not tell us as much as he presumably knew, what he does say is essentially accurate.

sight, out of the wintry storm and into it again. So this life of man appears but for a moment; what follows or indeed what went before, we know not at all. If this new doctrine [Christianity] brings us more certain information, it seems right that we should accept it.[55]

In its own right this is significant and instructive. But one could certainly wish for more, and there is little to be gleaned from the rest of Bede's account.[56]

In his works on chronology Bede tells us that the Romans associated both the days of the week and some of the months of the year with the gods of the pantheon,[57] but this is all that he has to say about the deities of classical religion. A discussion in *De temporum ratione* leaves us somewhat better informed about Anglo-Saxon paganism, although the amount learned is still relatively modest.[58] Among other things we read that February was called *Solmonath*, the month of cakes, after the offerings that were made to the gods at that time; and that March and April were named *Hredmonath* and *Eosturmonath* respectively, after the goddesses Hreda and Eostre, to whom festivals were then dedicated. Eostre, Bede goes on to say, has lent her name to the Easter season, the ancient and familiar words now being filled with new meaning.

If the sum total of information provided is disappointing, Wallace-Hadrill suggests that it is because Bede was following the conventions of ecclesiastical history. No matter how tenaciously it was held, he says, ecclesiastical historians were incapable of taking paganism, especially Germanic paganism, seriously. It was not a subject worthy of their attention. "If Bede had been writing a history of the English people, as distinct from their ecclesiastical history, he could scarcely have avoided some treatment of their paganism as part and parcel of their life, not only past but present. As it was, he could and did avoid it."[59] A more likely explanation, I think, is that, worthy or not, Bede simply did not

---

55 *HE* 2.13, p. 185.
56 From Gregory the Great's letter to Mellitus, which Bede quotes, one learns of idols, of the temples that housed them, and of cattle slaughtered in sacrifice. Bede also includes the letter in which Pope Boniface V preaches to King Edwin of Northumbria on the foolishness of idolatry. Cf. *HE* 1.30 & 2.10, pp. 106-108 & 168-170.
57 *De temporibus* 4 & 6, CCL 123C:586 & 589; *De temp. ratione* 8 & 12, CCL 123B:300-302 & 320-323.
58 See *De temp. ratione* 15, CCL 123B:331-332.
59 J.M. Wallace-Hadrill, "Bede and Plummer," in *Famulus Christi*, pp. 366-385; and in his *Early Medieval History*, pp. 76-95 at 81. Cf. Markus, *Bede and the Tradition of Ecclesiastical Historiography*, p. 10.

see paganism as a force to be reckoned with. One of the most striking features of his treatment of the subject, limited though it may be, is his casual, straightforward approach. It is difficult to believe that paganism was a source of anxiety for him. After observing that November was named *Blodmonath*, the month of sacrifices, because of the beasts that were slain and offered to the gods at that time, Bede does express gratitude that his people have now escaped such pagan error: "Gratias tibi, bone Iesu, qui nos ab his vanis avertens tibi sacrificia laudis offerre donasti." But one suspects that he was not very fearful of its revival.[60] If, as we have noted, he sees no need to hide paganism's attraction for Redwald and others, it is only because he does not consider it a major problem. Indeed, he makes no effort to disguise the fact that the Anglo-Saxons began the year on December 25, and that Christmas has replaced an important pagan festival,[61] candour improbable at best if he thought a recrudescence of heathen superstition at all likely.

Conceivably, rather than paganism, it was heresy that in Bede's estimation constituted the greatest danger to the Anglo-Saxon church. Pelagianism was *the* major British heresy, and Bede seems to have considered it a serious peril. Hence he prefaces his commentary on the Canticle of Canticles with a lengthy refutation of the errors of Julian of Eclanum. One has the sense, however, that the issue would have been given more prominent treatment had it represented a primary concern. More plausible perhaps is the suggestion that his major source of anxiety was the problem of pseudo-Christians, people who professed the Christian faith without really having absorbed its spirit.[62] This is a conspicuous Gregorian theme that has clearly left its impress on Bede, even if he does not give it the same emphasis. Many profess the Christian faith only because everyone else does, he claims, quoting verbatim Gregory's *Homilies on the Gospels*.[63] Elsewhere he expresses the same idea in his own words. In contrast to true Christians who, like the

---

60 *De temp. ratione* 15, CCL 123B:332. Cf. André Crépin, "Bede and the Vernacular," in *Famulus Christi*, pp. 170-192 at 176.

61 *De temp. ratione* 15, CCL 123B:330: "Incipiebant autem annum ab octavo kalendarum Ianuariarum die, ubi nunc natalem domini celebramus. Et ipsam noctem nunc nobis sacrosanctam, tunc gentili vocabulo Modranect, id est matrum noctem, appellabant, ob causam, ut suspicamur, ceremoniarum quas in ea pervigiles agebant."

62 Davidse, "Sense of History," p. 683.

63 *In Marc.* 2, CCL 120:540; *In Luc.* 3, CCL 120:203: "in hac plebe christiana sunt non nulli qui Christum ideo confitentur quia cunctos christianos esse conspiciunt." Cf. Gregory the Great, *Hom. in Evan.* 2.32.5, PL 76:1236.

apostle, glory only in the cross of Christ the Lord, there are those who are really false Christians. They profess to be Christians; they receive the sacraments of the Christian church; but ultimately they are concerned only about the joys of the present life.[64]

In the mind of Gregory the Great the existence of such false Christians is intimately tied to the matter of modern miracles. Miracles are necessary today for the same reason they were required in New Testament times. They support the work of evangelization, a process that by no means is complete. Many have not managed to get beyond simple professions of faith and external observance; they still need to experience the fundamental conversion that is a matter of the heart. Conceivably a similar kind of logic could have been at work in the thought of the Venerable Bede. Richter reminds us of the famous letter to Egbert of York, in which Bede laments the existence of many who still require instruction in the most basic elements of the Christian faith. "The English people, it is true, were formally Christian, but conversion, teaching, these tasks were not completed; they started anew with each generation."[65]

Wormald and others have pointed to one important consequence of the rapid evangelization of Anglo-Saxon society: however sincerely endorsed, Christianity had not been able to displace the traditional way of life. Even within the upper ranks of the ecclesiastical hierarchy, as the case of a St Wilfrid illustrates, the prevailing ethos was assimilated to the essentially pre-Christian *mores* of the lay aristocracy. For the most part, the pagan gods may have disappeared, but not the pagan Germanic heroes and the particular set of values with which they were associated.

---

64 *In Marc.* 4, CCL 120:633: "Quod vero Luca testante unus latro dominum blasphemat dicens, *Si tu es Christus, salvum fac temet ipsum et nos*, alter vero et illum digna invectione redarguit et dominum fideli supplicatione precatur dicens, *Domine memento mei cum veneris in regnum tuum*, usque hodie geri in ecclesia videmus cum mundanis tacti afflictionibus veri simul et falsi christiani, illi quidem qui ficta mente dominicae passionis sacramenta gestant ad praesentis vitae gaudia cupiunt liberari a domino, at qui simplici intentione cum apostolo non gloriantur nisi in cruce domini nostri ita potius a praesentibus aerumnis optant erui ut spiritum suum in manus sui commendent auctoris unaque cum ipso regni caelestis desiderant esse participes."

65 Michael Richter, "Practical Aspects of the Conversion of the Anglo-Saxons," in *Irland und die Christenheit. Ireland and Christendom*, ed. Próinséas Ní Chatháin & Michael Richter (Stuttgart, 1987), pp. 362-376 at 376.

Of this *Beowulf* is the proof.[66] Although he tells us relatively little about this situation, Bede of course was aware of it, and in the latter years of his life there is increasing evidence of his concern. But if both Bede and Gregory demonstrated anxiety about the spiritual health of the society in which they lived, the fundamental premises of their thought differed dramatically. Whereas Gregory conceives of evangelization as an ongoing process, Bede thinks of it as being essentially done. Whereas Gregory laments the fact that for many conviction has remained superficial and belief has not been translated into practice, Bede focuses more specifically on a failure of leadership in society's elite, and he does so only relatively late in his career. Gregory preaches to a society still in need of fundamental conversion; Bede decries episcopal neglect and avarice in a basically Christian society. The focus is different in the two cases, and for Bede the result is that modern miracles are left without the clear rationale that they possess in the thought of his famous predecessor.

---

66 Cf. Wormald, "Bede, 'Beowulf' and the Conversion," esp. pp. 66-68; James Campbell, "Bede," in *Latin Historians*, ed. T.A. Dorey (London, 1966), pp. 159-190, esp. 173-174.

5

The Virtue of the Saints

In the by now extensive literature devoted to Gregory the Great's conception of the spiritual life, there seems to be a broad consensus that the mixed life represented his highest ideal. In the strictest sense, of course, Gregory would have insisted that the life of contemplation was absolutely superior. In personal terms as well he was deeply attached to a monastic, contemplative brand of spirituality, and he was anguished by the fact that the myriad cares of the papal office had deprived him of all but a fading memory of the spiritual repose he once enjoyed. As he puts it in the preface to the *Dialogues*:

> I am tossed about on the waves of a heavy sea, and my soul is like a helpless ship buffeted by raging winds. When I recall my former way of life, it is as though I were once more looking back toward land and sighing as I beheld the shore. It only saddens me the more to find that, while flung about by the mighty waves that carry me along, I can hardly catch sight any longer of the harbor I have left.[1]

However, Gregory's was not a one-sided spirituality that failed to do justice to the life of active service. His own personal inclinations notwithstanding, the balanced life that combined and harmonized both active and contemplative elements was the one on which he placed the greatest value.[2]

Bede's view was substantially the same, although in his case as well the scale on which the balanced life is measured seems tilted in the

---

1 Gregory the Great, *Dial.* 1 Prol. 5, Zimmerman 4, SC 260:12. Cf. his letter of April 591 to Leander of Seville: "Tantis quippe in hoc loco huius mundi fluctibus quatior, ut vetustam ac putrescentem navim, quam regendam occulta Dei dispensatione suscepi, ad portum dirigere nullatenus possim" (*Epist.* 1.41, CCL 140:47-49 at 47).

2 See, for example, Claude Dagens, *Saint Grégoire le Grand. Culture et expérience chrétiennes* (Paris, 1977), pp. 135-163; G.R. Evans, *The Thought of Gregory the Great* (Cambridge, 1986), esp. pp. 105-111; and, most recently, Straw, *Gregory the Great: Perfection in Imperfection*. See also Claudio Leonardi, "Modelli di santità tra secolo V e VII," in *Santi e demoni nell'alto medioevo occidentale*, pp. 261-283, esp. 279-281. Leonardi argues that Gregory articulated the model of sanctity that would prevail in the West in the early medieval centuries. He also comments on its limitations.

direction of monastic spirituality. It is sometimes claimed that Bede does not privilege any one route to perfection, that in his judgment the Christian life can be lived in several different ways, all of value.[3] However, the Northumbrian church of which he was the son was largely the product of monastic impulses, from the Irish missionaries who first evangelized the countryside to the Roman mission that completed their work; and as he himself tells us, Bede's personal experience was also strongly shaped by monastic forces from the time in his earliest youth when he was committed to the monastery for his upbringing.[4] It is scarcely surprising, therefore, that Bede was positively influenced by the atmosphere of the cloister, and, like Gregory the Great, developed a strong personal predilection towards monasticism. On first glance at least it is perhaps the most striking feature of his thought. It clearly had a bearing on his treatment of the issue of the active and contemplative lives. Like Gregory, Bede argues that, strictly speaking, the contemplative life is of higher value, and for essentially the same reasons. Whereas death brings an end to active labours, it presents no such barrier to contemplation. On the contrary, physical death enables contemplation and praise of God to be raised to new levels of perfection.[5]

At one point in *De tabernaculo* Bede seems to suggest that, in the final analysis, the life of the pastor is superior to that of the monk. He is commenting on Exodus 25:32, where we read of the candelabrum of the tabernacle having three branches on each side of a central shaft. Bede informs us that these signify the three estates in each Testament—the *coniugati*, the *continentes* and the *rectores*—and then continues:

> Because in the company of the elect those who preach are of more exalted merit than those who commit themselves only to continence and not also the instruction of the faithful (*operi doctrinae*), and because the life of chastity in turn is of greater stature than married life, quite properly the uppermost arms branching out on either side of the shaft represent those who in either Testament among their other virtues have committed themselves to the work of spiritual instruction (*doctrinae studiis*). The arms in the middle position, also projecting from each side of the shaft, represent the life of the continent, devoted to God. The lowest branches, they too

---

3 See, for example, Edward P. Echlin, "Bede and the Church," *Irish Theological Quarterly* 40 (1973): 351-363 at 363.
4 *HE* 5.24, p. 566.
5 See *Hom. Evan.* 1.9, CCL 122:65; *In Luc.* 3, CCL 120:226. Cf. Gregory the Great, *Hom. in Ezech.* 2.2.9, CCL 142:231.

issuing from the same stem of the single candelabrum, designate figuratively the life of married couples, both in Old and in New Testament times, faithfully serving one and the same Lord.[6]

Pride of place, it would seem, is to be given to pastors.

There are two points that need to be made, however, to bring this passage into focus. First, the language Bede customarily uses presupposes that the relationship of pastors with the faithful at large is to be conceived essentially in monastic terms. As Thacker has observed, they are *rectores* or *magistri*, to whom the faithful, conceived as *subjecti* or *discipuli*, are bound to submit themselves for instruction in spiritual matters.[7] In the background, therefore, Bede's monastic predilection is evident. Secondly, it is equally important to notice the kind of monasticism being commended to us: a monasticism of service, a monastic pastorate, in which withdrawal and contemplation are combined with active ministry to the larger lay community. On this point Bede's message is reinforced by the *Ecclesiastical History*, where his heroes are virtually all monks committed to active service, monks like Aidan, Chad and perhaps most importantly Cuthbert, who joined the love of God to lives of teaching and preaching. Thacker has pointed out how the central books of the *Ecclesiastical History*, covering the period from Augustine's mission to the death of King Ecgfrith, offer a picture of a golden age in the history of Bede's people:

> Bede's depiction of that period and the great preachers and holy communities which adorned it was designed to recall his degenerate contemporaries to that path of righteousness from which he believed they had so seriously erred. It was above all a record of monastic achievement, of an ascetic pastorate which, in contrast to the luxurious and avaricious ecclesiastics condemned in the letter to Egbert, rejected worldly possessions, rich gifts,

---

6   *De tabernaculo* 1, CCL 119A:32: "quia vero in parte electorum sublimius est meritum praedicantium quam eorum qui solummodo continentiae et non etiam operi doctrinae student item sublimior continentium quam coniugatorum conversatio recte supremi calami qui hinc et inde de hastili procedebant eos qui in utroque testamento inter virtutes alias doctrinae studiis sese subdidere designant, recte inferiores calami qui aeque ex utroque hastilis latere prodeunt vitam continentium Deo devotam, recte infimi calami et ipsi ex eodem unius candelabri stipite orti bonorum vitam coniugum in utriusque testamenti tempore uni eidemque domino fideliter servientem typice demonstrant."

7   Thacker, "Bede's Ideal of Reform," p. 132. See also *Hom. Evan.* 1.7 & 2.22, CCL 122:46-47, 345; and *In Luc.* 4, CCL 120:260.

and ostentatious modes of travel, and was zealous in preaching, converting the pagan, and defeating the heretic.[8]

At the summit of the monastic life, of course, was the kind of spiritual withdrawal that in Cuthbert's case was brought to fulfillment on Farne Island. However, Bede avoids privileging the life of the recluse at the expense of other considerations. Only after long service to his monastic brethren and the larger Christian community did Cuthbert earn the right to devote himself more exclusively to monastic contemplation, and even then the privilege was a temporary one, soon to be interrupted by his summons to the episcopate. His fame as a solitary and a miracle worker attracted many visitors, and his own brethren continued to want to learn from his example. More than once, however, Cuthbert informed them that the life of withdrawal from the world ought not to be regarded as an especially exalted state. On the contrary, he said,

> the life of monks ought rightly to be admired, for they are in all things subject to the commands of the abbot and govern all their times of watching, praying, fasting and working to his judgment; and I have known many of those who, both in purity of heart and in loftiness of prophetic grace, far exceed me in my weakness.[9]

If Cuthbert's biography as reconstructed by Bede reveals a progressive strengthening of the spiritual, contemplative element that culminates in his experience on Farne, it is important to note that this is paralleled by another theme, one acknowledging a life of active service as guest-master, prior and ultimately bishop to the Christian community.[10]

In all of this Bede's views are a legitimate development of the Gregorian position, the central features of which he is prompt to endorse. Neither the active nor the contemplative life can be valued in isolation. Like two sides of a coin, they presuppose one another. Just as active Christian service would be incomplete without some admixture of contemplation, so the love of God cannot be held apart from the love of

---

8 Thacker, "Bede's Ideal of Reform," pp. 142-143. Cf. Gerald Bonner, "The Christian Life in the Thought of the Venerable Bede," *Durham University Journal* 63 (1970): 39-55 at 40-41.

9 *VCP*, chap. 22, pp. 229-231.

10 Cf. Lenore Abraham, "Bede's *Life of Cuthbert*: A Reassessment," *Proceedings of the PMR Conference* 1 (1976): 23-32 at 28-29; Thacker, "Bede's Ideal of Reform," pp. 137-138; and Stancliffe, "Cuthbert and the Polarity between Pastor and Solitary," pp. 21-44.

neighbour. His monastic inclinations notwithstanding, for Bede, as for Gregory, the highest ideal of sanctity requires a life in which active and contemplative elements are held in balance.[11] If there are some important differences between Bede and Gregory nonetheless, the most important of them arises at the personal rather than the doctrinal level, a product of the fact that, in Bede's case, the issue did not generate any of the anxiety that so afflicted Gregory.

Although Gregory and Bede each had a strong disposition to the cloistered life, they had not been required to compromise their monastic ideals to the same extent. In a lifetime devoted to the service of his brethren, Bede was never drawn to duties outside the monastery, and never had to assume responsibilities even remotely comparable to those of the papal office. He seems never, therefore, to have suffered—and seems scarcely capable of comprehending—the kind of spiritual malaise, the sense of loss, experienced by Gregory when he assumed the government of the Roman Church. In the short biography of Gregory contained in the *Ecclesiastical History* Bede does dutifully record Gregory's distress. But one wonders if he has fully grasped the import of his words, interpreting them as he does as a *confessio humilitatis*. Having never faced any form of spiritual crisis himself, he assures us that Gregory had nothing to lament:

> The holy man said all this in a spirit of great humility (*Haec quidem sanctus vir ex magnae humilitatis intentione dicebat*). We need not believe ... that he had lost any of his monastic perfection by reason of his pastoral cares. It would appear that he profited more by his efforts over the conversion of many than he had done from the quiet retirement of his earlier way of life.

If this leaves the impression that a loss of contemplation is not to be taken as seriously as Gregory takes it, Bede partially recovers by explaining that Gregory continued to surround himself with his monastic brethren: "through their unremitting example he could bind himself, as it were by an anchor cable, to the calm shores of prayer, while he was being tossed about on the ceaseless tide of secular affairs."[12] But one is still left with the sense that he has not really understood, that matters were much more straightforward for Bede than they had been for his

---

11 Cf. M. Thomas Aquinas Carroll, *The Venerable Bede: His Spiritual Teachings* (Washington, 1946), pp. 247-249.
12 *HE* 2.1, pp. 124-125.

celebrated predecessor, and that he could therefore opt for the Gregorian ideal of the mixed life without an acute sense—certainly, it would seem, without any strong personal sense—of the loss thereby entailed.[13]

There is also an additional and more substantive respect in which Bede's conception of sanctity is to be distinguished from Gregory's. Although he fully acknowledged the importance of disciplining both mind and body, Gregory's Roman instinct for moderation prevented him from endorsing the extremes of ascetic self-denial present in the tradition of the desert fathers. Despite the pull of the Roman tradition and the significance of Gregory's personal example, Bede did not distance himself from the spirituality of the desert to the same extent. One thinks of his portrait of Cuthbert spending the entire night in prayer, immersed to the neck in the cold waters of the sea,[14] or of the similar harshly penitential discipline to which Dryhthelm subjected himself after his chastening vision and withdrawal to the monastery at Melrose:

> As his retreat was on the banks of the river, he often used to enter it in his great longing to chastise his body, frequently immersing himself beneath the water; he would remain thus motionless, reciting prayers and psalms for as long as he could endure it, while the water of the river came up to his loins and sometimes up to his neck. When he came out of the water, he would never trouble to take off his cold, wet garments until the warmth of his body had dried them. When in winter time the broken pieces of ice were floating round him, which he himself had had to break in order to find a place to stand in the river or immerse himself, those who saw him would say, "Brother Dryhthelm, ... however can you bear such bitter cold?" He answered them simply, for he was a man of simple wit and few words, "I have known it colder."[15]

Bede describes these practices with evident approval. Gregory, however, would have had none of them.

The inspiration on which Bede draws here, of course, is the Irish tradition, which had been much more profoundly influenced by the asceticism of the desert than Roman spirituality had been. Kirby has suggested that the mediating influence may well have been King Ceolwulf,

---

13 Cf. Georges Tugène, "Rois moines et rois pasteurs dans l'*Histoire Ecclésiastique* de Bède," *Romanobarbarica* 8 (1984-1985): 111-147 at 142.

14 *VCP*, chap. 10, pp. 188-190.

15 *HE* 5.12, pp. 497-499. Dryhthelm's words are an allusion to the alternating cold and heat that were part of his vision of Purgatory. See below, pp. 180-183.

whose personal piety and spiritual sensibilities were clearly demonstrated by his abdication to the monastery of Lindisfarne. It was to this Ceolwulf that Bede sent the *Ecclesiastical History* for his blessing. "It may well be," argues Kirby, "that pressure from Ceolwulf obliged Bede to write more tolerantly of Aidan and his successors than he otherwise would."[16] Whether the positing of any such intermediary is necessary, however, is uncertain, for Bede seems genuinely to have admired the spiritual example of the Irish saints who were instrumental in the Christianization of Northumbria. Although harshly critical of his views on the Easter question, the product of either ignorance or culpable weakness on his part, of Aidan's sanctity Bede has no doubt. Miracles, he tells us, have provided divine confirmation of his merits, should any be needed.[17] Ultimately his judgment is a nuanced one. Hence he can use the words that St Paul reserves for the children of Israel: "aemulationem Dei habent, sed non secundum scientiam."[18] But he clearly acknowledges that Irish spirituality contains much that is admirable, including a more pronounced penchant for ascetic practices than the Roman, Benedictine and Gregorian traditions.

If Bede's ideal of sanctity was clearly influenced but not fully determined by Gregorian ideas, the same can be said of his thoughts on the relationship between saintly virtue and miracles. Although Bede shared the broadly based medieval conviction that miracles were performed by the saints, he had read Gregory carefully enough to realize that miracles were not essential to saintly status. Gregory, of course, had written his *Dialogues* with the express purpose of providing an account of the miracles being performed by the saints in Italy in his own time. But both there and elsewhere he had made it clear that not every saint was blessed with wonder-working powers. In the modern world, as he explains in his *Homilies on the Gospels*, miracles occur relatively less frequently than they did in the times of the apostolic church. Then they were required to ensure that the Gospel would receive

16   D.P. Kirby, "King Ceolwulf of Northumbria and the *Historia Ecclesiastica*," *Studia Celtica* 14-15 (1979-1980): 168-173, esp. 172.

17   *HE* 3.15, p. 260: "Qui cuius meriti fuerit, etiam miraculorum signis internus arbiter edocuit, e quibus tria memoriae causa ponere satis sit."

18   Rom. 10:2. Cf. *HE* 3.3, p. 218, where Aidan is described as "summae mansuetudinis et pietatis ac moderaminis virum habentemque zelum Dei, quamvis non plene secundum scientiam."

a fair hearing. Now that the faith has been established, many lead lives of virtue without demonstrating miraculous powers.[19]

Bede endorses the Gregorian view by quoting Gregory verbatim in his commentaries on both Mark and Luke.[20] In his *Ecclesiastical History* he again acknowledges the point by including an extensive extract from the famous letter of June 601 to Augustine of Canterbury. There Gregory cautions Augustine lest his miracles become an occasion for vainglory. When the apostles returned from their preaching overjoyed at the fact that even the devils had been subject to them, they were told to delight not in the possession of such miraculous power but rather in the fact that their names were inscribed in the book of life. "Not all the elect work miracles," says Gregory, "but nevertheless all their names are written in heaven. Therefore those who are true disciples ought not to rejoice except in that good thing which they have in common with all the elect and which they will enjoy for ever."[21]

Naturally enough, both Gregory and Bede tell us much more about those who combined personal sanctity with miraculous powers than they do about those known for their lives of virtue alone. But the admittedly unusual story of Sigeberht, king of the East Angles, clearly illustrates that Bede did not expect even profound personal sanctity always to be accompanied by miracles. Sigeberht was "a good and religious man" who resigned his earthly kingdom to his kinsman Ecgric and retired to a monastery that he himself had founded, resolved to fight thereafter for the Kingdom of Heaven. When the East Anglians were attacked by the Mercians under King Penda, they appealed to Sigeberht to assume command of the army, and ultimately dragged the unwilling and unarmed former monarch from his monastic retreat and placed him at the head of their forces. They assumed that their troops would take courage from the presence of one who had been a distinguished military leader. All was to no avail, however. Both Sigeberht and Ecgric were

---

19 Gregory the Great, *Hom. in Evan.* 1.4.3, PL 76:1090-1091.
20 *In Marc.* 1, CCL 120:470; *In Luc.* 3, CCL 120:194: "Nunc quoque cum fidelium numerositas excrevit intra sanctam ecclesiam multi sunt qui vitam virtutum tenent et signa virtutum non habent quia frustra miraculum foras ostenditur, si deest quod intus operetur. Nam iuxta magistri gentium vocem linguae in signum sunt non fidelibus sed infidelibus."
21 *HE* 1.31, p. 111; cf. Gregory the Great, *Epist.* 11.36, CCL 140A:925-929 at 926. Cf. also Luke 10:17-20.

killed in the battle, and the rest of the East Anglian army was either slain or routed by their heathen enemies.[22]

The story is memorable for a variety of reasons, not least of which the fact that it runs counter to the way events usually unfold in the *Ecclesiastical History*. Generally a beneficent Providence ensures the triumph of good over evil. Generally individuals of proven sanctity find their virtue, when put to the test, honoured by the grace of miracles. Clearly, however, this is not the way things must happen. Not all saints are blessed with miraculous powers, and indeed even those who are find that they can be withdrawn. Elsewhere Bede states that, like other divine benefits granted as aids to spiritual growth, the gift of miracles sometimes is taken away to preserve humility. Although the faithful have been promised the constant succour and support of the Holy Spirit, only the grace required for works of piety and charity is constantly and permanently available.[23] It is these that are essential to sanctity, not the miracles by which they may or may not be accompanied. Hence Bede points out that when the disciples took special pride in their miraculous powers as if they were intrinsically important, Christ corrected them with a stiff rebuke.[24]

Like Gregory, Bede was convinced of humanity's need for good examples; and so, again like Gregory, he readily acknowledged the centrality for ordinary Christians of the examples of the saints. Christ has not abandoned us to the darkness of this world, but for our guidance has provided the *exempla sanctorum* like so many stars illuminating the night.[25] Clearly, the kind of example that is required and that is given to us for imitation, although real imitation may be beyond the capacity of the simple faithful,[26] is that of a life transformed by Christ. The miracles of the saints are divinely bestowed gifts, and we are properly humbled before them. But it is veneration that they command, not imi-

22 *HE* 3.18, pp. 267-269.
23 *In Cant.* 5, CCL 119B:357-358; *In Marc.* 1, CCL 120:443; *Hom. Evan.* 1.15, CCL 122:110.
24 See *In Luc.* 3, CCL 120:218, where he comments on Luke 10:17-18.
25 *In Cant.* 3, CCL 119B:253. Cf. *In Cant.* 3 & 6, CCL 119B:273, 369; *De templo* 1, CCL 119A:164-165. See also Peter Brown, "The Saint as Exemplar in Late Antiquity," in *Saints and Virtues*, ed. John Stratton Hawley (Berkeley, 1987), pp. 3-14.
26 *De templo* 2, CCL 119A:195; *In Ezram et Neemiam* 3, CCL 119A:375: "Et nos sublimem vitam electorum quam sequi imitando non possumus congaudendo ac venerando nostram facere debemus."

tation,[27] whereas the holy lives of the saints are offered for our active emulation. Miracles are an adornment to works of virtue. They are a reward for the sanctified life, not its essence.[28] As Proverbs 15:17 informs us, a simple meal served with love is to be preferred to a more lavish repast where charity is missing. Bede explains: "It is much better to preserve the innocence of a simple life with charity, than to be outwardly resplendent with great miracles and not purge the heart of the filth of enmity."[29]

In his *Homilies on the Gospels*, as was noted earlier, Gregory the Great observes that the miracles performed when the church was in its infancy have now largely been replaced by spiritual wonders of much greater intrinsic value. The faithful of today may not be able to cure the physically ill by the simple laying on of hands, but they can strengthen the spiritually infirm by the force of their Christian example. They may be unable to speak in tongues like the apostles at Pentecost, but they have effected an even more profound transformation in their level of discourse by abandoning the worldly conversation of the old life to proclaim the sacred mysteries and to sing the praises of their Creator. Once again Bede reports Gregory's words extensively and verbatim, thereby giving the Gregorian view his own personal endorsement. To both Gregory and Bede these modern wonders are greater than their physical analogues precisely because of their spiritual nature, because by means of them souls are revived and not simply bodies.[30] To focus on the wonders of the saint, therefore, rather than the example of personal holiness provided would be to mistake what is secondary for the essen-

---

27 *In Luc.* 1, CCL 120:85: "miracula in exemplo operationis non sunt trahenda." See also *In Ezram et Neemiam* 2, CCL 119A:315-316.

28 See *De tabernaculo* 1, CCL 119A:11, where Bede refers to the "miracula sanctorum quibus cogitationes Deo devotas et opera virtutum ornavere." See also *HE* 1.17, p. 56, where he says of bishops Germanus of Auxerre and Lupus of Troyes: "Erat illis apostolorum instar et gloria et auctoritas per conscientiam, doctrina per litteras, virtutes [i.e. miracula] ex meritis."

29 *In Prov.* 2, CCL 119B:88: "multo est utilius simplicis vitae innocentiam cum caritate servare quam maioribus virtutum miraculis foras effulgere et interiora mentis ab odiorum sorde non expurgare."

30 Cf. Bede, *In Marc.* 4, CCL 120:645-646; and Gregory the Great, *Hom. in Evan.* 2.29.4, PL 76:1215-1216. Cf. also *In Marc.* 2, CCL 120:503, where, in reference to Mark 6:5-6, it is said of Christ: "Maiora autem signa cotidie in gentibus per apostolos facit non tam in sanatione corporum quam in animarum salute." Here Bede is quoting Jerome, *In Matth.* 2, CCL 77:116.

tial. It would also leave one open to the possibility of grievous error. Taken on their own and given independent value and status, miracles can deceive. In addition to the miracles of the saints, as Scripture itself informs us, miracles are sometimes performed by evil men.

Perhaps the most significant biblical passage in this regard is Matthew 7:21-23, where Christ is reported to have said:

> Not every one who says to me, "Lord, Lord," shall enter the kingdom of heaven, but he who does the will of my father who is in heaven. On that day many will say to me, "Lord, Lord, did we not prophesy in your name, and cast out demons in your name, and do many mighty works in your name?" And then will I declare to them, "I never knew you; depart from me, you evildoers."

To Bede, as to Gregory the Great, the virtually inescapable implication of such a pronouncement is that miracles cannot be considered an exclusive privilege of the saints. Impostors who will ultimately be rejected by Christ on the Day of Judgment can perform miracles in his name as well, a possibility that also seems to be envisaged by Luke 9:49-50.[31] In practice, both Gregory the Great and Gregory of Tours may well have been more familiar with such cases than Bede was. Gregory the Great tells us of the pseudo-monk Basilius, who was unmasked by Abbot Equitius; and Gregory of Tours acknowledges the miracles performed by spiritual charlatans like Desiderius.[32] Bede

---

31 *In Luc.* 3, CCL 120:210-211. Cf. *In Marc.* 3, CCL 120:552. Creider, "Bede's Understanding of the Miraculous," p. 211, points to the significance of the words attributed to Bishop Wilfrid in Bede's account of the Synod of Whitby. Bishop Colman had attempted to defend the Irish tradition of Easter by pointing to the practice of St Columba and his successors, men whose sanctity had been confirmed by the performance of miracles. In his reply Wilfrid readily acknowledges both the reality of their miracles and their status as men of God, but maintains at the same time that they were mistaken on the Easter question. Presumably they would quickly have changed their ways had someone been available to instruct them in the catholic tradition. In themselves, he argues, their miracles have no probative value: "at the judgment many will say to the Lord that they prophesied in His name and cast out devils and did many wonderful works, but the Lord will answer that He never knew them" (*HE* 3.25, pp. 305-307).

32 Gregory the Great, *Dial.* 1.4.3-6, SC 260:38-42; Gregory of Tours, *Historia Francorum* 9.6 & 10.25, MGH, SRM 1:417-420 & 517-519. Cf. *Vita S. Guthlaci*, chap. 46, ed. & trans. Bertram Colgrave (Cambridge, 1956), p. 142, where Felix reports the views of Wigfrith, secretary to a bishop Headda who had come to visit Guthlac. Like some others in Headda's retinue, says Felix, Wigfrith had doubts

reports no such examples. However, he clearly recognizes the possibility of pseudo-prophets. The source of their power would be the name of Christ, not any inherent merit of their own; and their wonders would also work to their own damnation. But Bede has no doubt that, unworthy though they may be, their miracles would be perfectly genuine. He even points out that Scripture gives us specific instances in the wonders performed by Judas and by the sons of Sceva, the high priest.[33]

In early medieval sources the miracles of false saints are generally attributed to the forces of evil.[34] Although occasionally Bede seems to conceive of them as divinely produced,[35] elsewhere it is clear that he considers them to be demonic rather than divine. Sometimes it is simply a question of tricks or illusions. The example of the witch of Endor could be a case in point. Bede suggests that it may simply have been some false shade that she conjured up at Saul's request, and not Samuel at all. The matter is uncertain, however, and the spirit of the departed prophet may actually have appeared, for as the trials of Job and the temptation of the Lord himself both indicate, Satan is sometimes allowed to exercise extraordinary power to accomplish some hidden purpose. If

---

about the source of Guthlac's miraculous powers. Before meeting him, he was unsure if he was dealing with a genuine saint or an imposter (*pseudo-sanctitatis simulator*): "Dicebat enim inter Scottorum se populos habitasse et illic pseudo-anachoritas diversarum religionum simulatores vidisse, quos praedicere futura et virtutes alias facere, quocumque numine nesciens conperit."

33 *In Luc.* 3, CCL 120:219. For the episode involving the sons of Sceva, see Acts 19:13-17. Bede also acknowledges the possibility of spiritual benefit being derived from such miracles by others. Some, he seems to suggest, might be brought to honour the divine authority while despising its unworthy human agents. Cf. *Exp. Act. Apost.* 19.13, CCL 121:77: "Refert Iosephus regem Salomonem excogitasse suamque gentem docuisse modos exorcismi, id est adiurationis, quibus immundi spiritus expulsi ab homine ulterius reverti non sint ausi. Fit autem hoc interdum etiam per reprobos ob condemnationem eorum qui faciunt, vel ob utilitatem eorum qui vident et audiunt, ut licet homines despiciant signa facientes, tamen deum honorent ad cuius invocationem fiant tanta miracula."

34 See, for example, Aron Gurevich, *Medieval Popular Culture: Problems of Belief and Perception* (Cambridge, 1988), pp. 65 & 69.

35 The claim that such miracles derive their power from the name of Christ, and that their purpose is either the damnation of those who perform them or the edification of others, could be taken to imply as much. Conceivably, however, Bede regards them as wonders performed by evil men and for essentially evil purposes, although such evildoers would have no power at all unless God permitted it, and although God ultimately is able to produce good from their evil designs.

we find the idea troublesome, Bede tells us, we should remember that the Devil's ability in such matters extends only as far as God's will permits.[36]

Bede's treatment of such miracles is largely limited to scriptural statements and examples. Neither demonic illusions nor genuine demonic miracles are frequent in the pages of the *Ecclesiastical History*. Nowhere is there a story to rival Adomnan's account of the sorcerer who by diabolic art (*arte diabulica*) managed to draw milk from a bull. St Columba, of course, unmasked the deception, and showed the liquid to be not true milk at all but "blood bleached by the imposture of demons, to deceive mankind."[37] However, Adomnan tells another story that does have a parallel in the *Ecclesiastical History*. Indeed, it is repeated there. Adomnan observes:

> Hosts of evil spirits once attack[ed] the holy bishop Germanus in the midst of the sea, when he was sailing from the bay of Gaul to Britain, in the cause of man's salvation. They put perils in his way, and stirred up storms; they covered sky and daylight with a mist of darkness. But more quickly than speech, at the prayer of Saint Germanus all these things were calmed, and ceased. And the mist was cleared away.[38]

The source of the story was the *Vita S. Germani* of Constantius of Lyons. Bede found it there as well, and chose to include it in the *Ecclesiastical History*.[39]

Of all evildoers, the one whose miracles attracted the greatest amount of interest was, of course, the Antichrist; and neither Gregory the Great nor St Augustine had had any doubt at all that his miracles would be genuine. There are several passages in which Bede seems to endorse this view. On more than one occasion he allows references to Antichrist's miracles to pass without commenting on their ontological

---

36 *In 1 Sam.* 4, CCL 119:256-257.
37 *Vita S. Columbae* 2.17, ed. & trans. Anderson & Anderson, p. 362. The story is a curious one, and illustrates that the line between miracle and illusion could be difficult to define. Adomnan considers it an imposture because the milk was really blood. Judging from his own account, however, it seems that the sorcerer did milk a bull like a cow, and did succeed in extracting a bucket of blood. There is no suggestion that the blood was illusory.
38 Ibid. 2.34, pp. 405-407.
39 *Vita S. Germani* 3.12-13, SC 112:144-148; *HE* 1.17, pp. 54-56.

status, thereby implying that they will be perfectly real.[40] At other times, however, he is more explicit. In the *Chronica Maiora* he refers to Antichrist as being entrusted with the fullness of Satan's power, and as accomplishing wonders sufficient to eclipse all others (*magica ceteris omnibus maiora*).[41] In his commentary on 1 Samuel he describes Antichrist as a son of the Devil, one of the fallen angels.[42] Elsewhere he is careful to explain that Antichrist will indeed be a man, but one in whom Satan will be totally present in a corporeal manner.[43] All this suggests miracles that are more than demoniacal sleight-of-hand. Combined with the savagery of Antichrist's persecution, they will constitute an unprecedented tribulation for the faithful:

> The holy martyrs frequently performed many and great miracles before their persecutors, who nonetheless were unwilling to believe or to cease from persecution. Who, therefore, will be converted to the faith, and who among those who already believe will not find his faith severely shaken, when the enemy of all that is holy becomes a worker of wonders, when the very one who rages against and tortures Christians so that Christ may be denied brings it about by his own miracles that faith be placed in him, the Antichrist, instead? In these circumstances what refuge, what hope will remain for the elect, save that the heavenly grace that distributes the virtue of patience to the faithful may very quickly deprive the forces of evil of the power to persecute and oppress?[44]

---

40 See, for example, *In Marc.* 4, CCL 120:600; and *Expl. Apoc.* 3.16, PL 93:181. In the latter passage he implies that Antichrist and his minions will be as capable of miracles as Pharaoh's magicians.

41 *Chronica Maiora* = *De temp. ratione* 69.602, CCL 123B:539: "*Et vidi*, inquit, *de mari bestiam ascendentem, et dedit illi draco virtutem suam et potestatem magnam* [Rev. 13:1-2], id est vidi hominem sevissimi ingenii de tumultuosa impiorum stirpe progenitum, cui mox nato et per magicas artes a pessimis inbuto magistris, adiungens se diabolus totam virtutis suae potentiam. Per quam magica ceteris omnibus maiora patraret, individuus comes attulit." This is a sloppy piece of editing; the two sentences need to be read together.

42 *In 1 Sam.* 4, CCL 119:242.

43 See *Expl. Apoc.* 2.13, PL 93:172, where he comments on Rev. 13:17-18: "Numerus enim hominis est, ne eum putemus, juxta quorumdam opinionem, vel diabolum esse vel daemonem, sed unum de hominibus, in quo totus Satanas habitaturus est corporaliter."

44 *In Marc.* 4, CCL 120:599: "Quanta enim saepe miracula quot virtutes sancti martyres coram persecutoribus fecerunt nec tamen credere illi neque a persequendo cessare voluerunt. Quis ergo ad fidem convertitur incredulus cuius iam credentis non pavit et concutitur fides quando persecutor pietatis fit etiam operator virtutis

In his most explicit treatment of the issue Bede avoids committing himself. In the Vulgate text of 2 Thess. 2:9 Antichrist's advent is described as being "secundum operationem Satanae in omni virtute, et signis, et prodigiis mendacibus." Bede comments as follows:

As has been said, his advent will be according to the working of Satan, in all power, and signs, and false prodigies. The issue is a matter of debate. Are his signs and prodigies said to be false because he will deceive the mortal senses through phantasms, and only appear to do what he does not in fact do? Or is it because these same prodigies, perfectly real, will deceive those who believe that they can be produced only on divine authority, unaware of the power of the Devil, who carried away the entire family of the blessed Job and all his flocks, not by any imaginary fire and whirlwind, but by real ones? Whether it is in this manner or that that they should be said to be false signs, this much is beyond doubt: that that trial will appear greater than all others, when the holy martyr submits his body to tortures only to have Antichrist perform so many miracles before his very eyes.[45]

---

idemque ipse qui tormentis saevit ut Christus negetur provocat miraculis ut antichristo credatur? Quod ergo in his suffugium quae spes remanebit electis, nisi ut superna gratia quae virtutem patientiae piis largitur potentiam persequendi ac tribulandi citius demat impiis?" Cf. Gregory the Great, *Mor.* 32.15.24, CCL 143B:1648: "Pensemus ergo quae erit humanae mentis illa temptatio, quando pius martyr et corpus tormentis subicit, et tamen ante eius oculos miracula tortor facit. Cuius tunc virtus non ab ipso cogitationum fundo quatiatur, quando is qui flagris cruciat signis coruscat?" Gregory also states that the miracles of Antichrist will be all the more troubling because the grace of miracles will be largely withdrawn from the church at the same time (see ibid. 34.3.7, p. 1738). Bede does not give the point the same emphasis. But cf. *Expl. Apoc.* 2.11, PL 93:163, where he maintains "quod tunc Ecclesia virtutum gratia destituenda credatur, adversario palam signis mendacii coruscante."

45 *Expl. Apoc.* 2.13, PL 93:171: "Adventus enim ejus erit, sicut dictum est, secundum operationem Satanae in omni virtute, et signis, et prodigiis mendacii. Quae solet ambigi utrum propterea dicta sint signa et prodigia mendacii, quoniam mortales sensus per phantasmata decepturus est, ut quod non facit, facere videatur; an quia illa ipsa etiam, si erunt vera prodigia, ad mendacium pertrahent credituros non ea potuisse nisi divinitus fieri, virtutem diaboli nescientes, qui non phantastico, sed vero igni et turbine tantam familiam sancti Job cum tantis gregibus absumpsit. Sive autem hoc, sive illo modo signa mendacii dicantur, hoc est, sine dubio, in quo illa tentatio cunctis major apparebit, quando pius martyr et corpus tormentis subjicit, et tamen ante ejus oculos miracula tot facit." Creider, "Bede's Understanding of the Miraculous," pp. 211-212, interprets this passage to mean that Antichrist's miracles may be either genuine or illusory, but that is not what Bede says. The question posed at the beginning, the question that Bede ultimately fails to answer, is which of these alternatives is the correct one.

Bede's ambivalence at this juncture is more than a little puzzling. Presumably it was his reading of Augustine that was responsible for his caution. Much of the passage quoted above, including Bede's statement of the alternative views of Antichrist's miracles, is borrowed verbally from *De civitate Dei*. But whereas Augustine's reference to Job's afflictions indicates a clear preference for the second alternative, Bede's does not.[46] Augustine does not expressly commit himself, and so Bede seems to have thought that the issue remained doubtful enough to justify his sitting on the fence. On the general issue of the miracles of evildoers, however, Bede's mind was clear. Miracles are not the exclusive privilege of the saints. They are neither a necessary condition for the state of sanctity nor incontrovertible proof of having achieved it.

In practice, of course, it was miracles that had been accomplished by saints that were of primary interest to Bede, just as they had been to Gregory the Great. The saints are almost as prominent in the *Historia ecclesiastica* as they are in Gregory's *Dialogues*. In Gregory's case, however, the realization that miracles cannot be considered irrefragable evidence of sanctity is thought through more clearly than it is in Bede's. Gregory does indeed forget himself occasionally, and speak as if miracles could establish someone's sanctity. This was the hagiographical tradition, and we should not be surprised that Gregory did not escape it completely. In general, however, the essential distinctions are preserved. The awareness that miracles cannot prove sanctity prevents the *Dialogues* from subordinating miracle stories to the purposes of cult, and functions instead to invest them with a higher spiritual significance. Although they are generally stories in which saints figure prominently,

---

46 See *De civitate Dei* 20.19, CCL 48:732-733: "*Praesentia* quippe *eius erit*, sicut dictum est, *secundum operationem satanae in omni virtute et signis et prodigiis mendacii et in omni seductione iniquitatis his, qui pereunt.* Tunc enim solvetur satanas et per illum Antichristum in omni sua virtute mirabiliter quidem, sed mendaciter operabitur. Quae solet ambigi utrum propterea dicta sint signa et prodigia mendacii, quoniam mortales sensus per phantasmata decepturus est, ut quod non facit facere videatur, an quia illa ipsa, etiamsi erunt vera prodigia, ad mendacium pertrahent credituros non ea potuisse nisi divinitus fieri, virtutem diaboli nescientes, maxime quando tantam, quantam numquam habuit, acceperit potestatem. Non enim quando de caelo ignis cecidit et tantam familiam cum tantis gregibus pecorum sancti Iob uno impetu absumpsit et turbo inruens et domum deiciens filios eius occidit, phantasmata fuerunt; quae tamen fuerunt opera satanae, cui Deus dederat hanc potestatem. Propter quid horum ergo dicta sint prodigia et signa mendacii, tunc potius apparebit.*"

this is not invariably the case. Even when it is, the intent is not generally to focus attention on the person of the saint himself. The value of miracles is located rather in the lessons they contain, lessons both doctrinal and moral that God has chosen to convey by means of them.

It has not infrequently been claimed that similar concerns are characteristic of Bede as well. Thacker, for example, points to the broad difference in approach that separates the anonymous life of St Cuthbert from Bede's reworked prose version. The former, says Thacker, offers us an image of St Cuthbert as wonder-worker. Very little attention is given to illustrating his pastoral activities, or to demonstrating the moral or spiritual relevance of his example to those for whom the life may have been intended. In contrast, says Thacker, Bede's approach is strongly didactic. Cuthbert is presented as the ideal monk and pastor, one modelled after the portrait of St Benedict in Gregory's *Dialogues*.[47] The contrast that Thacker sees between the two lives in general others have seen in the way their respective authors present the miracles of the saint. If the wonders in the anonymous account serve primarily to authenticate Cuthbert's sanctity, in Bede's account, or so it is argued, they teach spiritual lessons.[48]

That such claims have at least some basis in fact is illustrated by the contrasting ways in which the anonymous author and Bede handle the story of Cuthbert and the ravens. Bede tells us that the ravens had been stealing the thatch of the guest house on Farne Island, and that Cuthbert chased them off. He then continues:

> when three days had passed, one of a pair returned and found the servant of Christ digging. With its feathers sadly ruffled and its head drooping to its feet, and with humble cries it prayed for pardon, using such signs as it could; and the venerable father, understanding what it meant, gave it permission to return. And having got leave to come back, it soon went off in

---

47 Thacker, "Bede's Ideal of Reform," esp. pp. 137-138, 140. Rosenthal conceives of the distinction between the two lives in analogous but somewhat different terms, characterizing Bede's version as the first step in a transition from a personal, idiosyncratic portrait of the saint to one set in a more institutional context. See Joel T. Rosenthal, "Bede's *Life of Cuthbert*: Preparatory to *The Ecclesiastical History*," *Catholic Historical Review* 68 (1982): 599-611 at 602, 603-604. Cf. Goffart, *Narrators of Barbarian History*, pp. 292-293.

48 See, for example, Carroll, *Venerable Bede*, pp. 197-198; Wolpers, *Englische Heiligenlegende*, esp. p. 81; and Abraham, "Bede's *Life of Cuthbert*: A Reassessment," pp. 26-28. Cf. Creider, "Bede's Understanding of the Miraculous," pp. 161-162.

order to bring back its mate. Without delay they both returned bringing a worthy gift, namely a portion of hog's lard; and this the man of God used often afterwards to show to the brethren when they visited him, and to offer it to grease their shoes, declaring how carefully men should seek after obedience and humility, seeing that even a proud bird hastened to atone for the wrong that it had done to a man of God, by means of prayers, lamentations and gifts.[49]

The anonymous author recognized humble submission in the bird's request for pardon as well: it would have been hard to miss. But only Bede reports the spiritual lesson Cuthbert derived from the episode.[50] The kinds of significance that the two authors attached to the story were fundamentally different. What Bede conceived primarily as an object lesson in obedience and humility, his anonymous predecessor saw as an instance of the natural realm acknowledging Cuthbert's sanctity.[51]

One should not overestimate the importance of a single striking example. In particular, one should not be tempted to think that Bede disdained the anonymous author's simpler kind of point.[52] But the

49 *VCP*, chap. 20, p. 225. For the corresponding episode in the anonymous version see *VCA* 3.5, pp. 100-102.

50 Cf. *VCM* 18, pp. 91-92:
    Quid fera praetumido cervice superbia ferves?
    Cerne viam corvi et caecum depone furorem,
    Qui precibus noxam fletuque et munere purgat.
    Nec pudeat vitae volucrum de pectore formam
    Sumere, cum moneat Sapientia: respice calles,
    Quos formica ferat, sensumque addisce sagacem.

51 Bede introduces the story by saying: "Let us also tell of a miracle wrought by the blessed Cuthbert after the example of the above-mentioned father Benedict, in which human pride and contumacy are openly condemned by the obedience and humility of birds" (*VCP*, chap. 20, p. 223). At the corresponding point in the anonymous author's account we read: "We have told how the sea served the man of God; so also the birds of the air obeyed him" (*VCA* 3.5, p. 101).

52 Bede begins the next chapter, which corresponds to the preceding chapter in the anonymous account, as follows: "Moreover not only the creatures of the air but also of the sea, yes, and even the sea itself, as well as air and fire as we have shown above, did honour to the venerable man" (*VCP*, chap. 21, p. 225). The story that follows—an episode in which the tide miraculously provides some lumber needed by Cuthbert—illustrates the point. At the conclusion of the story Bede describes the reaction of Cuthbert's brethren: "they marvelled at the holiness of the venerable man for whom even the elements did service; and with fitting shame they blamed their slothful minds, for even the insensible elements taught them what obedience ought to be shown to saints" (*VCP*, chap. 21, p. 227). In addition to reinforcing the

contrast in their handling of this one episode is real nonetheless, and it clearly illustrates Bede's willingness to turn his material to the purposes of instruction when the opportunity presented itself. A similar example can be found in the *Vita Felicis*. Bede tells us that, after his miraculous release from prison, Felix sought to escape a second wave of persecution by taking refuge in an abandoned building. Although its crumbling wall offered very little in the way of protection, Providence came to the saint's assistance. *Divino nutu*, a spider disguised Felix's entrance with its webs, deceiving his enemies into thinking that no one could recently have been there. Bede comments:

> The great wisdom of our holy maker and protector is clear. Rather than defending them, the highest and best fortified of city walls sometimes deliver their citizens into the hands of the adversaries who have laid siege; and yet the humble Christ uses fragile spider webs to conceal his servant from pursuing armed enemies, so that he can be neither found nor captured. Truly, as the venerable father Paulinus says, speaking of these matters:
>
>> If Christ is present among us, then a spider's web becomes a wall. But if Christ is absent, then the wall is no more than a spider's web.[53]

As Mackay observes, "the moral lesson is clearly drawn: trust in God and not in the arm of the flesh."[54]

In the *Ecclesiastical History* Bede frequently is even more explicit in evoking the moral or doctrinal import of the story he relates. Hence the pedagogical purpose that it serves is mentioned at the very outset of his account of the vision of Dryhthelm. "In order to arouse the living from spiritual death," he says, "a certain man already dead came back to life

---

main point, these comments convey a larger spiritual lesson, at least in attenuated form. Similar traces, even more attenuated, are found in the anonymous account. In both versions, however, the primary objective is to show nature subservient to the man of God. Cf. *VCA* 3.4, pp. 98-100.

53 *Vita Felicis*, ed. Thomas William Mackay, in "A Critical Edition of Bede's *Vita Felicis*" (Ph.D. dissertation, Stanford University, 1972), pp. 16-17: "multa claruit sapientia pii conditoris ac protectoris nostri. Certe nonnumquam muri urbium altissimi ac munitissimi cives suos obsidentibus adversariis produnt magis quam liberant et humilis Christus famulum suum persequentibus armatis hostibus tremulis aranearum cassibus ne inveniri vel capi posset abscondit. Vere ut venerabilis pater Paulinus de his loquens ait, ubicumque

... Christus adest nobis et aranea murus fiet
at cui Christus abest et murus aranea fiet."

54 Ibid., p. 114.

and related many memorable things that he had seen, and I think that some of them ought briefly to be mentioned here."[55] Although the vision offers detailed instruction on the geography of the afterlife, Bede sees it primarily as an exhortation to penance, a theme that carries through the two immediately following chapters as well.[56] With the story of Imma it is the doctrinal content of the miracle that dominates. Every time his brother offered masses on his behalf, Imma's bonds were miraculously loosened. Says Bede:

> Many who heard about this from Imma were inspired in faith and pious devotion to prayer, to almsgiving or to the offering up of sacrifices of holy oblation to God for the deliverance of their kinsfolk who had departed from the world; for they realized that the saving sacrifice availed for the everlasting redemption of both soul and body.[57]

In its present form the story smacks of superstition, and has none of the subtlety of Gregory the Great's teaching. Whereas Gregory carefully explains that masses can benefit the departed only if their sins are such as to be pardonable in the afterlife,[58] Bede manages to suggest that they are the logical equivalent of spells, and work with the

---

55 *HE* 5.12, p. 489 (translation slightly revised).
56 The vision of Dryhthelm is followed by two stories of frightening death-bed visions. The man who had the first of these, Bede announces, "now ... suffers everlasting and fruitless punishment in torment because he failed to submit for a brief spell to the penance which would have brought him the fruit of pardon. From this it is clear, as the blessed Pope Gregory writes about certain people, that he saw this vision not for his own benefit, because it did not profit him, but for the sake of others; so that they, hearing of his fate, may fear to put off their time of repentance while they still have the opportunity, and not be cut off by sudden death and die impenitent" (*HE* 5.13, pp. 501-503). At the conclusion of the second episode Bede states: "This happened lately in the kingdom of Bernicia. The story spread far and wide and roused many people to do penance for their sins without delay. And may the reading of this account of ours have the same effect!" (ibid. 5.14, p. 505).
57 Ibid. 4.22, p. 405 (translation revised). Bede alerts us to the presence of spiritual significance in this episode in his opening comments, referring to it as "a remarkable incident ... which in my opinion should certainly not be passed over in silence, since the story may lead to the salvation of many" (p. 401).
58 Gregory the Great, *Dial.* 4.57.2, SC 265:184; & 4.59.6, SC 265:200. Cf. *Dial.* 4.41 & 42, SC 265:146-154.

same kind of automatic efficacy.[59] Nonetheless the Gregorian inspiration of the story is undeniable: it bears a strong resemblance to an episode in the *Dialogues* designed to convey the same lesson.[60] It is unsurprising, therefore, that Tugène can describe the approach Bede takes in the *Ecclesiastical History* in terms that would be entirely appropriate of his great predecessor: "ce qui compte pour lui, c'est la valeur du miracle en tant que 'signe', et non son côté merveilleux. ... Bède ne s'intéresse pas beaucoup à l'aspect anecdotique des choses. Qu'il s'agisse de batailles ou de miracles, c'est la leçon morale ou spirituelle de l'événement qui lui importe avant tout."[61]

If similar examples were needed to reinforce the point, they could be provided fairly easily. Like Gregory, Bede was clearly interested in the spiritual instruction that could be derived from the miracles he related. To the extent that it was moral instruction specifically that they provided, miracle stories were covered by the same rationale that applied to the

59 See *HE* 4.22, p. 403, where Bede tells us that Imma's captor suspected him of magic: "the *gesith* who kept him captive grew amazed and asked him why he could not be bound and whether he had about him any loosing spells (*litteras solutorias*) such as are described in stories. But Imma answered that he knew nothing of such arts. 'However,' said he, 'I have a brother in my country who is a priest and I know he believes me to be dead and offers frequent masses on my behalf; so if I had now been in another world, my soul would have been loosed from its punishment by his intercessions.'" Wallace-Hadrill, *Bede's Ecclesiastical History*, p. 162, points out that it is the thegn who believes in the efficacy of *litterae solutoriae*, not Imma and certainly not Bede. Although this is a fair comment, neither Imma nor Bede can escape all responsibility for suggesting that masses for the departed work in much the same way. Cf. Gurevich, *Medieval Popular Culture*, p. 54; and Flint, *Rise of Magic*, p. 289. In the vision of Dryhthelm, however, Dryhthelm's heavenly guide offers a view that is more theologically sound: "'The valley that you saw, with its awful flaming fire and freezing cold, is the place in which those souls have to be tried and chastened who delayed to confess and make restitution for the sins they had committed until they were on the point of death; and so they died. But because they did repent and confess, even though on their deathbed, they will all come to the kingdom of heaven on judgment day; and the prayers of those who are still alive, their alms and fastings and specially the celebration of masses, help many of them to get free even before the day of judgement" (*HE* 5.12, p. 495).
60 Gregory the Great, *Dial.* 4.59.1, SC 265:196; cf. his *Hom. in Evan.* 2.37.8, PL 76:1279. Cf. also *Dial.* 2.31, SC 260:222-226.
61 Tugène, "Histoire 'ecclésiastique' du peuple anglais," pp. 150-151. Cf. Ward, "Miracles and History," pp. 70-76.

writing of history in general. On the very first page of the *Ecclesiastical History* Bede announces a broad moral purpose for his work:

> Should history tell of good men and their good estate, the thoughtful listener is spurred on to imitate the good; should it record the evil ends of wicked men, no less effectually the devout and earnest listener or reader is kindled to eschew what is harmful and perverse, and himself with greater care pursue those things which he had learned to be good and pleasing in the sight of God.[62]

What also needs to be acknowledged, however, is that, in practice, the moral lesson that Bede would see in specific historical events is sometimes hard to detect. In practice, he often had other concerns in mind, including the simple desire to provide a record of some of the most broadly significant events in his people's past. As he puts it at the end of the preface to his history: "I have diligently sought to put on record concerning each of the kingdoms and the more important places those events which I believe to be worthy of remembrance and likely to be welcome to the inhabitants."[63] Not surprisingly, the same is true of miracle stories specifically, and the result is a contrast between the *Ecclesiastical History* and the Gregorian *Dialogues* that is considerable. In Gregory's *Dialogues* it is a relatively rare occurrence for a miracle story to be allowed to stand on its own without explanatory comment. Extensive stretches of exposition alternate with narrative passages, to ensure that the spiritual significance of the wonders being related is made as explicit as possible. The same cannot be said of the *Ecclesiastical History*. Bede's interest in pedagogy is undeniable, but so is the fact that teaching is not nearly as prominent as it is in the *Dialogues*.

Equally as significant is one other aspect of their approach in which Bede and Gregory are to be distinguished. When miracles are performed by people whose sanctity cannot be doubted, Gregory treats them as *exempla*. They are divinely sanctioned signs intended to encourage others to emulate saintly virtue. Peter, Gregory's interlocutor in the *Dialogues*, captures the point well at the outset, when he asks Gregory to tell him what he knows of the miracles performed by the saints of Italy:

---

62 *HE*, Praef., p. 3
63 Ibid., p. 7. Cf. Richard Vaughan, "The Past in the Middle Ages," *Journal of Medieval History* 12 (1986): 1-14 at 8-9.

Interrupting the study and explanation of the Scriptures for such a purpose should not cause grave concern, for the amount of edification to be gained from a description of miracles (*virtutum*) is just as great. An explanation of holy Scripture teaches us how to attain virtue (*virtus*) and persevere in it, whereas a description of miracles shows us how this acquired virtue reveals itself in those who persevere in it.[64]

The play on the word *virtus* is obvious, and helps to reinforce the point that, rather than having their own intrinsic importance, the miracles of the saints are to be valued because of their moral significance. Miracles are *ostensiones sanctitatis*, illustrations or revelations of the specific virtues that make a saint.

At times Bede seems close to perceiving miracles in a similar way. Hence he tells us that the miracles of the saints are *insignia virtutum*.[65] They are external manifestations of the grace by which the saints are internally resplendent.[66] In Cuthbert's case specifically the "signs and miracles whereby he shone outwardly gave witness to the inward virtues of his mind." All this sounds very Gregorian, including the interior/exterior contrast much favoured by Gregory.[67] There is also the description of the *Dialogues* themselves that Bede includes in the *Ecclesiastical History*. Speaking of Gregory, he says:

He composed forty *Homilies on the Gospel*, which he divided into two volumes of equal size, and made four books of *Dialogues* in which, at the request of Peter his deacon, he collected the miracles (*virtutes*) of the most famous saints he knew or could learn of in Italy, as an example of life to posterity: as in his expository works he taught what virtues (*virtutibus*) men

---

64 *Dial.* 1 Prol. 9, Zimmerman 5-6, SC 260:16: "neque hac pro re interrumpere expositionis studium grave videatur, quia non dispar aedificatio oritur ex memoria virtutum. In expositione quippe qualiter invenienda atque tenenda sit virtus agnoscitur, in narratione vero signorum cognoscimus inventa ac retenta qualiter declaratur."

65 *In Marc.* 1, CCL 120:443.

66 *Hom. Evan.* 1.15, CCL 122:110. Bede explains that in one sense the saints are in permanent possession of the Holy Spirit, and in another they are not: "Manet semper ut possint habere virtutem [qua?] mirabiliter ipsi vivant; venit ad tempus ut etiam aliis per miraculorum signa quales sint intus effulgeant." Cf. *In Cant.* 6, CCL 119B:368, where he says of the biblical saints: "quam pii quam humiles quam benigni exstiterint eorum testantur operationes." This is part of a lengthy quotation from Gregory the Great: cf. *Hom. in Ezech.* 2.3.23, CCL 142:255.

67 *VCP*, chap. 26, pp. 242-243: "Cuius internis id est animi virtutibus, ea quoque quibus foras effulgebat miraculorum signa testimonium dabant." Cf. *VCM* 8, p. 76: "pandunt miracula mentem." See also Dagens, *Saint Grégoire le Grand*, esp. pp. 133 & 231.

ought to strive after, so, by describing the miracles of the saints, he showed how glorious those virtues (*virtutum*) are.[68]

Here Bede seems clearly to have had in mind the passage from the prologue to the *Dialogues* noted above. There is the same play on the word *virtus*, and there is the claim that miracles offer us an example of life.[69] Since miracles are extraordinary events and can be performed only by the privileged few, in the strict sense we should not try to imitate them at all. If they are examples to emulate, presumably it is because at a deeper level there are specific moral lessons that they impart. In all likelihood, however, what we are dealing with here are simply vestiges of Gregorian usage. When Bede's words are examined more carefully, it is not at all clear that he has fully grasped the point. Whereas Gregory intends miracles to be object lessons in sanctity, Bede seems to suggest that their role is a more mechanical one. To Bede's mind, it would appear, they confirm the value of the saintly virtues in a purely external fashion.

This suspicion is borne out when the miracles attributed to Cuthbert and other saints in the *Vita Cuthberti* and the *Ecclesiastical History* are examined in greater detail. Bede tells us that Bishop Chad was buried in the church of St Mary at Lichfield. After its completion, his bones were translated to the church of St Peter. "In each place," says Bede, "frequent miracles of healing occur as a sign of his virtue" (*ad indicium virtutis illius*);[70] and he follows the claim with the confirming example of a madman who was restored to his senses after spending a night at Chad's tomb. The connection between this miracle and any virtues Chad may have possessed is entirely an external one. On the assumption that only saints possess such powers, the miracle confirms that Chad was a

---

68 *HE* 2.1, pp. 126-129: "Sed et Omelias evangelii numero XL conposuit, quas in duobus codicibus aequa sorte distinxit. Libros etiam Dialogorum IIII fecit, in quibus rogatu Petri diaconi sui virtutes sanctorum, quos in Italia clariores nosse vel audire poterat, ad exemplum vivendi posteris collegit ut, sicut in libris expositionum suarum quibus sit virtutibus insudandum edocuit, ita etiam descriptis sanctorum miraculis quae virtutum earundem sit claritas ostenderet."

69 On the varieties of meaning conveyed by the word *virtus* in Bede's usage, see Thomas, *Bede, Archaeology, and the Cult of Relics*, pp. 3-4. As in Gregory's case, *virtus* sometimes means "virtue," and it sometimes means "miracle" in a generic sense. However, Thomas points to a third sense, distinctive to Bede, in which it designates specifically a power of healing.

70 *HE* 4.3, pp. 344-345.

virtuous man. But it offers nothing in the form of specific moral instruction. In the case of King Oswald of Northumbria Bede seems to promise more, for he tells us that "his great faith in God and his devotion of heart" were illustrated by miracles that took place after his death.[71] Once again, however, what the miracles illustrate is only sanctity in general. We learn that the place where Oswald fell in battle became a pilgrimage site, and that soil from there, when mixed in water, brought great relief to the sick. The argument seems to be that, having established by means of the miracles that Oswald was indeed a saint, by extension one can conclude that he obviously possessed the saintly virtues, faith in God and devotion of heart among others. Certainly there is nothing in the miracles themselves to substantiate a reputation for these specific virtues.

Similar examples could be multiplied easily. "In order to illustrate his merits and the kind of life he lived" (Cuius ut meritum vel vita qualis fuerit certius clarescat),[72] Bede tells us of a miracle performed by the saintly Oethelwald. But the miracle in question, a case of Oethelwald calming stormy seas by means of prayer, offers no more in the form of specific spiritual instruction than the example of Chad cited above. The miracles in the Vita Cuthberti are of the same sort. In one well-known episode, for example, we are told that Cuthbert had asked his brethren to provide the wood he needed for a hut he was building on Farne Island. In their carelessness, the brethren forgot all about it. But the following morning they discovered that the required lumber had been miraculously produced:

> rising up in the morning, they saw that the night tide had carried up some tim-
> ber of the required length, and had placed it over the very spot whereon it was
> to be set for the building. As soon as they saw this, they marvelled at the holi-
> ness of the venerable man for whom even the elements did service.[73]

The miracle clearly helped bring home to the brethren that Cuthbert was indeed a holy man. But of the specific nature of his holiness they would have known no more after the miracle than they had grasped before.

At first glance at least, one of the miracles associated with King Oswald might be taken to suggest a more specifically Gregorian pattern.

71   Ibid. 3.9, p. 243.
72   Ibid. 5.1, pp. 454-455.
73   VCP, chap. 21, p. 227.

"Though he wielded supreme power over the whole land, he was always wonderfully humble, kind, and generous to the poor and to strangers," says Bede. The point is illustrated by a particular act of generosity on the king's part. He and Bishop Aidan had just sat down to dinner one Easter Day when it was announced that a multitude of the poor was at the gate requesting alms. The King offered them the rich meal that had been prepared for him and the bishop, and he ordered that the silver dish on which it was served be broken up and distributed to the needy as well. As subsequent events proved, the charity of the king was given a miraculous sanction:

> The bishop, who was sitting by, was delighted with this pious act, [and] grasped [the king] by the right hand, and said, "May this hand never decay." His blessing and his prayer were fulfilled in this way: when Oswald was killed in battle, his hand and arm were cut off from the rest of his body, and they have remained uncorrupt until this present time.[74]

Bede's handling of the example of Aethelburh, abbess of Brie, might be read as an even clearer example of Gregorian inspiration. He tells us that Aethelburh "lived a life of great self-denial, also preserving the glory of perpetual virginity which is well pleasing to God." Seven years after her death, he goes on to say, "the greatness of this virtue was more clearly revealed."[75] When her sepulchre was opened, her body was found to be "as untouched by decay as it had also been immune from the corruption of fleshly desires."[76] A similar story is told of Aethelthryth, wife of King Ecgfrith of Northumbria. Although she lived with the king for twelve years, the glory of her virginity was preserved intact, as subsequent events clearly demonstrated: "the divine miracle whereby her flesh would not corrupt after she was buried was token and proof that she had remained uncorrupted by contact with any man."[77] In both of these cases there is an evident parallelism between the miracles in question and the virtue for which Aethelburh and Aethelthryth were most celebrated.

---

74 *HE* 3.6, p. 231.
75 Ibid. 3.8, pp. 240-241: "et ipsa Deo dilectam perpetuae virginitatis gloriam in magna corporis continentia servavit; quae cuius esset virtutis magis post mortem claruit."
76 Ibid. 3.8, p. 241.
77 Ibid. 4.19, p. 393.

On closer inspection, however, the Gregorian overtones seem to have been a product of accident rather than design. The incorrupt body was a distinction shared by many medieval saints, and it generally pointed simply to saintly status, not any particular virtue. Bede himself informs us that this was the case with St Cuthbert, whose body also was preserved from physical corruption. The purpose was not to demonstrate any specific virtue he may have possessed, but rather "to show still further in what glory Saint Cuthbert lived after his death, whose sublime life had been attested before his death by frequent signs and miracles."[78] The standard relationship between miracles and virtue as Bede conceived it is well illustrated in the story of Peter, the first abbot of St Peter and St Paul's, later St Augustine's, at Canterbury. It is fundamentally different than the Gregorian pattern:

> Peter ... was sent on a mission to Gaul and was drowned in a bay of the sea known as *Amfleat* (Ambleteuse). He was given an unworthy burial by the inhabitants of the place but, in order that Almighty God might show how worthy a man he was (*ut qualis meriti vir fuerit demonstraret*), a heavenly light appeared every night above his grave until at last the people of the neighbourhood noticed it. They saw that it was a saint who had been buried there; so, after making inquiries as to who he was and whence he came, they removed his body and put it in a church in Boulogne with all the honour due to so great a man.[79]

In his treatment of the miracles of Bishop Aidan of Lindisfarne, Bede follows the general form. Although he introduces them by claiming that they reveal Aidan's merits for us,[80] the miracles that follow, one of them post-mortem, demonstrate his sanctity only in a very external way. They confirm *that* Aidan was a saint, but on the specific nature of his

---

78   Ibid. 4.30, p. 443. Cf. Arnold Angenendt, "Der «ganze» und «unverweste» Leib— eine Leitidee der Reliquienverehrung bei Gregor von Tours und Beda Venerabilis," in *Aus Archiven und Bibliotheken. Festschrift für Raymund Kottje zum 65. Geburtstag*, ed. Hubert Mordek (Frankfurt am Main, 1992), pp. 33-50.

79   *HE* 1.33, pp. 114-117. Cf. the entry for October 3 in the *Martyrologium*, ed. Quentin, pp. 105-106, ed. Dubois & Renaud, p. 181, where Bede tells us of the martyrdom of the two priests named Hewald: "qui cum Willibrordo episcopo venientes in Germaniam, transierunt ad Saxones; et cum ibi praedicare Christum coepissent, comprehensi sunt a paganis et sic occisi: ad quorum corpora noctu multa diu lux apparens, et ubi essent et cuius essent meriti declaravit."

80   *HE* 3.15, p. 260. Referring to Aidan he says: "Qui cuius meriti fuerit, etiam miraculorum signis internus arbiter edocuit."

sanctity they say very little. Immediately thereafter, however, Bede tells us that he chose to include in his history an account of Aidan's life and wonders, not to commend the position he took on the observance of Easter, which Bede heartily disapproved, but out of respect for his many good qualities:

> Such were his love of peace and charity, temperance and humility; his soul which triumphed over anger and greed and at the same time despised pride and vainglory; his industry in carrying out and teaching the divine commandments, his diligence in study and keeping vigil, his authority, such as became a priest, in reproving the proud and the mighty, and his tenderness in comforting the weak, in relieving and protecting the poor. To put it briefly, so far as one can learn from those who knew him, he made it his business to omit none of the commands of the evangelists, the apostles, and the prophets, but he set himself to carry them out in his deeds, so far as he was able. All these things I greatly admire and love in this bishop and I have no doubt that all this was pleasing to God.[81]

Like Gregory, Bede was interested in edification; and so, having completed his account of Aidan's miracles, he took full advantage of the opportunity to commend Aidan's virtues to his readers. In this case, as in others, however, any connection between his miracles and his virtues is tenuous at best. If Aidan's virtues are endorsed by his miracles, it is only in an external fashion; the miracles would be of no value whatever in identifying the precise set of qualities included in Bede's encomium.

Gregory the Great was not completely immune to the same tendencies that characterized Bede's approach. More than occasionally he too suggests nothing more than an external connection between the miracles of some saintly hero and his life of virtue. There is nothing surprising in this: it was the view of the relationship between miracle and virtue that dominated early medieval hagiography. It is the view to be found in the *Life of St Wilfrid*, the *Life of St Boniface*, the *Life of St Columba* and elsewhere.[82] It would have been truly extraordinary

---

81 Ibid. 3.17, p. 267.

82 See, for example, Felix, *Vita S. Guthlaci*, chap. 51, ed. Colgrave, p. 160; chap. 53, p. 168; Willibald, *Vita S. Bonifatii*, chap. 9, ed. Levison, p. 56; Eddius Stephanus, *Vita S. Wilfrithi*, chap. 66, ed. Colgrave, p. 142; Adomnan, *Vita S. Columbae* 2.9, ed. Anderson & Anderson, pp. 344-346; 2.45, p. 456. Several representative passages in the *Vita Columbae* take the same form: cf. 2.34, p. 406; 2.42, p. 446; & 3.23, p. 538: "Perpendat itaque lector quanti et qualis apud deum praedicabilis patronus honoris habeatur, cui aliquando

had Gregory escaped its influence completely. But Gregory also aspired to a more profound view of the relationship, one that transformed miracles into object lessons of saintly life and conduct in a deeper sense. This, combined with his overall interest in the edification of his audience, was what made the *Dialogues* unique in the hagiographical literature of their time.

Unfortunately, this was a view of the relationship between miracles and virtue that Bede grasped imperfectly, and it is present in his thought only in vestigial form. Lacking the clear sense of the rationale of miracles in the contemporary world that Gregory had, Bede largely echoed the traditional view. He did manage to avoid succumbing to the temptation to enlist miracles in the support of some particular cult.[83] At one point he remarks that the faith can actually be undermined when the power of a shrine is disparaged by those who are unworthy of a cure.[84] But rather than demonstrating the specifics of the saintly life *in concreto*, in Bede's thought miracles establish simply *that* the individual in question is a saint. This is the only point of most of the miracles recorded in both prose and metric versions of the *Vita Cuthberti*.[85] Despite his acknowledgment that miracles can be performed by evil men of all sorts, he even speaks as if they can be taken as proof

---

in carne mortali conversanti deo dignante oranti tempestates sedatae sunt et maria tranquillata."

83   Cf. Carroll, *Venerable Bede*, p. 197; Campbell, "Bede", p. 163.

84   *VCP*, chap. 23, pp. 232-234. Cf. chap. 37, pp. 279-281, where Cuthbert resists the desire of the brethren that his body be taken back to Lindisfarne for burial. He is concerned about it being a burden to them should his tomb attract "fugitives and guilty men of every sort." Ultimately he relents, but still shows his unease about a tomb generally accessible to the public: "'If', he said, 'you wish to set aside my plans and to take my body back there, it seems best that you entomb it in the interior of your church, so that while you yourselves can visit my sepulchre when you wish, it may be in your power to decide whether any of those who come thither should approach it.'"

85   Michael Lapidge, "Bede's Metrical *Vita S. Cuthberti*," in *St Cuthbert, His Cult and His Community*, pp. 77-93, argues that rather more than this is at issue in the VCM. In Lapidge's view, Bede's concern here was not to convey the story as story, but rather, having alluded in each chapter to the narrative available in the VCA by means of his prose *capitulum*, to develop its figural significance. For a fundamentally different view, however, see Wolpers, *Englische Heiligenlegende*, p. 77: "Bedas Anliegen ist hier poetischer, nicht stofflicher Art."

of sanctity.[86] When Bede informs us that, "through the merits of his holiness" (*ob meritum sanctitatis eius*), many miracles of healing happened on the spot where Bishop Haedde died,[87] the relationship between miracles and sanctity is clear. Sanctity is the cause; miracles are the effect.

---

86 See for example *HE* 4.6, p. 354, where we read of Eorcenwold, bishop of London: "Cuius videlicet viri et in episcopatu et ante episcopatum vita et conversatio fertur fuisse sanctissima, sicut etiam nunc caelestium signa virtutum indicio sunt." See also *VCP*, chap. 23, p. 232, where Bede says of two miracles performed by means of the girdle of St Cuthbert: "Quod divina dispensatione factum intelligitur, videlicet ut et per duo sanitatis miracula Deo dilecti patris sanctitas appareret credentibus, et deinceps dubitandi de sanctitate illius occasio tolleretur incredulis." The miracles of deceased saints, therefore, can establish the blessedness that they must currently enjoy in heaven. This is claimed of St Cuthbert (*HE* 4.30, p. 442; *VCP*, chap. 42, pp. 290-292) and of St Felix (*Vita Felicis*, ed. Mackay, p. 24, where he says of Felix: "Tali vivens pietate vir et nomine et merito Felix plenus dierum atque operum bonorum defunctus est ac viam patrum secutus aeterna est receptus in gloria sicut etiam signa quae in ecclesia in qua sepultus est sunt facta perplura testantur"). See also *HE* 4.10, p. 364, where we read of a miracle that confirmed the blessedness of the saints buried in the cemetery of the nuns of Barking. A woman was cured of blindness while praying there: "quasi ad hoc solummodo lucem amitteret temporalem, ut quanta sanctos Christi lux in caelis, quae gratia virtutis possideret, sua sanatione demonstraret."

87 *HE* 5.18, pp. 514-515.

6

Bede and the Hagiographical Tradition

In his essay in *Famulus Christi*, the special thirteenth centenary volume of Bede studies, Paul Meyvaert describes himself as having "often been struck by the absence of firsthand accounts of miracles from the pens of reliable authors. We always seem to encounter tales of miracles told to the author by others."[1] One could argue for one or more exception to the rule, by pointing to Gregory of Tours, for example. But the force of Meyvaert's observation would remain unimpaired, and could easily be illustrated. Meyvaert himself refers to Gregory the Great and the Venerable Bede. Although they had the privilege of recording the many wonders that God performed through the saints of their own time, neither seems to have had extensive personal experience of the miraculous. Indeed, their collected works inform us of only one miracle each of which they were the personal beneficiaries, and in neither case is the miracle in question among the most striking of those recorded.

In book three of his *Dialogues* Gregory tells us that, during the period before his summons to the papal office, while he was still living in the monastery of St Andrew, he was once stricken by a serious intestinal disorder. Not only was he prevented from keeping the fast on Holy Saturday, a matter that much distressed him, but his very life was in jeopardy. However, he asked Eleutherius of Spoleto to pray for him, and the effect was instantaneous. The holy man's prayer was scarcely completed when Gregory found himself completely restored to health and relieved of all anxiety. Bede also, it would seem, received a physical cure, although his ailment was not life-threatening. In the dedicatory epistle to the metrical *Vita Cuthberti* he informs us that he has not been able to record all the miracles performed by the saint. On a daily basis new ones are accomplished through the virtue of his relics, and older ones continue to come to light. Among these, Bede says, is a wonder he

1   "Bede the Scholar," p. 54.

experienced in his own person, a healing of the tongue received while singing the miracles of the saint.[2]

Gregory's account includes enough detail to provide a fairly clear indication of what he experienced. He tells us that physicians use the Greek term, *syncopin*, to refer to his ailment. At issue seems to have been at least some temporary relief from a chronic stomach problem that plagued him throughout his career. Unfortunately, Bede's brief comments are not nearly as informative. When he speaks of "singing" the miracles of the saint (*dum miracula eius canerem*), presumably he means the composition of the metrical life itself. Possibly, therefore, it was not physical healing of the tongue he received, but simply guidance from the saintly muse. As G.H. Brown points out, the Latin (*linguae curatio*) could bear either meaning.[3] On balance, however, it seems improbable that Bede here would use *curatio* to mean anything other than "cure." The context is one in which he is clearly thinking of the miracles of the saint, those newly effected or recently reported. Given the kind of wonders he judges worth recording elsewhere in the *Vita Cuthberti*, one doubts that he would have regarded a simple case of poetic inspiration as at all comparable. If this leaves us with a physical cure of some kind, regrettably not much else is clear. Reginald of Durham posits the healing of a speech impediment, but his testimony is late, from the twelfth century, and lacks corroboration.[4] Whether a cure of this magnitude is at issue, or the simple healing of a "sore tongue," as suggested by Levison, is impossible to determine.[5]

If their rather limited firsthand experience of the miraculous was a trait that both Gregory and Bede had in common with most other early medieval hagiographers, so was their insistence on the truthfulness of

2   *Dial.* 3.33.7-9, SC 260:396-398; *VCM, Epist. ad Johannem*, p. 57: "Scire autem debes, quod nequaquam omnia gesta illius exponere potui; cotidie namque et nova per reliquias eius aguntur et vetera noviter ab his qui scire poterant indicantur. Ex quibus unum est, quod in me ipso, sicut jam tibi dixi, per linguae curationem, dum miracula eius canerem, expertus sum."

3   Brown, *Bede the Venerable*, p. 69. Cf. Dorothy Whitelock, "Bede and His Teachers and Friends," in *Famulus Christi*, pp. 19-39 at 21.

4   Reginald of Durham, *Libellus de admirandis Beati Cuthberti virtutibus*, chap. 76, ed. J. Raine (London, 1835), p. 158: "Nam multos novimus a Beato Cuthberto donum scientiae expetisse, et uberioris quam expetierant dono gratiae inundasse. De quorum numero Beda Doctor magnificus exstitit, qui linguae impeditioris impedimento ipsius meritis absolvi meruit."

5   Levison, "Bede as Historian," p. 126.

what they related, and their appeal to witnesses. In the prologue to book one of the *Dialogues* Gregory informs us that what he is about to narrate he has received on the testimony of worthy men. He goes on to say that, in order to remove any possibility of doubt on the part of his readers, he will indicate the authority on which each account is based.[6] Bede prefaces his prose version of the *Vita Cuthberti* with similar assurances:

> I have not presumed to write down anything concerning so great a man without the most rigorous investigation of the facts nor, at the end, to hand on what I had written to be copied for general use, without the scrupulous examination of credible witnesses. Nay rather, it was only after first diligently investigating the beginning, the progress, and the end of his most glorious life and activity, with the help of those who knew him, that I began at last to set about making notes: and I have decided occasionally to place the names of these my authorities in the book itself, to show clearly how my knowledge of the truth has been gained.[7]

It has been observed more than once that, in the hagiographical tradition, such statements do not necessarily mean much. In a variation on the motif, Eddius Stephanus prefaces his life of St Wilfrid with similar assurances, beseeching his readers to take what he has written at face value. Everything, he says, has been received from and is attested to by trustworthy men; remaining silent would be better than stating what is false. The point of such statements was to enhance credibility. For modern readers the effect is quite different when they discover that Eddius's verbal guarantee is lifted directly from the Anonymous life of St Cuthbert, which in turn is dependent on the *Vita Martini* of Sulpicius Severus.[8] Indeed, the prologue to Bede's *Vita Cuthberti* quoted above itself served as a model for the author of the life of St Guthlac.[9]

---

6   *Dial.* 1 Prol. 10, SC 260:16.

7   *VCP*, Prol., pp. 143-145.

8   *Vita Wilfrithi*, Praef., ed. Colgrave, pp. 2-3: "*Obsecro itaque eos qui lecturi sunt, ut fidem dictis adhibeant,* relinquentes antiqui hostis millenos invidiae stimulos et recolentes, quod eloquentia pertonabat. Semper enim in propatulo fortitudo emulos habet: *feriuntque summos fulgora montes. Neque enim me quicquam* audaci temeritate, *nisi quod compertum et probatum a fidelibus sit, scripsisse arbitrentur; alioquin tacere quam false dicere maluissem.*" Cf. *VCA* 1.2, pp. 62-64; and *Vita Martini* 1.9, SC 133:252-254.

9   Cf. *VCP*, Prol., pp. 142-143; and *Vita S. Guthlaci*, Prol., ed. Colgrave, pp. 64-65. The Life of Guthlac cannot be dated precisely enough to ensure that it was Felix copying Bede and not the other way around, but it does seen likely. In his

If hagiographers cannot always be taken at their word on such matters, however, their claims cannot be routinely dismissed either. The point becomes clear when one examines closely Gregory the Great's practice in the *Dialogues*. Gregory's appeal to witnesses to corroborate his miracle stories could have been no more than a simple literary device, but that is not what the balance of the evidence suggests. In addition to the general claims standard to the genre, Gregory provides specifying detail. In the overriding majority of cases he identifies his sources by name. Moreover, the impression created by the *Dialogues* is reinforced by his register, which strongly suggests that he really did draw on the informants he mentions.[10] In Bede's case, therefore, we cannot simply assume either factual veracity or hagiographical invention. In order to determine whether it was the Gregorian model or the standard hagiographical pattern that prevailed, Bede's practice, both in the life of Cuthbert and in the *Ecclesiastical History*, needs to be subjected to a close analysis.

---

introduction Colgrave provides us with at least a few solid points of reference for dating the *Vita Guthlaci*. First of all, the prologue indicates that the life was dedicated to and written at the request of Aelfwald, king of the East Angles from about 713 to 749. The *terminus a quo* becomes clearer from the reference to the visit of Aethelbald to the saint's tomb, for this occurred "less than twelve months before the king's accession to the Mercian throne which was in 716" (p. 18). Colgrave argues that Felix's use of Bede's prose life of Cuthbert provides further refinement of the date, for the latter was not written before 721. This assumes the very point we would like to have corroborated. Significant in this regard, however, is the observation that "Bede nowhere mentions Guthlac in his *Ecclesiastical History*. In view of Bede's interest in East Anglian and Mercian affairs, it would be surprising if he had not come across Felix's Life, supposing it had been written before his *Ecclesiastical History* which appeared in 731. Bearing all these facts in mind, one might suggest a date [for the writing of the *Vita Guthlaci*] somewhere between 730 and 740" (p. 19).

10 On the sources of the *Dialogues*, see *Signs of Sanctity*, pp. 113-117. See also Gregory's letter of July 593 to Bishop Maximian of Syracuse: *Epist.* 3.50, CCL 140:195-196. Here Gregory asks Maximian for information about the miracles of the abbot Nonnosus, information that he subsequently reports at *Dial.* 1.7, SC 260:64-70. Meyvaert,"Enigma of Gregory the Great's *Dialogues*," p. 348, has recently pointed out that, if this letter appears unique, it is "only because so few letters from this indiction have survived. It is likely enough that Gregory was questioning others among his friends at this same period about miracles accomplished by Italian Fathers."

On first glance at least, the standard Bede employed in his prose life of St Cuthbert seems to have been less exacting than that of the Lindisfarne Anonymous who preceded him. If we exclude episodes that are just mentioned,[11] the anonymous life contains thirty miracle stories. For nine of these (roughly thirty percent of the total) we are given a named source, for four others (thirteen percent) an anonymous source. In the remaining cases (seventeen, or fifty-seven percent) no source is mentioned. Bede's version in comparison contains forty-three miracle stories in total,[12] only eleven of which (twenty-six percent) have a named source, and only three of which (an additional seven percent) have even an anonymous source. A full sixty-seven percent of the time (i.e. in twenty-nine of the forty-three cases) Bede provides no source whatever. On a cursory view at least, his practice seems to have been closer to Adomnan's than to Gregory the Great's.[13]

The cursory view, however, is probably misleading, since it fails to take account of the relationship between the two versions of Cuthbert's life. Berschin has argued that Bede's account was intended to replace the anonymous life, and that he deliberately chose not to mention it because he considered it nothing more than a quarry for the materials of his own building,[14] a view that would tend to reinforce the tentative conclusion reached above. On closer examination, however, this appears unlikely. Bede's account includes all thirty miracle stories in the anonymous

---

11 Cf. *VCA* 1.7 & 4.18, pp. 72 & 138.
12 Counting miracle stories is not a precise science. Some arbitrariness is involved in judging when a miracle is simply mentioned rather than related, or when one ends and another begins. In comparison to our forty-three miracles, Loomis counts thirty-eight, and Colgrave forty. Cf. Loomis, "Miracle Traditions," and Colgrave, *Two Lives*, p. 14.
13 Cf. *Vita S. Columbae*, 2a Praef., ed. Anderson & Anderson, p. 184, where Adomnan claims to be drawing on the evidence of knowledgeable and trustworthy informants: "Nemo itaque me de hoc tam praedicabili viro aut mentitum estimet aut quasi quaedam dubia vel incerta scripturum; sed ea quae majorum fideliumque virorum tradita expertorum cognovi relatione narraturum et sine ulla ambiguitate craxaturum sciat, et vel ex his quae ante nos inserta paginis repperire potuimus, vel ex his quae auditu ab expertis quibusdam fidelibus antiquis sine ulla dubitatione narrantibus diligentius sciscitantes didicimus." In point of fact, however, Adomnan is not particularly faithful in identifying his sources.
14 Berschin, *Biographie und Epochenstil im lateinischen Mittelalter* 2:270; idem, "*Opus deliberatum ac perfectum*," p. 96.

version, plus an additional thirteen.[15] Generally speaking, Bede omits any mention of the sources cited by the Anonymous, although in chapters one and thirty he does retain the references to Bishop Tumma and to Aethilwald, prior of Melrose. Tumma is now identified more formally, presumably for the benefit of an altered and possibly wider audience, as Trumwine; and Aethilwald is now credited with the change in his status wrought by his promotion to abbot. In chapter five, a named source, Ingwald, a priest and monk at Wearmouth, is provided for a story that is unattested in the anonymous account; in chapter twenty-five, a hitherto anonymous informant is identified as Baldhelm, priest of Lindisfarne; and in chapter thirty-eight, Herefrith, a priest and former abbot of Lindisfarne, is called upon to attest to a wonder originally received on the authority of the monk, Wahlstod. Elsewhere, however, it is basically a question of the references in the anonymous version, whether to named or anonymous informants, being suppressed.

What this strongly suggests is that Bede presupposed a continuing knowledge of the work of his anonymous predecessor, although his failure to refer to it does remain puzzling. Writing as he was, at least in the first instance, for the monks of Lindisfarne, he may have felt no need to mention a work that they all certainly would have known. Possibly as well he wished to spare the feelings of the anonymous Lindisfarne monk responsible for the first life. It would have been difficult to acknowledge that it provided the point of departure for his own account without implicitly at least suggesting its inadequacy.[16] Whatever the case, it seems improbable that Bede conceived of his own work as a replacement for the anonymous account. It was more likely intended to "supplement

---

15 The Anonymous mentions two of the thirteen along with a number of others, but does not relate them in detail. So they really are additions in Bede's account. Cf. *VCA* 4.18, p. 138; and *VCP*, chaps. 31, 35, pp. 254-256, 264-266. Instead of thirteen additional miracles, Colgrave, *Two Lives*, p. 14, counts only eight. In fact, however, he appears to have counted chapters rather than miracles, and he misses the miracle story in the second half of chapter twenty-seven.

16 Goffart, *Narrators of Barbarian History*, pp. 284-285, argues that, because of its appropriation by the author of the *Life of Wilfrid*, in the eyes of the Lindisfarne monks and of Bede himself "the original *Life of St. Cuthbert* had been soiled and devalued. ... Stephen [Eddius Stephanus] had befouled the original *Life of St. Cuthbert* by placing it in the service of the very different sanctity Wilfrid had embodied." See below, pp. 201-202.

the earlier version for a community ... in possession of both."[17] Bede's basic operating rule, therefore, was to say nothing about the informants already identified by the Anonymous unless he had something new to contribute: a clarification to offer, or an additional witness to confirm the story.[18] A general practice of continuing to identify the original sources could well have misled readers by creating the impression that these sources were his informants as well, that he had learned of the events in question from them directly, which, of course, he had not.

If we return, therefore, to our comparison of the Anonymous and Bede, assuming this time no need on Bede's part to identify sources already named in the anonymous life, and counting all of these as if they were named by Bede as well, the results are altered significantly. Bede now provides a named source thirty-nine percent of the time (seventeen times out of forty-three). Anonymous sources are cited in five percent of the miracle stories (two of forty-three), and stories for which no source is provided (twenty-four of forty-three) are reduced to fifty-six percent of the total. If we assume that Bede would have felt no need to mention already identified anonymous sources either, and count these as well as if they were cited by Bede himself (unless, of course, an anonymous is replaced by a named source), the results are even more favourable. Although named sources are unaffected, anonymous sources now account for twelve percent of the total (five episodes of forty-three), and episodes without attestation (twenty-one of forty-three) drop even further to forty-nine percent.

When Bede's practice is compared to Gregory the Great's, the results are inconclusive at best. In the *Dialogues* named sources are provided for a clear majority of the miracle stories related, and only a handful are left without even anonymous attestation. This is a record that Bede does not come close to matching. Although the sample is small, perhaps the best measurement of Bede's practice is provided by an analysis of the thirteen stories that he alone tells. However, the results are not altered significantly. Colgrave claims that "when he tells a fresh miracle not

---

17   Abraham, "Bede's *Life of Cuthbert*: A Reassessment," p. 24. Cf. Alan Thacker, "Lindisfarne and the Origins of the Cult of St Cuthbert," in *St Cuthbert, His Cult and His Community*, pp. 103-122 at 118-119.

18   The single exception occurs in chapter eleven, where the priest originally identified as Tydi remains in the narrative, but sinks to anonymity, although Bede clearly is thinking of the same man.

related in the other life, he refers to his witnesses, though not in every case by name."[19] This is imprecise enough to be misleading. Six of the thirteen miracles (forty-six percent) are credited to named sources, and an additional two (fifteen percent) to anonymous sources. The remaining five (thirty-eight percent) are related without any reference to sources or witnesses. It seems clear, however, that Bede was at least as exacting and probably more exacting in his standards than the Lindisfarne Anonymous. Not content with formulaic protestations of truthfulness, Bede seems to have felt an obligation to provide witnesses, witnesses that, in some cases at least, were clearly consulted just as he claims. A detailed analysis of the manner in which he reworked one of the episodes in the anonymous life illustrates the point well.

The story in question concerns the cure of a young woman who had been seriously ill with pain in her head and side that the physicians had not been able to relieve.[20] She was restored to good health, however, when Cuthbert took pity on her, and anointed her with chrism he had blessed. The Anonymous tells the story on the authority of Aethilwald, prior of the monastery of Melrose, who had been an eyewitness to the event. As mentioned above, Bede appeals to Aethilwald as well, but identifies him as the current abbot. Bede omits the name of the village in which the miracle occurred, *Bedesfeld*, possibly because it wasn't of compelling interest. But he explains why Cuthbert was there in the first place, although the point may well be implied in the anonymous account. He was making the rounds of several villages, says Bede, to instruct the inhabitants, presumably on the rudiments of the faith. More importantly, Bede clarifies the cured woman's status, explaining that she was one of a group of nuns who, just a short time previously, had had to flee before a ravaging army, and who had been given by Cuthbert himself a place of refuge in the village in question.

One additional difference between the two accounts concerns the term of the woman's illness. The affliction that the Anonymous says had lasted for almost a year (*pene per totum anni spatium*) Bede describes without qualification as having persisted for an entire year (*per integrum annum*). Certainty is elusive here, but one might guess that Bede missed the qualifying adverb and consequently offered a less precise account. Everything else, however, suggests that he checked the

19   Colgrave, *Two Lives*, p. 14.
20   Cf. *VCA* 4.4, pp. 116-117; *VCP*, chap. 30, pp. 254-255.

story with Aethilwald, whose status he upgraded, and from him learned additional significant detail. The nature of the wonder itself confirms this assessment, for both authors deemphasize its miraculous aspects. It was not a sudden and spectacular cure. Rather, as Bede explains, once the woman was anointed by the man of God, "she began to get better from that very hour, and after a few days was restored to complete health."[21] Instead of being a fantastic tale credited to some mythical source, it has the ring of an honest report derived from a credible witness still alive at Bede's time of writing.

When our enquiry is expanded to include the *Ecclesiastical History*, the evidence suggests that in this his masterpiece Bede worked to a more exacting standard, although perhaps still not one that would fully match the benchmark established by Gregory's *Dialogues*. In his Preface Bede addresses King Ceolwulf in words reminiscent of the Prologue to the *Dialogues*, informing him that

> in order to remove all occasions of doubt about those things I have written, either in your mind or in the minds of any others who listen to or read this history, I will make it my business to state briefly from what sources I have gained my information.[22]

This seems fully in character for a man who, as Plummer has pointed out, had "a much greater sense of literary property than is at all common among mediaeval writers."[23] In the prologue to his commentary on Luke he readily acknowledges his debts to Ambrose, Augustine, Jerome, Gregory the Great and others; and, anxious that he not be thought of as having stolen their comments and given them off as his own (*sollicitus per omnia ne maiorum dicta furari et haec quasi mea propria componere dicar*), he pleads with those who might have his work copied that they

21 "Quae ab illa mox hora meliorari incipiens, post dies paucos plena sospitate convaluit." In the anonymous version we read: "quae ab illa hora cito virtute proficiens, dolorem de die in diem deserens, sanitati pristinae reddita est."

22 *HE*, Praef., pp. 2-3: "Ut autem in his quae scripsi vel tibi vel ceteris auditoribus sive lectoribus huius historiae occasionem dubitandi subtraham, quibus haec maxime auctoribus didicerim, breviter intimare curabo." The verbal echo of *Dial.* 1 Prol. 10, sc 260:16, is clear: "Sed ut dubitationis occasionem legentibus subtraham, per singula quae describo, quibus mihi haec auctoribus sint conperta manifesto."

23 Plummer, *Opera Historica* 1:xxiii.

preserve the system of marginal notation he has devised to indicate precisely what he has borrowed from whom.[24]

In the remaining part of his Preface Bede fleshes out the general statement quoted above, telling us, among other things, that for the period up to the conversion of the English he derived his material "chiefly from the writings of earlier writers" (*ex priorum maxime scriptis*).[25] Contrary to expectations, none of these writers is identified by name, and neither here nor in the body of the history proper does Bede feel any great compulsion to give such sources proper credit.[26] The list of authors used without acknowledgment is quite extensive, and includes, among others, Orosius, Eutropius, Gildas, Prosper and Constantius of Lyons.[27] For the more recent period, however, he does identify a number of sources, chiefly Albinus, abbot of the monastery of Saints Peter and Paul (later St Augustine's) at Canterbury, and Nothhelm, a priest of the church in London. Albinus was a major source of information, both oral and documentary, and Nothhelm was his primary means of contact with Jarrow. Bede also mentions Daniel, bishop of Winchester; the monks of Lastingham; Abbot Esi, about whom nothing more is known; and Cyneberht, bishop of Lindsey. Since he comments as well on the areas or subjects about which all these various sources informed him, at least some conclusions can be safely drawn. His

---

24 *In Luc.*, Prol., CCL 120:7; cf. *In Marc.*, Prol., CCL 120:432.

25 *HE*, Praef., pp. 4-5.

26 The only written source explicitly referred to in the Preface is one Bede utilized for a later period, the Anonymous Life of St Cuthbert, and even it is not clearly identified as a completed literary work. Cf. *HE*, Praef., p. 6: "ea quae de sanctissimo patre et antistite Cudbercto vel in hoc volumine vel in libello gestorum ipsius conscripsi, partim ex eis quae de illo prius a fratribus ecclesiae Lindisfarnensis scripta repperi adsumsi, simpliciter fidem historiae quam legebam accommodans, partim vero ea quae certissima fidelium virorum adtestatione per me ipse cognoscere potui, sollerter adicere curavi." Berschin, "*Opus deliberatum ac perfectum*," p. 96, argues that, given the nature of Bede's reference, were it "not for some continental manuscripts in which the first life of St Cuthbert is handed down to us, we would have no idea that such a work ever existed."

27 Occasionally Bede mentions such sources. Hence at *HE* 1.8, p. 36, he cites Eutropius as the source of a detail; at 1.10, p. 38, he quotes Prosper on the rise of Pelagianism; and at 1.22, p. 68, he mentions (in a passing reference) Gildas as a source on the crimes of the Britons. But this disguises the true nature of his indebtedness. In the same first book of the *Ecclesiastical History* Bede borrows extensively and without acknowledgment from these same authors. See Plummer, *Opera Historica* 1:xxiv n.

language implies, for example, that he was highly dependent on Albinus and Nothhelm for Kent, and on the monks of Lastingham for Mercia and Essex, as well as what he knew of the holy fathers Cedd and Chad. In general, however, the list seems to be one of principal sources only, and I doubt that Bede would claim any more for it. For the most part, arguing from the location of a story or its subject matter back to the identity of Bede's informant would be a perilous undertaking.[28]

If the Preface to the *Ecclesiastical History* provides an essentially favourable impression of Bede's standards for the use of sources, it is reinforced by his handling of the miracle stories themselves. There are seventy-six such stories in the history.[29] When they are analyzed in terms of the kind of source to which he appeals in each case, the results can be displayed as follows:

Named	Written	Anonymous	No Source
18: 24%	17: 22%	7: 9%	34: 45%

The analysis rests on the assumption that the monks of Lastingham are to be given credit for the stories of Chad and Cedd as the Preface suggests, and are to be treated as named sources. It assumes as well that the five episodes also in the *Vita Cuthberti* are to be considered as being based on a written source. In point of fact, however, only three of these are also found in the anonymous account, and no sources of any kind are cited to attest to the other two. Appropriate adjustments, therefore, lead to the following revised totals:

Named	Written	Anonymous	No Source
18: 24%	15: 20%	7: 9%	36: 47%

A breakdown by individual book yields the following summary:

BOOK ONE: ELEVEN MIRACLES

Named	Written	Anonymous	No Source
0	0	0	11: 100%

---

28 For an attempted reconstruction of Bede's sources on a region-by-region basis, see D.P. Kirby, "Bede's Native Sources for the *Historia Ecclesiastica*," *Bulletin of the John Rylands Library* 48 (1965-1966): 341-371.

29 Cf. Loomis, "Miracle Traditions," who counts fifty-two miracles; and Rosenthal, "Bede's Use of Miracles," who counts fifty-one. Perhaps we are not counting the same thing. Whereas I have counted seventy-six different miracles, Rosenthal identifies "about 51 different *accounts* of miracles and the miraculous" (p. 329).

BOOK TWO: FOUR MIRACLES			
Named	Written	Anonymous	No Source
0	0	0	4: 100%

BOOK THREE: TWENTY-ONE MIRACLES			
Named	Written	Anonymous	No Source
4: 19%	3: 14%	4: 19%	10: 48%

BOOK FOUR: TWENTY-SEVEN MIRACLES			
Named	Written	Anonymous	No Source
5: 19%	12: 44%	2: 7%	8: 30%

BOOK FIVE: THIRTEEN MIRACLES			
Named	Written	Anonymous	No Source
9: 69%	0	1: 8%	3: 23%

The trend, already noted by Rosenthal, is clear.[30] Bede becomes increasingly more forthcoming in his citation of sources as he moves to the latter portions of his history.

The first three books, either individually or as a group, should probably not be considered as the best indicators. Book one offers a survey stretching from Roman times up to the Augustinian mission. Books two and three advance the account into the seventh century, the second book closing with the death in battle of King Edwin in 633, the third with the apostasy of Sigehere, king of Essex, in the plague of 664. With books four and five, however, the narrative moves into Bede's own time. The last major event recorded in book four is the death of Cuthbert in 687;[31] book five extends the account up to the point where the narrative breaks off in 731. If we limit ourselves to the last two books, on the premiss that for events much earlier there would have been a greater chance of his having had to rely on unsubstantiated general report, the forty miracles stories Bede relates can be classified as follows:

Named	Written	Anonymous	No Source
14: 35%	12: 30%	3: 7%	11: 28%

Although this does not match Gregorian practice, it comes close.

In his *Dialogues*, Gregory the Great provides named sources for fifty-two percent of his miracle stories, anonymous sources for an

---

30 Rosenthal, "Bede's Use of Miracles," p. 331.
31 The final chapter of book four contains a miracle at Cuthbert's tomb that Bede tells us took place just three years before his time of writing, i.e. in 728.

additional thirty-five percent, and no source at all for a mere thirteen percent.[32] All things considered, therefore, Bede seems to have been a successor reasonably faithful to Gregorian practice. However, the differences between them are perhaps as significant as the similarities. If in their use of clearly identified sources (named and written) Gregory and Bede seem comparable, Bede does not seem to have felt Gregory's compulsion, in the absence of anything better, to refer to at least an anonymous source, nor does he seem to have shared Gregory's horror at leaving a miracle story unattested. In short, he did not feel quite the same need as Gregory to marshall all the witnesses who could attest to the truth of his account. The reason for this is unclear, but it at least raises the possibility that his commitment to providing a factually accurate narrative was not as uncompromising as Gregory's.

It has frequently been claimed that historical veracity was not Gregory the Great's primary concern in writing his *Dialogues*. The spiritual value of his stories, it is said, was much more important to him than their historicity.[33] Provided that they could be enlisted in the service of edification, he felt no qualms in borrowing from earlier writers, attributing wonders described there to the saints of his own time. Although Gregory refers frequently to the witnesses who can confirm the truth of what he reports, his claims are not systematically to be taken at face value. As de Vogüé puts it:

> Si parfois des miracles de saints étrangers ont pu être attribués par la voix publique à des héroes italiens avant d'être recueillis de bonne foi par Grégoire, il n'est guère douteux que celui-ci, dans d'autres cas, a lui-même opéré le transfert des textes à la réalité, des narrations d'écrivains antécédents à l'existence de personnages vivant en Italie au vi^e siècle.[34]

Although de Vogüé's voice is not an isolated one, so far evidence has fallen somewhat short of the claims. If Gregory was indeed guilty of literary fraud, the case has not been demonstrated. Moreover, since such a practice would be difficult to reconcile with his strongly held Augustin-

---

32 See *Signs of Sanctity*, p. 114, n. 8. For reasons outlined there, these figures do not take into account book two, the Life of St Benedict. If they did, the percentage of stories having named sources would be even higher.

33 For a recent statement of this view, one that illustrates as well how it has entered the realm of generally received truth, see Janet Coleman, *Ancient and Medieval Memories: Studies in the Reconstruction of the Past* (Cambridge, 1992), pp. 125-126.

34 De Vogüé, *Grégoire le Grand, Dialogues* 1:135.

ian standards of truthfulness, in the absence of proof Gregory should be taken at his word.[35] Augustinian standards were not the only ones known to the medieval west, however, and more than one hagiographer clearly was willing to compromise factual veracity in the service of some greater good, be it only the celebration of his patron's merits. The precise nature of Bede's relationship to his sources, therefore, cannot be assumed in advance. The potential for literary invention clearly existed; and elsewhere, as we have seen, Bede could be strongly influenced by Gregory the Great while preserving independence of judgment. The case needs to be examined on its merits, subjecting each of several examples of possible literary borrowing on his part to close and careful scrutiny.

One interesting case of duplication has already been noticed by Colgrave.[36] The Lindisfarne Anonymous informs us that once, when he had been out preaching the Gospel in the surrounding countryside, Cuthbert came upon the village of a *gesith* of King Aldfrith by the name of Hemma, a man whose wife was ill to the point of death. After being welcomed by the *gesith* and informed of the seriousness of his wife's condition, Cuthbert blessed some water, and entrusted it to the priest, Beta, to administer to her. Beta sprinkled the water over the woman and over her bed, pouring some into her open mouth as well; and its effect was instantaneous. She recovered immediately; and like Peter's wife's mother, she ministered to her guests. "She was the first of the whole household to give the chalice of joy to the bishop (*episcopo poculum ... dedit*), who had taken away from her, as she lay dying, the cup of death." Bede's prose life, of course, contains the story as well; and although Bede chooses not to retain some interesting details bearing on the identity of the *gesith* and the location of his village, his version is substantially the same. "It was a fair sight to see," says Bede, "how she who had escaped the cup of death by the bishop's blessing, was the first of all the household of so great a man to offer him the cup of refreshment (*episcopo potum ... obtulit*). She thus followed the example of the mother-in-law of the Apostle Peter, who, when she was cured of a fever by the Lord, forthwith rose and ministered to Him and to His disciples."[37]

---

35 *Signs of Sanctity*, Chaps. 5 & 6.
36 Colgrave, "Bede's Miracle Stories," pp. 209-210.
37 Cf. *VCA* 4.3, pp. 114-115; *VCP*, chap. 29, pp. 252-255.

As Colgrave observes, there is a surprising degree of similarity between this incident and an episode that the *Ecclesiastical History* associates with St John of Beverley. In the latter case the story concerns a *gesith* named Puch, whose wife had been suffering from a serious illness for forty days. Puch decided to take advantage of Bishop John's presence in his village; and so, after John had finished consecrating the village church, he invited him, with much insistence, back to his home to dine. Ultimately the bishop agreed, and he sent as well one of his brethren to Puch's sick wife with some of the consecrated water left over from the dedication. Once again the healing effect of the water was immediate. After being anointed where the pain was greatest and being given some to drink,

> the woman at once rose cured, realizing that she was not only free from her protracted illness but had also recovered her long-lost strength; she brought the cup to the bishop (*obtulit poculum episcopo*) and to the rest of us and continued to serve us all with drink until dinner was finished. In this she imitated the mother-in-law of St Peter, who had been sick of a fever, but rose and ministered to them, having regained her health and strength at the touch of the Lord's hand.[38]

There is a little verbal similarity among the three passages, but only a very little, and not enough in itself to justify the conclusion that in the John of Beverley episode Bede was simply reusing material from the *Vita Cuthberti*. Noteworthy also is the fact that the story is quite well attested, Bede's source being Berhthun, abbot of Beverley, who was still alive when the *Ecclesiastical History* was written. The matter is complicated further, however, as Colgrave also notes, by the existence of another parallel episode in the *Vita Wilfrithi*. Eddius Stephanus tells us that while Wilfrid was languishing in prison on the orders of King Ecgfrith, the wife of the reeve of the town in which he was being detained was suddenly overcome by a serious palsy. Fearing for her life, the reeve hastened to enlist the aid of the saint. Bishop Wilfrid invoked divine assistance, sprinkling the face of the woman with consecrated water and, like both Cuthbert and John of Beverley, pouring some into her mouth. The cure, once again, followed without delay:

> She opened her mouth, drew in long breaths, unclosed her eyes, recovered consciousness and understanding, and shortly afterwards her limbs became

38   *HE* 5.4, pp. 462-463.

warm; she raised her head and moved her tongue to speak, and thanked God. Like Peter's wife's mother, she ministered to our holy bishop in all honour; she is still living and is now a holy abbess named Aebbe, and is wont to tell this story with tears.[39]

With one exception the verbal echoes among these four episodes are all quite weak. The exception is a significant parallelism between the *Vita Wilfrithi* and the anonymous *Vita Cuthberti* at that part of the narrative comparing the healed woman with Peter's wife's mother. Where the Lindisfarne Anonymous maintains that *sicut socrus Petri sanata, ministravit eis*, Eddius states: *sicut socrus Petri sanata sancto pontifici nostro honorifice ministrabat*. In all probability Eddius has borrowed from the anonymous Lindisfarne monk. Whether Bede has done anything comparable, however, is uncertain. The John of Beverley story, it seems clear, is a variation on a tale first articulated by the Anonymous. Conceivably, however, echoes of what he had written earlier when revising the anonymous life were still resounding in Bede's mind as he gave shape to Abbot Berhthun's story.

Another interesting case of duplication involves parallels between the two lives of St Cuthbert and Adomnan's *Vita Columbae*.[40] While he was still a monk at Melrose, Bede tells us, the abbess Aebbe—another Aebbe apparently—once invited Cuthbert to the monastery at Coldingham. Cuthbert accepted, devoting several days to his visit, and "opened up to them all the path of righteousness about which he preached, as much by his deeds as by his words." While there, the saint followed his customary practice of spending the night alone in prayer; and one night, one of the brethren, overcome by curiosity, followed after him secretly. He saw Cuthbert go down to the shore where, immersed in the waters of the sea up to his neck and arms, the saint passed the hours of darkness "watching and singing praises to the sound of the waves." What he witnessed in the morning was even more remarkable:

When daybreak was at hand, he [Cuthbert] went up on to the land and began to pray once more, kneeling (*flexis genibus*) on the shore. While he was doing this, there came forth from the depths of the sea two four-footed creatures which are commonly called otters. These, prostrate before him on the sand, began to warm his feet with their breath and sought to dry him

---

39 *Vita Wilfrithi*, chap. 37, ed. Colgrave, pp. 74-77.
40 Cf. *VCP*, chap. 10, pp. 188-190; *VCA* 2.3, pp. 78-82; *Vita S. Columbae* 3.16, ed. Anderson & Anderson, pp. 496-498.

with their fur, and when they had finished their ministrations, they received his blessing and slipped away into their native waters.[41]

Cuthbert hastened back to the monastery in time for the canonical hours; the brother, stricken with fear at what he had witnessed, had to struggle to accomplish as much. Ultimately, however, he humbled himself before the saint, who of course knew what he had done, and he received Cuthbert's forgiveness on the condition that no one be informed of what he had witnessed before Cuthbert's death.

Bede's account is substantially the same as the earlier version of the Lindisfarne Anonymous, although Bede does add some significant detail. Aebbe, described by the Anonymous simply as a widow, is now identified more exactly as the sister of King Oswiu of Northumbria. In the anonymous account small sea animals minister to the saint; as we have seen, Bede speaks more precisely of otters. The two authors also choose to emphasize different biblical parallels, thereby indicating the different aspects of the story they think noteworthy. Whereas the Anonymous mentions the lions that ministered to Daniel, and the spiritual sight that St Paul demonstrated when he detected the sin of Ananias and Sapphira, Bede points out how Cuthbert's actions mirrored those of the Saviour. After the Transfiguration the disciples were directed to "tell the vision to no man until the Son of Man be risen again from the dead" (Matt. 17:9). If we were to stop our enquiries at this point, the conclusion that would suggest itself is that Bede has obviously followed the Anonymous, but has given the story his own emphasis, and has been able to supply additional detail through his own enquiries.

Both stories, however, need to be compared with a strikingly similar episode in Adomnan's life of St Columba. One day, says Adomnan, Columba assembled the brethren of the monastery of Iona to inform them that he wished to go out alone to the western plain of their island, and he instructed that no one was to follow him. One of the brethren disobeyed, and following by a somewhat different route took up a position to spy upon the saint. What he witnessed was quite different from the ministration of the otters, but equally as astonishing:

> From the top of the little hill the spy saw him standing on a certain knoll of that plain and praying, with his hands outstretched to the sky, and his

---

41   *VCP*, chap. 10, pp. 189-191 (punctuation amended). On the identity of Aebbe, see the notes of Colgrave, *Life of Bishop Wilfrid*, pp. 174-175.

eyes raised to heaven, and then, strange to tell, behold suddenly a marvellous thing appeared. ... For holy angels, citizens of the heavenly country, flew down with marvellous suddenness, clothed in white raiment, and began to stand about the holy man as he prayed. And after some converse with the blessed man, that heavenly throng, as though perceiving that they were watched, quickly returned to the highest heaven.[42]

Like Cuthbert, Columba hurried back to the monastery. He reassembled the monks and demanded to know who had been spying upon him. Unable to conceal his guilt any longer, the offending brother prostrate himself before the saint, begging his pardon. Again like Cuthbert, Columba forgave the man on the condition that, for the duration of Columba's lifetime, he inform no one of this angelic visitation.

The parallels in the two lives are striking enough to preclude co-incidence. In the first instance at least, they suggest that the Lindisfarne Anonymous has borrowed from Adomnan's account. Thacker has already pointed to several themes that the two *vitae* have in common. If, in this most striking example of their interdependence, connections at the verbal level are difficult to document, it is nevertheless clear that "they were shaped by the same hagiographical conventions."[43] Somewhat earlier, Bullough ruled out as "unlikely" any direct connection between the *Vita Columbae* and the anonymous *Vita Cuthberti*. On the basis of similar use of sources and likeness in vocabulary, however, he postulated a connection none the less real. "The Lindisfarne monk may not have been familiar with Adomnan or the *Vita Columbae* itself, but ... he had links with the milieu in which it was written." Conceivably, he went on to argue, several of the texts used by the Anonymous came to him from Iona, rather than from English or Northumbrian sources as is commonly supposed.[44]

Hitherto any direct connection between Bede and the *Vita Columbae* has also been thought unlikely. Bede knew of Adomnan, of course, for he devotes a chapter of his *Ecclesiastical History* to him.[45] How much he knew, however, is a matter of conjecture. Picard argues that, due to

---

42 *Vita S. Columbae* 3.16, ed. Anderson & Anderson, p. 497.
43 Thacker, "Lindisfarne and the Origins of the Cult of St Cuthbert," p. 112.
44 Donald A. Bullough, "Columba, Adomnan and the Achievement of Iona," *The Scottish Historical Review* 43 (1964): 111-130, esp. 129-130; 44 (1965): 17-33, esp. 21. Cf. idem, "Hagiography as Patriotism: Alcuin's «York Poem» and the Early Northumbrian «Vitae sanctorum»," in *Hagiographie, cultures et sociétés*, pp. 339-359 at 344.
45 *HE* 5.15, pp. 504-508.

a lack of reliable information, Bede's version of Adomnan's later years is doubtful at best, owing more to "the tradition of Northumbrian propaganda" than anything else.[46] We know that Adomnan visited with King Aldfrith of Northumbria in 686, and with Ceolfrith at Jarrow two years later. The young Bede may actually have seen him. We know as well that Adomnan left a copy of his *De locis sanctis* with the king, and that, "through his kindness, it was circulated for lesser folk to read."[47] Bede himself was a beneficiary of this largesse, for he made his own abridgement of the volume, and included several extracts from it in the *Ecclesiastical History*.[48] Whether he knew the *Vita Columbae*, however, is another matter.

It has been argued that, when Bede and Adomnan are compared on the basic chronology of Columba's life, discrepancies occur, suggesting that Bede was dependent on another source.[49] Moreover, he nowhere explicitly mentions the *Vita*, referring instead to some records he apparently has not seen, "written records of his [i.e. Columba's] life and teachings [that] are said to have been preserved by his disciples."[50] With some plausibility Picard maintains that Bede "would certainly have mentioned ... the author of the *De locis sanctis* in this passage had he known about his hagiographical work."[51] On the other side is the curious fact that in both Bede's account and Adomnan's (but not the Anonymous) the offending brother who follows the saintly hero is identified as a spy (*explorator*). Suggestive as it is, however, this falls short of conclusive proof. At the point in the story where Cuthbert comes out of the sea and kneels on the shore, Bede uses some additional language (*flexis genibus*) that he could have derived from Adomnan. But

---

46 Jean-Michel Picard, "The Purpose of Adomnán's *Vita Columbae*," *Peritia* 1 (1982): 160-177, esp. 166.

47 *HE* 5.15, p. 509.

48 See Bede's *De locis sanctis*, CCL 175:245-280, which is based largely, although not exclusively, on Adomnan's work; and *HE* 5.16-17, pp. 508-512.

49 Introduction to *Vita S. Columbae*, ed. Anderson & Anderson, pp. 66-67.

50 *HE* 3.4, pp. 224-225: "de cuius vita et verbis nonnulla a discipulis eius feruntur scripta haberi." Cf. Ludwig Bieler, "Ireland's Contribution to the Culture of Northumbria," in *Famulus Christi*, pp. 210-228 at 222; Wallace-Hadrill, *Bede's Ecclesiastical History*, p. 94.

51 Picard, "Purpose of Adomnán's *Vita Columbae*," p. 164n. Cf. Bullough, "Columba, Adomnan and the Achievement of Iona," p. 116; and the editors' comment at *HE* 3.4, p. 225n.

in Adomnan's account these words are employed at a logically different place, to describe the attitude assumed by the penitent monk. Presumably as well Bede's wording could have been suggested by the Anonymous (*flectens genua*).

The likelihood of Bede having been dependent on Adomnan is increased by another and more striking instance of parallelism between the *Vita Columbae* and the *Vita Cuthberti*, although it too is inconclusive. Adomnan tells us that once, in order to facilitate the building of a guest house, Columba asked his monks to bring him wattle from the field of a layman named Findchan.[52] The monks did as they were asked, providing the saint with a ship-load of the desired material, but reporting as well Findchan's distress at his loss. To compensate him, Columba instructed that twice three measures of barley be sent to the layman, with instructions to sow it immediately. Findchan was sceptical that a crop sown after mid-summer, June 15, could issue successfully. But on the encouragement of his wife and the messengers of the saint, he did as instructed, and he was amply rewarded: "the harvest that, at the time spoken of above, he had sown without hope, he reaped, to the astonishment of all the neighbours, in the beginning of the month of August, fully ripe, according to the saint's word."

The first part of this tale is reminiscent of an episode contained in both the anonymous life of Cuthbert and Bede's version.[53] Cuthbert too asks his brethren for assistance in providing building materials. Rather than wattle, however, it is a timber twelve feet in length that Cuthbert requires; and rather than a guest house, it is a latrine that he proposes to construct. As the Lindisfarne Anonymous explains: "there was a rock hollowed by the waves, rising from the sea, near to the outermost part of his dwelling place; so he purposed to join the edge of this rock by a twelve-foot beam, as we have said, to the adjoining ground and on the beam he thought to build a little chamber." Unlike Columba's brethren, however, Cuthbert's let him down. In both versions of the life of Cuthbert, therefore, the story has a distinctive thrust that is paralleled only loosely at best in the cognate episode in the *Vita Columbae*. It serves to show nature subservient to the saint. Both Bede and the Anonymous report that, to compensate for the failings of the brethren, the night tide deposited a floating timber of exactly the right

---

52   *Vita S. Columbae* 2.3, ed. Anderson & Anderson, pp. 328-331.
53   *VCA* 3.4, pp. 98-101; *VCP*, chap. 21, pp. 224-227.

size to serve Cuthbert's needs, and at exactly the right place. "Waking in the morning," says the Anonymous, "the brethren saw it and gave thanks to God, marvelling that the sea in honour of Christ had accomplished more than men, in obedience to the hermit." Bede reports that "they marvelled at the holiness of the venerable man for whom even the elements did service; and with fitting shame they blamed their slothful minds, for even the insensible elements taught them what obedience ought to be shown to saints."[54]

Adomnan could have given a similar thrust to his story, but he does not. The miracle he reports demonstrates, not that nature is submissive to the holy man, but rather that God hears his prayers. When Findchan doubts Columba's promise, his wife says: "Do according to the bidding of the saint, to whom the Lord will grant whatever he may ask of him." The episodes of the *Vita Columbae* and the *Vita Cuthberti* are only broadly similar, therefore, and their relationship, one might be tempted to conclude, not worth pursuing.[55] What makes it significant is the parallelism that exists between the latter half of Adomnan's story and an episode that exists only in Bede's version of the life of Cuthbert. It is separated by only one chapter from the episode just considered; and it is a miracle for which Bede gives no source.[56]

Bede tells us that in the early stages of his retreat to Farne Island, Cuthbert survived on the bread that visitors brought to him. Considering it more fitting that he live by his own labour, he asked for tools, and he sowed wheat, but by midsummer the crop had failed to develop. Possibly, he thought, the land was inappropriate for wheat, or maybe it was simply not God's will that wheat grow for him. So he asked the brethren for barley to sow, and this time the results were different. "The

---

54 The purpose of the story is reinforced by the titles it bears in the two accounts: "De ligno quod mare serviens ei detulit" (*VCA*); "Qualiter eius necessitatibus etiam mare servierit" (*VCP*).

55 The "obvious and immediate literary model" for the episode in the *Vita Cuthberti*, says Mayr-Harting, is a story related by Gregory the Great. See Mayr-Harting, *Venerable Bede, the Rule of St. Benedict, and Social Class*, p. 9; and Gregory the Great, *Dial.* 3.10, Zimmerman 125, sc 260:289-291. When the River Po overflowed its banks, Bishop Sabinus of Piacenza ordered his deacon to go to it and demand that it return to its channel. The deacon laughed at the thought, but Sabinus issued a written command, which he had thrown into the waters directly; and the river obeyed immediately. To Gregory, the incident shows "the stubborn disobedience of man put to shame by the obedience of an unreasoning element."

56 Cf. *VCP*, chap. 19, pp. 220-223.

barley was brought long after the proper time for sowing it," says Bede, "and when there seemed no hope of any harvest, yet when he put it in the ground, it soon sprang up and brought forth a very abundant crop."

There is only a very modest amount of verbal similarity between Bede's account of miraculous harvest and Adomnan's,[57] and in Bede's case the story is developed in a manner without parallel in the *Vita Columbae*. Bede is mainly interested to tell of how, when the crop of barley began to ripen and some birds began to steal it, Cuthbert rebuked them, and they departed at his command. Indeed, he underlines the significance of Cuthbert's action by pointing to a saintly parallel. "In driving away the birds from the crops," says Bede, "he followed the example of the most reverend and holy father Antony, who with one exhortation restrained the wild asses from injuring the little garden that he himself had planted."[58] None of this has any parallel in Adomnan's text. For both Cuthbert and Columba, however, barley, sown late, after mid-summer, produces a miraculous harvest. The conclusion seems inescapable: directly or indirectly, Bede's account has been influenced by Adomnan. Quite possibly Bede has borrowed from Adomnan. Indeed, the cumulative weight of the evidence may even make it likely that he has done so.

---

57 Whereas Adomnan informs us, for example, that Findchan *contra spem seminavit*, Bede says that Cuthbert *ultra omnem spem ... terrae commendaret*.
58 The title of the chapter reflects Bede's interest: "Qualiter a messe quam sua manu seruerat, verbo volucres abegerit."

7

The Legacy of the *Dialogues*

If conclusive proof of Bede's dependence on Adomnan is lacking, an examination of his relationship to Gregory the Great yields a little more certainty. We have already referred in earlier chapters to Bede's story of Imma, a thegn of King Ecgfrith who was taken captive in battle.[1] Remarkably, fetters could not be kept on him. His brother, Tunna, was a priest, and because he believed him dead he offered masses on Imma's behalf. Every time he did so, Imma's chains miraculously fell to the ground. As background for the event, Wallace-Hadrill has pointed to the loosing of Peter's fetters when the angel rescued him from prison.[2] To this we might add the more recent precedent in the second book of Gregory's *Dialogues*, where we read that St Benedict, by his mere glance, once dissolved the bonds of a farmer who had been taken prisoner by Zalla, the Goth. The most striking anticipation of Bede's story, however, is provided by book four of the same *Dialogues*. There Gregory tells us of another man who, like Imma, was captured and bound in chains. Like Imma's brother, this man's wife had masses said for him, and they worked the same effect. After several years the man returned home, and was able to verify that his chains had been loosed on precisely those days when masses had been offered.[3]

Bede's tale of Imma is a well-developed story that occupies the equivalent of two full pages of Latin text, and at both beginning and end Bede expatiates on its spiritual significance. He regards it as a "remarkable incident," one that "should certainly not be passed over in silence, since the story may lead to the salvation of many." Several who heard about it, he tells us, were inspired to greater acts of piety and devotion. In particular they were encouraged to offer masses on behalf of departed loved ones, "for they realized that the saving sacrifice availed for the everlasting redemption of both body and soul." Although Gregory's story is also part of a series designed to illustrate the spiritual

---

1   *HE* 4.22, pp. 400-405. See above, pp. 44-45, 143-144.
2   Acts 12:7; cf. Wallace-Hadrill, *Bede's Ecclesiastical History*, p. 162.
3   *Dial.* 2.31, SC 260:222-226; 4.59, SC 265:196.

benefits of masses—a theological point, we have already noted, that Gregory makes with considerably more precision than Bede—the story itself seems a poor thing in comparison. It is offered without comment, which is unusual for the *Dialogues*, and in its entirety it occupies a mere seven lines. The similarity of the two stories, however, is still quite striking. Rather than being unique, it is symptomatic of a close relationship between the *Ecclesiastical History* and the *Dialogues* that can be detected at several other points as well.

One interesting example involves a story Bede relates about Bishop Mellitus of Canterbury and a parallel narrative in the *Dialogues* concerning Bishop Marcellinus of Ancona.[4] In each case the bishop provides miraculous assistance when his community is threatened with destruction by flames. As Bede tells it:

> On a certain occasion the city of Canterbury had been carelessly set on fire and was rapidly being consumed by the growing blaze. It could not be quenched by throwing water on it and no small part of the city had already been destroyed, while the raging fire was spreading towards the bishop's house. Mellitus, trusting in divine help since human aid had failed, ordered them to carry him into the path of the furious flames where tongues of fire were flying about hither and thither. The church of the Four Crowned Martyrs stood just where the fury of the flames was at its height; the bishop was carried to this spot by his followers, and, weak as he was, proceeded to avert by his prayers the peril which had defeated strong men in spite of all their efforts. Immediately the south wind, which had spread the conflagration over the city, veered round to the north and first of all prevented the fury of the flames from destroying those places which were in its path; then it soon ceased entirely and there was a calm, while the flames also sank and died out.

Gregory's story of Bishop Marcellinus lacks some of the distinctive detail—the reference to the church of the Four Crowned Martyrs, for example—that enhances verisimilitude in Bede's account. But in every other respect it is identical: Bede has simply replaced Marcellinus and Ancona with Mellitus and Canterbury respectively. In each case the fire is due to carelessness, described in precisely the same language: *per culpam incuriae*. In each case efforts to extinguish the flames have been in vain, with the result that a large part of the city has been destroyed;

---

4   Cf. *HE* 2.7, pp. 156-159; *Dial.* 1.6, Zimmerman 27-28, SC 260:62-64.

and once again the similarity in language is unmistakable.[5] In each case the bishop is carried into the midst of the conflagration,[6] and through his prayers extinguishes the blaze by forcing it to double back upon itself. Each author also closes his account by pointing to the moral of the story. Gregory regards the wonder as evidence of his hero's holiness, inviting Peter to "consider what great sanctity was required for a sick man to sit there and by prayers subdue the flames." Bede does the same. "So brightly," he says, "did the man of God burn with the fire of divine love, so often had he repelled the stormy powers of the air from harming him and his people by his prayers and exhortations, that it was right for him to be able to prevail over earthly winds and flames and to ensure that they should not injure him or his people."

Loomis has suggested that this kind of parallelism could have had its origin in Bede's use of the *Dialogues* as a touchstone of authenticity.[7] Presumably all sorts of tales came to Bede's attention while he was assembling the materials for his history, many of them quite fabulous. The *Dialogues*, whose authority was uncontested, provided a standard to help determine what should be retained and what rejected. If an otherwise suspect story had some cognate in Gregory's account, its credibility was thereby enhanced. Loomis's point is a good one: such a state of affairs was not only possible but likely. There was "a fundamental difference between medieval and modern canons of interpretation," as Zaleski has recently reminded us:

> Whereas modern readers might doubt the veracity of a narrative filled with easily recognized conventions, medieval readers considered the recurrence of well-known motifs a sign of authenticity. We tend to search for unprecedented elements, as if these were the kernels of truth masked by husks of borrowed formulas, but medieval readers believed that after all the proofs

---

5   In Gregory's text we read: *iamque urbis partem non modicam*; in Bede's: *iamque civitatis ... pars ... non minima*.

6   In Gregory's account we read: *deductus in manibus ... episcopus*; in Bede's: *perlatus obsequentium manibus episcopus*. Gregory tells us that Marcellinus was carried because he suffered from gout, and found walking extremely painful. Bede offers no such explanation, but nonetheless reports that Mellitus ordered that he be carried (*iussit se ... efferri*) into the path of the flames.

7   Loomis, "Miracle Traditions," p. 418. Cf. Wallace-Hadrill, *Bede's Ecclesiastical History*, p. 186.

have been tallied, there is no better index of an account's validity than its edifying qualities and its conformity to tradition.[8]

In these circumstances it is unsurprising that a number of the miracles Bede chooses to relate should have their counterparts in the work of his illustrious predecessor. When similarity verges on identity, however, one suspects dependence of a rather different order; and suspicion increases when, as is the case here, neither story is well attested.[9] Bede was certainly capable of borrowing verbatim from Gregory's work, and without acknowledgment. A case in point is provided by the eleventh chapter of his *Vita Cuthberti*, where Cuthbert's spiritual progress is described with words originally applied to St Benedict.[10] There only words have been shifted from one saint to another; elsewhere one suspects that the reality they describe has been transferred in a similar fashion.

Although conclusive proof is rarely attainable in these matters, a series of miracles in three consecutive chapters of book five of the *Ecclesiastical History* is worthy of special attention. It opens with the famous story of Dryhthelm's vision, "a memorable miracle," Bede tells us, "like those of ancient times."[11] A *paterfamilias* who had lived a devout and religious life with his family, Dryhthelm was stricken by a serious illness and died. But several hours later he suddenly revived, to the great consternation of the mourners who, with the exception of his faithful but trembling wife, all fled in terror. Dryhthelm explained that he was indeed risen from the dead, but from that point on needed to live

8 Zaleski, *Otherworld Journeys*, p. 85.
9 Gregory cites no source, but possibly would have us understand that his informant was the anonymous bishop (and former monk from Ancona) mentioned in the previous chapter. Bede mentions no source either. Given the Canterbury location, however, one might presume Albinus. See above, pp. 163-164.
10 Cf. *VCP*, chap. 11, p. 192; *Dial.* 2.11.3, sc 260:174: "Coepit vero inter ista vir Dei etiam prophetiae spiritu pollere, ventura praedicere, praesentibus absentia nuntiare." Cf. also *HE* 4.32, p. 446: "Nec silentio praetereundum, quod ante triennium per reliquias eius factum, nuper mihi per ipsum in quo factum est fratrem innotuit." Both Colgrave & Mynors, *HE*, p. 446n, and Wallace-Hadrill, *Bede's Ecclesiastical History*, p. 173, point to the verbal echoes of *Dial.* 4.57.8, sc 265:188: "Sed neque hoc silendum existimo, quod actum in meo monasterio ante hoc triennium reminiscor." Colgrave, "Earliest Saints' Lives Written in England," p. 39, claims that Bede was "particularly attracted" by the *Dialogues*: "There are at least 17 verbal borrowings ... in the course of the *Ecclesiastical History* and probably more."
11 *HE* 5.12, pp. 488-489: "miraculum memorabile et antiquorum simile." For the complete story see pp. 488-499.

a different kind of life. After distributing all his assets in equal shares to his wife, his sons, and the poor, he retired to the monastery of Melrose, where he became known for the rigid severity of his self-denial. "Until the day he was called away," says Bede, "in his unwearied longing for heavenly bliss, he subdued his aged body with daily fasts and led many to salvation by his words and life."[12]

What Dryhthelm experienced in the hours of death amounted to nothing less than a complete tour of the afterlife. His itinerary began with purgatory, which took the form of a deep, broad valley, infinite in length. The souls of the departed could be seen being tossed from the searing flames on one side to the freezing hail and snow on the other. Slightly further on he came upon "the very mouth of hell,"[13] a malodorous and fiery pit of torment. Here the flames surged and receded in alternating motion, tossing the souls of the damned on high and then drawing them back again into the abyss. Separating all this from the realm of the blessed was a very great wall, "endlessly long and endlessly high,"[14] and having neither gates nor windows. Transported to the top, Dryhthelm was able to see a paradise of repose for those who, while destined to enter into the presence of Christ at the Last Judgment, were not worthy of immediate reception into the Kingdom of Heaven. He describes it as

> a very broad and pleasant plain, full of such a fragrance of growing flowers that the marvellous sweetness of the scent quickly dispelled the foul stench of the gloomy furnace which had hung around me. So great was the light that flooded all this place that it seemed to be clearer than the brightness of daylight or the rays of the noontide sun. In this meadow there were innumerable bands of men in white robes, and many companies of happy people sat around.[15]

Heaven proper, when he finally glimpsed it, struck Dryhthelm as being even more glorious: its fragrance more delightful, its light more wondrous than what he had seen before.

Dryhthelm's vision is noteworthy in more ways than one. It is certainly remarkable in the curious fourfold structure of the afterlife that it

---

12 Ibid., p. 499.
13 Ibid., p. 495.
14 Ibid., p. 493.
15 Ibid.

presents,[16] although it would seem that at least one parallel can be found elsewhere in Bede's works.[17] It is also striking in its richness of detail, which has given rise to much speculation about the sources from which this or that feature may have been drawn. Precedent for the

16 Cf. Maria Pia Ciccarese, *Visioni dell'aldilà in occidente. Fonti, modelli, testi* (Firenze, 1987), p. 305: "assistiamo ad una sorta di «sdoppiamento» del purgatorio, situato in luoghi diversi e diversamente configurato." Claude Carozzi, "La géographie de l'au-delà et sa signification pendant le haut moyen âge," in *Popoli e paesi nella cultura altomedievale* (Spoleto, 1983), 2:423-481, esp. 448 and 453, also emphasizes the revolutionary nature of Dryhthelm's vision. However, cf. Michel Aubrun, "Caractères et portée religieuse et sociale des «Visiones» en Occident du VIe au XIe siècle," *Cahiers de civilisation médiévale* 23 (1980): 109-130, esp. 116-117. Bede's division of purgatory, Aubrun suggests, and the fourfold division of the hereafter to which it leads, are simply logical extensions of the basic idea of purgatory endorsed by Gregory the Great.

17 See *Hom. Evan.* 1.2, CCL 122:12-13: "Non tunc autem solum enarrabit unigenitus filius Deum, id est sanctae et individuae trinitatis quae est unus Deus gloriam manifestabit hominibus cum post universale iudicium omnes pariter electos ad visionem claritatis eius inducet; sed et cotidie narrat cum singulis quibusque fidelium perfectorum mox a carnis corruptione solutis implere coeperit quod promisit dicens: *Qui diligit me diligitur a patre meo, et ego diligam eum et manifestabo me ipsum illi.* Me ipsum, inquit, manifestabo dilectoribus meis ut quem in sua cognovere mortalem in mea iam natura patri et spiritui sancto videre possint aequalem. Verum hoc de apostolis martyribus confessoribus ceterisque artioris ac perfectioris vitae viris fieri credendum est quorum unus certaminum suorum conscius non dubitavit de se ipso testari: *Cupio dissolvi et cum Christo esse.* Ceterum sunt plures in ecclesia iusti qui post carnis solutionem continuo beata paradisi requie suscipiuntur expectantes in magno gaudio in magnis congaudentium choris quando recepto corpore veniant et appareant ante faciem Dei. At vero non nulli propter bona quidem opera ad electorum sortem praeordinati sed propter mala aliqua quibus polluti de corpore exierunt post mortem severe castigandi excipiuntur flammis ignis purgatorii et vel usque ad diem iudicii longa huius examinatione a vitiorum sorde mundantur vel certe prius amicorum fidelium precibus elemosinis ieiuniis fletibus et hostiae salutaris oblationibus absoluti a poenis et ipsi ad beatorum perveniunt requiem." In this text hell is not mentioned. But the context does not require it, and it can be taken as understood. The other three divisions of the hereafter described in Dryhthelm's vision all seem to be present. Apostles, martyrs, confessors and other saints whose lives of perfection would merit it are received directly into heaven to enjoy the immediate presence of Christ. Other members of the elect are received into the rest of paradise, but must await the resurrection before being summoned into the divine presence. Still other members of the elect are consigned to purgatory to be cleansed of the sins by which they were corrupted when they departed this life. Cf. Capelle, "Rôle théologique de Bède le Vénérable," p. 36n, who offers the judgment: "Très curieux stade de l'évolution qui mènera à la doctrine définitive."

vision of purgatory, for example, may be seen in the vision of hell related by the *Apocalypse of Paul*, where at least some of the same elements are present. There is fire, of course, although in the form of two rivers of fire. There are also two references to ice and cold, without, however, the accompanying theme of alternating forms of punishment.[18] Precedent may also be found in the vision of a house, "hot like fire and cold like ice," in the first book of Enoch, or in the black river of fire and ice in the version of Enoch's vision that appears in book two.[19] In the first of these texts the idea of punishment is lacking; the second, however, describes a frightful place, where every kind of torture and torment is to be found.

Among ancient texts, perhaps the closest cognate is in the vision of Thespesius. Plutarch records it as follows:

> There were lakes lying side by side, one a seething lake of gold, a second, piercing cold, of lead, and a third of rugged iron, with certain daemons in charge, who, like smiths, were using tongs to raise and lower alternately the souls of those whose wickedness was due to insatiable and overreaching avarice. Thus, when the souls had grown red hot in the gold from the blazing heat, the daemons plunged them into the lake of lead; when they had there been chilled and hardened, like hailstones, they were removed to the lake of iron. Here they turned an intense black and were altered in appearance, as their hardness caused them to become chipped and crushed; and after this they were once more taken to the gold, enduring, as he said, the most fearful agonies in the course of each change.[20]

In all probability, however, the answer lies closer at hand, in the weeping and gnashing of teeth mentioned at several points in the New

---

18   See *New Testament Apocrypha*, ed. Edgar Hennecke & Wilhelm Schneemelcher, English trans. ed. R.McL. Wilson, 2 vols. (London, 1963-1965), 2:755-798. See esp. pp. 779-780 (the rivers of fire), and pp. 783 & 786 (ice and snow). Of the latter two passages, the first describes the punishment of those who harmed widows, orphans and the poor; the second the punishment of those who denied the resurrection.

19   Cf. 1 Enoch 14:10-13 & 2 Enoch 10:1-3, in *The Old Testament Pseudepigrapha* 1: *Apocalyptic Literature and Testaments*, ed. James H. Charlesworth (Garden City NY, 1983), pp. 20-21 & 118-119.

20   Plutarch, "On the Delays of the Divine Vengeance," chap. 30 (*Moralia* 567C-D), in *Plutarch's Moralia in Fifteen Volumes*, vol. 7: 523C—612B, trans. Phillip H. De Lacy & Benedict Einarson (Cambridge MA, 1959), p. 295. Cf. Zaleski, *Otherworld Journeys*, pp. 33 & 55.

Testament.[21] Bede himself comments on the phrase in the context of Luke 13:28; and although he sees in it an image of the pains of hell rather than purgatory, he explains that the weeping and the gnashing of teeth are the product of excessive heat and extreme cold respectively.[22]

If we shift attention from the image of purgatory to Dryhthelm's vision of hell, it is noteworthy that a similar experience is recorded of a monk of Wenlock, in Shropshire, in a letter of 716 from St Boniface to Eadburga, abbess of Thanet. Boniface states that he had first learned of the vision from Hildelida, abbess of Barking, but subsequently was able to confirm it by speaking to the monk himself. Like Dryhthelm, this brother had died and returned to life. While he was in the hereafter he also witnessed aspects of the nether world that resemble, at least superficially, Dryhthelm's account. As Boniface explains:

> He reported further that he saw, as it were in the bowels of the earth, many fiery pits vomiting forth terrible flames; and as the foul fire arose, the souls of wretched men, in the likeness of black birds, flew through the flames, wailing and howling and shrieking with human cries. Mourning their past deeds and their present suffering, they sat upon the margins of the pits, clinging there for a while, and then they fell screaming back into the abyss.[23]

---

21 Cf. Matt. 8:12; 13:42,50; 22:13; 24:51; 25:30; Luke 13:28. The point has been noted more than once. See, for example, Plummer, *Opera Historica* 2:296; and Ciccarese, *Visioni dell'aldilà*, pp. 333-334, n. 10.

22 *In Luc.* 4, CCL 120:272: "*Ibi erit fletus et stridor dentium.* Fletus de ardore stridor dentium solet excitari de frigore. Ubi duplex ostenditur gehenna, id est nimii frigoris et intolerabilis esse fervoris. Cui beati Iob sententia [Job 24:19] consentit dicentis: *Ad calorem nimium transibunt ab aquis nivium.*" Cf. *De die iudicii*, CCL 122:439-444 at 442:

> Nec vox ulla valet miseras edicere poenas:
> Ignibus aeternae nigris loca plena gehennae,
> Frigora mixta simul ferventibus algida flammis:
> Nunc oculos nimio flentes ardore camini,
> Nunc iterum nimio stridentes frigore dentes.

23 Boniface, *Epist.* 10, ed. Michael Tangl, in *Die Briefe des heiligen Bonifatius und Lullus* (Berlin, 1916), pp. 7-15 at 11; trans. Ephraim Emerton, *The Letters of Saint Boniface* (New York, 1940), pp. 25-31 at 27-28 (significantly revised): "Inter ea referebat se quasi in inferioribus in hoc mundo vidisse igneos puteos horrendam eructantes flammam plurimos et erumpente tetra terribilis flamma ignis volitasse et miserorum hominum spiritus in similitudine nigrarum avium per flammam plorantes et ululantes et verbis et voce humana stridentes et lugentes propria merita et presens supplicium consedisse paululum herentes in marginibus puteorum et iterum heiulantes cecidisse in puteos."

There is no parallel in Dryhthelm's vision to the souls of the doomed being likened to birds. But the structural similarity between the two accounts is still obvious. In each case souls rise and fall as the flames surge and recede. Equally as significant, however, are the differences, and so Bede's direct dependence on Boniface's letter would be difficult to demonstrate.[24] Dryhthelm sees one pit, which he describes as the gateway to hell itself. The souls tossed on the tips of the flames are the souls of the very damned. The monk of Wenlock's vision describes many pits, and although they are the locus of fearsome torment, it is not the agony of eternal punishment. Indeed, the vision includes momentary respite from the flames, indicating that "Almighty God will give to these souls in the judgment day relief from their punishment and rest eternal." Hell itself is at a lower level, from which an "unspeakable groaning and weeping of souls in distress" can be heard.

Like Dryhthelm, the monk of Wenlock also attributes a fourfold structure to the hereafter, a fact that may lend the other points of contact in the two accounts added significance. On balance, however, a much more likely source than Boniface for any borrowing on Bede's part is Gregory the Great. The *Dialogues* contain a number of stories of people dying and then coming back to life to tell of what they have seen in the hereafter: some of the parallels with Dryhthelm's vision have already been noted.[25] The principal examples include the stories of Reparatus, Stephen and the anonymous soldier.[26] The last of these is probably the

---

24 Ciccarese, *Visioni dell'aldilà*, p. 363 n. 10, suggests that it was Boniface who was dependent on Bede: "La derivazione da Beda è fuori discussione, ma Bonifacio ha modificato l'immagine e il suo significato." However, the later date of the *Ecclesiastical History* would preclude this possibility. Sims-Williams, *Religion and Literature in Western England*, p. 250, argues that "the simplest way" of explaining the similarities is to suppose that "the priest Haemgisl's lost account of Dryhthelm, which Bede used in the 730s, was already in circulation in the south a few decades earlier."

25 See, for example, Colgrave, "Bede's Miracle Stories," p. 215; and Loomis, "Miracle Traditions," p. 409. See also Linda L. Miller, "Drythelm's Journey to the Other World: Bede's Literary Use of Tradition," *Comitatus* 2 (1971): 3-15 at 9-10.

26 Cf. *Dial.* 4.32, SC 265:106-108 (Reparatus); 4.37.5-6, SC 265:128 (Stephen); & 4.37.7-16, SC 265:128-134 (the anonymous soldier). Ciccarese, *Visioni dell'aldilà*, p. 332 n. 2, focuses on the fact that Dryhthelm is described as *paterfamilias*, and points to the parallel with *Dial.* 1.12.1-3, SC 260:112-114, which contains the story of another *paterfamilias* who died, was ushered into the afterworld, and was subsequently restored to life by the priest, Severus. Her conclusion: "il riscontro non è casuale, tanto più che in quest'epoca protagonisti di visioni sono quasi tutti monaci."

closest cognate. It concerns a soldier who had died three years earlier of the plague in Rome. Subsequently restored to life, he was able to explain what had happened to him. He had seen a dark river, whose foul waters were covered by noisome vapors. The river was crossed by a bridge, which functioned as a place of testing. The virtuous were able to pass over with ease; the unjust, assailed by evil spirits lurking beneath, slipped into the fetid waters. On the other side were pleasant meadows of green grass and fragrant flowers whose aroma filled the air. People arrayed in white robes were gathered there, for each of whom there was a dwelling of light.

Particularly noteworthy are the meadows, which function as a representation of heaven in the soldier's story, and which strongly resemble the plain in Dryhthelm's vision of paradise. Both are decorated with richly scented flowers;[27] both are occupied by men in white robes, described in strikingly similar language (Bede speaks of *hominum albatorum conventicula*, Gregory of *albatorum hominum conventicula*); and both are resplendent with light, although in the soldier's story it is attached to dwellings, unmentioned in Dryhthelm's account.[28] For the rest there is little in the soldier's story that suggests the much more detailed account of Dryhthelm, although there are a few points of contact. Thus the stench coming from the vaporous flames of Dryhthelm's hell (*fetor incomparabilis cum eisdem vaporibus ebulliens*) corresponds to the stench of vaporous waters in the soldier's account (*niger atque caligosus foetoris intolerabilis nebulam exhalans fluvius*). Perhaps most importantly, some of the most distinctive features of Gregory's story —the river, the bridge—have no counterpart in Bede's; and the guide that Bede's account does supply makes no appearance in Gregory's.

By Bede's time, as Ciccarese observes, Gregory's picture of the hereafter had exerted a wide-ranging influence, becoming part of a standard repertoire of images.[29] Hence not every parallel can be taken as *prima facie* evidence of conscious borrowing from the *Dialogues*. Moreover, in a study focusing on possible sources of Gregory's work

---

27 They are described in quite different language. Where Bede refers to a *campus ... latissimus ac laetissimus, ... flagrantia vernantium flosculorum plenus*, Gregory describes *amoena ... prata atque virentia, odoriferis herbarum floribus exornata*.

28 Bede does refer to the *beatorum mansiones spirituum*, but not to the *domus* of Gregory's account.

29 See Ciccarese, *Visioni dell'aldilà*, pp. 121, 167-168.

itself, Ciccarese observes that the same imagery—"da secoli divenuta ormai stereotipa per il convergente apporto di autori pagani e cristiani" —can easily be found in pre-Gregorian texts as well. Her example is the *Passio Perpetuae*, where the garden, the fragrant flowers, and the blessed clothed in white all figure prominently.[30] She might equally as well have cited the *Apocalypse of Peter*. There heaven is likened to "a great open garden ... full of the fragrance of perfume." It is also suffused with light, the raiment of the blessed "glistening" or "shining," their bodies being "whiter than any snow and redder than any rose."[31]

That such imagery was part of the common intellectual currency by Bede's time of writing argues for the substantial independence of his story. So does the fact that he gives us a named source—the monk and priest Haemgisl, whom Dryhthelm met after his retreat to Melrose— who was still alive at his time of writing. Bede also tells us that people as prominent as Aldfrith, king of Northumbria, and Aethilwald, one-time abbot of Melrose and the present bishop of Lindisfarne, were involved with Dryhthelm; and although he does not adduce them as sources, they lend weight to the substance of what he reports.[32] That he has also been influenced by Gregory the Great, however, seems undeniable. Bede's characterization of Dryhthelm's experience as *miraculum memorabile et antiquorum simile* is more than suggestive. If, as Wallace-Hadrill maintains, it functions to enhance the credibility of the account,[33] it also clearly demonstrates that Bede had some earlier wonder or wonders in mind. The similarities noted above (especially the verbal similarity) with the text of the soldier's story suggest that the precedent was Gregorian, as does another parallel with Gregory's text near the opening of Bede's account. After his retirement to Melrose, Bede tells us, Dryhthelm distinguished himself by his harsh, ascetic practices: "There, until the day of his death, he lived a life of such penance of mind and body that even if he had kept silence, his life would have declared that he had seen many things to be dreaded or

---

30 Maria Pia Ciccarese, "La genesi letteraria della visione dell'aldilà: Gregorio Magno e le sue fonti," *Augustinianum* 29 (1989): 435-449 at 446. Ciccarese concludes: "Abbiamo già qui elementi validi a sostenere la filiazione diretta della descrizione gregoriana."
31 See *New Testament Apocrypha* 2:663-683 at 680-682. In the *Apocalypse of Paul* (ibid. 2:755-798) paradise and its inhabitants are also characterized by brightness (hence the references to things golden). See esp. 2:796.
32 *HE* 5.12, p. 496.
33 Wallace-Hadrill, *Bede's Ecclesiastical History*, p. 185.

desired which had been hidden from other men." The words echo
Gregory's account of the hermit Peter, who also died, had a vision of
hell, and subsequently returned to life to tell his story.[34]

Bede follows the tale of Dryhthelm with a story about a man from
the kingdom of Mercia "whose visions and words, but not his way of
life, profited many but not himself."[35] The man refused to repent of
his evil ways until it was too late. Confined to his sick bed, he had a
vision of angels bearing a small volume listing all his merits, and of
demons carrying a huge book itemizing all his sins. Not long after the
vision, he expired. Says Bede:

> Now he suffers everlasting and fruitless punishment in torment because he
> failed to submit for a brief spell to the penance which would have brought
> him the fruit of pardon. From this it is clear, as the blessed Pope Gregory
> writes about certain people, that he saw this vision not for his own benefit,
> because it did not profit him, but for the sake of others; so that they, hearing
> of his fate, may fear to put off their time of repentance while they still have
> the opportunity, and not be cut off by sudden death and die impenitent.[36]

The open reference to Gregory's *Dialogues* is significant. It increases
the likelihood that it was the *Dialogues* Bede was thinking of when
likening Dryhthelm's vision to those of former times. Here the specific
passage he had in mind may have been Gregory's statement concerning
the experience of Reparatus: "His journey to hell, his return and
description of what he had seen, and his subsequent death, indicate that
all this did not happen for Reparatus' own benefit, but as a warning for

34 Cf. *HE* 5.12, pp. 488-489: "et ibi usque ad diem mortis in tanta mentis et corporis
contritione duravit, ut multa illum quae alios laterent vel horrenda vel desideranda
vidisse, *etiamsi lingua sileret, vita loqueretur*"; and *Dial.* 4.37.4, SC 265:126-128:
"tantisque se postmodum vigiliis ieiuniisque constrinxit, ut inferni eum vidisse et
pertimuisse tormenta, *etiam si taceret lingua, conversatio loqueretur*." Emphasis
added. See Miller, "Drythelm's Journey," p. 9; Zaleski, *Otherworld Journeys*,
pp. 76-78; and Ciccarese, *Visioni dell'aldilà*, p. 333 n. 8: "Qui la dipendenza dai
Dial. si spinge fino al calco letterale." Zaleski also points to the command to return
to life in each of these accounts, suggesting that the one is modelled on the other.
35 *HE* 5.13, pp. 498-503 at 499.
36 Ibid., pp. 500-503. The second sentence reads: "De quo constat quia, sicut beatus
papa Gregorius de quibusdam scribit, *non pro se ista, cui non profuere, sed pro
aliis viderit*, qui eius interitum cognoscentes differre tempus paenitentiae, dum
vacat, timerent, ne inproviso mortis articulo praeventi inpaenitentes perirent."
Emphasis added.

us that we should use the opportunities given us to correct our evil ways."[37] More likely, however, is *Dial.* 4.40, a chapter, with several illustrative examples, devoted to demonstrating that people are sometimes given visions of the punishment that awaits them, not for their own sake, but for others'.[38]

Like the story of Dryhthelm, the tale of the unrepentant man of Mercia is among the best attested in the *Ecclesiastical History.* Bede's source was Pehthelm, former monk at Malmesbury and bishop of Whithorn, who survived until 735, well after the *Ecclesiastical History* was completed. There is also no good cognate for the story in the *Dialogues,* and so whatever literary affiliations it has would have to be traced elsewhere. One possibility, first mentioned by Plummer, is the *Apocalypse of Paul,* where the angel of the sinful soul approaches the Lord with a document in his hands and says: "This, Lord, in my hands is the account of all the sins of this soul from its youth up to the present day."[39] Another is the *Apocalypse of Zephaniah,* where we find a more precise cognate:

37 *Dial.* 4.32.5, Zimmerman 229, SC 265:108: "Qui videlicet Reparatus, ductus ad loca poenarum, dum vidit, rediit, narravit et obiit, aperte monstratur quia *nobis illa, non sibi viderit,* quibus dum adhuc concessum est vivere, licet etiam a malis operibus emendare." Emphasis added.

38 *Dial.* 4.40, SC 265:138-146. The chapter begins as follows: "Sciendum quoque est quia nonumquam animae adhuc in suis corporibus positae poenale aliquid de spiritalibus vident, quod tamen quibusdam ad aedificationem suam, quibusdam vero contingere ad aedificationem audientium solet" (4.40.1, p. 138). Further on Gregory tells us of the rich man Chrysaurius: "De quo nimirum constat quia *pro nobis ista, non pro se viderat,* ut eius visio nobis proficiat, quos adhuc divina patientia longanimiter expectat" (4.40.9, p. 144; emphasis added). With regard to the monk in the monastery called Ton Galathon, he says: "statim defunctus est, atque ut paenitendo liberari potuisset a dracone quem viderat, expectatus non est. Quod nimirum constat quia ad solam utilitatem audientium viderit, qui eum hostem cui traditus fuerat et innotuit et non evasit" (4.40.12, p. 146). A comparison of Bede's and Gregory's language does not lead to definitive results, but generally supports the conclusion that Bede had this chapter in mind. The closest analogue to Bede's language is at *Dial.* 4.40.9.

39 *New Testament Apocrypha* 2:757. Cf. p. 761, where we read of angels informing God of both the good and the evil deeds performed by men: "For at that hour all the angels go to the Lord to worship him and bring before him all the deeds of men, whether good or evil, which each of them does from morning until evening." Cf. Plummer, *Opera Historica* 2:298; and Wallace-Hadrill, *Bede's Ecclesiastical History,* p. 186.

the angels of the Lord and the angels of the accuser record the good deeds of the righteous and the evil deeds of sinners respectively.[40]

Both these texts, however, were somewhat remote, and the main inspiration was probably closer at hand. Throughout Holy Scripture, particularly the Apocalypse, are many references to the book of life, where the names of the elect are recorded.[41] In Rev. 20:12 we read of books (in the plural) being opened, and the dead being judged by what was written therein. Conceivably, as Ciccarese suggests, Bede's story results from this theme being combined with one prominent in the hagiographical literature: angels and demons struggling for the souls of the departed.[42] In that case it may not be entirely fortuitous that such a conflict figures prominently in Gregory's account of the soldier's story, discussed above. Among the wonders witnessed by the soldier was a struggle of good and evil spirits for the soul of a man who had slipped while crossing the bridge, and was in danger of falling into the loathsome waters below.

Following immediately in Bede's text is the final episode in the trilogy mentioned above, the story of a monk whom Bede claims to have known personally.[43] Although he was a craftsman whose skill was much valued in his monastery, this nameless brother appears to have had no genuine religious calling. A drunkard also addicted to "the other pleasures of a loose life," he would remain in his workshop rather than joining the others for services. Frequently rebuked for his failures without effect, he ultimately reaped the consequences. He was stricken by serious illness, in which he had a vision of hell; and alongside Satan, Caiaphas and the others who slew the Lord, he saw a place reserved for himself in the fiery abyss. His brethren urged him to repent while there was still time, but to no avail. Concluding that his doom was sealed, the wretched man abandoned hope: "he died without receiving the saving viaticum and his body was buried in the furthest

---

40 *Apoc. of Zephaniah* 3:5-9, in *Old Testament Pseudepigrapha* 1:511; cf. 7:1-2, 10-11, p. 513. There is also an analogue in the vision of Abraham. See the *Testament of Abraham* 12:6-8, 12 (Recension A), in *Old Testament Pseudepigrapha* 1:889; cf. 13:9 (Recension A), p. 890, and 10:7-11 (Recension B), p. 900.

41 See, for example, Exod. 32:32-33; Ps. 68(69):29; Dan. 12:1; Luke 10:20; Phil. 4:3; Rev. 3:5; 13:8; 17:8; 20:12, 15; 21:27. Cf. the *Apocalypse of Peter*, in *New Testament Apocrypha* 2:683.

42 Ciccarese, *Visioni dell'aldilà*, pp. 306, 336 n. 32.

43 *HE* 5.14, pp. 502-505.

corner of the monastery; nor did anyone venture to say masses or sing psalms or even pray for him."

Bede contrasts this man's fate with that of the apostle Stephen:

> Oh, how far asunder has God divided light from darkness! The blessed protomartyr Stephen, when he was about to suffer death for the sake of the truth, saw the heavens opened and the glory of God, and Jesus standing at the right hand of God. The eyes of his mind were fixed before his death upon the place where he was to be after death, so that he might die more happily. But on the other hand this smith (*faber*), a man of dark mind and dark deeds, when he was at the point of death, saw hell opened and the damnation of the devil and his followers. The unhappy man also saw his own place of imprisonment among them, so that he might perish the more miserably in despair himself, and yet might leave behind him a reason why those who were still alive and knew of this, should seek their own salvation by his own perdition.

Bede closes by telling us that all of this happened recently in the kingdom of Bernicia. The news of it, he says, "spread far and wide and roused many people to do penance for their sins without delay. ... May the reading of this account of ours have the same effect!"

Bede clearly sees this, like the previous episode, as a case of someone receiving a vision of future punishment for the benefit of others, not his own. Hence it is unsurprising that it should bear some affinity to a couple of stories in *Dial.* 4.40, the chapter to which Bede probably alludes in the previous episode, the chapter that Gregory crafted with precisely such visions in mind. Beyond affinity, however, is the extensive parallelism between the *Dialogues* and the *Ecclesiastical History* that a close reading reveals. First of all, there is the case of Theodore, a young monk of Gregory's own monastery of St Andrew, and hence personally known to Gregory just as the unfortunate monk from Bernicia was known to Bede. Theodore too was entirely unsuited for the monastic life, having entered St Andrew's because of the force of circumstances rather than conviction, and he would chafe whenever any serious spiritual lesson was impressed upon him. He too became seriously ill, and was confined to his sick bed where his brethren surrounded him in prayer. As his life ebbed away, he suddenly reported the assaults of a dragon intent on devouring him; his body was held fast in the dragon's coils, his head already in his jaws. However, the brethren added tears to their fervent prayers, which happily had the intended effect. The dragon was routed and the brother restored to health, resolved to abandon his former ways. "After recovering from the partial death of his body," says Gregory, "this monk offered his life generously to God. With a complete change of heart, he now welcomed afflictions and endured them for a long time until his soul was finally freed from the body."[44]

This story has a happy ending, but another tale from the same chapter of the *Dialogues*, the story of the monk in the monastery called Ton Galathon, does not. Unlike Theodore or the monk of whom Bede informs us, this man appeared to be a model religious. Indeed, he was renowned for his sanctity. Ultimately, however, appearance and reality were proven to be quite different. Stricken by a mortal illness, he summoned the brethren to his bedside, where he unburdened himself of a confession:

> "You thought all along that I was fasting with you," he said, "but, unknown to you I took food secretly. For this reason I have been handed over to the dragon to be devoured. His tail is now coiled around my feet and knees and, with his head to my mouth, he is stealing the breath of life from me."

This time the brethren were denied the opportunity to offer prayers on his behalf. His death followed at once, clearly showing, says Gregory, that it was for the benefit of others that he was allowed to see the dragon that held him in his grasp. "He could point him out to others, but for himself there was no escape."[45]

Of course, the monk of Ton Galathon was a secret sinner, unlike the monk in Bede's story; and as in Theodore's case, it was a vision of the dragon that he saw, not a vision of hell with Satan and Caiaphas and company. But the vision that Bede reports is a logical equivalent, and most of the other features of Bede's story could have been drawn from Gregory's two accounts. The final detail of Bede's story—"his body was buried in the furthest corner of the monastery; nor did anyone venture to say masses or sing psalms or even pray for him"[46]—could have been suggested by Gregory's story of the dying monk, Justus, who, like Theodore, was a monk of Gregory's own monastery.[47] On

---

44 *Dial.* 4.40.2-5, Zimmerman 244-245 at 245, SC 265:140-142 at 142. The translation is a little loose: "Homo ergo qui, sicut iam dictum est, ab extrema corporis fuerat parte praemortuus, reservatus ad vitam toto ad Deum corde conversus est, et postquam mutatus mente diu est flagellis adtritus, tunc eius anima carne soluta est."

45 *Dial.* 4.40.10-12, Zimmerman 246-247, SC 265:144-146.

46 *HE* 5.14, p. 505.

47 *Dial.* 4.57.8-16, SC 265:188-194.

his death-bed he was revealed to have kept for himself and hidden away three gold pieces. In punishment Gregory ordered that, rather than being buried with the brethren, a grave should be dug for him in a manure pile. He also ordered, however, that masses be said for him, and ultimately they led to his deliverance.

The only remaining significant detail in Bede's story is the fact that the offending monk was a craftsman, a smith, as we learn when Bede goes on to compare his fate with that of St Stephen. The suspicion that the whole tale could be no more than a pastiche of elements drawn from the *Dialogues* is reinforced by the realization that this too, as well as the comparison with St Stephen, could have been suggested by Gregory's story of another Stephen, a man of high rank (*inlustris vir*) who fell ill and died while he was in Constantinople on a matter of business. Ushered into the underworld, this Stephen had his case come before the infernal court, where it was immediately dismissed because of mistaken identity. Rather than this man, it was his neighbour who had been ordered to appear. The error was corrected immediately. Stephen was restored to life, and in the same hour his neighbour, another Stephen who was a smith by trade, died.[48]

Could the monk in Bede's story have been given the identity of a smith because of Stephen the smith? Could St Stephen have come to mind because of this Stephen? The story of the two Stephens, although in a different chapter, is quite close to the other stories on which Bede might have drawn; and it also would have been reasonable for Bede to think of it in this context. It too tells the tale of a man who had a vision of the hereafter from which he was not able personally to benefit. This becomes clear in the immediately following story, the tale of the anonymous soldier, in which the noble Stephen figures once again. In the soldier's vision it is this Stephen who has slipped while trying to cross the bridge, and who finds himself being pulled in different directions by the good and evil spirits contending for his soul. Even though he had seen a vision of hell, says Gregory, he had not fully amended his life, and therefore had to undergo this test before his fate could be decided. "We might say, then," Gregory concludes, "that a vision of hell and its torments is helpful for some, but for others it is the cause of even graver condemnation. Some are forewarned by these visions and turn from evil. Others, on the contrary,

---

48   *Dial.* 4.37.5-6, SC 265:128.

unwilling to avoid hell even after seeing and considering its torments, become all the more blameworthy."[49]

When the three consecutive chapters of the *Ecclesiastical History* that we have been considering are viewed together, the influence of Gregory the Great seems beyond doubt. In its substance, the second story appears to be independent of Gregory. The same can probably be said of the first one as well, although Bede's memory of the *Dialogues* seems to have coloured some of the details. He may also have consciously chosen to reproduce some of the language of the *Dialogues* in order to describe an essentially similar situation. Elsewhere I have argued that clear textual evidence should be required before we conclude of two similar episodes that one has been derived from the other.[50] Equally clear, however, is the fact that verbal dependence in itself is not conclusive evidence of literary invention. Earlier we referred to Loomis's point: that Bede employed the *Dialogues* as a gauge of authenticity.[51] Faced with the report of some doubtful wonder, he was reassured if he could find an analogue in Gregory's account. Gregory's endorsement constituted proof that such a miracle was indeed within the range of the possible. In such circumstances, why not reinforce the point by appropriating some of Gregory's language as well? In the *Vita Cuthberti*, as we have seen, Bede uses words that Gregory originally intended for St Benedict to describe a parallel phase in Cuthbert's spiritual progress.[52] Conceivably, therefore, he would have felt no compunction in employing Gregorian language to describe wonders essentially similar to those recorded in the *Dialogues*, wonders, like Dryhthelm's vision, that he nonetheless regarded as perfectly genuine.

When the third story in Bede's Gregorian triptych is factored into the analysis, however, the balance of judgment shifts. Whereas the first two

---

49 *Dial.* 4.37.14, Zimmerman 241, SC 265:134: "Qua de re colligitur quia ipsa quoque inferni supplicia cum demonstrantur, aliis hoc ad adiutorium, aliis vero ad testimonium fiat, ut isti videant mala quae caveant, illi vero eo amplius puniantur, quo inferni supplicia nec visa et cognita vitare voluerunt."

50 *Signs of Sanctity*, p. 125. For a similar view, see René Latourelle, *The Miracles of Jesus and the Theology of Miracles*, trans. Matthew J. O'Connell (New York, 1988), pp. 108 & 166: "there is a vast distance between literary affinity and the invention of [an] incident on the basis of [an] old story. Analogy is not genealogy" (p. 108).

51 See above, p. 178, n. 7.

52 See above, p. 179, n. 10.

stories are well attested, the third is not. Bede tells us that it took place recently at an unnamed monastery somewhere in the kingdom of Bernicia. Other than that he provides no identifying names and places, and no indication of the source of his information. In stating that "the story spread far and wide," he implies that it became common knowledge. Although he claims to have known the monk involved—"I myself knew a brother, and I would that I have not known him, whose name I could mention if it were any use"[53]—he could not have had a firsthand report of the man's story, because he did not survive to tell it. In short, Bede had ample opportunity to draw creatively on the *Dialogues* in order to fashion a narrative from which his contemporaries could derive spiritual benefit. On balance, it would seem that that is precisely what he did.

---

53 *HE* 5.14, pp. 503-505.

8

Vera Lex Historiae

If we were to expand the enquiry of Chapter Seven in the search for additional texts on which Bede may have been dependent, a promising candidate for further investigation would be the *Vita Martini* of Sulpicius Severus. The parallels between the life of Martin and the various lives of Cuthbert have been noted more than once. On first glance at least they would suggest that, either directly through Sulpicius or indirectly through Venantius Fortunatus, the literary portrait of Cuthbert has been strongly influenced by Martinian elements. In the case of the Lindisfarne Anonymous conscious borrowing can be demonstrated.[1] In Bede's case there is nothing comparable, although Wallace-Hadrill argues that his use of the Martinian material may have been even more extensive.[2] In the final analysis the situation is not as clear as we would like. We need to acknowledge that most of what Bede knew about Cuthbert he derived from the Anonymous. We also need to allow for the possibility of Cuthbert himself being influenced by the *Vita Martini*, and consciously choosing it as a model for his own life.[3] For our immediate purposes, however, the point is not crucial. From what we have already established the probability seems high that, whether here or elsewhere, Bede engaged in the kind of literary invention that was broadly characteristic of medieval hagiography as a whole.[4]

1   The very words in which he promises to provide a truthful account are lifted verbatim from the *Vita Martini*. See above, p. 156, n. 8.

2   Wallace-Hadrill, "Bede and Plummer," in his *Early Medieval History*, pp. 91-92.

3   See John Corbett, "Two Early Anglo-Saxon Holy Men: Oswald and Cuthbert," in *The Anglo-Saxons: Synthesis and Achievement*, ed. J. Douglas Woods & David A.E. Pelteret (Waterloo, 1985), pp. 63-75, who cautions against "the dangers implicit in a shallow scepticism regarding the commonplaces so often found in the lives of the saints" (p. 66). In Corbett's view, both "King Oswald and Saint Cuthbert modelled their conduct as Holy Men, saints and patrons, in large part after the pattern set by their great predecessor, St. Martin" (p. 75). Cf. Gerald Bonner, "Saint Cuthbert: Soul Friend," in *Cuthbert: Saint and Patron*, ed. D.W. Rollason (Durham, 1987), pp. 23-44, esp. 28-30.

4   Donald K. Fry, "The Art of Bede: Edwin's Council," in *Saints, Scholars and Heroes* 1:191-207, argues that Bede supplied the controlling imagery for the speech of the unnamed counselor at Edwin's council (*HE* 2.13) by drawing on Psalm 83

Medieval hagiography, it is usually argued, was not a genre in which factual accuracy was highly valued. Its principal objective was to abstract from normal human failures and limitations, and to present an idealized portrait of the saint that would cast his or her spiritual qualities in the clearest possible relief. Therefore, more than one scholar has warned us against the mistake of confusing the saint's life with a modern biography. Despite superficial similarities, the differences are profound; "we should no more look to [the saint's life] for historical or psychological truth than we would to a medieval romance."[5] To the mind of the medieval hagiographer, as one recent commentator sees it, the details of the saint's earthly, physical existence had no intrinsic importance. They took on meaning only as touched by the grace of God, and hence as bearers of a greater allegorical or spiritual significance. Medieval hagiography was a characteristically Christian expression of the quest for the absolute; in assessing its character and import, we must not confuse metahistory with history, images or figures with facts.[6] Hence, the truth to which the medieval hagiographer aspired, it is sometimes said, was truth of a higher order. According to a recent articulation of the idea, the medieval *vita* was "ethically rather than factually true. To move men to the love of God was such a noble purpose that other considerations (such as truthfulness) paled before it."[7]

The question of truth and falsity in the Middle Ages has been much debated, although for the most part attention has focused on the medieval

---

(84). However, the similarities are pretty slight: the words *passer* and *domum*, and what Fry sees as a pun on the Psalm's *tabernacula* in the counselor's *cenaculo*. Fry himself acknowledges that the connection seems "rather slender," and it is not much strengthened by his appeal to the role of the Psalter in monastic life (p. 200).

5   Woolf, "Saints' Lives," p. 40.

6   Cf. Georg Scheibelreiter, "Die Verfälschung der Wirklichkeit: Hagiographie und Historizität," in *Fälschungen im Mittelalter* (Hannover, 1988), 5:283-319 at 285; and Claudio Leonardi, "Il problema storiografico dell'agiografia," in *Storia della Sicilia e tradizione agiografica nella tarda antichità* (Soveria Mannelli (CZ), 1988), pp. 13-23, esp. 16. See also Réginald Grégoire, *Manuale di agiologia: introduzione alla letteratura agiografica* (Fabriano, 1987), pp. 318-319.

7   Alison Goddard Elliott, *Roads to Paradise: Reading the Lives of the Early Saints* (Hanover NH, 1987), p. 6. Cf. Heffernan, *Sacred Biography*, pp. 70-71; and Franz-Josef Schmale, "Fälschungen in der Geschichtsschreibung," in *Fälschungen im Mittelalter* 1:121-132, who refers to hagiographical sources "deren Wahrheit nicht das Erzählte, aber erfundene Geschehen ist, sondern im tropologischen Sinn der Erzählung liegt" (p. 128).

forger, whose excesses were even greater than the hagiographer's. The most recent trend seems to be against the idea of a conception of truth any different from our modern one,[8] but it would be premature to suggest that the issue has finally been resolved. As part of the larger debate, Bede's notion of truth has been and continues to be the focus of much discussion. Several years ago now Charles W. Jones opened the argument by observing that Bede never adduces authorities in support of "factual" statements, but only for miracles. The witnesses cited to verify the latter, therefore, were intended to attest not to factual accuracy but to "ethical" truth. At the time of the thirteenth centenary celebrations of Bede's birth, Ward advanced a view substantially the same. Without denying Bede's belief in miracles, Ward maintains that, like Gregory the Great, he was much more interested in what the miracle meant than he was in the wonder itself. It was to this spiritual significance, she suggests, that he would have his witnesses attest. Although Bede's miracle stories undoubtedly contain factual information, we need to be conscious of the layers of interpretation that have been superimposed: "Bede is using his miracle material from the inside, and he shapes it according to his purposes. If we try to see the miracles as a simple record of facts we show ourselves more credulous and naive than Bede himself."[9]

The Jones thesis has not gone entirely unchallenged. Creider, for instance, has argued that Bede's use of witnesses is indeed a sign of his commitment to factual truthfulness. His practice is to provide authorities wherever he expects doubt on the part of his readers, and not just with regard to miracle stories.[10] However, it is the opposite reaction, the suspicion that Bede was frequently being governed by a different kind of truth, that is prominent in the remarks of some of the most recent

---

8 See, for example, Elizabeth A.R. Brown, *"Falsitas pia sive reprehensibilis*: Medieval Forgers and their Intentions," in *Fälschungen im Mittelalter* 1:101-119, esp. 112; and Frantisek Graus, "Fälschungen im Gewand der Frömmigkeit," in *Fälschungen im Mittelalter* 5:261-282, esp. 268. See also Nicholas P. Brooks, *History and Myth, Forgery and Truth* (Birmingham, 1986), esp. p. 11 [unnumbered]; and Anthony Grafton, *Forgers and Critics: Creativity and Duplicity in Western Scholarship* (Princeton NJ, 1990), esp. p. 49.

9 Cf. Jones, *Saints' Lives and Chronicles*, pp. 75-76; and Ward, "Miracles and History," pp. 72, 76. See also Jones, "Bede as Early Medieval Historian," *Medievalia et Humanistica* 4 (1946): 26-36 at 31.

10 Creider, "Bede's Understanding of the Miraculous," pp. 152-153; cf. Musca, *Venerabile Beda*, pp. 166-167.

commentators. Rollason argues of the lives of St Cuthbert in general that it was a higher, moral truth to which they aspired: "They are first and foremost works of spiritual rather than historical literature and the witnesses invoked are surely attesting to the ethical validity of the miracle stories rather than to the reality of the events described." Distinguishing between the anonymous *Vita Cuthberti* and Bede's, Stancliffe warns us against the pedagogical bias of the latter. Although in many respects he was a better historian than the Anonymous, "Bede's didactic concerns did lead him to portray Cuthbert in an essentially Gregorian mould, and this occasionally led him to alter the anonymous's account in the interests of didacticism, rather than truth."[11] The point has been repeated often enough to suggest a broadly based scholarly consensus. According to Fry, the confidence Bede has inspired among many modern readers of his works results from his mastery of sophisticated narrative techniques. In reality, "the *Ecclesiastical History* is an immense artifice, drawing stories from deep time and remotest shires, welded into a chronological and moral framework for our spiritual benefit."[12]

Somewhat surprising in view of the strength of the received view is the weakness of the evidential foundation on which it frequently rests. It has been argued, for example, that a clear illustration of Bede's disregard for factual veracity can be found in the latter stages of the prose *Vita Cuthberti*. There he informs us of the miraculous cure effected by a piece of calfskin that Oethelwald, Cuthbert's successor at the hermitage on Farne Island, had attached to the wall to keep out the drafts. Says Bede:

> Whether this ought to be ascribed to the merits of the same blessed father Cuthbert or of his successor Aethilwald, a man equally devoted to God, He knows who judges the heart. Nor does any reason forbid us to believe that it was wrought by the merits of both, accompanied also by the faith of the most reverend father Felgild, through whom and in whom the miracle of healing, to which I refer, was wrought. He is the third heir of that dwelling

11 David W. Rollason, "Why Was St Cuthbert So Popular?" in *Cuthbert: Saint and Patron*, pp. 9-22 at 13; Stancliffe, "Cuthbert and the Polarity between Pastor and Solitary," p. 28. Campbell, "Bede," p. 182, says that the *Ecclesiastical History* was written "not only in the Eusebian tradition but also in that of hagiography. ... Moral truth, not literal truth, was what mattered."

12 Donald K. Fry, "The Art of Bede II: The Reliable Narrator as Persona," in *The Early Middle Ages*, ed. William H. Snyder (Binghamton NY, 1982), pp. 63-82 at 80.

and of that spiritual warfare and today, more than seventy years of age, he awaits the end of the present life, eagerly longing for the life to come.[13]

These comments, says Jones, indicate that "Bede was unconcerned about the facts when he was writing didactic works." To another scholar they suggest that "even factual accuracy could be winked at, provided the narrative added to the dignity and holiness of the subject."[14] Surely, however, this is to get it precisely wrong. Bede is simply saying that, since they were all meritorious, he does not know to which of the saints involved the miracle should be credited. In the face of insufficient evidence, it is not a willingness to leave a question unanswered that threatens to compromise factual veracity, but rather an unwarranted haste to pronounce definitive judgment.[15]

When Bede's own methodological statements are consulted, what they seem to suggest, on a *prima facie* view at least, is a standard of factual veracity scarcely less exacting than our modern one. In the prologue to the prose life of Cuthbert, which is dedicated to Bishop Eadfrith and the brethren at Lindisfarne, he states:

> I have not presumed to write down anything concerning so great a man without the most rigorous investigation of the facts (*sine certissima exquisitione rerum gestarum*) nor, at the end, to hand on what I had written to be copied for general use, without the scrupulous examination of credible witnesses (*sine subtili examinatione testium indubiorum*). ... Thus I have made it my business to put down on parchment the results of my rigorous investigation of the truth (*certam veritatis indaginem*), expressed in simple language quite free from all obscurities and subtleties, and to bring what was written into the presence of your brotherhood, in order that it might be corrected if false, or if true, approved by the authority of your judgment.[16]

The truth to which Bede says he aspired seems clearly to have been objective truth, factual veracity that was to be determined by the evidence, precisely what we should expect given the concern for correctness and accuracy evident in his scriptural commentaries.[17] His handling of

---

13 *VCP*, chap. 46, pp. 301-303.
14 Jones, "Bede as Early Medieval Historian," p. 31; Thomas W. Mackay, "Bede's Hagiographical Method: His Knowledge and Use of Paulinus of Nola," in *Famulus Christi*, pp. 77-92 at 87.
15 Cf. Creider, "Bede's Understanding of the Miraculous," pp. 142-143.
16 *VCP*, Prol., pp. 142-145 (translation slightly amended).
17 See Carroll, *Venerable Bede*, p. 50.

Acts 1:13 provides an example of the extent to which even a minor factual error distressed him. In his commentary Bede tells us that the Judas Jacobi there numbered among the apostles was also known as Thaddaeus; and that, as Eusebius relates, it was this Thaddaeus who was sent to heal King Abgar at Edessa. In his *Retractions*, however, he issues a correction. Earlier he had simply been following Jerome, and he had not realized his mistake until he had had an opportunity to check Eusebius for himself. The Thaddaeus sent to King Abgar was not an apostle at all, but one of the seventy-two disciples. Bede's distress is clearly revealed by the need he felt to exculpate himself. The error should not be held to his account, he suggests. Surely he cannot be faulted for assuming the correctness of one of the great doctors of the church.[18]

In what immediately follows in the prologue to the *Vita Cuthberti* Anderson detects a rather different perspective, that of a mind closed to the evidence and intent upon presenting a predetermined picture of the saint. Here Bede reminds the brethren at Lindisfarne that after his work had been examined for two days by their elders and teachers, it was given their unqualified endorsement. Not a word had to be changed. But, he continues,

> consulting together in our presence, you brought forward many other facts concerning the life and virtues of the blessed man no less important than those which we have written down, which would have well deserved to be mentioned if it had not seemed scarcely fitting and proper to insert new matter or add to a work which was planned and complete.[19]

Anderson is startled by the passage. "According to Bede," she says, "the pattern has been perceived and woven, and its truth should not be disturbed. The *vita* has been written and has now, it appears, a life of its own."[20] However, this does Bede a disservice. Bede says only that, additional information notwithstanding, he saw no need to reopen a work that had been finished and given the *imprimatur* of the brethren. In view of every historian's need to make some selection from the material to hand, this seems perfectly reasonable. There is no reason to believe that

---

18 Cf. *Exp. Act. Apost.* 1.13, CCL 121:11; and *Retr.* 1.13, CCL 121:107: "Non autem mihi imputandum errorem reor, ubi auctoritatem magnorum sequens doctorum, quae in illorum opusculis inveni, absque scrupulo suscipienda credidi."

19 *VCP*, Prol., p. 145 (translation slightly amended).

20 Judith H. Anderson, *Biographical Truth: The Representation of Historical Persons in Tudor-Stuart Writing* (New Haven, 1984), p. 12.

Bede would stubbornly have refused to amend what he had written if it had been shown to be incorrect, or if something essential had been omitted. Although it would undoubtedly have distressed him, it would not likely have surprised Bede to learn that modern historical scholarship has managed to detect errors in his account of events. Picard, for example, argues that his version of Adomnan's later years contains major inaccuracies. Since Picard also acknowledges that Bede was probably simply reporting the best information that he had, his errors point more clearly to the limitations of his sources than to any lack of commitment on Bede's own part to factual history.[21] His best efforts notwithstanding, Bede's knowledge of early English history could not have been anything other than fragmentary. Although he had access to some documents, for the most part he was dependent on an oral tradition given more to panegyric than objective history, and both highly localized and evanescent as well. "The traditions even about kings could fade quickly if not cultivated by an interested party, and if Bede failed to contact the right monastery information would elude him."[22]

Of course, the accuracy of Bede's account may also have been compromised by the limitations of his own perspective or biases, potentially a more serious matter. The presence of the Roman point of view that animates his history has been remarked on more than once. Picard complains of Bede's prejudicial treatment of the Irish,[23] Barnard of his distorted view of the Britons as well.[24] Recently Goffart

---

21 Picard, "Purpose of Adomnán's *Vita Columbae*," pp. 160-177. Cf. idem, "Bede, Adomnán, and the Writing of History," where Picard again argues that Bede gives a partial and misleading account in the chapter devoted to Adomnán. Judging from the general tone of his remarks, here as well Picard seems to be of the view that Bede was simply misinformed. Although he characterizes the chapter in question as "the work of the historian as propagandist" (p. 69), he also admits that the evidence for deliberate falsification on Bede's part is at best inconclusive (p. 70).

22 Kirby, "Bede's Native Sources for the *Historia Ecclesiastica*," p. 355; cf. idem, "Northumbria in the Time of Wilfrid," in *Saint Wilfrid at Hexham*, ed. D.P. Kirby (Newcastle upon Tyne, 1974), pp. 1-34 at 4-5.

23 Picard, "Bede, Adomnán, and the Writing of History," p. 57. Cf. Margaret W. Pepperdene, "Bede's *Historia Ecclesiastica*: A New Perspective," *Celtica* 4 (1958): 253-262; and Friedrich Prinz, "Von der Bekehrung der Angelsachsen bis zu ihrer Missionstätigkeit im Frankenreich," in *Angli e Sassoni al di qua e al di là del mare*, pp. 701-734.

24 L.W. Barnard, "Bede and Eusebius as Church Historians," in *Famulus Christi*, pp. 106-124 at 120. Cf. Nora K. Chadwick, "The Conversion of Northumbria: A

has argued that he was more immediately involved in the controversies of his day than may formerly have been suspected. If the monks of Lindisfarne were keen to have Bede rewrite the anonymous *Vita Cuthberti*, it was because it had been compromised beyond redemption by being quarried for the *Life of Wilfrid*. The anti-Wilfridian stance, says Goffart, was one that Bede shared: it dominates the main narrative line of the *Ecclesiastical History*, and in the *Historia abbatum* leads him deliberately to deemphasize Wilfrid's role in Wearmouth-Jarrow's foundation.[25] Approaching the matter from a very different angle, Kirby has argued that, rather than activism, it was Bede's very detachment from the events of his day that gave rise to a distorting element in his narrative. Noting that when compared with Eddius Stephanus Bede offers a rather roseate picture of Anglo-Saxon life, Kirby claims that part of the explanation at least is to be found in Bede's personality:

> Bede was a monk, a scholar, a quietly devout and pious man, writing of a lay world he hardly knew in praise of kings who appeared to him, from what he was told, to possess definite virtues as rulers and individuals. ... The serenity which Bede brings to the ecclesiastical personalities of the period of the Conversion does not derive necessarily from their individual lives, nor is their apparent mildness and humility purely the result of Celtic piety or Roman devotion: it is a mirror of the peace and charity of Bede himself and of the timeless quiet of his own life, the melodious unison of plainsong and the contemplative observance of the canonical hours during which, as Bede believed (and a delightful belief too), angels visited the congregations of the brethren.[26]

Without attempting to adjudicate these claims, one might simply note that their conflicting nature is reassuring. Furthermore, no working, modern historian would be too distressed by them. Just as all his-

---

Comparison of Sources," and "The Battle of Chester: A Study of Sources," in *Celt and Saxon: Studies in the Early British Border*, ed. Nora K. Chadwick (Cambridge, 1963), pp. 138-166, 167-185.

25 Goffart, *Narrators of Barbarian History*, pp. 283-285, 296-328 (esp. 320), & 294-295. Cf. Thacker, "Lindisfarne and the Origins of the Cult of St Cuthbert," pp. 117-122; Rollason, *Saints and Relics*, pp. 112-113. For a contrasting view, see D.P. Kirby, "Bede, Eddius Stephanus and the 'Life of Wilfrid,'" *English Historical Review* 98 (1983): 101-114. Bede's active involvement in current affairs—this time the politics of the early 730s—is an idea that Goffart pursues further in "The *Historia Ecclesiastica*: Bede's Agenda and Ours," *Haskins Society Journal* 2 (1990): 29-45.

26 Kirby, "Northumbria in the Time of Wilfrid," p. 4.

torians make mistakes, all are equally required to view the evidence from some particular vantage point, some point of view that may be more or less successful in doing it justice. Having a perspective on the issues does not automatically result in a tendentious treatment of them. It becomes an offence only when it leads to wilful distortion. In Bede's case, however, suspicions may be further aroused because of the explicitly moral purpose with which he invests his historical work. Its imprint is clearly evident in the Preface of the *Ecclesiastical History*:

> Should history relate good things concerning good men, the thoughtful listener is spurred on to imitate the good; should it record evil things of wicked men, no less effectually the devout and earnest listener or reader is kindled to eschew what is harmful and perverse, and himself with greater care pursue those things which he has learned to be good and pleasing in the sight of God.[27]

Here Bede gives voice to a tradition that stretched back into classical times, when history was considered a branch of rhetoric that could stir the emotions by means of effective examples.

Bede's primary objective in the *Ecclesiastical History* was simply to tell the story of the Church in England from the time of the conversion up to his own day; and because he was considerably more scholarly in his approach than most other early medieval historians, he has justifiably earned the esteem of modern commentators. Knowles describes him as "the father of English history," largely because of the critical capacity he brought to his task: "The pains he took to acquire and check reliable information, to secure genuine documents, and to criticize and present all this, the care he took to have it read and revised before finally giving it to the world, would be admirable in the most scholarly historian of today."[28] But Bede also clearly intended to treat the material he assembled as a potential gallery of examples, and by appropriate words of praise or censure educate his readers in the good to be emulated or the evil to be avoided. In practice, Bede also seems to have been

---

27 *HE*, Praef., pp. 2-3 (translation revised): "Sive enim historia de bonis bona referat, ad imitandum bonum auditor sollicitus instigatur; seu mala commemoret de pravis, nihilominus religiosus ac pius auditor sive lector devitando quod noxium est ac perversum, ipse sollertius ad exsequenda ea quae bona ac Deo digna esse cognoverit, accenditur."

28 David Knowles, *Saints and Scholars: Twenty-Five Medieval Portraits* (Cambridge, 1962), p. 15.

materially influenced by Orosius and Gildas, earlier Christian adepts of the moral-pedagogical school of historiography. Hence throughout the *Ecclesiastical History* he reinforces his lessons by means of a strong sense of immanent justice, according to which God intervenes actively in the historical process by rewarding goodness and punishing sin.[29] His account of the fire that razed the monastery at Coldingham, divinely produced in response to the wickedness of the inmates, is a case in point. "It seemed desirable," says Bede, "to include this story in our *History* in order to warn the reader about the workings of the Lord, how terrible he is in his dealings with the children of men, lest perhaps indulging in fleshly delights or paying little heed to the judgment of God, his sudden wrath at some time should fall upon us, and either his righteous anger afflict us with temporal loss, or he judge us still more sternly and bear us away to everlasting perdition."[30]

Not surprisingly, some would see a tension between the demands of this kind of historiography and a commitment to factual veracity. To paraphrase Hunter Blair, history is recorded not for its own sake, but as a means to the achievement of spiritual objectives. It is not written so that people may be better informed, but rather to inspire them to greater depths of devotion and piety.[31] To a large extent, however, Bede's view is a simple reflection of the standard medieval view, which he endorses without reservation, and we should be careful before we rule it inconsistent with a concern for factual truthfulness. Distinctive to Bede's approach, it has been claimed, is the manner in which he addresses, not simply individual Christians, but the Anglo-Saxon people as a whole. In addition to fostering moral and religious development at the personal level, says Musca, Bede also wished to stimulate a collective sense of national identity premised on shared cultural and religious values.[32] If this was indeed Bede's intention (the point has been con-

---

29 Cf. Mayr-Harting, *Coming of Christianity to England*, p. 44.

30 *HE* 4.25, p. 427.

31 Peter Hunter Blair, "The Historical Writings of Bede," in *La storiografia altomedievale* (Spoleto, 1970), 1:197-221 at 201.

32 Musca, *Venerabile Beda*, pp. 180, 262-264. Cf. H.E.J. Cowdrey, "Bede and the 'English People,'" *Journal of Religious History* 11 (1981): 501-523; R.H.C. Davis, "Bede After Bede," in *Studies in Medieval History Presented to R. Allen Brown*, ed. Christopher Harper-Bill, Christopher J. Holdsworth & Janet L. Nelson (Woodbridge, Suffolk, 1989), pp. 103-116; and Patrick Wormald, "Bede, the *Bretwaldas* and the Origins of the *Gens Anglorum*," in *Ideal and Reality in Frankish and Anglo-*

tested[33]), to some it might suggest that his statements must be approached with an even greater degree of suspicion. However, this is not the conclusion that Musca himself draws. Musca argues that the moral purpose or purposes Bede set for his work would not have required him consciously to jeopardize factual veracity, and in this he is almost certainly correct.

Bede's choices were very different from those of a modern historian, and while searching out points of moral relevance he undoubtedly ignored much that the modern reader would have found significant. Possibly as well there were occasions when he suppressed details that, if included, could have created a different impression of the events in question. Bonner suggests that avoiding the bad and dwelling on what made for edification was a basic principle of ecclesiastical history that Bede could have learned from Eusebius,[34] and Campbell argues that the lesson was applied in his treatment of St Wilfrid. Bede highlights the more edifying aspects of Wilfrid's career, says Campbell, while deemphasizing or omitting entirely what was less clearly to the saint's credit. Hence "the veneration which [Bede] has so long and so rightly been accorded ought to be tempered by some mistrust."[35] Once again, however, Bede's own statements offer an important corrective. His portrait of Bishop Aidan, for example, is introduced with the following words:

> I have written these things about the character and work of Aidan, not by any means commending or praising his lack of knowledge in the matter of the observance of Easter; indeed I heartily detest it, as I have clearly shown in the book which I wrote called *De temporibus*, but, as a truthful historian (*quasi verax historicus*), I have described in a straightforward manner those things which were done by him or through him, praising such of his qualities as are worthy of praise and preserving their memory for the benefit of my readers. Such were his love of peace and charity, temperance and humility.[36]

Saxon Society, pp. 99-129, esp. 120-121. Wormald argues that, in encouraging a common English identity, Bede was endorsing the vision of Gregory the Great. Cf. Michael Richter, "Bede's *Angli*: Angles or English?" *Peritia* 3 (1984): 99-114.

33 See Steven Fanning, "Bede, *Imperium*, and the Bretwaldas," *Speculum* 66 (1991): 1-26.

34 Gerald Bonner, "Bede and His Legacy," *Durham University Journal* 78 (n.s. 47) (1986): 219-230, esp. 227.

35 Campbell, "Bede," pp. 179, 183.

36 *HE* 3.17, pp. 265-267.

If selectivity produced distortion, Bede would have us believe that it was not something of which he was aware. What he was very much conscious of was his responsibility to be truthful. Hence, he says, he will tell things as they were, praising only what was genuinely praiseworthy in Aidan's case for the guidance of his readers. Indeed, far from being jeopardized by Bede's didacticism, one might argue that the factual accuracy of his account would have been a precondition for any moral purpose it was intended to serve.

One of the most important dividends of recent Bedan scholarship is an increased realization that his historical and hagiographical work cannot be appraised in isolation from his scriptural commentaries. In the short biographical statement at the end of the *Ecclesiastical History* Bede tells us that, having been committed to the care of Abbot Benedict as a young boy, he has spent virtually his entire life at the monastery of Jarrow, applying himself completely to the study of the Scriptures: *omnem meditandis scripturis operam dedi.*[37] Coming where it does at the conclusion of a major piece of historical scholarship that could not conceivably qualify as the study of Scripture, this statement obviously cannot be taken too literally. But it is an important indication nonetheless of the primacy Bede attached to biblical studies, and hence of the likely influence they had on every other task to which he directed his attention, his historical work included.

To Bede's mind the biblical narratives were exemplary historical literature, and so they profoundly affected the language, style and structure of his *Ecclesiastical History.*[38] The influence of the Old Testament seems to have been especially pronounced. Recently McClure has argued that it was in the books of Samuel and Kings specifically that Bede found the key to his conception of history and of himself as an historian.[39]

---

37 Ibid. 5.24, p. 566.
38 Roger D. Ray, "Bede, the Exegete, as Historian," in *Famulus Christi*, pp. 125-140. Cf. Leonardi, "Venerabile Beda e la cultura del secolo VIII," esp. pp. 635-639; and Mayr-Harting, *Venerable Bede, the Rule of St Benedict, and Social Class*, pp. 12-22.
39 McClure, "Bede's Old Testament Kings," pp. 76-98. Cf. Thacker, "Bede's Ideal of Reform," esp. pp. 142-143, who suggests that the Old Testament provided Bede with a central narrative theme, that of the chosen nation that had failed to fulfill its divinely established destiny. See also Schoebe, "Was gilt im frühen Mittelalter als Geschichtliche Wirklichkeit?" Schoebe argues that the basic categories of Bede's analysis were derived from the Old Testament. Indeed, it so shaped his perspective that Bede saw the world in essentially Old Testament terms.

The lessons that Bede would have learned from the historical books of the Bible were manifold, not the least of them being that history served a moral-pedagogical purpose. In addition to providing a narrative in which virtue is rewarded and vice punished, on closer inspection they also revealed hidden allegorical depths beneath the literal surface. Alongside the allegorical sense proper, in which Old Testament characters or events were shown to prefigure Christ or the church, there was also the tropological sense, in which they became vehicles for moral instruction. Bede also would have learned, however, the importance of a truthful and accurate account of the past, for unlike the allegories of the classical poets, the spiritual senses of Scripture were written into the fabric of events that actually occurred.[40]

There is one additional major passage that has some bearing on the question of the value Bede attached to factual veracity; it is also the one that in the recent past has attracted the most comment. It occurs in the Preface to his *Ecclesiastical History*, and it comes at the conclusion of an extensive treatment of the sources of the history, of their relative importance and of the reliability that Bede attached to them. Bede states:

> As to the kingdom of Lindsey, I learned of the growth of their faith in Christ and of the succession of bishops, either through a letter from the reverend Bishop Cyneberht or from the lips of other trustworthy men (*aliorum fidelium virorum*). But what happened in the church in the various parts of the kingdom of Northumbria, from the time when they received the faith of Christ up to the present, apart from those matters of which I had personal knowledge, I have learned not from any one source but from the faithful testimony of innumerable witnesses (*fideli innumerorum testium ... adsertione*), who either knew or remembered these things. In this respect it is to be noted that what I have written about the most holy father Bishop Cuthbert, either in this volume or in his biography, I took partly from what I had previously found written about him by the brethren of the church at Lindisfarne, accepting the story I read in simple faith; but in part I also made it my business to add with care what I was able to learn myself from the trustworthy testimony of reliable witnesses (*certissima fidelium virorum adtestatione*). So I humbly beg the reader, if he finds anything other than the truth set down in what I have written, not to impute it to me. For in accordance with the true law of history (*quod vera lex historiae est*), I have

---

40 Cf. Musca, *Venerabile Beda*, pp. 126, 251-252; and de Lubac, *Exégèse médiévale* 1.2:384-396, 513-522; 2.2:125-149.

sought simply to commit to writing what I have collected from common report (*ea quae fama vulgante collegimus*) for the instruction of posterity.[41]

Recent discussion of this passage began with Jones, who argues that
it is far from representing the commitment to factual veracity that earlier
commentators thought. Jones explains that the *vera lex historiae* to which
Bede appeals was borrowed from Jerome's *Adversus Helvidium*, and that
Bede had employed it earlier in his commentary on Luke to help explain
how the Evangelist, his knowledge of the virgin birth notwithstanding,
could have referred to Joseph as the father of Christ. The answer: St
Luke was simply expressing the popularly held view, *quae vera lex
historiae est*. As Jones sees it, therefore, the point of the true law of
history is "to express the common view—to use accepted symbols as
tools for attaining the ideal end, though the words may not be factually
true." By invoking it in the Preface to his *Ecclesiastical History*, "Bede
directly absolved himself from the blame of any reader who would want
him to write *ad litteram*, or from our objections should we want to read
as fact a story never so intended."[42] Others have been prompt to endorse a similar view. According to Schreiner, Bede did not believe that
exercising his critical capacities and assuming responsibility for the facts
reported were part of his task. Hence the Preface to the *Ecclesiastical
History* shows him avoiding accountability for its contents and shoving
responsibility off onto the sources themselves. Rather than providing a
factually accurate account, says Hunter Blair, his function as an historian was simply to record what was popularly believed. Indeed, there
is reason to suspect that he did not always himself believe what he
chose to report.[43]

The example to which Hunter Blair points is the account in book
two of the *Ecclesiastical History* of the meeting of Gregory the Great,
who was not yet pope, and some Northumbrian slave boys in the market

---

41 *HE*, Praef., pp. 6-7 (revised slightly).
42 Jones, *Saints' Lives and Chronicles*, p. 88.
43 Klaus Schreiner, "'*Discrimen veri ac falsi*.' Ansätze und Formen der Kritik in der
    Heiligen- und Reliquienverehrung des Mittelalters," *Archiv für Kulturgeschichte* 48
    (1966): 1-53 at 2; Hunter Blair, "Historical Writings of Bede," p. 202. Cf.
    Peter Hunter Blair, *Bede's Ecclesiastical History of the English Nation and Its
    Importance Today* (Jarrow Lecture, 1959), p. 10; idem, *World of Bede*, p. 303. See
    also Ray, "Bede, the Exegete, as Historian," esp. pp. 129-130; Spencer Cosmos,
    "Oral Tradition and Literary Convention in Bede's Life of St. Aidan," *Classical
    Folia* 31 (1977): 47-63 at 51-52; and Ward, *Venerable Bede*, pp. 113-114.

place in Rome. The boys were handsome, and of fair complexion, and Gregory took an interest in them. Having enquired about their place of origin and their spiritual state, he was distressed to learn that they were still heathens:

> With a deep-drawn sigh he said, "Alas that the author of darkness should have men so bright of face in his grip, and that minds devoid of inward grace should bear so graceful an outward form." Again he asked for the name of the race. He was told that they were called *Angli*. "Good," he said, "they have the face of angels, and such men should be fellow-heirs of the angels in heaven." "What is the name," he asked, "of the kingdom from which they have been brought?" He was told that the men of the kingdom were called *Deiri*. "*Deiri*," he replied, "*De ira*! Good! Snatched from the wrath of Christ and called to his mercy. And what is the name of the king of the land?" He was told that it was Aelle; and playing on the name, he said, "Alleluia! The praise of God the Creator must be sung in those parts."[44]

Bede goes on to say that Gregory went to the Bishop of Rome to ask that missionaries be sent to the *Angli*. Indeed, he was anxious to undertake the mission himself, and the pope approved, but the people of Rome were unprepared to see him journey so far. Soon after he became pope himself, however, Gregory was able to realize his ambition, at least vicariously through St Augustine and his companions, whose efforts he supported through his encouragement and his prayers.

Hunter Blair maintains that it would be perilous to conclude that Bede believed the story. He reports it, not because he was convinced it was true, but rather because it was widely held to be true.[45] That it was indeed a popular story is clear: Bede himself emphasizes its status as a traditional tale. At the very outset he says: "We must not fail to relate the story about St. Gregory which has come down to us as a tradition of our forefathers." And to reinforce the point, he returns to it once again at the end: "I have thought it proper," he says, "to insert this story, ... based as it is on the tradition which we have received from our ancestors." Were it not for these explicit statements, we might have suspected that Bede was drawing on a written source. The story

44 *HE* 2.1, pp. 133-135.
45 Hunter Blair, "Historical Writings of Bede," p. 202. Cf. Wallace-Hadrill, *Bede's Ecclesiastical History*, p. 51; and Ward, *Venerable Bede*, p. 119, who regards the episode as an instance of "Bede's preference for the significant over the factual."

appears in the anonymous Whitby life of St. Gregory as well, and for the most part in substantially the same form. Taken together with Bede's comments, however, the differences that do exist between the two versions confirm their mutual independence.[46] In the Whitby account, unlike Bede's, Gregory does set out to convert the *Angli*, but in order to placate the anger of the Roman citizens has to be recalled before reaching his destination. Indeed, he is able to anticipate the arrival of messengers commanding his return when a locust (*locusta*) settles on him while he is reading, for he sees in the event a command to remain in place (*sta in loco*).

Hunter Blair suggests that, since the episode of the locust is lacking in the *Ecclesiastical History*, Bede evidently chose to suppress the more blatantly superstitious elements of the tale. Indeed, says Hunter Blair, his omission of this episode suggests that "he had reservations about the historical truth of the whole tradition, but he conceived it to be his duty as a historian to record not merely what had happened, but also what was widely believed to have happened."[47] It is also quite possible, however, that the locust story was unique to the Whitby account, and that Bede was simply unaware of it. Even if he did actually reject it, his decision to retain the other major elements of the story is no reason to suspect a lack of concern on his part about factual accuracy. Because it was unverified legend, he did have some doubts, and so in the actual telling of the tale he is careful to distance himself from it. He describes it as *opinio*, and twice chooses other wording—*Dicunt, ut aiunt*—that reminds us of its status as hearsay.[48] However, the story does cohere with the allegorical style of Gregory's thought as Bede would have known it; and as Bede himself suggests, it does provide some context for the conversion of the *Angli* by demonstrating Gregory's interest in the matter from early in his career.[49] These factors would have argued

---

46 On the relationship between Bede's account and the Whitby life, see Colgrave, "Earliest Saints' Lives Written in England," pp. 35-60; idem, "The Earliest Life of St Gregory the Great, Written by a Whitby Monk," in *Celt and Saxon: Studies in the Early British Border*, pp. 119-137.

47 Hunter Blair, *World of Bede*, p. 78.

48 Cf. Plummer, *Opera Historica* 1:xlv; Levison, "Bede as Historian," pp. 140-141; Creider, "Bede's Understanding of the Miraculous," pp. 145-146.

49 *HE* 2.1, p. 132: "Nec silentio praetereunda opinio, quae de beato Gregorio traditione maiorum ad nos usque perlata est, qua videlicet ex causa admonitus tam sedulam erga salutem nostrae gentis curam gesserit."

in its favour, and would have disposed Bede to give it some credence. Since the conversion is the central event of the *Ecclesiastical History*, Bede probably thought it important to include all relevant information that came to his attention, provided that it met some minimal standard of credibility. Since he was also candid enough to inform his readers of the quality of his information, in the circumstances nothing more could reasonably have been expected of him.

As a product of popular tradition, the episode of the Anglo-Saxon slave boys was by no means unique. Elsewhere as well in the *Ecclesiastical History* Bede had to work with facts of less than absolute certainty. Hence he takes advantage of the opportunity that the Preface provides to register a general disclaimer. He has done the best he can, he wishes to tell us, to ensure the accuracy of what he has reported, and so he cannot be held responsible for any errors or misinformation that remain. His comments have to be read in context if their import is properly to be appraised. Bede spends most of the Preface identifying his principal sources, repeatedly emphasizing the personal qualities of all those on whose testimony he has been dependent. Only then does he beg the reader, if he finds anything at variance with the truth, not to charge it to his account. "In accordance with the principles of true history," he says, "I have simply sought to commit to writing what I have collected from common report, for the instruction of posterity."[50] It is mistaken to see in these words a challenge to the idea of factual veracity. Common report—*fama vulgans*—is not street gossip; it is the product of informants uniformly identified as trustworthy, faithful and reliable, and it is therefore worthy of belief. Despite a superficial similarity, it is to be distinguished from *opinio vulgi*, the clearly erroneous and misguided popular opinion to which Bede refers in his commentary on Luke 2:33-34.

When the Evangelist, despite his knowledge of the virgin birth, chose to refer to Joseph as the father of Christ, Bede tells us, it was *opinio vulgi* that he was articulating, *quae vera lex historiae est*. He knew perfectly well that Joseph was not the father of Christ, but chose not to controvert the popularly held view.[51] The verbal similarity of *opinio vulgi* and *fama vulgans*, both linked to *vera lex historiae*, has tempted more than one scholar to conflate the two expressions, and to read the passage from the *Ecclesiastical History* in light of the earlier

---

50 Ibid., Praef., pp. 6-7.
51 *In Luc*. 1, CCL 120:67-68.

passage from the commentary on Luke. In point of fact, *opinio vulgi* and *fama vulgans* are intrinsically different, and it is two different laws of history to which they are related. The law that the Evangelist employed permits the conscious abandonment of literal truth in certain circumstances. As Ray points out, it is a product of the rhetorical doctrine of probability, according to which "the narrator may momentarily state erroneous common opinion if it is somehow congruous with other elements of his story." If this seems an odd doctrine for Bede to invoke, it is one that he discovered in Jerome, who in turn allowed it only limited use; and it is one that Bede used, not to describe his own work, but rather to solve an exegetical problem in the text of Luke. The very different law to which he appeals in the *Ecclesiastical History*, the one that articulates *fama vulgans*, is a law that allows for the use of unverified oral report in historical narrative when other and better sources are lacking. It involves no compromise with the historian's commitment to factual veracity, which remains unimpaired.[52] Whereas *opinio vulgi* is false, *fama vulgans* can be presumed to be true.[53] But its truth is not certain, and it cannot be confirmed; and so in the Preface to his *Ecclesiastical History* Bede issues a disclaimer to protect himself from the accusation of falsehood, and to warn his readers about possible errors of which he is unaware.[54]

The conclusion seems clear, although perhaps not without paradox. Indeed, it leaves a major problem unresolved. As noted in Chapter Seven, the probability is high that at least one of the miracle stories in the *Ecclesiastical History* is a product of artifice rather than empirical research. Although offered as a factual report, it is more likely a literary construct, fashioned of elements drawn from the *Dialogues* of Gregory the Great. Indeed, it is likely that Bede engaged in similar borrowing,

---

52 Ray, "Bede's *vera lex historiae*," esp. pp. 4 & 14.
53 The point is intended to apply only to the specific texts under consideration. However, for additional examples of *opinio vulgi* being mistaken, see *In Luc.* 3, CCL 120:201; *Exp. Act. Apost.* 7.16, CCL 121:34-35; and *Retr.* 13.21, CCL 121:146-147. Cf. *Hom. Evan.* 1.20, CCL 122:142, where *opinio vulgata* is clearly erroneous. There is a certain amount of fluidity in Bede's usage. Hence, for a passage suggesting that *opinio vulgata* can be quite correct, see *In Gen.* 3, CCL 118A:143. Conversely, for an instance of *fama vulgaris* being conceived as misguided, see *Retr.* 13.19, CCL 121:146.
54 Cf. Musca, *Venerabile Beda*, pp. 251-257; Creider, "Bede's Understanding of the Miraculous," pp. 123-124; Brown, *Bede the Venerable*, p. 89.

either from Gregory or from the *Vita Columbae* of Adomnan, on one or two other occasions as well. If this indeed is what he did, it was not because he had a view of history according to which factual veracity, as a matter of course, could be sacrificed to other, higher considerations; nor was it because he thought that his obligations as an historian could be fulfilled simply by passing on what was popularly, and conveniently, thought to be true. Neither Bede nor Jerome before him would have maintained that the historian's chief purpose was to record popular and misguided opinion. The explanation will have to be sought elsewhere. Ray puts it well. For both Bede and Jerome, "the true law of history was to write instructive factual narrative, whether of kings or of saints."[55]

---

55 Ray, "Bede's *vera lex historiae*," p. 13.

9

Truth and Its Limits

In a relatively recent statement on the matter, as we have seen, Roger Ray maintains that Bede the historian was committed to the highest standards of factual veracity.[1] In an earlier pair of articles, however, he advances a different view. Bede's conception of his role as an historian, he argues, was primarily a product of biblical study. But his understanding of and appreciation for the kind of history to be found in the Gospels was in turn shaped by the tradition of the Fathers, and in particular by the influence of Augustine's *De consensu Evangelistarum*. The use of classical narrative theory to interpret sacred history was common among the Fathers, and Augustine appeals to it as well in his analysis of biblical narrative technique. Among the principles he elucidates, says Ray, are several that would become commonplaces in medieval historiography, among them the notion that, in the final analysis, the truth of historical narrative is doctrinal and moral truth.[2]

One of the fundamental distinctions of *De consensu*, says Ray, is the one between *res* and *verba*. *Res* is of fundamental importance; *verba* have only relative significance. However,

> *res* is no neutral datum: it is inseparable from *sententia, voluntas, veritas*. It is an event that actually happened, but it is primarily something that speaks, that signifies. To report *res* is therefore to record the event not so much in itself as in its signifying power, not so much in literal manifestation as in intention. ... The underlying principle is that narrative technique must above all be rhetorically sufficient. Whether it is also empirically exact is at best a secondary issue.

Although there is no indication that Augustine would countenance the invention of "a rhetoric of historical circumstances," in Ray's judgment the historiography that he advocates is still one in which "moral interiors" take precedence over "literal exteriors." The implications for Bede are clear. What is prescribed for the *Ecclesiastical History* is "a

---

1   "Bede's *vera lex historiae*," *Speculum* 55 (1980): 1-21.
2   Ray, "Bede, the Exegete, as Historian," p. 130.

historiography which selects and molds external details as internal aims dictate."[3]

The extent to which Ray would still commit himself to such an interpretation of *De consensu Evangelistarum* is unclear. At best, however, it represents an idiosyncratic reading. Augustine's primary purpose is to defend the four Evangelists from the accusation of various detractors claiming that they contradict one another.[4] Although the strategy Ray outlines would have been possible, it is not the one Augustine adopts. Rather than seeking to reconcile apparently conflicting accounts by appealing to a unifying moral or spiritual sense, it is at the level of the literal, historical sense itself that Augustine chooses to stand and fight. Far from threatening the literal integrity of the Gospel texts, the main thrust of *De consensu Evangelistarum* is to demonstrate that, apparent tensions notwithstanding, the four Gospels possess an internal consistency precisely on the literal level.

One of Augustine's fundamental points, and one that he refers to at frequent intervals throughout the treatise, is that care should be taken not to overestimate the significance of purely verbal dissimilarities. The Evangelists sometimes differ in the order of the comments attributed to Christ, the apostles, or some other character in the narrative. Indeed, sometimes they differ in the very words themselves. But rather than the words, it is their meaning that is important; rather than the specific utterance, it is the sense that it conveys to which we must be attentive. Hence the following principle, which he describes as *res plane utilissima ... et pernecessaria*:

> There is nothing in anyone's words to which we ought to be attentive other than their meaning, which the words themselves ought to serve; nor is anyone to be regarded as a liar for using other language to convey someone's thought and not that individual's own precise language. Wretched, nit-picking word-chasers ought not to think that the truth is somehow bound by letters, since in fact it is not in words alone that the

---

3   Roger Ray, "Augustine's *De Consensu Evangelistarum* and the Historical Education of the Venerable Bede," *Studia Patristica* 16.2 (1985): 557-563 at 561, 562, 563. This paper was originally delivered in 1975, although not published until a decade later, after the appearance of Ray's *Speculum* article.

4   *De cons. Evan.* 1.7.10, CSEL 43:11.

true meaning is to be sought but in all the other indications of the mind [of their author] as well.[5]

Occasionally Augustine's comments might be taken to suggest that verbal accuracy does not matter at all. With regard to the differences between Matt. 12:38-45 and Luke 11:16-36, for example, he states simply that the manner in which the Evangelists have arranged the Lord's words is of no importance: "Quis autem non videat *superfluo* quaeri, quo illa ordine dominus dixerit, ... cum ipsius ordinis *nihil intersit* ad rem, sive ita sive ita sit?" In the context of the feeding of the five thousand he states that, in view of their uniformity of meaning, the specific words the Evangelists report are not worth attention: "*nihil quaerendum* in verbis nisi loquentium voluntatem, cui demonstrandae invigilare debent omnes veridici narratores, cum de homine vel de angelo vel de deo aliquid narrant."[6] Provided that the meaning is not in jeopardy, one can readily understand Augustine's willingness to excuse the Evangelists for recalling specific words differently. More puzzling is the absence of any mention of their best effort being required to record comments precisely and accurately. If such was not the expectation, then the Evangelists had both the licence and the opportunity to create freely.

All things considered, however, this reads too much into Augustine's text. His point in the passages quoted above is not so much to defend the integrity of the Evangelists as to demonstrate their substantive agreement. Presumably, therefore, he felt no need to insist repeatedly on what bears only on the former. In an absolute sense, of course, words do not matter at all: Christ and the angels are capable of understanding and communicating without them. But this provides no licence to devalue the words actually spoken by Christ and the apostles, for in this

---

5   Ibid. 2.28.67, CSEL 43:172: "nihil in cuiusque verbis nos debere inspicere nisi voluntatem, cui debent verba servire, nec mentiri quemquam, si aliis verbis dixerit quid ille voluerit cuius verba non dicit, ne miseri aucupes vocum apicibus quodammodo litterarum putent ligandam esse veritatem, cum utique non in verbis tantum, sed etiam in caeteris omnibus signis animorum non sit nisi ipse animus inquirendus." Cf. ibid. 2.66.128, CSEL 43:230: "... qua nobis ostenditur non esse mendacium, si quisquam ita diverso modo aliquid narret, ut ab eius voluntate, cui consonandum et consentiendum est, non recedat."

6   Ibid. 2.39.86 & 2.46.97, CSEL 43:188-189, 205. Emphasis added.

world the constraints of language are inescapable.[7] Christ's discussion with the Pharisees is reported in different words in Matt. 19:1-12 and Mark 10:1-12, a point without interest, says Augustine, because meaning has not been compromised:

> Since the intent of the speakers, which their words ought to reflect, has been demonstrated by each Evangelist, it is of no interest (*nihil interest*) how different the actual narrative is in the two cases. In each version one and the same truth is preserved.[8]

Lest we take *nihil interest* too literally, however, Augustine goes on immediately to argue that the differences in the two Evangelists' accounts were due to their reporting different portions of the same conversation. Indeed, he expends considerable energy to show how their differences can be reconciled in a reconstructed dialogue.[9]

In what is perhaps his most important statement on the issues, Augustine comments on the various words attributed to John the Baptist in Matt. 3:7-12, Mark 1:7-8, and Luke 3:7-17. In these three passages the Evangelists differ in the order they assign to the Baptist's comments, in the specific remarks they choose to include in their accounts, and in the individual words they put into his mouth as well. Not unexpectedly, Augustine argues that the overall sense is what matters, and that in this regard the Evangelists are in substantive agreement. More interesting is the fact that he goes on to comment on the reasons for the variations in the three accounts as we have them. He implies that the Evangelists may have differed in their judgments about what needed to be rendered explicitly and what could be left implicit in the text, or about what might have needed to be said in order to make the import of the Baptist's statements clear. Beyond that, however, he makes no appeal to any conscious choices on the Evangelists' part, and he certainly does not suggest a role for purely rhetorical considerations, as if the precise words did not matter at all. In Augustine's view, the differences in the

---

7 Ibid. 2.66.128, CSEL 43:231: "ita res, quae discenda est, sermonibus, per quos discenda est, praeferatur, ut istos omnino quaerere non deberemus, si eam sine his nosse possemus, sicut illam novit deus et in ipso angeli eius."
8 Ibid. 2.62.121, CSEL 43:224: "Cum ergo voluntas loquentium, cui debent verba servire, ab evangelista utroque monstrata sit, nihil interest, quam diversus inter ambos fuerit narrandi modus, dum ab eadem veritate neuter abscederet."
9 Ibid. 2.62.122, CSEL 43:224-225.

three accounts are due primarily to differences in the Evangelists' memories of what they saw and heard.[10]

Augustine is clearly not prepared to admit that any of the Evangelists either lied or was mistaken. Hence, after offering his own preferred solution to the puzzle of how Mark could say that Christ was crucified at the third hour when John says it was at the sixth, he states that he is open to any other suggestion that is consistent with the Evangelists' moral and intellectual integrity. What he will not consider is the possibility of either error or misrepresentation in the Gospels.[11] He is, however, prepared to recognize the possibility of significant variation in the Evangelists' recollection of events, confident that such differences are subject to and governed by the will of God. The Evangelists did not remember things differently, but they did remember different things; and they did so at different points when composing their Gospels. Hence more than once Augustine argues that apparent inconsistencies in narrative order disappear when we recall the Evangelists' tendency to mention events before their occurrence by anticipation, or afterwards by recapitulation. While their accounts may differ, therefore, they do not conflict; and since the differences that do exist are part of the plan of Providence, it would be temerarious to question them:

> Their memories have been governed by the hand of him who rules the waters, as it is written, according to his pleasure [cf. Ps. 134(135):6]. Human memory wavers amidst changing thoughts, nor is it in anyone's power to determine what will come to mind or when. For the purposes of the structure of their narrative, these saintly and truthful men entrusted the vagaries of their memories to the hidden power of God, to which nothing is fortuitous. It is hardly appropriate, therefore, for someone else, cast out from the sight of God and a stranger to him, to say: "This ought to be placed at this point in the narrative," clearly failing to take into account why God wished it to be placed elsewhere. [12]

---

10 Ibid. 2.12.27-28, CSEL 43:127-128.

11 Ibid. 3.13.43, CSEL 43:327.

12 Ibid. 3.13.48, CSEL 43:333-334: "recordationes enim eorum eius manu gubernatae sunt qui gubernat aquam, sicut scriptum est, qualiter illi placuerit. fluitat enim humana memoria per varias cogitationes, nec in cuiusquam potestate est, quid et quando ei veniat in mentem. cum ergo illi sancti et veraces viri quasi fortuita recordationum suarum propter narrationis ordinem occultae dei potestati, cui nihil fortuitum est, commisissent, non oportet quemquam hominum dicere longe abiectum ab oculis dei et longe peregrinantem: hoc loco poni debuit, quod valde ignorat, cur eo loco Deus poni voluerit."

Because the Evangelists' memories were controlled by God, says Augustine, the contradictions that others have discovered disappear in the light of close scrutiny. A case in point is provided by the words of John the Baptist referred to above. In Matthew's account the Baptist claims that he is unworthy to carry Christ's sandals. In both Mark's and Luke's it is the thong of Christ's sandals that is at issue, and the Baptist is unworthy to untie it. For his own part, Augustine seems untroubled, for the intent of the Baptist is clear. What is at stake is a simple metaphor adopted to express both Christ's sublimity and the Baptist's own humility. However, others may see things differently, Augustine admits. Untying the thong of Christ's sandals, after all, is different from carrying the sandals themselves. Some might think it important to know precisely which of these John the Baptist considered himself unworthy of. Accordingly, if the point is indeed a substantive one, says Augustine, we can be assured in advance that the Gospels are free of error: "omnem autem falsitatem abesse ab evangelistis decet, non solum eam quae mentiendo promitur, sed etiam eam quae obliviscendo." If the difference is significant, John the Baptist must have said both, whether at the same or at different times. He claimed that he was unworthy both of loosening the thong of Christ's sandals and of carrying them. Whereas Mark and Luke remembered and reported the first half of his comment, Matthew picked up on the second.[13]

If we were to summarize the lessons Augustine derives from this example, we could do so in terms of the following principle: whenever any two Evangelists cannot be reconciled, they must be talking about different things, for both accounts must be true. Indeed, Augustine's reflections on the miracle(s) of the loaves and fishes lead him to express the point in precisely these terms himself. Whereas the miracle of the five loaves is reported by all four Evangelists, the miracle of the seven loaves is found in Matthew and Mark alone. If only one Evangelist had reported the latter event, says Augustine, and if at the same time he had omitted the miracle of the five loaves, we would be tempted to think that he was reporting the same episode as the others, but that mistakes obviously had been made. Were there seven loaves or five? Were there twelve baskets of fragments or seven? Did the multitude number four thousand or five? Because, however, the Gospels that relate the story of the seven loaves also contain the cognate miracle, no one has any doubt

---

13   Ibid. 2.12.29, CSEL 43:129-130.

that a similar wonder was performed twice. The lesson is salutary, says Augustine, and it occasions the rule that if two Evangelists are in clear conflict, they must be reporting different events.[14] Here as elsewhere the reader is left with a strong sense of Augustine's respect for the literal meaning of the Gospel narrative. To the extent, therefore, that Bede's idea of history was shaped by *De consensu Evangelistarum*, to that same extent it was premised on a fundamental commitment to the standards of factual veracity. If, as I believe was the case, there were occasions when Bede was tempted to compromise those standards in the name of edification, it was not because of Augustine, but rather because of his abandonment of Augustine in favour of other guides, not the least of them being Jerome.

Jerome's influence is clearly discernible in Bede's comments on Luke 2:33-34, the passage in which St Luke casually refers to Joseph as the father of Christ. Following Jerome's *Adversus Helvidium*, Bede argues that Luke does not call Joseph Christ's father because, like the Photinians, he literally believed this to be true. He clearly knew better, for he had just finished stating in chapter one of his Gospel that Christ was conceived of the Holy Spirit and born of a virgin. What he was doing, therefore, was simply repeating the popular, although mistaken, view, *quae vera lex historiae est*; for in the interests of preserving Mary's reputation, Joseph was considered Christ's father by virtually everyone.

Having said that much, Bede promptly switches gears and, following Augustine's *De consensu Evangelistarum*, attempts to provide a more positive explanation for St Luke's choice of words. In a sense, he argues, Joseph can quite properly be considered the father of Christ, just as he can properly be considered the husband of Mary: not in virtue of any physical union, but by means of the bond of matrimony. Being the husband of Christ's mother, Joseph was much more intimately and effectively Christ's father than he would have been had he simply adopted him.[15] The line of argument is promising, and one can only

---

14   Ibid. 2.50.105, CSEL 43:214: "hoc ideo diximus, ut sicubi simile invenitur factum a Domino, quod in aliquo alteri evangelistae ita repugnare videatur, ut omnino solvi non possit, nihil aliud intellegatur quam utrumque factum esse et aliud ab alio commemoratum."

15   *In Luc.* 1, CCL 120:67-68: "*Et erat pater eius et mater mirantes super his quae dicebantur de illo, et benedixit illis Symeon.* Patrem salvatoris appellat Ioseph non quo vere iuxta Fotinianos pater fuerit eius sed quo ad famam Mariae conservandam pater sit ab omnibus aestimatus. Neque enim oblitus evangelista quod eam de spiritu

wish that Bede had pursued it. As things stand, however, it is simply appended to his initial statement on the matter, and no effort is made to develop a unified, coherent view. As Ponton puts it: "Notre maître anglo-saxon s'inspire ici de deux courants divers de pensée, ceux de Jérôme et d'Augustin; il juxtapose tout simplement leurs explications, sans se soucier d'établir une synthèse. Et en dernière analyse, ce n'est pas l'exposé du docteur d'Hippone qui prédomine."[16]

The clumsy treatment here given to the paternity of Joseph, and the consequent negative light it casts on the Evangelist, is especially puzzling in view of Bede's relatively deft handling of the issue elsewhere. He returns to the matter just a few pages later in his commentary on Luke, in the context of Luke 2:48-49, where Mary herself speaks of Joseph as Christ's father. This time his comments betray none of the tension noted above. In view of his love for both mother and son and the support that he provided them, says Bede, not only does Mary refer to Joseph as Christ's father, but Christ himself does not correct her. What he does is simply intimate that his true father is his Father in heaven.[17] In the *Homilies on the Gospels* Bede raises the issue once again while commenting on John 1:45, where it is Philip who refers to Jesus as the son of Joseph. Says Bede:

> He calls him the son of Joseph, not to proclaim that he whom he had learned in the prophets would be born of a virgin was begotten from the joining of man and woman, but to teach that he had come, as the prophets had foretold, from the house and family of David, whence he knew that Joseph had descended. It is unsurprising that Philip calls him the son of Joseph, whom he knew to be the husband of his virgin mother, since we read that this chaste and ever virgin mother herself, following the common

---

sancto concepisse et virginem peperisse narrarit sed opinionem vulgi exprimens quae vera historiae lex est patrem Ioseph nuncupat Christi. Quamvis et eo modo pater illius valeat dici quo et vir Mariae recte intellegitur *sine commixtione carnis ipsa copulatione coniugii multo* videlicet *coniunctius quam si esset aliunde adoptatus. Neque enim propterea non erat appellandus Ioseph pater Christi quia non eum concumbendo genuerat quando quidem recte pater esset etiam eius quem non ex sua coniuge procreatum alicubi adoptasset.*" Cf. Jerome, *Adversus Helvidium* 4, PL 23:196-197; Augustine, *De cons. Evan.* 2.1.2-3, CSEL 43:82-84.

16 Georges Ponton, "Saint Joseph d'après l'oeuvre de Bède le Vénérable," *Cahiers de Joséphologie* 19 (1971): 196-219 at 218.

17 *In Luc.* 1, CCL 120:73.

custom, spoke as follows: 'Son, why have you treated us so? Behold, your father and I have been looking for you anxiously' [Luke 2:48].[18]

Here once more, positive reasons are given for what was clearly a rather common practice, perhaps the most significant of them being that in referring to Joseph as Christ's father Mary was simply adopting the popular idiom (*consuetudo vulgi*).

From the outset the simplest explanation Bede could have provided would have been to say that the Evangelist (like Mary and Philip) had the good sense not continually to be challenging ordinary language. In everything other than the biological sense, Joseph did, after all, function as the father of Christ. Systematically denying him the title would have been tedious in the extreme. In the commentary on Luke 2:33-34, however, this and the other more positive approaches to the issue largely escape him, with the result that the dominant image is one of St Luke indulging in a fiction. The Evangelist was consciously passing on a popular misconception, says Bede, rather than taking the time and effort to correct it. Although the reasons for his handling (or mishandling) of the issue are not entirely clear, Ponton points to Bede's primary concern to defend the virginity of Mary. This was of much greater import than assessing the value of her marriage to Joseph, or defining in positive terms the paternity of the latter, issues that consequently suffered from a lack of attention.[19] Of equal or even greater significance, however, was the influence of Jerome, who was clearly pulling Bede into pathways very different from those traversed by Augustine.[20]

---

18 *Hom. Evan.* 1.17, CCL 122:122: "Filium Ioseph appellat non ut hunc ex coniunctione maris et feminae natum asseveret quem de virgine nasciturum in prophetis didicerit sed ut de domo ac familia David unde Ioseph ortum noverat secundum vaticinia prophetarum eum venisse doceret. Neque enim mirandum si Philippus eum filium Ioseph quem intemeratae genetricis illius virum noverat vocet cum et ipsa genetrix intemerata semperque virgo consuetudinem vulgi sequens sic locuta legatur: *Fili, quid fecisti nobis sic? ecce pater tuus et ego dolentes quaerebamus te.*"
19 Ponton, "Saint Joseph," p. 206.
20 Cf. *In Marc.* 2, CCL 120:508-509. Here Bede quotes Jerome while commenting on Mark 6:26-27, where Herod sends for the head of John the Baptist: "*Et contristatus rex propter ius iurandum et propter simul recumbentes noluit eam contristare sed misso speculatore praecepit adferri caput eius in disco,* et cetera. *Consuetudinis scripturarum est ut opinionem multorum sic narret historicus quo modo eo tempore ab omnibus credebatur sicut Ioseph ab ipsa quoque Maria appellatur pater Iesu ita et nunc Herodes dicitur contristatus quia hoc discumbentes putabant.*" Cf. Jerome, *In Matth.* 2, CCL 77:118.

On matters of truth and falsity Bede more than once did identify Augustine as an authority,[21] and it is clear that he wished to render more than lip service to the bishop of Hippo. In addition to the observations scattered throughout his exegetical work, Augustine had written a couple of seminal treatises on the issue. Like most subsequent thinkers, Bede had not entirely escaped his influence. A case in point is provided by his commentary on David's behaviour in 1 Sam. 27:10. Although David and his men had slaughtered and pillaged among the Geshurites, the Girzites and the Amalekites, who dwelt in the land of the Philistines, David tells Achish, his Philistine host, that his raids were directed against the people of Judah instead. Rather than dwelling on the lie, Bede argues that no deception whatever is involved when the text is read on the spiritual level. Allegorically David represents the Lord, and his raiding expeditions are really figures for the conversion of the Gentiles. At the spiritual level, therefore, they can quite properly be described as having been directed against Judah:

> He appears to have been lying when he is taken literally. Having risen up against the Philistines and laid waste to their neighbouring province, he responded to the enquiries of their king by stating that he had attacked his own people. In the figural sense, however, his words involve no deception, for in drawing the nations of the world to the faith, Christ attacks the manifest and impetuous blasphemy of the Jews.[22]

Although Bede does not explicitly say so, the implication is that David can be excused for a conscious lie on the literal level because of the deeper meaning his words possessed on the spiritual level. If we find this puzzling, Bede should not be required to bear responsibility alone, for the inspiration was Augustinian. Augustine's strongest conviction was that lying is nowhere tolerated in Sacred Scripture. Hence he avails himself of the same kind of exegesis to explain that the lie by which Jacob won the blessing of the first-born was not really a lie at all.[23]

---

21 See, for example, *In 1 Sam.* 3, CCL 119:194; and *In Prov.* 1, CCL 119B:55.

22 *In 1 Sam.* 4, CCL 119:251: "Quamvis fallere videatur ad litteram qui contra Palestinos insurgens eorumque provinciam non longe positam devastans sciscitanti eorum regi contra suam gentem se inruisse dicebat, non tamen fallit figura sermonis quia dum gentes ad fidem protrahit contra manifestam ferventemque Iudaeorum blasphemiam Christus inruit."

23 *Contra mendacium* 10.24, CSEL 41:499, 501-502.

More persuasively, Augustine had argued that the examples of lying contained in Scripture are not recorded for our emulation.[24] Once again Bede follows suit in his interpretation of 1 Sam. 21:1-3, another example involving David. There is nothing astonishing, Bede suggests, at the prospect of the saints being guilty of sinful conduct. As Scripture itself informs us: "If we say we have not sinned, we make him a liar, and his word is not in us" [1 John 1:10]. The faults of the saints are not recorded to teach us to sin, but to caution us against presuming on our own righteousness, and to instruct us by the example of their repentance to seek the grace of penance. Having said that much, he goes on to argue that, in this particular case, David did not really lie at all, but under the pressure of necessity simply used carefully chosen words to disguise the truth; and for that line of argument as well there was ample Augustinian precedent. Lying is to be distinguished from withholding some portion of the truth, even if the result is to mislead.[25] Not so clearly in the Augustinian tradition, however, are the comments with which he concludes this particular discussion of the issue, even though once again Bede appeals to Augustine himself as an authority:

> If anyone should wish to know whether a man who is steadfast and upright should ever, out of necessity as it were, invoke the assistance of lying, let him read the book by St Augustine *On the eight kinds of lying*, a work of extraordinary and salutary discernment, and also the *Collations of the Fathers*, where Joseph, who was distinguished among the Fathers, ... takes up, considers thoroughly and resolves part of this question. For the present suffice it briefly to say only this: that beyond any doubt the truth is always to be preferred to falsehood. On occasion, however, because of the circumstances that apply, the latter may be employed for a time to good effect, and the former profitably may be suppressed.[26]

24 *De mendacio* 5.9, CSEL 41:425; *Contra mendacium* 12.26, CSEL 41:504-505.
25 Cf. *In Gen.* 3, CCL 118A:175, where Bede follows Augustine in arguing that Abraham was not guilty of lying when he counseled Sarah to say that she was his sister (Gen. 12:10-20): *"Nihil mentitus est Abram quia uxorem suam dixit sororem. Erat enim et hoc quia propinqua sanguine, sicut etiam Loth eadem propinquitate, cum fratris eius esset filius, frater eius est dictus. Itaque uxorem tacuit, non negavit sororem, coniugis tuendam pudicitiam committens Deo, et humanas insidias cavens ut homo, quoniam si periculum quantum caveri poterat non caveret, magis temptaret Deum quam speraret in eum."* Cf. Augustine, *De civitate Dei* 16.19, CCL 48:522.
26 *In 1 Sam.* 3, CCL 119:194: "si qui de mendacio an iusti viri constantia eius aliquando debeat quasi necessarium flagitare praesidium scire velit, legat sancti Augustini librum de mendacii generibus octo mirifica salubrique discretione

The two texts to which Bede refers are Augustine's *De mendacio* and Cassian's *Collations*, more specifically the seventeenth book of the latter.[27] The title he gives suggests that it may have been the florilegium of Eugippius rather than Augustine himself that he used.[28]

Since either source, however, conveys essentially the same message, we can only be puzzled at what Bede does with it. Apparently Bede either misunderstood the main thrust of *De mendacio* or chose to misrepresent it. Beginning with a reference to Augustine's book, described very positively as *librum ... mirifica salubrique discretione moderatum*, he then passes on immediately to Cassian's treatment of the issues, which he clearly considers equally definitive. The impression created is that the two reinforce one another, whereas in fact they describe fundamentally different approaches. Ultimately it is Cassian's that is endorsed. Whereas Augustine maintains that lying is always sinful and never warranted in any circumstances, a position endorsed by Gregory the Great as well, Cassian, like Jerome, is prepared to recognize that in certain circumstances lying can be justified.[29]

Cassian supports his doctrine of the justifiable lie by appealing to Sacred Scripture. Bede does the same. In his comments on Prov. 16:10: "Divinatio in labiis regis, in iudicio non errabit os eius," Bede refers to the curious episode in 2 Chron. 18, in which God sends a lying spirit to

---

moderatum sed et collationes patrum ubi Ioseph non ignobilis inter patres ... huius quaestiunculae partem plenissime assumpsit proposuit solvit. Hoc tantum inpraesentiarum breviter dicere sufficiat cum absque ulla dubietate praeferenda sit semper mendacio veritas aliquando tamen propter rerum circumstantiam hoc utiliter ad tempus usurpandum et illa e contra sit occulenda salubriter."

27 See Augustine, *De mendacio*, CSEL 41:411-466; Cassian, *Coll.* 17.19, CSEL 13:478-481.
28 Eugippius, *Excerpta ex operibus S. Augustini*, chap. 181, CSEL 9:613-616. This section bears the title: "Ex libro De mendacio. De mendacii generibus octo." On Bede's dependence on Eugippius, see most recently Fransen, "D'Eugippius à Bède le Vénérable, pp. 187-194. Joseph F. Kelly, "Augustine and Bede on the Gospels," in *Congresso internazionale su S. Agostino nel XVI centenario della conversione* (Rome, 1987), 3:159-165, argues that Bede's references to *De mendacio* are "general and peripheral, and they offer no solid proof that he knew the book well or even that he knew it at all" (p. 161).
29 On the general issue, see Gregor Müller, *Die Wahrhaftigkeitspflicht und die Problematik der Lüge* (Freiburg, 1962), esp. pp. 27-93; and Wolfgang Speyer, *Die literarische Fälschung im heidnischen und christlichen Altertum. Ein Versuch ihrer Deutung* (München, 1971), pp. 94-96.

deceive King Ahab of Israel.[30] With the exception of Micaiah, all the king's prophets are filled with this spirit. Consequently they counsel Ahab to attack the Syrians, assuring him of victory, and Ahab is slain. Despite his insistence elsewhere that Christ could not have indulged in fictions,[31] Bede's initial remarks suggest that on this occasion God himself did precisely that. Although Ahab received only his just reward, God had actively deceived the king and his prophets.

However, God clearly did not constrain the king: Ahab also received the truth from Micaiah, but was disinclined to accept what he did not want to hear. Perhaps for this reason Bede's more considered view seems to be that, as a penalty for Ahab's sins, God simply permitted the evil spirit to work its influence: "Neque enim in hoc iudicio erravit os regis aeterni sed quod rex impius audire peccatis praecedentibus meruit ipse hoc prophetas erraticos ei loqui permisit." In the final analysis, therefore, this is perhaps only an equivocal instance of biblically sanctioned, divinely authorized lying. However, Bede is not at a loss for a more straightforward example, finding it in Rahab the harlot, whose behaviour in hiding the spies sent by Joshua, and subsequently lying to the King of Jericho, he clearly considers meritorious. Conversely, Doeg the Edomite sinned precisely because he was truthful in revealing David to Saul, and as a consequence Bede likens him to the betrayer of the Lord: "in typum Iudae Scariothis ... eradicari meruit de terra viventium."[32]

If lying is justifiable in certain circumstances, and if Scripture itself provides illustrative examples, then the image conveyed by Luke 2:33-34 of the Evangelist indulging in a fiction appears less anomalous than when viewed in isolation. Indeed, St Luke can be joined by St. Paul. In the sermon that he delivered in the synagogue in Antioch of Pisidia, as it is recorded in Acts 13, Paul too glossed over the truth in crediting King Saul with having reigned for forty years. In fact, says Bede, Saul's reign lasted only twenty. In giving a different number, Paul was following, quite consciously it would seem, mistaken popular opinion.[33] Why he would not have suggested that St Paul simply made a mistake is not

---

30 *In Prov.* 2, CCL 119B:91.

31 *In Luc.* 6, CCL 120:416: "Nihil simplex veritas per duplicitatem fecit." Cf. Gregory the Great, *Hom. in Evan.* 2.23.1, PL 76:1182.

32 *In 1 Sam.* 3, CCL 119:194-195.

33 *Exp. Act. Apost.* 13.19-21, CCL 121:61-62, esp. 62: "Credo quia liber Regum non aperte quot annis Saul regnaverit exponit, apostolum vulgo loquentem hoc quod fama crebrior haberet dicere voluisse."

immediately clear. But in fact it is not a possibility Bede seems seriously to have considered. In his *Retractions* he returns to the passage in question and revises some of his calculations, having in the interim examined Josephus; but his overall assessment remains the same. Indeed, rather than having simply blundered, Bede argues, on a second point as well St Paul chose instead to adopt the popular view. Bede's conclusion is unequivocal: "He followed common report in his sermon, which the blessed Stephen is proven to have done [as well] in the meeting that he had with the Jews, when he spoke about the burial of the twelve patriarchs."[34]

As Bede understands it, Stephen clearly and consciously sacrificed historical veracity in the address to the Jerusalem council recorded in Acts 7. There Stephen claims that the patriarchs were laid to rest in the tomb that Abraham bought from the sons of Hamor, the son of Shechem, whereas Genesis 23 makes it clear that the tomb was bought from Ephron the Hittite, the son of Zohar. In Stephen's version the story has become confused with the one recorded ten chapters later, according to which Jacob camped before the city of Shechem and there purchased from the sons of Hamor (Bede says from Hamor himself), Shechem's father, a piece of land on which to pitch his tent. Whereas the modern mind might find the likeliest explanation in simple confusion on Stephen's part, again this is not how Bede sees it. In fact, he explicitly rejects the suggestion:

> Speaking to the public, the blessed Stephen chose to follow popular opinion. Equally joining together two narratives, he considered not so much the relevant historical record as the cause that was at issue.[35]

That cause, of course, was the charge of blasphemy that had been levelled against him. Hence, Stephen decided to forsake historical accuracy and to focus on the essential point in his own defence: that Christ was prophesied in the Old Testament, but that the Hebrew people had been no more prompt in heeding Moses and the prophets in times past than they were in heeding Christ now. If these tactics were legitimate for the

---

34 *Retr.* 13.19-21, CCL 121:146-147, esp. 146: "vulgarem in loquendo famam secutus est, quod fecisse beatus Stephanus in contione cum Iudaeis habita de sepultura duodecim patriarcharum probatur."

35 *Exp. Act. Apost.* 7.16, CCL 121:34-35: "beatus Stephanus vulgo loquens vulgi magis in dicendo sequitur opinionem; duas enim pariter narrationes coniungens, non tam ordinem circumstantis historiae quam causam de qua agebatur intendit."

protomartyr Stephen, one can only wonder at the opportunity they would have provided for a highly motivated historian like Bede himself.

In a recent essay Ray argues that what we witness in Bede's handling of the Stephen episode is nothing short of the triumph of rhetorical historiography, the tradition of which continued virtually without interruption from classical times into the early Middle Ages. Isidore of Seville, he says, argued for a stricter commitment to truthful narrative in the tradition of Thucydides, but Isidore's view was an idiosyncratic one, and it was without a future. In Bede's treatment of Stephen's speech to the Sanhedrin, any vestiges of a similar view are ultimately sacrificed on the altar of rhetorical pragmatism. Indeed, in Ray's judgment the passage provides *prima facie* evidence for Bede's firsthand knowledge of Cicero's *De inventione*, or at least of Victorinus's commentary.[36]

That Bede was not entirely unschooled in classical rhetoric goes without saying. Like the Hellenistic historians before him, he records speeches that his protagonists could not possibly have delivered. However, an authority no less eminent than St Luke does the same in both Luke and Acts, taking full advantage of his literary skills to make the points he thinks essential for his audience.[37] Against this background, to speak of the triumph of rhetorical historiography in Bede's case is an exaggeration. Suggestive though his treatment of Stephen's speech may be, it is important to note that Bede was not entirely happy with it, and I suspect more than a little uneasy. I have done the best I can, he proclaims, and anyone who is capable is welcome to do better. "Haec, ut potui, dixi, non praeiudicans sententiae meliori si adsit."[38]

Under those circumstances, why did he not admit simply that Stephen had made a mistake? Primarily, I suspect, because of his overriding concern to preserve the inspiration and inerrancy of Scripture, however ironical that may seem. In part at least a similar explanation may help elucidate his exegesis of Luke 2:33-34 as well.[39] In view of

---

36 Roger Ray, "The Triumph of Greco-Roman Rhetorical Assumptions in Pre-Carolingian Historiography," in *The Inheritance of Historiography, 350-900* (Exeter, 1986), pp. 67-84; cf. idem, "Bede and Cicero," pp. 1-15. For recent support of such a view, see Coleman, *Ancient and Medieval Memories*, esp. pp. 59, 276.

37 See, for example, Howard Clark Kee, *Miracle in the Early Christian World: A Study in Sociohistorical Method* (New Haven, 1983), pp. 191-192.

38 *Exp. Act. Apost.* 7.16, CCL 121:35.

39 Cf. Creider, "Bede's Understanding of the Miraculous," pp. 123-124.

his belief that the Evangelist cannot have written anything false,[40] it was important to insist that Luke, who knew that Joseph was not really the father of Christ, had not made a mistake. Similarly, in view of his insistence that Scripture cannot contain any errors,[41] obvious blunders in Stephen's statement to the Sanhedrin have to turn out to be cases of him quite deliberately endorsing the mistaken popular view. Regrettably, Bede may simply have been confused on the issue. In order to be free of error, Scripture would simply have to report accurately what Stephen said. It would not be essential for Stephen's words themselves to be error-free. However, Bede appraises the words of Stephen as if they were the words of the divinely inspired Evangelist himself, and therefore has no option, if he is to avoid recognizing error in Sacred Scripture for what it is, but to prefer Stephen's endorsement of *fama vulgaris*. It was not a choice without consequences for the author of the *Ecclesiastical History*. Bede's fundamental instinct was to be a truthful historian. But he did have the example of Stephen to draw on, who, in order to make a spiritual point, compromised with the truth. It should not astonish us to discover that occasionally Bede himself may have done the same.

40 See, for example, *Exp. Act. Apost.*, Praef., CCL 121:4: "ipse Lucas, qui spiritu sancto calamum regente nullatenus falsum scribere potuit." Cf. his commentary on Luke 7:1-10, the healing of the centurion's servant: *In Luc.* 2, CCL 120:154.
41 See, for example, *In 1 Sam.* 2 Praef., CCL 119:69.

Conclusion

The time has come to draw together the principal results of our nine chapters, even if such an exercise does require painting in much broader strokes than one would desire.

Despite the extensive library at his disposal, the education of the Venerable Bede was much more narrowly focused than that of St Augustine or Gregory the Great. Although he was not entirely ignorant of the classics, it was overwhelmingly Christian literature that shaped his outlook, primarily works of Biblical exegesis. He was not, however, hostile to the world of classical, literary culture. Like both Augustine and Gregory, he acknowledged its legitimacy when it was properly subordinated to the elucidation of Christian doctrine. He was even more attracted to the legacy of ancient science, which he was able to enrich with his own personal contributions. Bede believed that the universe designed and called into being by the Creator was an orderly place, one in which the causes of phenomena could be investigated and explained in rational terms. It was not, however, completely self-contained. The same phenomena treated by science could be viewed from a theological perspective and seen as instruments in the hands of Providence. They were also subject to the more direct divine intervention that resulted in miraculous suspensions of the natural order (Chapter One).

Although Bede has sometimes been credited with being more reserved in his acceptance of miracles than other early medieval thinkers, the idea does not stand up under close scrutiny. Indeed, his comments on the miracles of Scripture reveal a greater literal-mindedness than is usual among the Fathers. Bede's invariable tendency is to highlight the miraculous aspects of the biblical account. Whenever presented with an opportunity for the rational explanation of a biblical miracle, he rejects it. If the modern miracle stories in the *Ecclesiastical History* and the *Life of St Cuthbert* are not particularly extravagant, they are entirely in keeping with what is found in similar early medieval texts. Bede used the *Dialogues* of Gregory the Great as his touchstone of authenticity. The miracles he records, therefore, are fully as astonishing as any attributed by Gregory to the saints of sixth-century Italy (Chapter Two). In Bede's case, however, the continued occurrence of miracles in his own day is not thought out as carefully as it is in Gregory's. While materially influenced by Gregory, therefore, his treatment of the matter takes on a character of its own.

Despite the modern miracles he records elsewhere, in his exegetical works Bede suggests that the age of miracles is over. Miracles were required only when the church was in its infancy, to confirm the new faith. Now they have been replaced by spiritual analogues of far greater intrinsic significance. Although the same tension appears in the thought of Gregory the Great, there it is more apparent than real. The same theological works that seem to deny modern wonders themselves contain many modern miracle stories, several of which are repeated in the *Dialogues*. What Gregory means, therefore, is simply that in the contemporary church miracles are less striking and less frequent than once was the case. Essentially this is Bede's position as well. But in Bede's case the tension between his historical and hagiographical works on the one hand and his more strictly theological works on the other cannot be resolved quite as easily as in Gregory's. Bede's theological works contain no modern miracle stories at all. Where such stories do appear, it is in a virtual theological vacuum (Chapter Three).

Bede clearly shares Gregory's view of the role of miracles in the early church. In New Testament times miracles served an apologetic purpose. They were vital to the establishment of the church, for they confirmed the truth of the Gospel. In Gregory's view, their purpose in modern times is the same, for the work of evangelization is incomplete. Many, while superficially Christian, are still in need of fundamental conversion, having never progressed beyond the level of external observance. The result is an identity of purpose linking miracles ancient and modern in one coherent view. In Bede's case, the same cannot be said. Although he does not articulate an alternative view of modern miracles, he does not share Gregory's either. While acutely aware of society's ills, Bede conceives the process of conversion in Anglo-Saxon England as being essentially complete (Chapter Four).

Like Gregory, Bede posits an important link between miracles and sanctity. But once again Gregory develops the idea more consistently than Bede. Because miracles are not essential to saintly status, they cannot be used to prove that someone is a saint. Hence Gregory's focus is not so much on the saint who performs them as on the lessons, whether of morals or of doctrine, that they provide. Bede was clearly interested in lessons as well, but not as much as Gregory, and not in the same way. In the *Dialogues* the miracles performed by saints function as *exempla*. They are *ostensiones sanctitatis*, illustrations or revelations of specific saintly virtues. In Bede's works miracles demonstrate virtue only in an external fashion, by confirming that the individual in question was indeed a saint. Lacking a clear sense of the rationale of miracles in the modern world, Bede echoes the traditional hagiographical view (Chapter Five).

While Gregory was not totally immune to the hagiographer's perspective either, it is his efforts to articulate a different approach that make the *Dialogues* unique. Nowhere is this clearer than in his commitment to providing a factually truthful account, one based on the reports of trustworthy sources usually identified by name. Although he has been accused of creating freely by drawing on established saintly *vitae* and other texts, invention of this sort has not clearly been demonstrated in Gregory's case, and it would be difficult to reconcile with his deepest convictions about matters of truth and falsity. In both his *Ecclesiastical History* and his *Vita Cuthberti* Bede too promises a truthful narrative; and while not equalling Gregorian practice, like Gregory he also cites witnesses for his miracle stories, witnesses who, in some cases at least, were clearly consulted. The force of his guarantees, however, is not the same. The cumulative weight of the evidence suggests that one episode in the life of St Cuthbert was borrowed from the *Vita S. Columbae* of Adomnan. At another point the evidence of his borrowing from Gregory's *Dialogues* is even greater (Chapters Six and Seven).

If this in fact is what Bede did, it was not because he thought that factual veracity was unimportant and could routinely be subordinated to other interests. Bede was an historian as well as a Christian teacher and exegete. His fundamental instinct was to provide as accurate and as truthful a narrative as possible (Chapter Eight). However, his position on the relative importance of truthfulness was different from Gregory's. Gregory's view was governed by Augustine, for whom lying is always sinful and never warranted. Bede's was governed by Jerome and Cassian, for whom lying can indeed be justified in certain circumstances. Indeed, like Jerome and Cassian, he supports his position by invoking Sacred Scripture itself. On Bede's reading, St Luke, St Paul and St Stephen all deliberately suppressed the truth in order to endorse popular but mistaken opinion. He nowhere suggests that such compromises with factual veracity were a standard practice among the saints, or could ever be defended in those terms. They were exceptional incidents. But given such instances of sanctified behaviour, Bede's commitment to factual veracity necessarily was something other than Gregory's. Gregory could not, in order to make some spiritual point, have allowed fiction to pass disguised as fact without violating his highest principles. Bede could have done so; and indications are that on a few, rare occasions that is precisely what he did (Chapter Nine).

Select Bibliography

PRIMARY SOURCES

Only the editions and translations that have been used are listed.

Adomnan. *Vita S. Columbae.* Ed. and trans. Alan Orr Anderson and Marjorie Ogilvie Anderson. *Adomnan's Life of Columba.* London: Nelson, 1961.

Ambrose, Saint. *Explanatio Psalmorum XII.* Ed. Michael Petschenig. 1919. CSEL 64.

——. *Expositio Evangelii secundum Lucam.* Ed. M. Adriaen. 1957. CCL 14.

Augustine, Saint. *Contra mendacium.* Ed. Joseph Zycha. 1900. CSEL 41:467-528.

——. *De civitate Dei.* Ed. Bernard Dombart and Alphonse Kalb. 1955. CCL 47, 48.

——. ——. Trans. Gerald G. Walsh and Daniel J. Honan (books 17-22). Fathers of the Church 24. Washington DC: Catholic University of America, 1954.

——. *De consensu Evangelistarum libri quattuor.* Ed. Franciscus Weihrich. 1904. CSEL 43.

——. *De doctrina christiana.* Ed. Joseph Martin. 1962. CCL 32:1-167.

——. *De Genesi ad litteram.* Ed. Joseph Zycha. 1894. CSEL 28.1:1-456.

——. *De mendacio.* Ed. Joseph Zycha. 1900. CSEL 41:411-466.

——. *Enarrationes in Psalmos.* Ed. D. Eligius Dekkers and Iohannes Fraipont. 1956. CCL 38-40.

——. *Epistulae.* Ed. Al. Goldbacher. 1895-1923. CSEL 34, 44, 57, 58.

——. *Quaestiones Evangeliorum.* Ed. Almut Mutzenbecher. 1980. CCL 44B.

——. *Quaestionum in Heptateuchum libri VII.* Ed. Iohannes Fraipont. 1958. CCL 33:1-377.

——. *Sermones.* PL 38, 39.

Augustinus Hibernicus. *De mirabilibus Sacrae Scripturae.* PL 35:2149-2200.

Bede the Venerable. *Aliquot quaestionum liber.* PL 93:455-462.

——. *De arte metrica et de schematibus et tropis.* Ed. Calvin B. Kendall. 1975. CCL 123A:59-171.

——. ——. Trans. (*De schematibus et tropis*) Gussie Hecht Tannenhaus. In *Readings in Medieval Rhetoric.* Ed. Joseph M. Miller, Michael H. Prosser and Thomas W. Benson, pp. 96-122. Bloomington: Indiana University Press, 1973.

——. *De eo quod ait Isaias: "Et claudentur ibi in carcere et post dies multos visitabuntur."* PL 94:702-710.

——. *De locis sanctis.* Ed. Iohannes Fraipont. 1965. CCL 175:245-280.

——. *De mansionibus filiorum Israel.* PL 94:699-702.

——. *De natura rerum.* Ed. Charles W. Jones. 1975. CCL 123A:173-234.

——. *De tabernaculo et vasis eius ac vestibus sacerdotum libri III.* Ed. David Hurst. 1969. CCL 119A:1-139.

——. *De templo libri II.* Ed. David Hurst. 1969. CCL 119A:141-234.

——. *De temporibus liber Chronica Minora includens (id est capita xvii-xxii) a Th. Mommsen divulgata.* Ed. Charles W. Jones. 1980. CCL 123C:579-611.

——. *De temporum ratione liber Chronica Maiora includens (id est capita lxvi-lxxi) transcripta ex editione a Th. Mommsen divulgata.* Ed. Charles W. Jones and Th. Mommsen. 1977. CCL 123B.

——. *Epistola ad Albinum.* Ed. Carolus Plummer. *Venerabilis Baedae Opera Historica.* 1:3. Oxford: Oxford University Press, 1896.

——. *Epistola ad Ecgbertum episcopum.* Ed. Carolus Plummer. *Venerabilis Baedae Opera Historica.* 1:405-423. Oxford: Oxford University Press, 1896.

——. ——. Trans. Dorothy Whitelock. *English Historical Documents* 1: c. 500-1042. 2nd edition, pp. 799-810. New York: Oxford University Press, 1979.

——. *Epistola ad Helmuualdum.* Ed. Charles W. Jones. 1980. CCL 123C: 627-629.

——. *Epistola ad Pleguinam.* Ed. Charles W. Jones. 1980. CCL 123C:613-626.

——. *Epistola ad VVicthedum.* Ed. Charles W. Jones. 1980. CCL 123C: 631-642.

——. *Explanatio Apocalypsis.* PL 93:129-206.

——. *Expositio Actuum Apostolorum.* Ed. M.L.W. Laistner. 1983. CCL 121: 1-99.

——. *Expositio in Canticum Abacuc prophetae.* Ed. J.E. Hudson. 1983. CCL 119B:377-409.

——. *Historia abbatum (Vita beatorum abbatum Benedicti, Ceolfridi, Eosterwini, Sigfridi, atque Hwaetberhti).* Ed. Carolus Plummer. *Venerabilis Baedae Opera Historica.* 1:364-387. Oxford: Oxford University Press, 1896.

——. *Historia ecclesiastica gentis Anglorum.* Ed. and trans. Bertram Colgrave and R.A.B. Mynors. Oxford: Clarendon, 1969.

——. *Homeliarum Evangelii libri II.* Ed. David Hurst. 1955. CCL 122.

——. *In Cantica Canticorum libri VI.* Ed. David Hurst. 1983. CCL 119B:165-375.

——. *In epistolas septem catholicas.* Ed. David Hurst. 1983. CCL 121:179-342.

———. ———. Trans. David Hurst. *Bede the Venerable: Commentary on the Seven Catholic Epistles.* Cistercian Studies Series 82. Kalamazoo: Cistercian Publications, 1985.

———. *In Ezram et Neemiam libri III.* Ed. David Hurst. 1969. CCL 119A:235-392.

———. *In librum beati patris Tobias.* Ed. David Hurst. 1983. CCL 119B:1-19.

———. *In Lucae Evangelium expositio.* Ed. David Hurst. 1960. CCL 120:1-425.

———. *In Marci Evangelium expositio.* Ed. David Hurst. 1960. CCL 120:427-648.

———. *In primam partem Samuhelis libri IIII.* Ed. David Hurst. 1962. CCL 119:1-272.

———. *In Proverbia Salomonis libri III.* Ed. David Hurst. 1983. CCL 119B:21-163.

———. *In Regum Librum XXX quaestiones.* Ed. David Hurst. 1962. CCL 119:289-322.

———. *Liber hymnorum, rhythmi, variae preces.* Ed. Iohannes Fraipont. 1955. CCL 122:405-470.

———. *Libri quatuor in principium Genesis usque ad nativitatem Isaac et eiectionem Ismahelis adnotationum.* Ed. Charles W. Jones. 1967. CCL 118A.

———. *Martyrologium.* Identified by Henri Quentin. *Les martyrologes historiques du moyen âge. Etude sur la formation du Martyrologe Romain,* pp. 17-119. 1908. Reprint. Darmstadt: Scientia Verlag, 1969.

———. ———. Ed. Jacques Dubois and Geneviève Renaud. *Edition pratique des martyrologes de Bède, de l'Anonyme lyonnais et de Florus.* Paris: C.N.R.S., 1976.

———. *Retractatio in Actus Apostolorum.* Ed. M.L.W. Laistner. 1983. CCL 121:101-163.

———. *Vita Felicis.* Ed. Thomas William Mackay. In "A Critical Edition of Bede's *Vita Felicis.*" Ph.D. dissertation, Stanford University, 1972.

———. *Vita S. Cuthberti (metrica).* Ed. Werner Jaager. *Bedas metrische Vita sancti Cuthberti.* Palaestra 198. Leipzig: Mayer & Müller, 1935.

———. *Vita S. Cuthberti (prosaica).* Ed. and trans. Bertram Colgrave. *Two Lives of Saint Cuthbert,* pp. 141-307. Cambridge: Cambridge University Press, 1940.

Boniface, Saint. *Epistolae.* Ed. Michael Tangl. *Die Briefe des heiligen Bonifatius und Lullus.* Epistolae selectae in usum scholarum ex Monumentis Germaniae Historicis separatim editae 1. Berlin: Weidmannsche Buchhandlung, 1916.

———. ———. Trans. Ephraim Emerton. *The Letters of Saint Boniface.* Records of Civilization 31. New York: Columbia University Press, 1940. Reprint. New York: Octagon Books, 1973.

Constantius of Lyons. *Vita S. Germani*. Ed. René Borius. 1965. SC 112.
Cuthbert. *Epistola de obitu Bedae*. Ed. and trans. Bertram Colgrave and
R.A.B. Mynors. *Bede's Ecclesiastical History of the English People*,
pp. 579-587. Oxford: Clarendon, 1969.

Eddius Stephanus. *Vita S. Wilfrithi*. Ed. and trans. Bertram Colgrave. *The
Life of Bishop Wilfrid by Eddius Stephanus*. Cambridge: Cambridge Uni-
versity Press, 1927.
Eugippius. *Excerpta ex operibus S. Augustini*. Ed. Pius Knoell. 1885. CSEL 9.
Eusebius. *Commentaria in Psalmos*. PG 23.
———. *Historia ecclesiastica*. Ed. Eduard Schwartz; Latin version of Rufinus
ed. Theodor Mommsen. *Eusebius Werke 2: Die Kirchengeschichte*. 3 vols.
Die griechischen christlichen Schriftsteller der ersten drei Jahrhunderte 9.
Leipzig: J.C. Hinrichs'sche Buchhandlung, 1903-1909.

Felix. *Vita S. Guthlaci*. Ed. and trans. Bertram Colgrave. *Felix's Life of
Saint Guthlac*. Cambridge: Cambridge University Press, 1956.

Gregory of Nyssa. *Commentarius in Canticum Canticorum*. PG 44:755-1120.
Gregory of Tours. *Historia Francorum (Historiarum libri X)*. Ed. Bruno
Krusch and Wilhelm Levison. 1937-1951. MGH, SRM 1.
———. *Liber vitae patrum*. Ed. Bruno Krusch. 1885. MGH, SRM 1.2:211-294.
Gregory the Great. *Dialogorum libri quatuor de miraculis patrum italicorum*.
Ed. Adalbert de Vogüé. 1978-1980. SC 251, 260, 265.
———. ———. Trans. Odo John Zimmerman. Fathers of the Church 39. New
York: Fathers of the Church Inc., 1959.
———. *Homiliae in Evangelia*. PL 76:1075-1312.
———. *Homiliae in Hiezechihelem prophetam*. Ed. M. Adriaen. 1971. CCL 142.
———. *In librum primum Regum expositionum libri VI*. Ed. Patricius Verbraken.
1963. CCL 144:47-614.
———. *Moralia in Iob*. Ed. Marcus Adriaen. 1979-1985. CCL 143-143B.
———. *Registrum epistularum*. Ed. Dag Norberg. 1982. CCL 140, 140A.

Hilary of Poitiers. *In Matthaeum*. Ed. Jean Doignon. 1978-1979. SC 254, 258.

Isidore of Seville. *Etymologiarum sive originum libri XX*. Ed. W.M. Lindsay.
2 vols. Oxford: Clarendon, 1911.

Jerome, Saint. *Commentariorum in Hiezechielem libri XIV*. Ed. Franciscus
Glorie. 1964. CCL 75.

———. *Commentariorum in Matheum libri IV*. Ed. D. Hurst and M. Adriaen. 1969. CCL 77.
———. *Commentarii in Zachariam Prophetam*. Ed. M. Adriaen. 1970. CCL 76A: 747-900.
———. *De perpetua virginitate B. Mariae adversus Helvidium liber unus*. PL 23: 191-216.
———. *De viris illustribus*. PL 23:631-760.
———. *Epistulae*. Ed. Isidorus Hilberg. 1910-1918. CSEL 54-56.
———. *Vita S. Hilarionis eremitae*. PL 23:29-54.
———. ———. Ed. A.A.R. Bastiaensen. In *Vite dei santi* 4:69-142. Milan: Fondazione Lorenzo Valla, Arnoldo Mondadori Editore, 1975.
———. *Vita S. Pauli primi eremitae*. PL 23:17-30.
John Cassian. *Collationes*. Ed. Michael Petschenig. 1886. CSEL 13.
John Chrysostom. *Homiliae in Epistolam primam ad Corinthios*. PG 61:9-382.
———. *Homiliae in Epistolam secundam ad Corinthios*. PG 61:381-610.
———. *Homiliae in Matthaeum*. PG 57, 58.
Josephus, Flavius. *Jewish Antiquities*. Loeb Classical Library. 6 vols. London: Heinemann, 1930-1965.
———. ———. Ed. Franz Blatt. *The Latin Josephus 1: Introduction and Text (The Antiquities: Books i-v)*. Acta Jutlandica 31. Aarhus: The University of Aarhus, 1958.

New Testament Apocrypha. Ed. Edgar Hennecke and Wilhelm Schneemelcher. English translation ed. R. McL. Wilson. 2 vols. London: Lutterworth, 1963-1965.

The Old Testament Pseudepigrapha 1: *Apocalyptic Literature and Testaments*. Ed. James H. Charlesworth. Garden City NY: Doubleday, 1983.
Origen. *Commentaria in Evangelium secundum Matthaeum*. PG 13:829-1800.
———. *Homiliae in Ieremiam*. PG 13:253-544.
———. ———. Ed. Pierre Husson and Pierre Nautin. 1976-1977. SC 232, 238.
Orosius, Paulus. *Historiarum adversum paganos libri VII*. Ed. Carolus Zangemeister. 1882. CSEL 5.
———. ———. Trans. Roy J. Deferrari. Fathers of the Church 50. Washington DC: Catholic University of America, 1964.

Plutarch. "On the Delays of the Divine Vengeance" (*Moralia* 548-568). Trans. Phillip H. De Lacy and Benedict Einarson. *Plutarch's Moralia in Fifteen Volumes*. Loeb Classical Library. 7:523C-612B; pp. 169-299. Cambridge MA: Harvard University Press, 1959.

Pseudo-Dionysius Areopagita. *De divinis nominibus*. PG 3:585-996.
Pseudo-Isidore. *De ordine creaturarum*. Ed. Manuel C. Díaz y Díaz. Santiago de Compostela: Universidad de Santiago de Compostela, 1972.

Reginald of Durham. *Libellus de admirandis Beati Cuthberti virtutibus quae novellis patratae sunt temporibus*. Ed. J. Raine. Publications of the Surtees Society 1. London: J.B. Nichols and Son, William Pickering, 1835.
Rufinus of Aquileia. *See* Eusebius.

Solinus. *Collectanea rerum memorabilium*. Ed. Theodor Mommsen. Berolini: Apud Weidmannos, 1895.
Sulpicius Severus. *Dialogi*. Ed. Carolus Halm. 1866. CSEL 1:152-216.
——. *Epistulae*. Ed. Jacques Fontaine. 1967. SC 133:316-345.
——. *Vita S. Martini*. Ed. Jacques Fontaine. 1967-1969. SC 133-135.

Vita Ceolfridi Abbatis (Historia abbatum auctore anonymo). Ed. Carolus Plummer. *Venerabilis Baedae Opera Historica*. 1:388-404. Oxford: Oxford University Press, 1896.
——. Trans. Dorothy Whitelock. *English Historical Documents* 1: *c. 500-1042*, pp. 758-770. 2nd edition. New York: Oxford University Press, 1979.
Vita S. Cuthberti auctore anonymo. Ed. and trans. Bertram Colgrave. *Two Lives of Saint Cuthbert*, 59-139. Cambridge: Cambridge University Press, 1940.
Vita S. Gregorii. Ed. and trans. Bertram Colgrave. *The Earliest Life of Gregory the Great by an Anonymous Monk of Whitby*. Lawrence, Kansas: University of Kansas Press, 1968.

Willibald. *Vita S. Bonifatii*. Ed. Wilhelm Levison. Scriptores rerum Germanicarum in usum scholarum ex Monumentis Germaniae Historicis separatim editi. 1905. Reprint. Hannover: Hahn, 1977.

SECONDARY SOURCES

Abraham, Lenore. "Bede's *Life of Cuthbert*: A Reassessment." *Proceedings of the PMR [Patristic, Medieval & Renaissance] Conference* 1 (1976): 23-32.
Amat, Jacqueline. *Songes et visions: l'au-delà dans la littérature latine tardive*. Paris: Etudes Augustiniennes, 1985.
Amos, Thomas L. "Monks and Pastoral Care in the Early Middle Ages." In *Religion, Culture, and Society in the Early Middle Ages: Studies in Honor of Richard E. Sullivan*. Ed. Thomas F.X. Noble and John J. Contreni, pp. 165-180. Studies in Medieval Culture 23. Kalamazoo: Western Michigan University, Medieval Institute Publications, 1987.

Anderson, Carol Susan. "Divine Governance, Miracles and Laws of Nature in the Early Middle Ages: The *De mirabilibus Sacrae Scripturae*." Ph.D. dissertation, University of California, Los Angeles, 1982.

Anderson, Judith H. *Biographical Truth: The Representation of Historical Persons in Tudor-Stuart Writing*. New Haven: Yale University Press, 1984.

Angenendt, Arnold. "Der «ganze» und «unverweste» Leib—eine Leitidee der Reliquienverehrung bei Gregor von Tours und Beda Venerabilis." In *Aus Archiven und Bibliotheken. Festschrift für Raymund Kottje zum 65. Geburtstag*. Ed. Hubert Mordek, pp. 33-50. Freiburger Beiträge zur Mittelalterlichen Geschichte 3. Frankfurt am Main: Peter Lang, 1992.

Angli e Sassoni al di qua e al di là del mare (26 aprile — 1 maggio 1984). Settimane di studio del Centro italiano di studi sull'alto medioevo 32. Spoleto, 1986.

Archambault, Paul. "The Ages of Man and the Ages of the World: A Study of Two Traditions." *Revue des études augustiniennes* 12 (1966): 193-228.

Atwell, R.R. "From Augustine to Gregory the Great: An Evaluation of the Emergence of the Doctrine of Purgatory." *Journal of Ecclesiastical History* 38 (1987): 173-186.

Aubrun, Michel. "Caractères et portée religieuse et sociale des «Visiones» en Occident du VIe au XIe siècle." *Cahiers de civilisation médiévale* 23 (1980): 109-130.

Barnard, L.W. "Bede and Eusebius as Church Historians." In *Famulus Christi*, pp. 106-124.

Bede and Anglo-Saxon England. Papers in Honour of the 1300th Anniversary of the Birth of Bede, given at Cornell University in 1973 and 1974. Ed. Robert T. Farrell. British Archaeological Reports 46. Oxford: British Archaeological Reports, 1978.

Bede: His Life, Times, and Writings. Essays in Commemoration of the Twelfth Centenary of His Death. Ed. A. Hamilton Thompson. 1935. Reprint. Oxford: Clarendon Press, 1969.

Benedict's Disciples. Ed. D.H. Farmer. Leominster, Herefordshire: Fowler Wright Books Ltd., 1980.

Berlin, Gail Ivy. "Bede's Miracle Stories: Notions of Evidence and Authority in Old English History." *Neophilologus* 74 (1990): 434-443.

Berschin, Walter. *Biographie und Epochenstil im lateinischen Mittelalter*. 3 vols. Quellen und Untersuchungen zur lateinischen Philologie des Mittelalters 8-10. Stuttgart: Anton Hiersemann Verlag, 1986-1991.

——. "*Opus deliberatum ac perfectum*: Why Did the Venerable Bede Write a Second Prose Life of St Cuthbert?" In *St Cuthbert, His Cult and His Community*, pp. 95-102.

Beumer, Johannes. "Das Kirchenbild in den Schriftkommentaren Bedas des Ehrwürdigen." *Scholastik* 28 (1953): 40-56.

Bieler, Ludwig. "Ireland's Contribution to the Culture of Northumbria." In *Famulus Christi*, pp. 210-228.

Bischoff, Bernhard. "Turning-Points in the History of Latin Exegesis in the Early Middle Ages." In *Biblical Studies: The Medieval Irish Contribution.* Ed. Martin McNamara, pp. 73-160. Proceedings of the Irish Biblical Association 1. Dublin: Dominican Publications, 1976.

Bitel, Lisa M. *Isle of the Saints: Monastic Settlement and Christian Community in Early Ireland.* Ithaca: Cornell University Press, 1990.

Black, Jonathan. "*De Civitate Dei* and the Commentaries of Gregory the Great, Isidore, Bede, and Hrabanus Maurus on the Book of Samuel." *Augustinian Studies* 15 (1984): 114-127.

Boesch Gajano, Sofia. "Uso e abuso del miracolo nella cultura altomedioevale." In *Les fonctions des saints dans le monde occidental (IIIe-XIIIe siècle)*, pp. 109-122.

Boglioni, Pierre. "Miracle et nature chez Grégoire le Grand." In *Cahiers d'études médiévales* 1: *Epopées, légendes et miracles*, pp. 11-102. Montreal: Institut d'études médiévales, 1974.

Bolton, W.F. "The Supra-Historical Sense in the Dialogues of Gregory I." *Aevum* 33 (1959): 206-213.

——. "A Bede Bibliography: 1935-1960." *Traditio* 18 (1962): 436-445.

——. "An Aspect of Bede's Later Knowledge of Greek." *Classical Review* n.s. 13 (1963): 17-18.

——. *A History of Anglo-Saxon Literature, 597-1066.* Princeton: Princeton University Press, 1967.

Bonner, Gerald. *Saint Bede in the Tradition of Western Apocalyptic Commentary.* Jarrow Lecture. Jarrow, 1966.

——. "The Christian Life in the Thought of the Venerable Bede." *Durham University Journal* 63 (1970): 39-55.

——. "Bedan Studies in 1973." *Clergy Review* 58 (1973): 689-696.

——. "Bede and Medieval Civilization." *Anglo-Saxon England* 2 (1973): 71-90.

——. "Bede and His Legacy." *Durham University Journal* 78 (n.s. 47) (1986): 219-230.

——. "Saint Cuthbert: Soul Friend." In *Cuthbert: Saint and Patron*, pp. 23-44.

Brooke, Christopher N.L. "Historical Writing in England Between 850 and 1150." In *La storiografia altomedievale* 1:223-247.

Brooks, Nicholas P. *History and Myth, Forgery and Truth.* Inaugural Lecture. Birmingham: University of Birmingham, 1986.

Brown, Elizabeth A.R. "*Falsitas pia sive reprehensibilis*: Medieval Forgers and Their Intentions." In *Fälschungen im Mittelalter* 1:101-119.

Brown, George Hardin. "The Age of Bede." In *Anglo-Latin in the Context of Old English Literature*. Ed. Paul E. Szarmach, pp. 1-6. Old English Newsletter, Subsidia 9. Binghamton NY: Centre for Medieval and Early Renaissance Studies, State University of New York, 1983.
———. *Bede the Venerable*. Twayne's English Authors Series 443. Boston: Twayne Publishers, 1987.
Brown, Peter. "The Saint as Exemplar in Late Antiquity." In *Saints and Virtues*. Ed. John Stratton Hawley, pp. 3-14. Berkeley: University of California Press, 1987.
Brown, T.J. "An Historical Introduction to the Use of Classical Latin Authors in the British Isles from the Fifth to the Eleventh Century." In *La cultura antica nell'Occidente latino dal VII all'XI secolo* 1:237-293, with discussion 295-299. Settimane di studio del Centro italiano di studi sull'alto medioevo 22. Spoleto, 1975.
Bullough, Donald A. "Columba, Adomnan and the Achievement of Iona." *The Scottish Historical Review* 43 (1964): 111-130; 44 (1965): 17-33.
———. "Hagiography as Patriotism: Alcuin's «York Poem» and the Early Northumbrian «Vitae Sanctorum»." In *Hagiographie, cultures et sociétés*, pp. 339-359.
Burrow, J.A. *The Ages of Man: A Study in Medieval Writing and Thought*. Oxford: Clarendon Press, 1986.

Cameron, Averil. *Christianity and the Rhetoric of Empire: The Development of Christian Discourse*. Sather Classical Lectures 55. Berkeley: University of California Press, 1991.
Campbell, James. "Bede." In *Latin Historians*. Ed. T.A. Dorey, pp. 159-190. London: Routledge and Kegan Paul, 1966.
———. "Elements in the Background to the Life of St Cuthbert and His Early Cult." In *St Cuthbert, His Cult and His Community*, pp. 3-19.
Capelle, D. Bernard. "Le rôle théologique de Bède le Vénérable." *Studia Anselmiana* 6 (1936): 1-40.
Carozzi, Claude. "La géographie de l'au-delà et sa signification pendant le haut moyen âge." In *Popoli e paesi nella cultura altomedievale* 2:423-481. Settimane di studio del Centro italiano di studi sull'alto medioevo 29. Spoleto, 1983.
Carroll, Sister M. Thomas Aquinas. *The Venerable Bede: His Spiritual Teachings*. Studies in Mediaeval History, n.s. 9. Washington DC: Catholic University of America Press, 1946.
Celt and Saxon: Studies in the Early British Border. Ed. Nora K. Chadwick. Cambridge: Cambridge University Press, 1963.

Chadwick, Nora K. "The Battle of Chester: A Study of Sources." In *Celt and Saxon*, pp. 167-185.

———. "The Conversion of Northumbria: A Comparison of Sources." In *Celt and Saxon*, pp. 138-166.

Ciccarese, Maria Pia. "Le più antiche rappresentazioni del purgatorio, dalla *Passio Perpetuae* alla fine del IX sec." *Romanobarbarica* 7 (1982-1983): 33-76.

———. *Visioni dell'aldilà in occidente. Fonti, modelli, testi.* Biblioteca Patristica 8. Firenze: Nardini Editore, Centro Internazionale del Libro, 1987.

———. "La genesi letteraria della visione dell'aldilà: Gregorio Magno e le sue fonti." *Augustinianum* 29 (1989): 435-449.

Clark, Francis. *The Pseudo-Gregorian Dialogues.* 2 vols. Studies in the History of Christian Thought 37-38. Leiden: E.J. Brill, 1987.

———. "The Authorship of the Gregorian Dialogues: An Old Controversy Renewed." *Heythrop Journal* 30 (1989): 257-272.

———. "St Gregory and the Enigma of the Dialogues: A Response to Paul Meyvaert." *Journal of Ecclesiastical History* 40 (1989): 323-343.

———. "The Renewed Debate on the Authenticity of the Gregorian Dialogues." *Augustinianum* 30 (1990): 75-105.

———. "The Renewed Controversy about the Authorship of the Dialogues." In *Gregorio Magno e il suo tempo* 2:5-25.

Clayton, Mary. "Homiliaries and Preaching in Anglo-Saxon England." *Peritia* 4 (1985): 207-242.

Coleman, Janet. *Ancient and Medieval Memories: Studies in the Reconstruction of the Past.* Cambridge: Cambridge University Press, 1992.

Colgrave, Bertram. "Bede's Miracle Stories." In *Bede: His Life, Times, and Writings*, pp. 201-229.

———. *Two Lives of St Cuthbert.* Cambridge: Cambridge University Press, 1940.

———. "The Earliest Saints' Lives Written in England." *Proceedings of the British Academy* 44 (1958): 35-60.

———. *The Venerable Bede and His Times.* Jarrow Lecture. Jarrow, 1958.

———. "The Earliest Life of St Gregory the Great, Written by a Whitby Monk." In *Celt and Saxon*, pp. 119-137.

Collins, Richard. "Observations on the Form, Language and Public of the Prose Biographies of Venantius Fortunatus in the Hagiography of Merovingian Gaul." In *Columbanus and Merovingian Monasticism*, pp. 105-131.

Columbanus and Merovingian Monasticism. Ed. H.B. Clarke and Mary Brennan. BAR International Series 113. Oxford: British Archaeological Reports, 1981.

Consolino, Franca Ela. "Sogni e visioni nell'agiografia tardoantica: modelli e variazioni sul tema." *Augustinianum* 29 (1989): 237-256.

Constable, Giles. "Forged Letters in the Middle Ages." In *Fälschungen im Mittelalter* 5:11-37.

Corbett, John. "Two Early Anglo-Saxon Holy Men: Oswald and Cuthbert." In *The Anglo-Saxons: Synthesis and Achievement.* Ed. J. Douglas Woods and David A.E. Pelteret, pp. 63-75. Waterloo: Wilfrid Laurier University Press, 1985.

Cosmos, Spencer. "Oral Tradition and Literary Convention in Bede's Life of St. Aidan." *Classical Folia* 31 (1977): 47-63.

Cowdrey, H.E.J. "Bede and the 'English People.'" *Journal of Religious History* 11 (1981): 501-523.

Cracco Ruggini, Lellia. "Il miracolo nella cultura del tardo impero: concetto e funzione." In *Hagiographie, cultures et sociétés*, pp. 161-202, with discussion 202-204.

Cramp, Rosemary. *The Background to St Cuthbert's Life.* Durham Cathedral Lecture. Durham: The Dean and Chapter, 1980.

Creider, Laurence Stearns. "Bede's Understanding of the Miraculous." Ph.D. dissertation, Yale University, 1979.

Cremascoli, Giuseppe. "Se i *Dialogi* siano opera di Gregorio Magno: due volumi per una *vexata quaestio.*" *Benedictina* 36 (1989): 179-192.

Crépin, André. "Bede and the Vernacular." In *Famulus Christi*, pp. 170-192.

Cusack, Pearse Aidan. "Authenticity of the Dialogues of Gregory the Great." *Cistercian Studies* 24 (1989): 339-342.

Cuthbert: Saint and Patron. Ed. D.W. Rollason. Durham: The Dean and Chapter, 1987.

Dagens, Claude. *Saint Grégoire le Grand. Culture et expérience chrétiennes.* Paris: Etudes Augustiniennes, 1977.

Dall'Olmo, Umberto. "*Eclypsis naturalis* ed *eclypsis prodigialis* nelle cronache medioevali." *Bullettino dell'Istituto storico italiano per il medio evo e Archivio Muratoriano* 87 (1978): 154-172.

Darby, H.C. "The Geographical Ideas of the Venerable Bede." *Scottish Geographical Magazine* 51 (1935): 84-89.

Davidse, Jan. "The Sense of History in the Works of the Venerable Bede." *Studi Medievali* 3rd ser. 23 (1982): 647-695.

Davis, R.H.C. "Bede After Bede." In *Studies in Medieval History Presented to R. Allen Brown.* Ed. Christopher Harper-Bill, Christopher J. Holdsworth, and Janet L. Nelson, pp. 103-116. Woodbridge, Suffolk: The Boydell Press-Boydell and Brewer, 1989.

Dean, Paul. "Three Episodes in Bede's 'History.'" *Durham University Journal* n.s. 50 (1988): 81-85.

Diesner, Hans-Joachim. "Das christliche Bildungsprogramm des Beda Vene-rabilis (672/73–735)." *Theologische Literaturzeitung* 12 (1981): 865-872.

———. "Inkarnationsjahre, 'Militia Christi' und anglische Königsporträts bei Beda Venerabilis." *Mittellateinisches Jahrbuch* 16 (1981): 17-34.

Dinzelbacher, Peter. *Vision und Visionsliteratur im Mittelalter.* Monographien zur Geschichte des Mittelalters 23. Stuttgart: Anton Hiersemann, 1981.

———. "Der Kampf der Heiligen mit den Dämonen." In *Santi e demoni nell'alto medioevo occidentale*, pp. 647-695.

Dionisotti, Anna Carlotta. "On Bede, Grammars, and Greek." *Revue Bénédictine* 92 (1982): 111-141.

Dudden, Frederick Homes. *Gregory the Great: His Place in History and Thought.* 2 vols. 1905. Reprint. New York: Russell and Russell, 1967.

Duval, Yvette. *Auprès des saints corps et âme. L'inhumation 'ad sanctos' dans la chrétienté d'Orient et d'Occident du IIIe au VIIe siècle.* Paris: Etudes Augustiniennes, 1988.

Echlin, Edward P. "Bede and the Church." *Irish Theological Quarterly* 40 (1973): 351-363.

Eckenrode, Thomas R. "Venerable Bede as a Scientist." *American Benedictine Review* 22 (1971): 486-507.

———. "Venerable Bede's Theory of Ocean Tides." *American Benedictine Review* 25 (1974): 56-74.

———. "The Growth of a Scientific Mind: Bede's Early and Late Scientific Writings." *Downside Review* 94 (1976): 197-212.

———. "The Venerable Bede and the Pastoral Affirmation of the Christian Message in Anglo-Saxon England." *Downside Review* 99 (1981): 258-278.

———. "The Venerable Bede: A Bibliographical Essay, 1970-81." *American Benedictine Review* 36 (1985): 172-194.

Elliott, Alison Goddard. *Roads to Paradise: Reading the Lives of the Early Saints.* Hanover NH: University Press of New England, 1987.

Engelbert, Pius. "Hat Papst Gregor der Große die «Dialoge» geschrieben? Bemerkungen zu einem neuen Buch." *Erbe und Auftrag* 64 (1988): 255-265.

———. "Neue Forschungen zu den «Dialogen» Gregors des Großen. Antworten auf Clarks These." *Erbe und Auftrag* 65 (1989): 376-393.

Evans, G.R. *The Thought of Gregory the Great.* Cambridge Studies in Medieval Life and Thought, fourth series 2. Cambridge: Cambridge University Press, 1986.

Fälschungen im Mittelalter. 5 vols. Internationaler Kongress der Monumenta Germaniae Historica, München, 16.-19. Sept. 1986. Monumenta Germaniae Historica, Schriften 33,1-5. Hannover: Hahnsche Buchhandlung, 1988.

Famulus Christi: Essays in Commemoration of the Thirteenth Centenary of the Birth of the Venerable Bede. Ed. Gerald Bonner. London: SPCK, 1976.

Fanning, Steven. "Bede, *Imperium,* and the Bretwaldas." *Speculum* 66 (1991): 1-26.

Farmer, D.H. "Saint Wilfrid." In *Saint Wilfrid at Hexham,* pp. 35-59.

Flint, Valerie I.J. *The Rise of Magic in Early Medieval Europe.* Princeton: Princeton University Press, 1991.

Les fonctions des saints dans le monde occidental (IIIe-XIIIe siècle). Actes du colloque organisé par l'Ecole française de Rome avec le concours de l'Université de Rome «La Sapienza», Rome, 27-29 octobre 1988. Collection de l'Ecole française de Rome, 149. Rome, 1991.

Foot, Sarah. "Parochial Ministry in Early Anglo-Saxon England: The Role of Monastic Communities." *Studies in Church History* 26 (1989): 43-54.

Franklin, Carmela Vircillo, and Paul Meyvaert. "Has Bede's Version of the «Passio S. Anastasii» Come Down to Us in «BHL» 408?" *Analecta Bollandiana* 100 (1982): 373-400.

Fransen, Paul-Irénée. "D'Eugippius à Bède le Vénérable: à propos de leurs florilèges augustiniens." *Revue Bénédictine* 97 (1987): 187-194.

Frantzen, Allen J. "The Penitentials Attributed to Bede." *Speculum* 58 (1983): 573-597.

Fros, Henricus. "L'eschatologie médiévale dans quelques écrits hagiographiques (IV-IX s.)." In *The Use and Abuse of Eschatology,* pp. 212-220.

Fry, Donald K. "The Art of Bede: Edwin's Council." In *Saints, Scholars and Heroes* 1:191-207.

——. "The Art of Bede II: The Reliable Narrator as Persona." In *The Early Middle Ages.* Ed. William H. Snyder, pp. 63-82. Acta 6. Binghamton NY: State University of New York, The Center for Medieval and Early Renaissance Studies, 1982.

——. "Bede Fortunate in His Translator: The Barking Nuns." In *Studies in Earlier Old English Prose.* Ed. Paul E. Szarmach, pp. 345-362. Albany: State University of New York Press, 1986.

Fuhrmann, Horst. "Von der Wahrheit der Fälscher." In *Fälschungen im Mittelalter* 1:83-98.

Fuhrmann, Manfred. "Die Mönchsgeschichten des Hieronymus: Formexperimente in erzählender Literatur." In *Christianisme et formes littéraires de l'antiquité tardive en Occident,* pp. 41-89. Entretiens sur l'antiquité classique 23. Genève: Fondation Hardt, 1977.

Gardner, Rex. "Miracles of Healing in Anglo-Celtic Northumbria as Recorded by the Venerable Bede and His Contemporaries: A Reappraisal in the Light of Twentieth Century Experience." *British Medical Journal* 287 (1983): 1927-1933.

Gewalt, Dietfried. "Der entstummte Bettler. Zu Beda Venerabilis, Historia Ecclesiastica Gentis Anglorum V, 2." *Linguistica Biblica* 54 (1983): 53-60.

Gillet, Robert. "Les *Dialogues* sont-ils de Grégoire?" *Revue des études augustiniennes* 36 (1990): 309-314.

Gneuss, Helmut. "The Study of Language in Anglo-Saxon England." *Bulletin of the John Rylands University Library* 72 (1990): 3-32.

Godding, Robert. "Les *Dialogues* ... de Grégoire le Grand. A propos d'un livre récent." *Analecta Bollandiana* 106 (1988): 201-229.

Godman, Peter. "The Anglo-Latin *Opus Geminatum*: From Aldhelm to Alcuin." *Medium Aevum* 50 (1981): 215-229.

Goffart, Walter. *The Narrators of Barbarian History (A.D. 550-800): Jordanes, Gregory of Tours, Bede, and Paul the Deacon.* Princeton NJ: Princeton University Press, 1988.

——. "The *Historia Ecclesiastica*: Bede's Agenda and Ours." *Haskins Society Journal* 2 (1990): 29-45.

Grafton, Anthony. *Forgers and Critics: Creativity and Duplicity in Western Scholarship.* Princeton NJ: Princeton University Press, 1990.

Gransden, Antonia. *Historical Writing in England* 1: *c. 550 to c. 1307.* Ithaca NY: Cornell University Press, 1974.

——. "Bede's Reputation as an Historian in Medieval England." *Journal of Ecclesiastical History* 32 (1981): 397-425.

Graus, Frantisek. "Fälschungen im Gewand der Frömmigkeit." In *Fälschungen im Mittelalter* 5:261-282.

——. "Hagiographie und Dämonenglauben — zu ihren Funktionen in der Merowingerzeit." In *Santi e demoni nell'alto medioevo occidentale*, pp. 93-120.

Gray, P. "Forgery as an Instrument of Progress: Reconstructing the Theological Tradition in the Sixth Century." *Byzantinische Zeitschrift* 81 (1988): 284-289.

Grégoire, Réginald. *Manuale di agiologia: introduzione alla letteratura agiografica.* Bibliotheca Montisfani 12. Fabriano: Monastero San Silvestro Abate, 1987.

Gregorio Magno e il suo tempo. 2 Vols. XIX Incontro di studiosi dell'antichità cristiana in collaborazione con l'Ecole Française de Rome, Roma, 9-12 maggio 1990. Studia EphemeridIs «Augustinianum» 33-34. Rome: Institutum Patristicum «Augustinianum», 1991.

Gribomont, Jean. "Saint Bède et ses dictionnaires grecs." *Revue Bénédictine* 89 (1979): 271-280.

Gurevich, Aron. *Medieval Popular Culture: Problems of Belief and Perception.* Cambridge: Cambridge University Press, 1988.

Hagiographie, cultures et sociétés, IVᵉ-XIIᵉ siècles. Actes du Colloque organisé à Nanterre et à Paris, 2-5 mai 1979. Paris: Etudes Augustiniennes, 1981.

Hamilton Thompson, A. "Northumbrian Monasticism." In *Bede: His Life, Times, and Writings,* pp. 60-101.

Hanning, Robert W. *The Vision of History in Early Britain: From Gildas to Geoffrey of Monmouth.* New York: Columbia University Press, 1966.

Heffernan, Thomas J. *Sacred Biography: Saints and Their Biographers in the Middle Ages.* New York and Oxford: Oxford University Press, 1988.

Herbert, Máire. *Iona, Kells and Derry: The History and Hagiography of the Monastic familia of Columba.* Oxford: Clarendon, 1988.

Hill, Rosalind. "Bede and the Boors." In *Famulus Christi,* pp. 93-105.

Holder, Arthur G. "Allegory and History in Bede's Interpretation of Sacred Architecture." *American Benedictine Review* 40 (1989): 115-131.

——. "New Treasures and Old in Bede's 'De Tabernaculo' and 'De Templo.'" *Revue Bénédictine* 99 (1989): 237-249.

——. "Bede and the Tradition of Patristic Exegesis." *Anglican Theological Review* 72 (1990): 399-411.

——. "The Venerable Bede on the Mysteries of Our Salvation." *American Benedictine Review* 42 (1991): 140-162.

Howe, Nicholas. *Migration and Mythmaking in Anglo-Saxon England.* New Haven: Yale University Press, 1989.

Hunter Blair, Peter. *Bede's Ecclesiastical History of the English Nation and Its Importance Today.* Jarrow Lecture. Jarrow, 1959.

——. "The Historical Writings of Bede." In *La storiografia altomedievale* 1:197-221.

——. *The World of Bede.* London: Secker and Warburg, 1970.

——. "From Bede to Alcuin." In *Famulus Christi,* pp. 239-260.

——. *Northumbria in the Days of Bede.* London: Victor Gollancz, 1976.

Hunter, Michael. "Germanic and Roman Antiquity and the Sense of the Past in Anglo-Saxon England." *Anglo-Saxon England* 3 (1974): 29-50.

Ideal and Reality in Frankish and Anglo-Saxon Society: Studies Presented to J.M. Wallace-Hadrill. Ed. Patrick Wormald, Donald Bullough and Roger Collins. Oxford: Basil Blackwell, 1983.

Insular Latin Studies: Papers on Latin Texts and Manuscripts of the British Isles, 550-1066. Ed. Michael W. Herren. Papers in Medieval Studies 1. Toronto: Pontifical Institute of Mediaeval Studies, 1981.

Irland und die Christenheit, Ireland and Christendom. Ed. Próinséas Ní Chatháin and Michael Richter. Stuttgart: Klett-Cotta, 1987.

Irvine, Martin. "Bede the Grammarian and the Scope of Grammatical Studies in Eighth-Century Northumbria." *Anglo-Saxon England* 15 (1986): 15-44.

Isola, Antonio. "Il *De schematibus et tropis* di Beda in rapporto al *De doctrina Christiana* di Agostino." *Romanobarbarica* 1 (1976): 71-82.

Jenkins, Claude. "Bede as Exegete and Theologian." In *Bede: His Life, Times, and Writings*, pp. 152-200.

Jones, Charles W. "Bede as Early Medieval Historian." *Medievalia et Humanistica* 4 (1946): 26-36.

———. *Saints' Lives and Chronicles in Early England.* Ithaca NY: Cornell University Press, 1947. Reprint. Hamden, Conn.: Archon Books, 1968.

———. "Some Introductory Remarks on Bede's Commentary on Genesis." *Sacris Erudiri* 14 (1969/70): 115-198.

———. "Bede's Place in Medieval Schools." In *Famulus Christi*, pp. 261-285.

Jones, Michael E. "The Historicity of the Alleluja Victory." *Albion* 18 (1986): 363-373.

Kee, Howard Clark. *Miracle in the Early Christian World: A Study in Sociohistorical Method.* New Haven: Yale University Press, 1983.

———. *Medicine, Miracle and Magic in New Testament Times.* Society for New Testament Studies, Monograph Series 55. Cambridge: Cambridge University Press, 1986.

Kelly, Joseph F. "Bede and the Irish Exegetical Tradition on the Apocalypse." *Revue Bénédictine* 92 (1982): 393-406.

———. "The Venerable Bede and Hiberno-Latin Exegesis." In *Sources of Anglo-Saxon Culture.* Ed. Paul E. Szarmach and Virginia Darrow Oggins, pp. 65-75. Studies in Medieval Culture 20. Kalamazoo: Western Michigan University, Medieval Institute Publications, 1986.

———. "Augustine and Bede on the Gospels." In *Congresso internazionale su S. Agostino nel XVI centenario della conversione*, Roma, 15-20 settembre 1986, 3:159-165. Studia Ephemeridis «Augustinianum» 24-26. Rome, 1987.

———. "The Venerable Bede's Sense of Scripture." In *Studies in Honour of René Derolez.* Ed. A.M. Simon-Vandenbergen, pp. 276-282. Ghent: Seminarie voor Engelse en Oud-Germaanse Taalkunde R.U.G., 1987.

Kendall, Calvin B. "Bede's *Historia ecclesiastica*: The Rhetoric of Faith." In *Medieval Eloquence: Studies in the Theory and Practice of Medieval*

Rhetoric. Ed. James J. Murphy, pp. 145-172. Berkeley: University of California Press, 1978.

——. "Imitation and the Venerable Bede's *Historia ecclesiastica*." In *Saints, Scholars and Heroes* 1:161-190.

King, Margot H. "*Grammatica mystica*: A Study of Bede's Grammatical Curriculum." In *Saints, Scholars and Heroes* 1:145-159.

Kirby, D.P. "Bede's Native Sources for the *Historia Ecclesiastica*." *Bulletin of the John Rylands Library* 48 (1965-1966): 341-371.

——. "Northumbria in the Time of Wilfrid." In *Saint Wilfrid at Hexham*, pp. 1-34.

——. "King Ceolwulf of Northumbria and the *Historia Ecclesiastica*." *Studia Celtica* 14-15 (1979-1980): 168-173.

——. "Bede, Eddius Stephanus and the 'Life of Wilfrid.'" *English Historical Review* 98 (1983): 101-114.

Knowles, David. *Saints and Scholars: Twenty-Five Medieval Portraits*. Cambridge: Cambridge University Press, 1962.

Laistner, M.L.W. "The Library of the Venerable Bede." In *Bede: His Life, Times, and Writings*, pp. 237-266.

Landes, Richard. "Lest the Millennium Be Fulfilled: Apocalyptic Expectations and the Pattern of Western Chronography 100-800 CE." In *The Use and Abuse of Eschatology*, pp. 137-211.

Lapidge, Michael. "The Study of Greek at the School of Canterbury in the Seventh Century." In *The Sacred Nectar of the Greeks: The Study of Greek in the West in the Early Middle Ages*. Ed. Michael W. Herren and Shirley Ann Brown, pp. 169-194. London: King's College, 1988.

——. "Bede's Metrical *Vita S. Cuthberti*." In *St Cuthbert, His Cult and His Community*, pp. 77-93.

Latourelle, René. *The Miracles of Jesus and the Theology of Miracles*. Trans. Matthew J. O'Connell. New York: Paulist, 1988.

Lauwers, Michel. "La mort et le corps des saints: la scène de la mort dans les *Vitae* du haut moyen âge." *Le Moyen Age* 94 (1988): 21-50.

Le Goff, Jacques. *The Birth of Purgatory*. Trans. Arthur Goldhammer. Chicago: University of Chicago Press, 1984.

——. *The Medieval Imagination*. Trans. Arthur Goldhammer. Chicago: University of Chicago Press, 1988.

Leclerc, Pierre. "Antoine et Paul: métamorphose d'un héros." In *Jérôme entre l'Occident et l'Orient*. Actes du colloque de Chantilly (septembre 1986). Ed. Yves-Marie Duval, pp. 257-265. Paris: Etudes Augustiniennes, 1988.

Leonardi, Claudio. "Il Venerabile Beda e la cultura del secolo VIII." In *I problemi dell'occidente nel secolo VIII*, pp. 603-658. Settimane di studio del Centro italiano di studi sull'alto medioevo 20. Spoleto, 1973.

——. "Il problema storiografico dell'agiografia." In *Storia della Sicilia e tradizione agiografica nella tarda antichità*. Atti del convegno di studi, Catania, 20-22 maggio 1986. Ed. Salvatore Pricoco, pp. 13-23. Soveria Mannelli (CZ): Rubbettino Editore, 1988.

——. "Modelli di santità tra secolo V e VII." In *Santi e demoni nell'alto medioevo occidentale*, pp. 261-283.

——. "Modelli agiografici nel secolo VIII: da Beda a Ugeburga." In *Les fonctions des saints dans le monde occidental (IIIe-XIIIe siècle)*, pp. 507-516.

Lerer, Seth. *Literacy and Power in Anglo-Saxon Literature*. Lincoln, Nebraska, and London: University of Nebraska Press, 1991.

Levison, Wilhelm. "Bede as Historian." In *Bede: His Life, Times, and Writings*, pp. 111-151.

——. *England and the Continent in the Eighth Century*. Oxford: Oxford University Press, 1946.

Löfstedt, Bengt. "Zu Bedas Evangelienkommentaren." *Arctos* 21 (1987): 61-72.

Loomis, C. Grant. "The Miracle Traditions of the Venerable Bede." *Speculum* 21 (1946): 404-418.

Lubac, Henri de. *Exégèse médiévale. Les quatre sens de l'Ecriture*. 2 parts in 4 vols. Paris: Aubier, 1959-1964.

Luiselli, Bruno. "Il *De arte metrica* di Beda di fronte alla tradizione metricologica tardo-latina." In *Grammatici latini d'età imperiale: Miscellanea filologica*, pp. 169-180. Genova: Istituto di filologia classica e medievale, 1976.

Lynch, Kevin M. "The Venerable Bede's Knowledge of Greek." *Traditio* 39 (1983): 432-439.

McClure, Judith. "Bede's Old Testament Kings." In *Ideal and Reality in Frankish and Anglo-Saxon Society*, pp. 76-98.

——. "Bede and the Life of Ceolfrid." *Peritia* 3 (1984): 71-84.

——. "Bede's *Notes on Genesis* and the Training of the Anglo-Saxon Clergy." In *The Bible in the Medieval World: Essays in Memory of Beryl Smalley*. Ed. Katherine Walsh and Diana Wood, pp. 17-30. Studies in Church History, Subsidia 4. Oxford: Basil Blackwell, for the Ecclesiastical History Society, 1985.

McCready, William David. *Signs of Sanctity: Miracles in the Thought of Gregory the Great*. Studies and Texts 91. Toronto: Pontifical Institute of Mediaeval Studies, 1989.

Mackay, Thomas W. "Bede's Hagiographical Method: His Knowledge and Use of Paulinus of Nola." In *Famulus Christi*, pp. 77-92.

——. "Bede's Biblical Criticism: The Venerable Bede's Summary of Tyconius' *Liber Regularum.*" In *Saints, Scholars and Heroes* 1:209-231.

Markus, R.A. *Bede and the Tradition of Ecclesiastical Historiography.* Jarrow Lecture. Jarrow, 1975.

——. "Church History and the Early Church Historians." *Studies in Church History* 11 (1975): 1-17.

——. *The End of Ancient Christianity.* Cambridge: Cambridge University Press, 1990.

Martin, Lawrence T. "Bede as a Linguistic Scholar." *American Benedictine Review* 35 (1984): 204-217.

——. "Bede's Structural Use of Wordplay as a Way to Teach." In *From Cloister to Classroom: Monastic and Scholastic Approaches to Truth.* Ed. E. Rozanne Elder, pp. 27-46. Cistercian Studies Series 90. Kalamazoo: Cistercian Publications, 1986.

——. "The Two Worlds in Bede's Homilies: The Biblical Event and the Listeners' Experience." In *De Ore Domini: Preacher and Word in the Middle Ages.* Ed. Thomas L. Amos, Eugene A. Green, and Beverly Mayne Kienzle, pp. 27-40. Studies in Medieval Culture 27. Kalamazoo: Western Michigan University, Medieval Institute Publications, 1989.

Mayr-Harting, Henry M.R.E. *The Coming of Christianity to England.* New York: Schocken, 1972.

——. *The Venerable Bede, the Rule of St Benedict, and Social Class.* Jarrow Lecture. Jarrow, 1976.

Meaney, Audrey L. "Bede and Anglo-Saxon Paganism." *Parergon* n.s. 3 (1985): 1-29.

Meyvaert, Paul. *Bede and Gregory the Great.* Jarrow Lecture. Jarrow, 1964.

——. "A New Edition of Gregory the Great's Commentaries on the Canticle and 1 Kings." *Journal of Theological Studies* n.s. 19 (1968): 215-225.

——. "Bede the Scholar." In *Famulus Christi*, pp. 40-69.

——. *Benedict, Gregory, Bede and Others.* London: Variorum Reprints, 1977.

——. "The Enigma of Gregory the Great's *Dialogues*: A Response to Francis Clark." *Journal of Ecclesiastical History* 39 (1988): 335-381.

Miller, Linda L. "Drythelm's Journey to the Other World: Bede's Literary Use of Tradition." *Comitatus* 2 (1971): 3-15.

Miller, Molly. "Starting to Write History: Gildas, Bede and 'Nennius.'" *Welsh Historical Review* 8 (1977): 456-465.

Minard, Pierre. "Les Dialogues de Saint Grégoire et les origines du monachisme bénédictin. A propos d'un livre récent." *Revue Mabillon* 61 (1986-1988): 471-481.

Miquel, Pierre. "Le diable dans les 'Vies' des saints moines. 'Vie de Saint Antoine' par Athanase, 'Vie de Saint Martin' par Sulpice Sévère, 'Vie de

Saint Benoît' par Grégoire le Grand." *Collectanea Cisterciensia* 49 (1987): 246-259.

Morse, Ruth. *Truth and Convention in the Middle Ages: Rhetoric, Representation, and Reality.* Cambridge: Cambridge University Press, 1991.

Müller, Gregor. *Die Wahrhaftigkeitspflicht und die Problematik der Lüge.* Freiburger Theologische Studien 78. Freiburg: Herder, 1962.

Musca, Giosué. *Il Venerabile Beda, storico dell'Alto Medioevo.* Storia e civiltà 9. Bari: Dedalo Libri, 1973.

Nie, Giselle de. *Views from a Many-Windowed Tower: Studies of Imagination in the Works of Gregory of Tours.* Studies in Classical Antiquity 7. Amsterdam: Rodopi, 1987.

Olsen, Alexandra Hennessey. "'De Historiis Sanctorum': A Generic Study of Hagiography." *Genre* 13 (1980): 407-429.

Olsen, Glenn W. "Bede as Historian: The Evidence from His Observations on the Life of the First Christian Community at Jerusalem." *Journal of Ecclesiastical History* 33 (1982): 519-530.

——. "From Bede to the Anglo-Saxon Presence in the Carolingian Empire." In *Angli e Sassoni al di qua e al di là del mare,* pp. 305-382.

Parabiaghi, Mario. "Pitture ed apparato di culto nelle opere del Venerabile Beda." *Ecclesia Orans* 4 (1987): 203-234.

Parkes, M.B. *The Scriptorium of Wearmouth-Jarrow.* Jarrow Lecture. Jarrow, 1982.

Pepperdene, Margaret W. "Bede's *Historia Ecclesiastica*: A New Perspective." *Celtica* 4 (1958): 253-262.

Piacente, Luigi. "Un nuovo frammento ciceroniano in Beda." *Romanobarbarica* 9 (1986-1987): 229-245.

Picard, Jean-Michel. "The Marvellous in Irish and Continental Saints' Lives of the Merovingian Period." In *Columbanus and Merovingian Monasticism,* pp. 91-103.

——. "The Purpose of Adomnán's *Vita Columbae*." *Peritia* 1 (1982): 160-177.

——. "Bede, Adomnán, and the Writing of History." *Peritia* 3 (1984): 50-70.

——. "Structural Patterns in Early Hiberno-Latin Hagiography." *Peritia* 4 (1985): 67-82.

Plummer, Carolus. *Venerabilis Baedae Opera Historica.* 2 vols. Oxford: Oxford University Press, 1896.

Ponton, Georges. "Saint Joseph d'après l'oeuvre de Bède le Vénérable." *Cahiers de Joséphologie* 19 (1971): 196-219.

Power, D. Edmund. "St Cuthbert and St Wilfrid." In *Benedict's Disciples*, pp. 52-69.

Price, Mary R. *Bede and Dunstan*. Clarendon Biographies. London: Oxford University Press, 1968.

Prinz, Friedrich. "Von der Bekehrung der Angelsachsen bis zu ihrer Missionstätigkeit im Frankenreich." In *Angli e Sassoni al di qua e al di là del mare*, pp. 701-734.

———. "Der Heilige und seine Lebenswelt: Überlegungen zum gesellschafts- und kulturgeschichtlichen Aussagewert von Viten und Wundererzählungen." In *Santi e demoni nell'alto medioevo occidentale*, pp. 285-311.

Ray, Roger D. "Medieval Historiography Through the Twelfth Century: Problems and Progress of Research." *Viator* 5 (1974): 33-59.

———. "Bede, the Exegete, as Historian." In *Famulus Christi*, pp. 125-140.

———. "Bede's *vera lex historiae*." *Speculum* 55 (1980): 1-21.

———. "What Do We Know About Bede's Commentaries?" *Recherches de théologie ancienne et médiévale* 49 (1982): 5-20.

———. "Augustine's *De Consensu Evangelistarum* and the Historical Education of the Venerable Bede." *Studia Patristica* 16.2 (1985): 557-563.

———. "The Triumph of Greco-Roman Rhetorical Assumptions in Pre-Carolingian Historiography." In *The Inheritance of Historiography, 350-900*. Ed. Christopher Holdsworth and T.P. Wiseman, pp. 67-84. Exeter Studies in History 12. Exeter: University of Exeter, 1986.

———. "Bede and Cicero." *Anglo-Saxon England* 16 (1987): 1-15.

Rector, Hampton Joel. "The Influence of St. Augustine's Philosophy of History on the Venerable Bede in the *Ecclesiastical History of the English People*." Ph.D. dissertation, Duke University, 1975.

Riché, Pierre. *Education and Culture in the Barbarian West: Sixth Through Eighth Centuries*. Trans. John J. Contreni. Columbia SC: University of South Carolina Press 1976.

Richter, Michael. "Bede's *Angli*: Angles or English?" *Peritia* 3 (1984): 99-114.

———. "Practical Aspects of the Conversion of the Anglo-Saxons." In *Irland und die Christenheit, Ireland and Christendom*, pp. 362-376.

Ridyard, Susan J. *The Royal Saints of Anglo-Saxon England: A Study of West Saxon and East Anglian Cults*. Cambridge Studies in Medieval Life and Thought, fourth series 9. Cambridge: Cambridge University Press, 1988.

Rollason, David W. "Why Was St Cuthbert So Popular?" In *Cuthbert: Saint and Patron*, pp. 9-22.

———. *Saints and Relics in Anglo-Saxon England*. Oxford: Basil Blackwell Ltd., 1989.

Rosenthal, Joel T. "Bede's Use of Miracles in 'The Ecclesiastical History.'" *Traditio* 31 (1975): 328-335.

———. "Bede's Ecclesiastical History and the Material Conditions of Anglo-Saxon Life." *Journal of British Studies* 19.1 (1979): 1-17.

———. "Bede's *Life of Cuthbert*: Preparatory to *The Ecclesiastical History.*" *Catholic Historical Review* 68 (1982): 599-611.

Rousselle, Aline. *Croire et guérir. La foi en Gaule dans l'Antiquité tardive.* n.p.: Fayard, 1990.

Rubin, Stanley. "St. Cuthbert of Lindisfarne: A Medical Reconstruction." *Transactions of the Architectural and Archaeological Society of Durham and Northumberland* n.s. 4 (1978): 101-103.

Saints, Scholars and Heroes: Studies in Medieval Culture in Honor of Charles W. Jones. Ed. Margot H. King and Wesley M. Stevens. Vol. 1: *The Anglo-Saxon Heritage.* Collegeville, Minn.: Hill Monastic Manuscript Library, Saint John's Abbey and University, 1979.

Saint Wilfrid at Hexham. Ed. D.P. Kirby. Newcastle upon Tyne: Oriel, 1974.

Santi e demoni nell'alto medioevo occidentale (secoli V-XI). Settimane di studio del Centro italiano di studi sull'alto medioevo 36. Spoleto, 1989.

Scharer, Anton. "Gesellschaftliche Zustände im Spiegel des Heiligenlebens: einige Folgerungen aus den Lebensbeschreibungen des heiligen Cuthberht." *Mitteilungen des Instituts für österreichische Geschichtsforschung* 100 (1992): 103-116.

Scheibelreiter, Georg. "Die Verfälschung der Wirklichkeit. Hagiographie und Historizität." In *Fälschungen im Mittelalter* 5:283-319.

Schindel, Ulrich. "Die Quellen von Bedas Figurenlehre." *Classica et Mediaevalia* 29 (1968): 169-186.

Schmale, Franz-Josef. "Fälschungen in der Geschichtsschreibung." In *Fälschungen im Mittelalter* 1:121-132.

Schoebe, Gerhard. "Was gilt im frühen Mittelalter als Geschichtliche Wirklichkeit? Ein Versuch zur 'Kirchengeschichte' des Baeda Venerabilis." In *Festschrift Hermann Aubin zum 80. Geburtstag.* Ed. O. Brunner et al., 2:625-651. Wiesbaden: Franz Steiner Verlag GMBH, 1965.

Schreiner, Klaus. "'*Discrimen veri ac falsi.*' Ansätze und Formen der Kritik in der Heiligen- und Reliquienverehrung des Mittelalters." *Archiv für Kulturgeschichte* 48 (1966): 1-53.

———. "Zum Wahrheitsverständnis im Heiligen- und Reliquienwesen des Mittelalters." *Saeculum* 17 (1966): 131-169.

Simonetti, Manlio. "*De mirabilibus sacrae scripturae.* Un trattato irlandese sui miracoli della Sacra Scrittura." *Romanobarbarica* 4 (1979): 225-251.

——. "La tecnica esegetica di Beda nel *Commento a 1 Samuele.*" *Romanobarbarica* 8 (1984-1985): 75-110.

Sims-Williams, Patrick. *Religion and Literature in Western England: 600-800.* Cambridge Studies in Anglo-Saxon England 4. Cambridge: Cambridge University Press, 1990.

Siniscalco, Paolo. "Le età del mondo in Beda." *Romanobarbarica* 3 (1978): 297-332.

Smalley, Beryl. *Historians in the Middle Ages.* London: Thames and Hudson, 1974.

Smith, Julia M.H. "Oral and Written: Saints, Miracles, and Relics in Brittany, c. 850-1250." *Speculum* 65 (1990): 309-343.

Southern, R.W. "Aspects of the European Tradition of Historical Writing 2: Hugh of St Victor and the Idea of Historical Development." *Transactions of the Royal Historical Society* 5th ser. 21 (1971): 159-179.

Speyer, Wolfgang. *Die literarische Fälschung im heidnischen und christlichen Altertum. Ein Versuch ihrer Deutung.* Handbuch der Altertumswissenschaft 1,2. München: Beck, 1971.

——. "Religiöse Betrüger. Falsche göttliche Menschen und Heilige in Antike und Christentum." In *Fälschungen im Mittelalter* 5:321-343.

Sprandel, Rolf. "Vorwissenschaftliches Naturverstehen und Entstehung von Naturwissenschaften." *Sudhoffs Archiv* 63 (1979): 313-325.

Stacpoole, Alberic. "St Bede the Venerable, Monk of Jarrow." In *Benedict's Disciples*, pp. 86-104.

Stancliffe, Clare. "Cuthbert and the Polarity Between Pastor and Solitary." In *St Cuthbert, His Cult and His Community*, pp. 21-44.

St Cuthbert, His Cult and His Community to AD 1200. Ed. Gerald Bonner, David Rollason and Clare Stancliffe. Woodbridge, Suffolk: The Boydell Press-Boydell and Brewer Ltd., 1989.

Stephens, J.N. "Bede's Ecclesiastical History." *History* 62 (1977): 1-14.

Stevens, Clifford. "Saint Cuthbert: The Early Years." *Cistercian Studies* 23 (1988): 3-13.

——. "Saint Cuthbert: Crisis in Northumbria (II)." *Cistercian Studies* 24 (1989): 280-292.

——. "St Cuthbert: The Lindisfarne Years (III)." *Cistercian Studies* 26 (1991): 25-39.

Stevens, Wesley M. *Bede's Scientific Achievement.* Jarrow Lecture. Jarrow, 1985.

La storiografia altomedievale. Settimane di studio del Centro italiano di studi sull'alto medioevo 17. Spoleto, 1970.

Stranks, C.J. *The Venerable Bede.* London: SPCK, 1955.

——. *The Life and Death of St Cuthbert*. London: SPCK, 1964.

Straw, Carole. *Gregory the Great: Perfection in Imperfection*. Transformation of the Classical Heritage 14. Berkeley: University of California Press 1988.

Strubel, Armand. "«Allegoria in factis» et «Allegoria in verbis»." *Poétique* 23 (1975): 342-357.

Strunz, Franz. "Beda in der Geschichte der Naturbetrachtung und Natur-forschung." *Zeitschrift für deutsche Geistesgeschichte* 1 (1935): 311-321.

Thacker, Alan. "Bede's Ideal of Reform." In *Ideal and Reality in Frankish and Anglo-Saxon Society*, pp. 130-153.

——. "Lindisfarne and the Origins of the Cult of St Cuthbert." In *St Cuthbert, His Cult and His Community*, pp. 103-122.

Theissen, Gerd. *The Miracle Stories of the Early Christian Tradition*. Trans. Francis McDonagh. Ed. John Riches. Philadelphia: Fortress, 1983.

Thomas, Charles. *The Early Christian Archaeology of North Britain*. The Hunter Marshall Lectures delivered at the University of Glasgow in January and February 1968. London: Oxford University Press, 1971.

——. *Bede, Archaeology, and the Cult of Relics*. Jarrow Lecture. Jarrow, 1973.

Tugène, Georges. "L'histoire 'ecclésiastique' du peuple anglais. Réflexions sur le particularisme et l'universalisme chez Bède." *Recherches augustiniennes* 17 (1982): 129-172.

——. "Rois moines et rois pasteurs dans l'*Histoire ecclésiastique* de Bède." *Romanobarbarica* 8 (1984-1985): 111-147.

The Use and Abuse of Eschatology in the Middle Ages. Ed. Werner Verbeke, Daniel Verhelst and Andries Welkenhuysen. Mediaevalia Lovaniensia, Series 1: Studia 15. Leuven: University Press, 1988.

Vaesen, Jos. "Sulpice Sévère et la fin des temps." In *The Use and Abuse of Eschatology*, pp. 49-71.

Van der Walt, A.G.P. "Reflections on the Benedictine Rule in Bede's Homiliary." *Journal of Ecclesiastical History* 37 (1986): 367-376.

Van Uytfanghe, Marc. "L'hagiographie et son public à l'époque mérovingi-enne." *Studia Patristica* 16.2 (1985): 54-62.

——. *Stylisation biblique et condition humaine dans l'hagiographie mérovingi-enne [600-750]*. Verhandelingen van de Koninklijke Academie voor Wetenschappen, Letteren en Schone Kunsten van België, Klasse der Letteren, Jaargang 49, Nr 120. Brussels: Paleis der Academiën, 1987.

——. "Le culte des saints et l'hagiographie face à l'Ecriture: les avatars d'une relation ambiguë." In *Santi e demoni nell'alto medioevo occidentale*, pp. 155-202.

Vaughan, Richard. "The Past in the Middle Ages." *Journal of Medieval History* 12 (1986): 1-14.

Verbraken, Pierre-Patrick. "Le commentaire de Saint Grégoire sur le Premier Livre des Rois." *Revue Bénédictine* 66 (1956): 159-217.

———. "Les Dialogues de saint Grégoire le Grand sont-ils apocryphes? A propos d'un ouvrage récent." *Revue Bénédictine* 98 (1988): 272-277.

Vogüé, Adalbert de. *Grégoire le Grand, Dialogues* 1: *Introduction, bibliographie et cartes.* SC 251. Paris: Editions du Cerf, 1978.

———. "Les plus anciens exégètes du Premier Livre des Rois: Origène, Augustin et leurs épigones." *Sacris Erudiri* 29 (1986): 5-12.

———. "Grégoire le Grand et ses 'Dialogues' d'après deux ouvrages récents." *Revue d'histoire ecclésiastique* 83 (1988): 281-348.

———. "La mort dans les monastères: Jonas de Bobbio et les Dialogues de Grégoire le Grand." In *Mémorial Dom Jean Gribomont (1920-1986),* pp. 593-619. Studia Ephemeridis «Augustinianum» 27. Rome: Institutum Patristicum «Augustinianum», 1988.

———. "'Martyrium in occulto'. Le martyre du temps de paix chez Grégoire le Grand, Isidore de Séville et Valerius du Bierzo." In *Fructus Centesimus. Mélanges offerts à Gerard J. M. Bartelink à l'occasion de son soixante-cinquième anniversaire.* Ed. A.A.R. Bastiaensen, A. Hilhorst and C.H. Kneepkens, pp. 125-140. Instrumenta Patristica 19. Dordrecht: Kluwer, 1989.

———. "Les dialogues, oeuvre authentique et publiée par Grégoire lui-même." In *Gregorio Magno e il suo tempo* 2:27-40.

Wallace-Hadrill, J.M. *Bede's Europe.* Jarrow Lecture. Jarrow, 1962. Also in his *Early Medieval History,* pp. 60-75.

———. "Gregory of Tours and Bede: Their Views on the Personal Qualities of Kings." *Frühmittelalterliche Studien* 2 (1968): 31-44.

———. *Early Medieval History.* Oxford: Basil Blackwell, 1975.

———. "Bede and Plummer." In *Famulus Christi,* pp. 366-385. Also in his *Early Medieval History,* pp. 76-95.

———. *The Frankish Church.* Oxford: Clarendon, 1983.

———. *Bede's Ecclesiastical History of the English People: A Historical Commentary.* Oxford: Clarendon, 1988.

Ward, Benedicta. "Miracles and History: A Reconsideration of the Miracle Stories Used by Bede." In *Famulus Christi,* pp. 70-76.

———. *Miracles and the Medieval Mind: Theory, Record and Event, 1000-1215.* Philadelphia: University of Pennsylvania Press 1982.

———. "Bede and the Conversion of the Anglo-Saxons." *Word and Spirit* 7 (1985): 34-46.

——. "The Spirituality of St Cuthbert." In *St Cuthbert, His Cult and His Community*, pp. 65-76.

——. *The Venerable Bede. Outstanding Christian Thinkers.* Harrisburg PA: Morehouse Publishing, 1990.

——. *Signs and Wonders: Saints, Miracles and Prayers from the Fourth Century to the Fourteenth.* Collected Studies Series. Hampshire: Variorum, 1992.

Waterhouse, Ruth. "'Wæter æddre asprang': How Cuthbert's Miracle Pours Cold Water on Source Study." *Parergon* n.s. 5 (1987): 1-27.

Watson, E.W. "The Age of Bede." In *Bede: His Life, Times, and Writings*, pp. 39-59.

Weber, Hugo. "Der heilige Kirchenlehrer Beda der Ehrwürdige als Exeget." *Theologie und Glaube* 59 (1969): 360-365.

West, Philip J. "Liturgical Style and Structure in Bede's Homily for the Easter Vigil." *American Benedictine Review* 23 (1972): 1-8.

——. "Liturgical Style and Structure in Bede's Christmas Homilies." *American Benedictine Review* 23 (1972): 424-438.

Wetherbee, Winthrop. "Some Implications of Bede's Latin Style." In *Bede and Anglo-Saxon England*, pp. 23-31.

Whitelock, Dorothy. *After Bede.* Jarrow Lecture. Jarrow, 1960.

——. "Bede and His Teachers and Friends." In *Famulus Christi*, pp. 19-39.

Whiting, C.E. "The Life of the Venerable Bede." In *Bede: His Life, Times, and Writings*, pp. 1-38.

Wieland, Gernot. "*Geminus stilus*: Studies in Anglo-Latin Hagiography." In *Insular Latin Studies*, pp. 113-133.

Wildhaber, Robert. "Beda Venerabilis and the Snakes." In *Folklore Today: A Festschrift for Richard M. Dorson.* Ed. Linda Dégh, Henry Glassie and Felix J. Oinas. Bloomington: The Research Center for Language and Semiotic Studies, Indiana University, 1976. 497-506.

Willmes, Ansgar. "Bedas Bibelauslegung." *Archiv für Kulturgeschichte* 44 (1963): 281-314.

Wilson, David M. "The Art and Archaeology of Bedan Northumbria." In *Bede and Anglo-Saxon England*, pp. 1-22.

Winstead, Karen A. "The Transformation of the Miracle Story in the *Libri Historiarum* of Gregory of Tours." *Medium Aevum* 59 (1990): 1-15.

Wolpers, Theodor. *Die englische Heiligenlegende des Mittelalters: Eine Formgeschichte des Legendenerzählens von der spätantiken lateinischen Tradition bis zur Mitte des 16. Jahrhunderts.* Tübingen: Max Niemeyer Verlag, 1964.

Wood, Ian N. "Pagans and Holy Men, 600-800." In *Irland und die Christenheit, Ireland and Christendom*, pp. 347-361.

——. "Forgery in Merovingian Hagiography." In *Fälschungen im Mittelalter* 5:369-384.

Woolf, Rosemary. "Saints' Lives." In *Continuations and Beginnings: Studies in Old English Literature*. Ed. Eric Gerald Stanley, pp. 37-66. London: Nelson, 1966.

Wormald, Patrick. "Bede and Benedict Biscop." In *Famulus Christi*. London, 1976. 141-169.

——. "Bede, 'Beowulf' and the Conversion of the Anglo-Saxon Aristocracy." In *Bede and Anglo-Saxon England*, pp. 32-95.

——. "Bede, the Bretwaldas and the Origins of the Gens Anglorum." In *Ideal and Reality in Frankish and Anglo-Saxon Society*, pp. 99-129.

Wright, Neil. "Bede and Vergil." *Romanobarbarica* 6 (1981): 361-379.

Zaleski, Carol. *Otherworld Journeys: Accounts of Near-Death Experience in Medieval and Modern Times*. New York: Oxford University Press, 1987.

Zwick, Jochen. "Zur Form und Funktion übernatürlicher Kommunikationsweisen in der Frankengeschichte des Gregor von Tours." *Mediaevistik* 1 (1988): 193-206.

Index of Citations
Scriptural, Ancient, Patristic and Medieval Texts

ADOMNAN:
Vita S. Columbae:

2a Praef.	158
1.1	25
2.3	173
2.9	151
2.17	136
2.33	25
2.34	136, 151
2.42	151
2.45	151
3.5	45
3.16	169, 171
3.23	151

AMBROSE:
Explanatio Psalmorum:

36,77.2	66
45,9.4	66

Expositio Evangelii secundum Lucam:

7.176	66
8.28-29	66

APOCRYPHA, NEW TESTAMENT:
Apocalypse of Paul: 182, 186, 188
Apocalypse of Peter: 186, 189

APOCRYPHA, OLD TESTAMENT:
1 Enoch:

14:10-13	182

2 Enoch:

10:1-3	182

Apocalypse of Zephaniah: 189
Testament of Abraham: 189

AUGUSTINE:
Contra mendacium:

10.24	223
12.26	224

De civitate Dei:

15.27	62
16.19	224
16.28	55
20.19	139
22.30	94

De consensu Evangelistarum:

1.7.10	215
2.1.2-3	221
2.12.27-28	218
2.12.29	219
2.28.67	216
2.39.86	216
2.49.97	216
2.50.105	220
2.62.121	217
2.62.122	217
2.66.128	216, 217
3.13.43	218
3.13.48	218

De doctrina christiana:

3.29.40	13

De Genesi ad litteram:

9.17	20

De mendacio: 225

5.9	224

Enarrationes in Psalmos:

45.6	68

Epistulae:

199.6.17	93

Quaestiones Evangeliorum:

1.29	68
2.39.1, 2-4	68

Quaestiones in Heptateuchum:
 1.4   62
Sermones:
 89.2 68

AUGUSTINUS HIBERNICUS:
De mirabilibus Sacrae Scripturae:
 1.4-9 62
 1.7   62

BEDE:
Aliquot quaestionum liber:
 3   63
Chronica Maiora (De temp. ratione 66-71):
 66.1-8 94
 66.379 70
 66.383 17
 66.389 17
 66.491 30, 113
 67.594-597 97
 68.598 94
 69.600 95
 69.600-603 95
 69.602 137
Chronica Minora (De temporibus 17-22):
 22   103
De arte metrica:
 3   12
 14   12
 24   14
De die iudicii: 90, 183
De natura rerum:
 1   20
 24   29
 28-29 27
 37   28
 39   62
De schematibus et tropis:
 1   13
 2   57

De tabernaculo:
 1   57, 96, 126, 133
 2   57
De templo:
 1   22, 58, 96, 132
 2   101, 132
De temporibus:
 4   120
 6   120
 16   94, 96
De temporum ratione:
 8   120
 10   94
 12   120
 15   120, 121
 27   61
Epistola ad Ecgbertum:
 4   99
 10   100
 11   100
Epistola ad Pleguinam:
 14-15 97
Explanatio Apocalypsis:
 2.9   112
 2.11   138
 2.13   137, 138
 3.16   137
Expositio Actuum Apostolorum:
 Praef. 229
 1.13   200
 2.6   60
 2.19   24
 7.16   212, 227, 228
 10.36-37 105
 13.19-21 226
 17.28 21
 19.13   135
 20.9   106, 109
Expositio in Cant. Abacuc: 56, 105, 106, 111

Historia abbatum:
1.1   7
1.8   51
1.13   26
2.14   52
2.15   53
Historia ecclesiastica:
Praef.   72, 74, 102, 145, 162, 163, 203, 208, 211
1.1   46, 47
1.7   75, 113
1.8   163
1.10   163
1.14   29
1.15   29
1.17   26, 133, 136
1.18   113
1.19   33
1.20   30
1.21   113
1.22   163
1.26   115
1.30   120
1.31   114, 131
1.32   90
1.33   150
2.1   6, 45, 114, 128, 147, 209, 210
2.6   44, 115
2.7   34, 177
2.10   120
2.13   120, 195
2.14   116
2.15   118
2.16   75
3.2   47, 76
3.3   130
3.4   172
3.6   149
3.8   149

3.9   47, 76, 148
3.13   47
3.15   70, 130, 150
3.16   34
3.17   47, 151, 205
3.18   132
3.19   22, 49
3.22   116
3.23   37
3.25   134
3.26   101
3.27   28, 70, 117
3.30   117
4.2   10
4.3   25, 47, 71, 75, 147
4.6   76, 153
4.10   35, 153
4.12   29
4.13   36, 116
4.19   80, 149
4.20   46, 50
4.22   44, 143, 144, 176
4.23   26
4.25   31, 204
4.26   30, 101
4.27   117
4.28   42
4.30   150, 153
4.31   22
4.32   179
5.1   38, 148
5.2   40, 70
5.4   168
5.6   37, 41
5.12   129, 143, 144, 179, 180, 186, 187
5.13   49, 143, 187
5.14   143, 189, 191, 194
5.15   171, 172
5.16-17   172
5.18   47, 153

Historia ecclesiastica (cont.):
5.23   29, 102, 103
5.24   1, 3, 10, 28, 88,
        125, 206
Homeliarum Evangelii libri duo:
1.2   181
1.7   126
1.8   105
1.9   125
1.14   24, 105, 108
1.15   132, 146
1.17   222
1.20   212
1.23   21, 26
1.24   91
2.2   58, 108
2.6   108
2.8   84
2.11   86, 112
2.22   126
Hymnus de opere sex dierum: 94
In Cantica Canticorum:
2   16, 86, 106
3   57, 108, 132
4   22, 106
5   17, 112, 132
6   6, 81, 82, 86, 105,
        106, 132, 146
In epistolas septem catholicas:
  In epist. I Pet.:
  4.7   93
  In epist. II Pet.:
  3.3-4   96
  In epist. I Ioh.:
  1.2   106
  2.18   93
  3.24   84
  4.3   95
  In epist. Judae:
  6   92

In Ezram et Neemiam:
1   16, 109
2   16, 17, 26, 56, 92,
        101, 133
3   16, 101, 108, 112,
        132
In librum Tobias: 105
In Lucae Evangelium:
Prol.   163
1   24, 84, 133, 211,
        220, 221
2   22, 23, 58, 106,
        108, 109, 229
3   55, 81, 87, 91, 106,
        108, 109, 121, 125,
        131, 132, 134, 135,
        212
4   15, 83, 84, 92, 110,
        126, 183
5   94, 96, 98, 108, 111
6   58, 91, 111, 226
In Marci Evangelium:
Prol.   163
1   22, 23, 26, 56, 57,
        81, 105, 106, 107,
        111, 131, 132, 146
2   22, 23, 24, 54, 55,
        60, 91, 107, 108,
        109, 112, 121, 133,
        222
3   65, 69, 70, 87, 108,
        134
4   57, 84, 91, 105,
        122, 133, 137
In natali SS. Petri et Pauli: 63
In primam partem Samuhelis:
1   16, 105
2 Praef. 229
2   17, 18, 24, 37,
        55, 57

3   57, 223, 224, 226
4   98, 136, 137, 223
In Proverbia Salomonis:
1   106, 223
2   16, 56, 133, 226
3   21, 57, 58
In Reg. Quaestiones:
1   95
25   21
Libri IV in principium Genesis:
Praef.   2
1   20, 21, 99
2   16, 62, 99
3   15, 24, 37, 212, 224
4   24, 25, 55, 57, 60,
         61
Martyrologium: 45, 46, 112, 113,
         150
Retractatio in Actus Apostolorum:
1.13   3, 200
2.6   60
2.19   24
13.19   212
13.19-21   227
13.21   212
Vita Felicis: 142, 153
Vita S. Cuthberti (metrica):
Epist. ad Johannem 76, 155
8   146
18   141
44   76
Vita S. Cuthberti (prosaica):
Prol.   73, 156, 199, 200
1   79, 159
2   32, 78
3   38, 70, 115, 117
5   39, 79, 159
9   117
10   79, 129, 169, 170
11   79, 160, 179

14   33, 35, 79
18   79
19   79, 115, 174
20   79, 141
21   141, 148, 173
22   127
23   152, 153
25   159
26   146
29   79, 167
30   159, 161
31   159
35   79, 159
36   70
37   152
38   79, 159
42   153
43   76
45   42
46   199

BIBLE:
Genesis:
3   48
7:20   16
8:1   62
12:10-20   224
18:1-15   60
18:11   55
23   227
Exodus:
25:32   125
32:32-33   189
Numbers:
12:10   26
1 Samuel:
12:16-18   24, 55
14:24ff   17
21:1-3   224
27:10   223

1 Kings:
5:16	58
17:6	40

2 Chronicles:
2:2, 18	58
18	225

Ezra:
4:14-15	16
10:9	25

Nehemiah:
13:23-24	16

Tobias:
11	32, 78

Job:
24:19	183

Psalms:
45(46):2-3	67
68(69):29	189
83(84)	195, 196
83(84):3	36
103(104):15	15
106(107):25	62
118(119):85-86	18
134(135):6	218
147:12	57

Proverbs:
15:2	16
15:17	133
16:10	225

Canticle of Canticles:
5:14	22
6:6	86
8:9	17

Isaiah:
2:2	67, 68
43:2	35

Jeremiah:
51:25	67

Daniel:
12:1	189

Zacharias:
4:7	66

2 Machabees:
11:6-8	78

Matthew:
3:7-12	217
7:21-23	134
8:1-3	106
8:12	183
12:22	82
12:38-45	216
13:31-32	66
13:42	183
13:50	183
17:9	170
17:19	66, 67
17:19-20	65, 66, 68
19:1-12	217
20:1-16	92
21:21	66, 67, 68, 69
22:13	183
24:12	98
24:36	96
24:51	183
25:30	183
28:20	80

Mark:
1:7-8	217
1:27	111
1:30-31	22
1:40-42	23
1:43-45	107
2:3-12	23, 26, 105
2:22	56
3:11-12	106
3:14-15	81
4:30-32	66
5:21-43	107
5:43	55
6:5-6	133

6:26-27	222		10:20	189
6:30-43	108		11:14	82
6:37	55		11:15-16	110
6:45-52	54		11:16-36	216
7	108		11:29	110
7:24	107		12:35-36	97
7:31-37	107		12:40	91
7:32-37	41		13:18-19	66
8	108		13:28	183
8:22-26	23, 107		13:32	84
8:30	106		14:15-24	92
8:39(9:1)	91		15:16-17	15
10:1-12	217		17:5-6	68
11:22-23	65, 69		17:6	66
11:23	67		17:7-10	68
13:30	91		21:32	91
13:32	96		22:44	24
16:17-18	83		*John*:	
Luke:			1:1	34
1:36-37	24		1:45	221
2:33-34	211, 220, 222,		2:1-11	105
	226, 228		5:8-9	22
2:48	222		5:17	21
2:48-49	221		6:1-14	108
3:7-17	217		9:3	26
4:35	106		11:4	26
4:38-39	22		16:13	85
5:12-13	23		21:25	65
5:17-26	23		*Acts*:	
5:18-26	26		1:7	94, 96
7:1-10	229		1:13	199, 200
7:11ff	106		2:19	24
8:55	55		3:2-8	41
9:1-2	80		3:10	56, 111
9:10-17	108		4:4	111
9:13	5		7	227
9:27	91		9:36-41	109
9:49-50	134		12:7	176
10:17-18	132		13	226
10:17-20	131		19:13-17	135
			20:7-12	106, 109

Romans:
10:2   130
1 Corinthians:
10:11   92
13:2   66
14:22   81
2 Corinthians:
11:25   62, 64
12:7   26
Galatians:
4:22-23   24
Ephesians:
6:16   35
Philippians:
4:3   189
2 Thessalonians:
2:2   94
2:9   138
1 Peter:
4:7   93
2 Peter:
2:16   79
3:8   97
1 John:
1:10   224
2:18   92
4:3   95
Revelation:
3:5   189
13:1-2   137
13:8   189
13:17-18   137
17:8   189
20:12   189
20:13   59
20:15   189
21:27   189

BONIFACE:
Epistolae:
10   183

CONSTANTIUS OF LYONS:
Vita S. Germani:
3.12-13   136
3.13   26
3.17   30

CUTHBERT:
Epistola de obitu Bedae: 1

EDDIUS STEPHANUS:
Vita S. Wilfrithi:
Praef.   156
37   169
66   151
67   25

EUGIPPIUS:
Excerpta ex operibus S. Augustini:
181   225

EUSEBIUS:
Commentaria in Psalmos:
45.4   66
Historia ecclesiastica:
5.28   45

FELIX:
Vita S. Guthlaci:
Prol.   156
46   134
51   151
53   151

GREGORY OF NYSSA:
Com. in Canticum Canticorum:
5   66

GREGORY OF TOURS:
Historia Francorum:
9.6   134
10.25   134

Liber vitae patrum:
3 Prol.   69

GREGORY THE GREAT:
Dialogues:
1 Prol. 4   45
1 Prol. 5   124
1 Prol. 9   146
1 Prol. 10   50, 156, 162
1.4.3-6   134
1.6   177
1.7   157
1.7.3   70
1.12.1-3   184
1.12.4-5   64
2 Prol. 1   7
2.11.3   179
2.31   144, 176
2.35.3-4   53
3.10   174
3.33.7-9   155
4.32   184
4.32.5   188
4.37.4   187
4.37.5-6   184, 192
4.37.7-16   184
4.37.14   193
4.40   188, 190
4.40.1   188
4.40.2-5   191
4.40.9   188
4.40.10-12   191
4.40.12   188
4.41   143
4.42   143
4.43.2   89
4.57.2   143
4.57.8   179
4.57.8-16   191
4.59   45, 176
4.59.1   144
4.59.6   143

Homiliae in Evangelia:
1.4.3   81, 131
1.13.5-6   92
2.23.1   226
2.29.4   84, 105, 133
2.32.5   121
2.32.6   91
2.36.2   92
2.37.8   144
Homiliae in Hiezechihelem:
2.2.9   125
2.3.23   81, 106, 146
2.4.8   86
In librum primum Regum:
5.84-85   18
Moralia in Iob:
27.11.21   114
32.15.24   138
33.35.59   95
34.3.7   138
Registrum epistularum:
1.41   124
3.29   98
3.50   157
11.36   114, 131
11.37   90

HILARY OF POITIERS:
In Matthaeum:
17.7   69
17.8   68
21.6-7   69

ISIDORE OF SEVILLE:
Etymologiae:
14.6.3   47
14.6.6   47

JEROME:
Adversus Helvidium:
4   221

De viris illustribus:
71   17
Epistulae:
22.30   18, 45
In Hiezechielem:
13   66
In Matheum:
2   66, 83, 133, 222
3   65, 66, 67
4   61
In Zachariam:
1   66
Vita S. Hilarionis:
29.5-6 69

JOHN CASSIAN:
Collationes:
17.19   225

JOHN CHRYSOSTOM:
Homiliae in Epist. I ad Corinthios:
32.4   65
Homiliae in Epist. II ad Corinthios:
25.1   64
Homiliae in Matthaeum:
57(58).3   65

JOSEPHUS:
Jewish Antiquities:
1.11.4(203) 60

ORIGEN:
Commentaria in Matthaeum:
13.7   66
Homiliae in Ieremiam:
12.12   66

OROSIUS:
*Historiarum adversum paganos
libri VII*:
7.3   31
7.39   31

PLUTARCH:
Moralia:
567C-D   182

PSEUDO-AUGUSTINE:
Sermo 203.3   63

PSEUDO-DIONYSIUS:
De divinis nominibus:
2.9   24

PSEUDO-ISIDORE:
De ordine creaturarum:
9.4-7   62

REGINALD OF DURHAM:
*Libellus de admirandis Beati Cuth-
berti virtutibus*:
76   155

SOLINUS:
Collectanea:
22.4(6)   47
22.8(10)   47

SULPICIUS SEVERUS:
Dialogi:
2.14   95
Epistulae:
1.6   63
Vita S. Martini:
1.9   156

VITA CEOLFRIDI ABBATIS:
14   1
19   52
40   53

**VITA S. CUTHBERTI AUCTORE
ANONYMO:**
1.2   156
1.4   33

1.6	39, 79	4.4	161
1.7	158	4.17	42
2.3	79, 169	4.18	79, 158, 159
2.4	79		
2.7	33	**WILLIBALD:**	
3.3	79	*Vita S. Bonifatii:*	
3.4	142, 173	6	118
3.5	141	9	151
4.3	79, 167		

General Index

Aaron 26

Abgar, king of Edessa 200

Abraham 24, 55, 60, 92, 94, 224, 227; vision of 189n

Abraham, Lenore 127n, 140n, 160n

Acca, bishop of Hexham 2n

Achish, king of Gath 223

Adam 94

Adomnan, abbot of Iona 136, 151, 158, 169-176, 201, 213, 232

Aebbe, abbess 169

Aebbe, abbess of Coldingham 169-170

Aelfwald, king of East Anglia 157n

Aelle, king of Deira 209

Aethelbald, king of Mercia 157n

Aethelbert, king of Kent 90, 115

Aethelburh, abbess of Brie 149

Aethelfrith, king of Northumbria 119

Aethelthryth, queen, wife of Ecgfrith 46n, 50, 80, 149

Aethilwald, hermit of Farne. *See* Oethelwald

Aethilwald, prior and abbot of Melrose, bishop of Lindisfarne 159, 161-162, 186

Ahab, king of Israel 226

Aidan, bishop of Lindisfarne 33-34, 70n, 126, 130, 149-151, 205-206

Alaric, king of the Visigoths 31

Alban, Saint 75, 113

Albinus, abbot of St Peter and St Paul's, Canterbury 163-164, 179n

Aldfrith, king of Northumbria 167, 172, 186

Alleluia victory 29-30

Amalekites 223

Amat, Jacqueline 18n

Ambleteuse 150

Ambrose, Saint 2, 4, 66, 68, 162

Amos, Thomas L. 100n

analogy 34-36

Anatholia, virgin and martyr 112n

Ancona 177, 179n

Anderson, Carol Susan 62n

Anderson, Judith H. 200

angels 60-61, 78, 187-189, 216

Angenendt, Arnold 150n

Angles 119

Angli 209-210

Anglo-Saxons 100n, 101, 103-104, 121-122, 202, 204; conversion of 6, 113-119, 163, 210-211, 231; paganism of 119-121; sense of the past 77

Anthony, Saint 79n, 175

Antichrist 93, 95-96; miracles of 136-139

Antioch of Pisidia 226

Antioch, school of 57

Apocalypse of Paul 182, 186n, 188

Apocalypse of Peter 186

Apocalypse of Zephaniah 188

apostles 106, 181n, 215-216; miracles of 22, 81, 83-84, 106, 133

Archambault, Paul 94n
Ark, of Noah 61-62
Aubrun, Michel 181n
Augustine, archbishop of Canterbury 113, 114n, 115, 126, 131, 165, 209
Augustine, Saint, bishop of Hippo x, 2, 19-20, 61, 67-68, 79n, 93, 96, 107n, 110, 112, 136, 139, 162, 230; attitude toward secular culture 18-19; concept of history 93-94; influence on Bede 4-5, 214, 220-221, 223-225; knowledge of classical literature 12
——, teachings on: the interpretation of Scripture 56, 58, 215-220; the seminal reasons 20; the six ages of the world 93-94; truth and falsity 166-167, 223-225, 232
——, writings: Contra Faustum 5n; De consensu Evangelistarum 214-220; De doctrina christiana 5n; De Genesi ad litteram 20
Augustinus Hibernicus 62n

Babylon 15n, 94
Baduthegn, monk of Lindisfarne 22
Balaam 79
Baldhelm, priest of Lindisfarne 159
Bamburgh 33
Barking, nuns of 35, 153n
Barnard, L.W. 201
Basil of Caesarea 2n
Basilius, pseudo-monk 134
Bede, the Venerable: analogical imagination 34-36; ascetic instincts 129; attitude toward secular culture 14-19, 230;

biases 201-202; biblical foundation of his work 88-89, 206-207; claims of truthfulness 73, 155-156, 199, 205-208, 211, 232; concept of history 30-32, 76-78, 93-94, 145, 203-207, 214; critique of contemporary society 99-101; distinctions among his writings 51-54, 87-88; education of 9-14, 230; healing of, by St Cuthbert 154-155; influence of 3n; influenced by Irish spirituality 129-130; knowledge of classical texts 11-14, 230; knowledge of Greek 9-10; knowledge of rhetoric 12n, 212, 228; knowledge of the Vita Columbae 172-175; library of 2, 11, 21, 230; monastic predilections of 125-128; respect for the Fathers 3-5; role in controversies of the day 202; scientific interests 19-21, 230; scriptural scholarship 3-4, 6-7; veneration of Gregory the Great xiv, 5-7. See also Augustine, Saint, bishop of Hippo; Gregory the Great; Jerome, Saint; Dialogues
——, teachings on: the benefit of masses 143-144, 177; the examples of the saints 132-133; the interpretation of Scripture 56-59, 107-109; the paternity of St Joseph 220-222; pseudo-prophets 134-135; the six ages of the world 93-94, 96-97, 99n; the spiritual life 124-128; truth and falsity 223-228, 232-233

——, writings: *De arte metrica* 12, 14; *De locis sanctis* 172; *De orthographia* 14n; *De schematibus et tropis* 12-13, 14n; *De tabernaculo* 4; *De templo* 4, 58-59; *Explanatio Apocalypsis* 59; *Expositio Actuum Apostolorum* 10, 59; *Historia abbatum* 7, 51-54, 87-88; *In Cantica Canticorum* 81-82; *In epistulas Pauli Apostoli* 5n; *In Lucae Evangelium* 98; *In primam partem Samuhelis* 59n, 98; *In principium Genesis* 98; *Retractatio in Actus Apostolorum* 10, 59; *Vita Anastasii* 10n, 88; *Vita Felicis* 88. See also *Historia ecclesiastica*; *Vita Cuthberti*

Bedesfeld 161
Benedict Biscop 1, 2, 7, 9, 26n, 52, 88, 206
Benedict of Nursia xi, 7, 51, 53, 79n, 140, 141n, 176, 179, 193
Beowulf 123
Berhthun, abbot of Beverley 70, 168-169
Berlin, Gail Ivy xiiin, 71n
Bernicia 143n, 190, 194
Berschin, Walter 50n, 158, 163n
Beta, priest 167
Bethsaida 23
Bieler, Ludwig 172n
Bischoff, Bernhard 58n
Black, Jonathan 59n
Boglioni, Pierre ix
Bolton, W.F. ix, 10n, 45n, 88n
Boniface v, pope 120n
Boniface, Saint 118, 183-184
Bonner, Gerald 11, 14n, 59n, 89n, 127n, 195n, 205

Bothelm, monk of Hexham 76n
Boulogne 150
Britain 46-48, 113, 136
Britons 29-30, 103, 163n, 201
Brooks, Nicholas P. 197n
Brown, Elizabeth A.R. 197n
Brown, George Hardin 14n, 103n, 155, 212n
Brown, Peter 132n
Bullough, Donald A. 171, 172n
Burrow, J.A. 94n

Caesarius, deacon and martyr 113n
Caiaphas 189, 191
Campbell, James 123n, 152n, 198n, 205
Cana, miracle at 24n, 79n, 105, 107-108
Canterbury 33-34, 44, 150, 163, 177, 179n; school of 10n, 57-58
Capelle, D. Bernard 14n, 181n
Carozzi, Claude 181n
Carroll, M. Thomas Aquinas 128n, 140n, 152n, 199n
Cassiodorus 11
Cedd, bishop of Essex 37, 71, 164
Ceolfrith, abbot of Wearmouth and Jarrow 1-2, 52-54, 88, 172
Ceolwulf, king of Northumbria 50n, 101, 102n, 129-130, 162
Chad, bishop of York and Lichfield 25, 28n, 71, 75, 76n, 126, 147-148, 164
Chadwick, Nora K. 201n
Chaldaeans 18
chance 36-37
Charles Martel 29n
Christ, Jesus 22, 215-217, 219, 221-222, 226-227, 229; calms the storm 60, 112; changes

Christ, Jesus (*cont.*) water into wine 24n, 79n, 105, 107-108; cleanses the temple 64, 66; commissions the apostles 80-81, 83; curses the fig tree 64, 66, 69; divinity of 105, 110, 112; expels demons 65, 82, 106, 111; feeds the multitude 55, 108, 112, 216, 219-220; heals the blind 23, 108; heals a deaf mute 107n, 108; heals a leper 22-23, 106; heals a paralytic 23, 26, 105; heals Peter's mother-in-law 22-23, 79n, 167-169; incarnation of 93-94, 110; passion of 61, 92, 105-107, 110, 218; raises the dead 55, 106n, 107n, 108-109; resurrection of 84n, 110; second coming of 91-92, 94-97; sermon on the mount 106; temptation of 135; transfiguration of 91, 110, 170; virgin birth of 24n, 208, 211, 220-221; walks on water 24n, 54, 112
Christmas 121
chronology 19, 77, 120
Chrysaurius, a rich man 188n
Ciccarese, Maria Pia 181n, 183n, 184n, 185-186, 187n, 189
Cicero, *De inventione* 12n, 228
Clark, Francis x-xiii
Clement I, pope 113n
Clovesho, Council of 118
Coifi, pagan priest 119
Coldingham, monastery 31, 169-170, 204
Coleman, Janet 166n, 228n
Colgrave, Bertram xiiin, 1, 29n, 30n, 32, 44, 72n, 74n, 76n, 79n, 85n, 87, 118n, 157n,

158n, 159n, 160, 161n, 167-168, 170n, 179n, 184n, 210n; and R.A.B. Mynors 102n, 118n, 172n, 179n
Colman, bishop of Lindisfarne 28n, 101n, 134n
Columba, Saint 45n, 134n, 136, 170-175
comets 28n-29n, 101
Constantinople 9, 192
Constantius of Lyons 136, 163
Corbett, John 195n
cosmology 19
Cosmos, Spencer 208n
Cowdrey, H.E.J. 204n
Cracco Ruggini, Lellia 114n
Creation 20, 47-48; six days of 94, 97, 99n
Creider, Laurence Stearns xiiin, 28n, 54n, 59n, 85n, 89n, 108n, 112n, 115n, 116, 134n, 138n, 140n, 197, 199n, 210n, 212n, 228n
Cremascoli, Giuseppe xin
Crépin, Andre 121n
Cusack, Pearse Aidan xiin
Cuthbert, abbot of Wearmouth and Jarrow 1
Cuthbert, Saint 51n, 70, 79n, 117, 126-127, 140, 146, 152n, 153n, 165, 179, 193, 195, 198, 207; calms a storm 38, 115-117; changes water into wine 79n; chastised as a boy 78-79; divinely fed 38-40, 79n; healed by an angel 32-33, 78; heals paralyzed monk 42; heals the wife of a *gesith* 79n, 167-168; heals a young woman 161-162; ministered to by otters 169-170, 172; performs

miracles at his tomb 22, 165n;
performs miracles through his
relics 42-43, 76, 154-155;
penitential discipline of 129,
169; preserved from bodily
corruption 150; provided with
bountiful harvest 42n, 174-
175; provided with timber by
the tide 141n, 148, 173-174;
rebukes and pardons raven
140-141, 175; saves house
from fire 33
Cyneberht, bishop of Lindsey 163,
207
Cynemund, priest and monk of
Jarrow 70n
Cynemund, priest and monk of
Lindisfarne 70
Cyprian of Carthage 2

Dagens, Claude 124n, 146n
Dall'Olmo, Umberto 28n
Daniel 18, 170
Daniel, bishop of Winchester 163
Dante 4n
David 94, 221, 223-224, 226
Davidse, Jan 77, 78n, 89n, 102n,
103n, 121n
Davis, R.H.C. 204n
Deira 209
demons 26n, 65-66, 83-84, 106,
135-136, 187, 189
Deorulf, Germanic chief 118
Desert Fathers 129
Desiderius, spiritual imposter 134
Dettic, Germanic chief 118
dialectic 16
Dialogues, of Gregory the Great:
ix-x, 32, 50, 54, 64, 75, 86,
88-89, 130, 146-147, 152,
157, 160, 162, 165-166; au-

thenticity of x-xiii; influence of
7n, 185; influence on Bede 7,
45, 53n, 79n, 178-179, 186-
188, 190-194, 212-213, 230,
232; pedagogical purpose of
139-140, 145
Diesner, Hans-Joachim 118n
Dionisotti, Anna Carlotta 10, 14n
Doeg the Edomite 226
Donatus 13n
Dryhthelm 129, 180, 186-187;
vision of 142-143, 144n, 179-
188, 193
Dubois, Jacques, and Geneviève
Renaud 46n
Dudden, Frederick Homes ix

Eadbald, king of Kent 44, 115n
Eadburga, abbess of Thanet 183
Eadfrith, bishop of Lindisfarne 199
East Anglia 131-132, 157n
Easter 120, 149; disputes concern-
ing 101n, 103, 130, 134n,
151, 205
Eastorwine, abbot of Wearmouth
51-52
Ecgfrith, king of Northumbria 29-
30, 44, 80, 101, 126, 149,
168, 176
Ecgric, king of East Anglia 131-
132
Echlin, Edward P. 125n
Eckenrode, Thomas R. 5n, 19n,
27n, 62n
eclipses 28, 61
Eddius Stephanus, Life of Wilfrid
151, 156, 159n, 168-169,
202
Edessa 200
Edwin, king of Northumbria 116,
119, 120n, 165, 195n

Egbert, archbishop of York 99, 102, 122, 126
Egbert, monk 29n, 30, 71
Egyptians 18, 61
Elafius, British chief 113n
Eleutherius, abbot of St Mark's at Spoleto 154
Elijah 40, 95-96
Elliott, Alison Goddard 196n
Engelbert, Pius xin, xii
Enoch 95-96, 182
Eorcenberht, king of Kent 28n
Eorcenwald, bishop of London 76, 153n
Eostre, pagan goddess 120
Ephron the Hittite 227
Equitius, abbot 134
eschatology, in Scripture 90-91
Esi, abbot 163
Essex 37, 164; conversion of 116-117
Eugippius 5n, 225
Eusebius 200, 205
Eutropius 163
Eutychus, revived by St Paul 106n, 109n
Evangelists, the four 215-220
Evans, G.R. 124n
Evilasius, martyr 112n
exempla 145-146, 231
exorcism, sacrament of 83

Famulus Christi 154
Fanning, Steven 205n
Farne Island 37, 127, 140, 148, 174, 198
fasting 40
Fausta, virgin and martyr 112n
Felgild, hermit of Farne 198
Felix of Nola, Saint 142, 153n

Felix, *Vita Guthlaci* 134n, 156, 157n
Findchan, layman 173-174, 175n
Flint, Valerie I.J. 118n, 144n
Flood 16n, 62n, 94
Florus 46n
Folcard, *Life of John of Beverley* 42n
Foot, Sarah 100n
Franklin, Carmela Vircillo 10n
Fransen, Paul-Irénée 5n, 225n
Fry, Donald K. 35n, 195n-196n, 198
Fuhrmann, Manfred 46n
Fursa 22, 49n, 88

Galilee, sea of 60
Garden of Eden 47-48
Gaul 29n, 101, 136, 150
genre, in medieval texts 51, 87-88
Gentiles 56, 67-68
Germanus, bishop of Auxerre 26n, 29-30, 33, 113, 133n, 136
Germanus, bishop of Capua 53
Geshurites 223
Gewalt, Dietfried 41n
Gildas 163, 204
Gillet, Robert xin
Girzites 223
Gneuss, Helmut 12n
Godding, Robert xin
Goffart, Walter 27n, 88, 93n, 103n, 140n, 159n, 201-202
Grafton, Anthony 197n
grammar 9, 11-13
Gransden, Antonia 31n
Graus, Frantisek 197n
Greek, language 9-10
Grégoire, Réginald 196n
Gregory Nazianzen 2, 60n

Gregory of Tours 27, 28n, 31n, 34, 48, 87n, 93n, 119, 134, 154

Gregory Thaumaturgus 69-70, 87

Gregory the Great ix-xiv, 2-3, 9, 19-20, 25, 27, 32, 34-35, 45, 50-51, 61, 64, 80, 85-86, 91-92, 95, 97-99, 103, 110, 112-113, 114n, 116, 121-125, 127-134, 136, 139-140, 145-147, 151-152, 162, 174n, 176, 181n, 184-186, 197, 205n, 208-210, 230-231; appeals to witnesses 156-157, 160, 165-166; attitude toward secular culture 14, 18-19; claims of truthfulness 155-156, 232; concept of history 78; healed of an intestinal disorder 154- 155; influence on Bede 4-8, 81-85, 89, 105, 130-133; knowledge of classical literature 12-13; knowledge of Greek 9; scriptural scholarship 6-7

——, teachings on: the benefit of masses 143-144, 176-177; the interpretation of Scripture 56-58, 109; the spiritual life 124-125; truth and falsity 166-167, 225, 232-233

——, writings: *In librum primum Regum* 7; *Homiliae in Evangelia* 86; *Registrum epistularum* 157. See also *Dialogues*

Gribomont, Jean 9, 10n

Gurevich, Aron 135n, 144n

Guthfrith, abbot of Lindisfarne 38

Guthlac, Saint 134n-135n, 157n

Hadrian, abbot of St Augustine's 10n, 57

Haedde, bishop of Wessex 153

Haemgisl, monk of Melrose 184n, 186

hagiography, ancient and medieval 26n, 31n, 71-73, 77n, 79n, 87-88, 155-157, 189, 195-196; concept of truth in 167, 196-197, 198n; miracles in 22, 25, 51, 139, 151-152, 154-155, 232

Hamor 227

Headda, bishop 134n

heaven 48, 91n, 180, 181n, 185-186

Heavenfield 76

Heffernan, Thomas J. 72, 196n

hell 35, 91n, 180, 181n, 182-185, 189-193

Hemma, *gesith* 167

Herebald, abbot of Tynemouth 36-37, 41-42

Herefrith, priest and former abbot of Lindisfarne 159

heresy 16, 121

Herod Antipas 222n

Hessians 118n

Hewald, two priests named 150n

Hilary of Poitiers 2, 68-69

Hild, abbess of Whitby 26n

Hildelida, abbess of Barking 183

Hill, Rosalind 117n

Historia ecclesiastica, of Bede: 1, 7, 22, 29n, 51-52, 75, 87-88, 116, 132, 157n, 162-165; allegory in 47-50; audience of 49-51; continues the Bible 78; influenced by the Old Testament 206; pedagogical purpose of 142-145

historiography, ancient and medieval 30-31, 71, 77, 87-88, 120, 203-205, 214, 228

Holder, Arthur G. 4, 49n
Holy Saturday 154
Howe, Nicholas 50n
Hreda, pagan goddess 120
Hunter Blair, Peter 11n, 20n, 204, 208-210
Hunter, Michael 77
Hurst, David 18n

idolatry and idols 36, 117-118, 120n
illness 26-28
Imma, thegn 44-45, 143, 144n, 176
Incarnation, doctrine of 60
Ingwald, monk of Wearmouth 39, 159
Iona 170-171
Ireland and the Irish 30, 46-48, 51, 57, 101n, 103, 125, 129-130, 134n, 201
Irvine, Martin 11, 12n, 14n
Isaac 24, 55
Ishmael 24
Isidore of Seville xi, 3, 4n, 19, 46-47, 48n, 228
Isola, Antonio 13n
Israel 67-69, 95, 101, 130
Italy 130, 146, 166

Jacob 223, 227
Jairus, daughter of 55, 107n, 108
Jarrow 1, 52, 163, 172, 206. See also Wearmouth-Jarrow
Jericho 226
Jerome, Saint 2, 18, 45, 46n, 65-68, 69n, 80, 162, 212-213, 225; influence on Bede 4-5, 61, 83, 200, 208, 212, 220-222, 232
Jerusalem 15n, 77-78, 227

Jews 56, 67-68, 78, 91, 95, 111, 223, 227
Job 26, 135, 138-139
John Cassian 224-225, 232
John Chrysostom 2, 63, 65
John of Beverley 1, 36, 40-42, 70, 168-169
John the Baptist 217, 219, 222n
John, Saint, the Evangelist 41, 56, 65, 67, 110, 218
Jonah 110
Jonas of Bobbio xi
Jonathan 17
Jones, Charles W. 44, 71, 197, 199, 208
Jones, Michael E. 30n
Joseph, Saint 208, 211, 220-222, 229
Josephus, Flavius 58, 60, 227
Joshua 226
Judah 223
Judas Iscariot 135, 226
Judas Maccabaeus 78
Judas, the son of James 200
Judgment, Day of 90, 91n, 93, 96-97, 99, 134, 144n, 180, 184
Julian of Eclanum 5, 82n, 121
Julian, emperor 16
Julian, priest and martyr 113n
Justus, monk of St Andrew's 191-192
Jutes 119

Kee, Howard Clark 109-110, 228n
Kelly, Joseph F. 225n
Kendall, Calvin B. 14n, 34, 47-50
Kent 117, 119, 164
Keturah 55
King, Margot H. 12n, 13
Kirby, D.P. 129-130, 164n, 201n, 202

Knowles, David 203

Laistner, M.L.W. 2, 4, 5n, 24n
Landes, Richard 97n
Langres 52-53
Lapidge, Michael 10n, 152n
Lastingham, monastery 37; monks
   of 163-164
Lateran Council of 649, Acts 24n
Latin, language 9, 11, 13
Latourelle, René 193n
Laurence, archbishop of Canter-
   bury 44-45, 115n
Lazarus 26, 109
Leander, bishop of Seville 124n
Leonardi, Claudio 114n, 124n,
   196n, 206n
Lerer, Seth 44n
Levison, Wilhelm 53n, 155, 210n
Lichfield 76n, 147
Life of Ceolfrith 1, 52-54
Lincoln 75
Lindisfarne 42-43, 130, 152n;
   monks of 33, 73, 159, 199-
   200, 202, 207
Lindisfarne Anonymous 33, 39,
   42-43, 79n, 140-141, 158-162,
   169- 171, 173-174, 195, 198
Lindsey, kingdom of 207
London 163
Loomis, C. Grant xiiin, 7, 44n,
   79n, 158n, 164n, 178, 184n,
   193
Lot's wife 59-60
Lubac, Henri de 59n, 207n
Luiselli, Bruno 12n
Luke, Saint 50, 208, 211-212,
   219-222, 226, 228-229, 232
Lupus, bishop of Troyes 26n, 30,
   113n, 133n
Lynch, Kevin M. 10

McClure, Judith 18n, 52n, 206
Maccabees 78
Mackay, Thomas W. 142, 199n
magic 118n, 144n
Malchion (Marcion), priest of
   Antioch 17n
Malmesbury 188
Mamre 60
Marcellinus, bishop of Ancona 35,
   79n, 177-178
Marcellinus, priest and martyr
   112n
Marcion. See Malchion
Mark, Saint 50, 218-219
Markus, R.A. 48n, 87-88, 89n,
   98, 103n, 118n, 120n
Martin, bishop of Tours 95n, 195n
martyrs 112, 137-138, 181n
Mary, the Virgin 220-222
mass 44, 143-144, 176-177, 190-
   192
Matthew, Saint 219
Maximian, bishop of Syracuse xi,
   157n
Mayr-Harting, Henry 38, 46, 47n,
   89n, 100n, 116, 174n, 204n,
   206n
Meaney, Audrey L. 119n
Mellitus, archbishop of Canterbury
   33-34, 120n, 177-178
Melrose 117, 129, 169, 180, 186
Mercia 157n, 164, 187-188
Meyvaert, Paul xin, xii, 2n, 3n, 4,
   5n, 6, 10n, 19n, 47, 51n, 52,
   54n, 59, 88n, 154, 157n
Micaiah 226
Milan 97, 103
millennialism 96-97
Miller, Linda L. 184n, 187n
Minard, Pierre xin
Miriam 26

Morse, Ruth 51n
Moses 18, 49, 61, 108, 227
Müller, Gregor 225n
Musca, Giosué 31n, 44n, 51, 72n, 197n, 204-205, 207n, 212n
Mynors, R.A.B. *See* Colgrave, Bertram

Nain, widow of 109
Natalius, false bishop 45n
nature, order in 19-21, 23-25
Nechtansmere 101
Nie, Giselle de 22n, 27n, 28n, 31n, 34, 35n, 93n
Nineveh 31, 110
Noah 92
Nonnosus, abbot 157n
Northumbria 2, 37, 102-103, 119, 207-208; Christianization of 116, 125, 130
Nothhelm, priest of London 62, 163-164

Odo, duke of Aquitaine 29n
Oethelwald (Aethilwald), hermit of Farne 37-38, 148, 198
Olsen, Glenn W. 59n, 77, 78n
Origen 61
Orosius, Paulus 31, 48, 163, 204
Osric, king of Northumbria 29n
Oswald, king of Northumbria 76, 148-149, 195n
Oswiu, king of Northumbria 170
Ovid, *Metamorphoses* 11-12

paganism 116-121
Parkes, M.B. 3n
Passio Perpetuae 186
Passover 61
Paterius xi
Paul of Samosata 17n

Paul the Deacon 119
Paul, Saint, the Apostle 18, 26, 46n, 66, 81, 92, 130, 226-227, 232; detects the sin of Ananias and Sapphira 170; raises Eutychus from the dead 106n, 109n; spends a day and night in the depths of the sea 62-64
Paulinus of Nola 142
Paulinus, archbishop of York 75
Pehthelm, bishop of Whithorn 188
Pelagianism 113, 121, 163n
Penda, king of Mercia 33, 131
Pentecost, miracle of 60, 112n, 133
Pepperdene, Margaret W. 201n
Peter, abbot of St Peter and St Paul's, Canterbury 150
Peter, hermit 187
Peter, exorcist and martyr 112n
Peter, Saint, the Apostle 22-23, 44, 64, 79n, 111, 167-169, 176; heals lame man 41, 56, 110; raises Tabitha from the dead 109n; walks on water 63-64
Pharaoh, magicians of 137n
Pharisees 68, 111n, 217
Philip, apostle 221-222
Philistines 17, 223
philosophy 15-17
Photinians 220
physicians 41-43, 155, 161
Piacente, Luigi 12n
Picard, Jean-Michel 88n, 171-172, 201
Picts 29-30, 101, 103
Pliny the Elder 11, 19, 28n
Plummer, Charles (Carolus) 25, 26n, 29n, 32, 42n, 45n, 47n, 49n, 89n, 101n, 102n, 118n, 162, 163n, 183n, 188, 210n

Plutarch 182
Po, river 174n
Ponton, Georges 221-222
Porphyrius, poet 14
Porphyry 16
Prinz, Friedrich 201n
Prodigal Son 15
Promised Land 48
Prosper of Aquitaine 163
Pseudo-Dionysius 24n
Puch, *gesith* 168
Purgatory 91n, 129n, 180-183

Quintilian, *Institutio oratoria* 40-41

Rahab 226
Raphael, archangel 32-33, 78
rationes seminales 20
Ray, Roger 2n, 3, 4n, 12n, 18n,
    59n, 206n, 208n, 212-215,
    228
Redwald, king of East Anglia 117-
    119, 121
Reginald of Durham 155
Renaud, Geneviève. *See* Dubois,
    Jacques
Reparatus, *spectabilis vir* 184, 187
resurrection, doctrine of 181n,
    182n
rhetoric 12n, 13, 16-17, 203, 212,
    214, 228
Riché, Pierre 18n
Richter, Michael 122, 205n
Rollason, David W. 7n, 75n, 76n,
    198, 202n
Rome 2, 31, 52, 118n, 185, 201,
    209-210
Rosenthal, Joel T. xiiin, 42, 89n,
    102, 114-115, 140n, 164n, 165
Rubin, Stanley 32
Rufinus of Aquileia 70n

Sabinus, bishop of Piacenza 174n
Samaritans 118
Samuel 24n, 55, 135
Sanhedrin 227-229
Saracens 29n, 101
Sarah 24, 55, 224
Satan 65-69, 105-106, 135-138,
    189-191
Saul, king of Israel 17, 135, 226
Saxons 29-30, 119
Sceva, high priest 135
Scheibelreiter, Georg 196n
Schindel, Ulrich 13n
Schmale, Franz-Josef 196n
Schoebe, Gerhard 30, 72n, 77,
    206n
Schreiner, Klaus 208
science, ancient and mediaeval 19-
    20, 230
Scientific Revolution 20
scribes 56, 68, 106, 111n
Sebbi, king of Essex 117
Sedulius 12
Seneca, *Epistulae* 11-12
Severus, priest 184n
Shechem 227
Shropshire 183
Sigeberht, king of East Anglia
    131-132
Sigefrith, abbot of Wearmouth 26n
Sigehere, king of Essex 117, 165
Signs of Sanctity ix-x, xiii, 8, 9n,
    25n, 50n, 54n, 71n, 82n, 85n,
    116n, 157n, 166n, 167n, 193n
Simonetti, Manlio 18n, 59n, 62n
Sims-Williams, Patrick 100n, 184n
Siniscalco, Paolo 94n
Sodom 59
Solinus 47n
Solomon 58, 61
Southern, R.W. 93

Spain 48n
Speyer, Wolfgang 225n
St Andrew's, monastery 154, 190
Stacpoole, Alberic 44n
Stancliffe, Clare 117n, 127n, 198
Stephen, *inlustris vir* 184, 192
Stephen, Saint 190, 192, 227-228, 232
Stephen, smith 192
Stephens, J.N. 50n, 116
Stevens, Wesley M. 19n
storms 25-28
Stranks, C.J. 39
Straw, Carole 27n, 124n
Strubel, Armand 57n
Strunz, Franz 19n
Sulpicius Severus x, 95, 156, 195
Sussex, evangelization of 36, 116
syncretism 118
Syrians 226

Tabernacle 61, 125
Tabitha, raised by St Peter 109n
Tajo, bishop of Saragossa xi
Temple, of Solomon 58, 61
Tertullian 46n
Thacker, Alan 5n, 101n, 126, 127n, 140, 160n, 171, 202n, 206n
Thaddaeus, apostle 200
Thaddaeus, disciple 200
Thanet 47n
Thecla, Saint 46n
Theodore, archbishop of Canterbury 10n, 57, 63; penitential attributed to 118
Theodore, monk of St Andrew's 190-191
Thespesius, vision of 182
Thomas Aquinas 3, 20
Thomas, Charles 75n-76n, 147n

Thucydides 228
tides, ocean 19, 62n
Tobias 26, 32-33, 78
Ton Galathon, monastery 188n, 191
Tours 29n
Tower of Babel 15
Trumwine (Tumma), bishop of the Picts 159
truth, medieval conception of 196-197
Tuda, bishop of Lindisfarne 117
Tugène, Georges 78, 129n, 144
Tunna, priest 44, 176
Turin, Biblioteca Nazionale 10n
Tyconius 59n
Tydi, priest 160n
Tynemouth, monastery 38

Utta, priest 70n

Vaesen, Jos 95n
Van Uytfanghe, Marc 31n, 50n, 69n, 77n
Vaughan, Richard 145n
Venantius Fortunatus 195
Verbraken, Pierre-Patrick xin, 18n
Vergil 11-12
Victoria, virgin and martyr 113n
Victorinus, rhetorician 228
Vita Cuthberti, anonymous: 72n, 73-74, 140, 156, 163n, 164, 202. *See also* Lindisfarne Anonymous
Vita Cuthberti, of Bede: 22, 51-52, 73, 87-88, 140, 152, 155, 157n, 164; hidden meaning of 50n; relationship to the anonymous life 158-161, 202
Vivarium 11

Vogüé, Adalbert de xin, xiin, 19n,
86n, 166
Vortigern, king of the Britons 29

Wahlstod, monk 159
Wallace-Hadrill, J.M. 7, 29n, 40-
41, 42n, 49n, 76n, 89n, 103n,
118n, 120, 144n, 172n, 176,
178n, 179n, 186, 188n, 195,
209n
Ward, Benedicta xiiin, 46n, 50n,
144n, 197, 208n, 209n
Wearmouth 1, 52
Wearmouth-Jarrow 1-2, 9, 11,
202. *See also* Jarrow
Wenlock, monk of 183-184
Wetherbee, Winthrop 9
Whitby: *Life of Gregory* 210;
Synod of 134n
Whitelock, Dorothy 3n, 155n
Wigfrith, cleric 134n-135n

Wildhaber, Robert 47n
Wilfrid, bishop of York 28n, 36,
101n, 116, 122, 134n, 159n,
168, 202, 205
Willibald, *Life of St Boniface* 118,
151
Willmes, Ansgar 3n, 7n, 58n
Wilson, David M. 2n
Winstead, Karen A. 87n
Witch of Endor 135
Wolpers, Theodor 7n, 140n, 152n
Woolf, Rosemary 85n, 87, 196n
Wormald, Patrick 100, 101n, 119,
123n, 204n-205n
Wright, Neil 11, 12n, 14n

Zaleski, Carol 72n, 178, 179n,
182n, 187n
Zalla, the Goth 176
Zephyrinus, pope 45n
Zizicus 631

DATE DUE

JUL 9 1998		
OCT 1999		
OCT 2000		
OCT		
JUN		
OCT		
OCT 0		
OCT 1		
SEP 1		
10 10		
10 5		